TERMINOLOGY AND LANGUAGE PLANNING

TERMINOLOGY AND LEXICOGRAPHY RESEARCH AND PRACTICE

Terminology and Lexicography Research and Practice aims to provide in-depth studies and background information pertaining to Lexicography and Terminology. General works will include philosophical, historical, theoretical, computational and cognitive approaches. Other works will focus on structures for purpose- and domain-specific compilation (LSP), dictionary design, and training. The series will include monographs, state-of-the-art volumes and course books in the English language.

Series Editors
Helmi Sonneveld
Sue Ellen Wright

Consulting Editor
Juan C. Sager

Volume 2

Bassey Edem Antia

Terminology and Language Planning
An alternative framework of practice and discourse

TERMINOLOGY AND LANGUAGE PLANNING

AN ALTERNATIVE FRAMEWORK OF PRACTICE AND DISCOURSE

BASSEY EDEM ANTIA
University of Maiduguri

JOHN BENJAMINS PUBLISHING COMPANY
AMSTERDAM/PHILADELPHIA

The paper used in this publication meets the minimum requirements of American National Standard for Information Sciences — Permanence of Paper for Printed Library Materials, ANSI Z39.48-1984.

Library of Congress Cataloging-in-Publication Data

Antia, Bassey Edem
   Terminology and language planning : an alternative framework of practice and discourse / Bassey Edem Antia.
       p.   cm. -- (Terminology and lexicography research and practice, ISSN 1388-8455 ; v. 2)
   A slight revision of v. 1 of the author's thesis (doctoral)--University of Bielefeld, Germany.
   Includes bibliographical references and indexes.
   1. Terms and phrases. 2. Language planning. 3. Knowledge representation (Information theory) I. Title. II. Series.
P305 .A58   2000
306.44'9--dc21   99-086614
ISBN 90 272 2325 4 (Eur.) / 1 55619 771 3 (US) (alk. paper)   CIP

© 2000 – John Benjamins B.V.
No part of this book may be reproduced in any form, by print, photoprint, microfilm, or any other means, without written permission from the publisher.

John Benjamins Publishing Co. • P.O.Box 75577 • 1070 AN Amsterdam • The Netherlands
John Benjamins North America • P.O.Box 27519 • Philadelphia, PA 19118 • USA

To Edem Hogan Antia

Table of Contents

Acknowledgments xiii

Introduction xv
Globalisation, Language Planning and Terminology xvi
About this book: Specific motivations and contents xxi

CHAPTER 1
Terminology in Language Planning Theory 1
1.1 Models of Language Planning 1
1.2 Terminology in Language Planning Theory 9
    1.2.1 *Who plans terminology?* 10
    1.2.2 *Modelling rationales for success in terminology* 11
    1.2.3 *Where is what done on terminology?* 15

CHAPTER 2
Terminology Discourse and Practice in Africa
Issues, Players and Arenas 17
2.1 Motivation, Players and Arenas: Case Studies 17
    2.1.1 *Somalia* 17
    2.1.2 *Tanzania* 19
    2.1.3 *Nigeria* 22
    2.1.4 *Ethiopia* 25
    2.1.5 *Francophone Africa* 26
2.2 Combating cynicism 29
2.3 Terminology Planning Process 33
    2.3.1 *Focus of the planning effort* 33
    2.3.2 *Integration of the terminology planning effort within other
          processes* 35

TABLE OF CONTENTS

    2.3.3   *The plenary and committee sessions* 36
    2.3.4   *Collaborators* 36
2.4 Critical Metadiscourse 38
    2.4.1   *Linguistic strategy* 39
    2.4.2   *Terminological system approach* 41
    2.4.3   *Sociological approach* 42
    2.4.4   *Communication approach* 44
    2.4.5   *Knowledge approach* 45
2.5 Sociological validations of terminology resources: A critique 46

CHAPTER 3
Evaluation of a Terminology Resource 49
3.1 Translation experiments 50
    3.1.1   *Experimental text, Pre-analysis & Research questions* 51
    3.1.2   *Findings* 53
    3.1.3   *Conclusion to translation experiment* 63
3.2 Knowledge experiment 65
    3.2.1   *Theoretical framework: Text, mediation and knowledge* 65
    3.2.2   *Findings* 66
    3.2.3   *Conclusion to knowledge experiment* 73
3.3 Miscellaneous 73
    3.3.1   *Adequacy of term motivations* 74
    3.3.2   *Inter(target)language variation* 76
    3.3.3   *Selection policy and coverage* 77
3.4 Consolidated summary 78

CHAPTER 4
Concept Theory in Terminology 81
4.1 Parameters for a concept theory 82
4.2 Relationship of the concept to its symbol 83
4.3 Relationship of concept to object (an object theory in terminology) 86
    4.3.1   *Epistemological positions for an object theory in terminology* .. 89
    4.3.2   *Types of objects* 90
4.4 Creation of specialised concepts 93
4.5 Typology of concept characteristics 96
4.6 Knowledge and terminology 100
    4.6.1   *Concept relations* 101
    4.6.2   *Concept system* 102

4.7	Concept system and semantic field	104
4.8	Critical perspectives on concept theory	106
	4.8.1 *A humanistic critique*	106
	4.8.2 *A prototypicalist critique*	108
4.9	Implications of concept theory in terminology	112
	4.9.1 *Designation*	112
	4.9.2 *Definition*	113
	4.9.3 *Conception of domain*	114
	4.9.4 *Knowledge transfer*	115

CHAPTER 5
Collocations and Communication 117
5.1	LGP views on word combinations	117
	5.1.1 *Communication perspective*	117
	5.1.2 *Knowledge perspective*	119
5.2	LSP views on collocations and other word combinations	119
	5.2.1 *Communication perspective*	120
	5.2.2 *Knowledge perspective*	120
5.3	Theoretical accounts in perspective	121
	5.3.1 *LGP theories of word combinations*	122
	5.3.2 *An LSP theory of word combinations*	127
5.4	Appraisal, and an eclectic framework for LSP	129
	5.4.1 *Variously conditioned term environments*	129
	5.4.2 *Problems of term delimitation*	132
	5.4.3 *Rethinking the trivialisation of grammatical collocations*	134
5.5	Sources of collocates	137
	5.5.1 *Introspection and reference*	137
	5.5.2 *Concept modelling and systematic elicitation*	137

CHAPTER 6
Terminography and Knowledge Representation 139
6.1	Notional representation in lexicography	140
	6.1.1 *Motivations and theoretical premises of non-alphabetical representation*	140
	6.1.2 *A plan of classification: Roget's Thesaurus*	142
6.2	Non-alphabetical representation in document classification	144
	6.2.1 *Motivation for information retrieval thesauri*	145
	6.2.2 *Structure of information retrieval thesauri*	145
6.3	A (systematic) thesaurus model for terminography	150

Chapter 7
Terminology, Text and Technology 153
7.1 Complementary frameworks 153
7.2 Knowledge in text: Inferences from text linguistics 154
7.3 Objectifying knowledge in text: Insights from corpus linguistics 157
7.4 Specialised text and Artificial Intelligence: Heuristics and tools for terminological knowledge acquisition 158
    7.4.1 *Statistics, LSP texts and term extraction* 159
    7.4.2 *Statistics, LSP texts and concept relations* 161
    7.4.3 *LSP texts and extraction of term collocates* 164
7.5 Knowledge structure-simulated representation of terminology 166
    7.5.1 *Conceptual graphs* 168
    7.5.2 *Hypertext* 170
7.6 Terminology management systems 170
    7.6.1 *An overview* 171
    7.6.2 *MultiTerm: A Case Description of a TMS* 172
7.7 Language engineering applications: Implications for Africa 175

Chapter 8
Applications
The Making of a Legislative Terminology Resource 179
8.1 Set of justifications 179
8.2 Delimitation of domain 182
8.3 From initiation corpus to definitive corpus 183
8.4 Manual processing 184
8.5 Semi-automatic processing 184
8.6 Knowledge modelling 185
8.7 Preliminaries for the target language version 194
    8.7.1 *Collaborators, briefing and process documentation* 194
    8.7.2 *Efik: Orthography and writing challenges* 195
8.8 Process analysis of the target language version 197
    8.8.1 *Term motivation* 197
    8.8.2 *Constraints on term decision* 201
    8.8.3 *The old and the new: Conflict and accommodation* 205
    8.8.4 *More terms than bargained for* 208
    8.8.5 *Knowledge of language, subject-matter and of translating* 210

8.9 Linguistic analysis of target language terms 211
    8.9.1   *Simple adjectives* 213
    8.9.2   *Partially and totally reduplicated adjectives* 213
    8.9.3   *Adjectival phrases* 214
    8.9.4   *Simple nouns* 214
    8.9.5   *Complex noun phrases* 215
    8.9.6   *Agentive prefix* 215
8.10 Creation of a MultiTerm database 216
8.11 The terminology resource, MultiTerm and the experiments 220

Conclusion 227

Bibliography 235

Subject Index 259

Name Index 263

Acknowledgments

This book is a slight revision of Volume 1 of my doctoral dissertation submitted to the Faculty of Linguistics and Literature of the University of Bielefeld, Germany. The dissertation and the published book have seen me incur huge debts of gratitude which I may never be able to clear. I am beholden to:
- the German Academic Exchange Service (DAAD) for financing my doctoral studies;
- Bernd Stefanink and Werner Kummer for supervising my dissertation;
- Khurshid Ahmad, head of the Artificial Intelligence Research Group at the University of Surrey, U.K., members and collaborators of the Group (Margaret Rogers, Andy Salway, Lee Gillam, Caroline Jones), and to Gerhard Oswald of the firm, Trados, for access to their language engineering technologies;
- reviewers of the dissertation as well as of the book manuscript;
- Trixi Stefanink, Wilhelm Seidensticker (late), Norbert Cyffer, Conrad Max Benedict Brann, Ekkehard Zöfgen, Rotimi Badejo, Peter Gottschligg, Margarita Krommer-Benz, Deborah Fry, Roberta Schwarz, Abdullahi Alkali (late), Shua'ibu Mohammed, Anna Aguilar-Amat, Khaled Yassin, Christy Antia for being important facilitators;
- resource persons in several national legislatures and at the Interparliamentary Union Headquarters; to experimental subjects; to Chiefs B. E. Bassey and E. U. Aye, the Association for the Promotion of Efik Language, Literature and Culture (APELLAC) as well as to Ofioñ Akak, Awaii Efio-Oyo, Stella Ekpo, Bernadette Etetta, Alice Hogan and Jean Slessor — collaborators on the Efik terminology resource that provided part of the material for Volume 2 of the original dissertation;
- Gunter Gerzelkesky, Frank Stuckmann and Hung-Tu Lin for always being there whenever the computers acted up;
- the University of Maiduguri for the grant of a study leave;

- Helmi Sonneveld, Bertie Kaal, Ingrid Seebus — managing editors at John Benjamins Publishers — for their expertise and professionalism;
- Inyang, Allan, Victoria, Richard, Victor, Hogan, Effiom for support and examples.

Bassey E. Antia
Bielefeld, September 1999.

Introduction

This book draws new outlines for a paradigm that may be referred to as *language planning (LP) oriented terminology management*, with such variant or synonymous designations as *LP-oriented terminology(management)* and *term(inology)planning*. Central to this paradigm is the discourse and practice of terminology in the context of LP. Terminology and LP, as academic communities, have had precious little contact between them. As a result, neither has been able to benefit from the other at that point where objects and needs demonstrably coincide.

The terminology community focuses, not on Latin, Greek or some such misconception, but on specialised or specific subject areas within which it studies knowledge (units, structure, representation, evolution, acquisition, etc.) in its relation to expression. As labels (linguistic or non-linguistic) for specialised concepts, terms are a means of acquiring, retrieving, creating, communicating, storing, representing and operationalising specialised knowledge. If the field of terminology is occasionally associated with language regulation, it must be in the third sense of the verb, *regulate*, as stated in the *Oxford English Reference Dictionary*: "adapt to requirements". On the other hand, the LP community, seen from the most abstract of levels, is interested in the co-evolution of society and language, under conditions specified or constraints manifested by one or the other co-variable, and along a transformation path that is at some point controlled.[1] An example of a specific research object in LP would be the functional extension of a less widely used language as a planned response to aspirations or ideology, expressed as social policy. Clearly, the implementation of a decision to extend the range of functions of a language into a specialised domain would

---

1. As increasingly used in the social sciences, *evolution* is not strictly Darwinian in its acceptation (that is, selection). Interestingly, Durham (1991:21) has defined it negatively as not being coterminous with progress or improvement, nor the preserve of genetic systems. Applying the disclaimer on improvement to LP would, for instance, enable one to restate the point made already by Haugen that LP could also aim at suppressing, rather than promoting, a language.

benefit from insights offered by an academic community that has knowledge and expression in specialised areas as its research object.

But the foregoing perhaps belies the scope of the book. Constructs or positions in both fields are subjected to sustained scrutiny in a way that allows for independent contributions to be made to each. Translation process analysis, text linguistics, LSP theory, epistemology, documentation science, lexical semantics, concept theory, corpus linguistics, artificial intelligence, knowledge representation, language engineering technologies are some of the areas dealt with. It is in the nature of the enterprise for the goal to be as important as the means.

Globalisation, Language Planning and Terminology

In any case, why the interest in *terminology, planning, less widely used languages* and the like, when many of the momentous events and topical issues of the late 20th century point to, or are believed to point to, the dismantling of frontiers, non-interventionism, etc.?

With the lowering, shifting or redefinition of disciplinary borders (referred to severally as inter-, trans-, cross-, multi-, para-disciplinarity), it has indeed become more compelling than ever before to relate one's research in a specific area to a broader intellectual framework. In the *Gutenberg Galaxy*, where electronic technology is seen as recasting the globe in the mould of a village in a pre-literate era, Marshall McLuhan writes that "compartmentalizing of human potential by single cultures will soon be as absurd as specialism in subject or discipline has become" (McLuhan & Zingrone 1997). Incidentally, globalisation could very well be one of the strongest candidates for interdisciplinary paradigm status on the eve of the 21st century.[2] In the sense adopted here, such a status would not refer to the scientific achievements that constitute the orthodoxy prevailing in any single discipline, as the first occurrence of *paradigm* is understood by Thomas Kuhn in his book, *The Structure of Scientific Revolutions*. Rather, this status would refer to that broad thematic framework into which research in many fields is collapsible. Pretty much like conservation or democra-

---

2. Globalisation is used here in a broad and in a narrow sense. In the latter acceptation, it occurs in the context of a world-wide development and marketing strategy that calls for culture-sensitive product design, documentation and client support. In the former acceptation, globalisation is an all embracing phenomenon, and an issue in sociological theory, economic theory, political theory and the like. Deborah Fry's assistance is acknowledged here. She is working on a useful glossary of terms in the translation and localisation industries.

tisation, globalisation may be seen as the construct in terms of which many model problems and solutions are contemporaneously defined by scholarly communities of various descriptions.

A book that seeks to provide a framework for enhancing the terminological development of less widely used languages might be viewed as running against the centripetal grain of globalisation. In the broader sense of space-time compression, globalisation is a phenomenon that is frequently seen in terms of increased mobility of capital, goods and labour, the formation of trans-national economic and trade blocs, interlinkage of money markets, increased information sharing across national frontiers, world-wide action plans, the increasing substitution of residency for nationality, hegemonisation of the English language, faster means of transportation, advances in information technology, etc. But these oft-cited features engender great illusions of a global village to whose square or centre-stage all are guaranteed access. Let us consider three different scenarios.

The first has to do with trade. The Manager in charge of South Asia for computer software giant, Microsoft, has been cited as saying that because "most Indians have to first learn English to use a computer [...] the use of computers could go up tenfold if programs were made in local languages".[3] Had the former situation not obtained, Microsoft just might have been able to reap huge profits in this potentially huge market of one-sixth of humanity without doing anything (translating out of English, adapting user interface, etc.) to its U.S. product releases and the accompanying documentation. The fact that Microsoft's shipments to countries where English is a dominant language are outstripped by sales in countries where English has no such status is perhaps partial evidence that the company's success resides, not in fostering U.S. hegemonies, but in a measure of sensitivity to local environments. And there is no shortage of clamours. In the July 1, 1998 telecast of *Europe Direct*, a programme on BBC World, Microsoft was taken on by the President of the Icelandic Association in the United Kingdom for the company's alleged refusal to localise its applications into Icelandic.[4] Interestingly, the question was not so much one of the ability or inability of Icelanders to use applications in English as that of checking the erosion of cultural identity. In an apparent appreciation of how business could be affected by the assertion of cultural rights, even in a country of 270,000 inhabitants, Microsoft stated its willingness to enter into localisation talks with governmental authorities in Iceland, as it had done previously with the Catalan

---

3. *AsiaWeek* (6–9–96) quoted by Björn Jernudd (1997).
4. A similar Icelandic campaign is documented in *Language International* 9.4 (1997).

and Basque governments.

The second scenario has to do with international travel. In her book, *The Coming Industry of Teletranslation*, Minako O'Hagan points out that through (and in spite of) information technology, the backbone on which many facets of globalisation ride, language problems arise today with a poignancy that was unknown in the age of limited cross-border transactions. Consider the following example which she cites:

> March 1989, an international hotel in Auckland, New Zealand. A Japanese businessman with very limited English is experiencing some frustration on the phone. As he doesn't know the correct number to dial he calls the hotel reception. The English-speaking receptionist can't understand her Japanese guest, but assumes he wants to make an international call to Japan. She connects him with the international operator. The operator also has difficulty communicating with him, but is able to determine that he is Japanese and puts him through to an international operator in Japan. There is a brief conversation in Japanese. The bilingual Japanese operator passes a message to the New Zealand operator who then informs the hotel reception that the man would like to order breakfast delivered to his room.

The third scenario deals with programmes requiring world-wide synergies. The increasing numbers of global summits and action plans on the environment reflect awareness that environmental problems do not know national frontiers. The forest-fires induced smog in Indonesia recently made nonsense of Malaysia's territorial integrity. If rural communities in Indonesia are not given alternative means of land-clearing as well as environmental education in a language they understand — not the working languages of Rio, Kyoto, Buenos — summit recommendations will remain just what they are. To the extent that language is the only means of receiving information, linguistic access is critical to the success of plans requiring global synergies. Seun Ogunseitan of the Nigeria-based African Centre for Science and Development Information might have mentioned language in warning that:

> An uninformed Africa is as much a threat to Europe, the Americas and Japan as it is to Africa and the Africans themselves. Access to information is vital for every country, but there is an enormous imbalance in the world in which one part lacks even the most basic information. [And] the lack of adequate and effective information flows to developing countries has made a holistic approach to global problems essentially impossible (quoted by Beaugrande 1992).

The foregoing scenarios — global product marketing, international business travel and world-wide (environmental) action plans — show that there are important linguistic correlates of globalisation. It is a moot point whether the gap between the *haves* and the *have-nots* in some of these scenarios is increasing or has only become accentuated and better appreciated. What is not in doubt is that, for many peoples around the world, only the obverse side of the stunning strides associated with globalisation is seen, and this side spells as i-n-s-u-l-a-r-i-s-m. Interestingly, this insularism is source of frustration for the major actors in the global village square.

Localisation, a solution to the challenge of globally marketing computer software requires, among others, research into the culture and languages of target-markets. For instance, terms have to be created, and issues of iconicity (*sensu* preferential information staging or presentation patterns) need to be researched into. Terms being the information and knowledge control centres which they are, there is little hope that without attention and resources being apportioned to terminology, the following piece of knowledge on protecting the environment, taken from the *Oxford Reference Dictionary*, could be readily expressed in more than a few hundred of the world's six thousand languages (and understood by those who might otherwise have been expected to):

> CFCs are nonflammable, non-toxic, and unreactive synthetic compounds which have been used since the 1930s as working fluids in refrigerators and propellants for aerosol sprays. They have now been shown to be harmful to the earth's ozone layer, as well as being major contributors to the greenhouse effect [...]. CFC molecules which have been released into the environment are broken down by the sun's ultraviolet radiation in the upper atmosphere, forming chlorine which reacts with ozone.

That many national populations speak more than one language must not be seen as suggesting that a language of modern science is comprised in such repertoires. If the speculation over the number of languages that can readily express the above text has some merit, it would show just how ludicrous it is to expect meaningful and informed debates in the world's legislatures — debates that are meant to ratify the Rio, Kyoto or Buenos protocols. In consonance with the democratic spirit, some legislatures in the developing world have ceased to make knowledge of English or other colonial languages an eligibility criterion for membership.

It follows from the foregoing that investment in local eco-systems by way of creating or planning terminology in less widely used languages is actually very much in tune with globalisation. It is perhaps no odd quirk that in the software industry, localisation and globalisation or internationalisation aim at the same goal. An electronic search for literature on globalisation at the Bielefeld University Library turned up the felicitous book subtitle, *Globalization is a Local*

Process.[5,6] Further search of the literature on sociological theory revealed an on-going debate as to whether globalisation is reducible to hegemonisation, as to whether locality is overridden by globalisation, etc. A leading scholar, Robertson, answers these questions in the negative.[7] In positing the concept of *glocalisation* (note spelling), Robertson seeks to make the oft-missed point that, as social processes, globalisation and localisation are not antithetical, and that the relationship into which they enter is not unidirectional.

The reflexivity of both processes, when seen from a linguistic standpoint, allows for the argument that there is no conflict between the terminological enhancement of less widely used languages and much of what globalisation is generally believed to represent.

In an age of globalisation, the patron-saint of the terminology planner in a less widely used language could very well be Leibniz, the 17th century German philosopher. Leibniz did not only cultivate a *universal* symbolic language but also a natural one, his native German, which was then an impoverished and *restricted* language.[8] Many of Leibniz's reasons for urging the terminological enrichment of German, in an era of the hegemony of Latin and French, bear striking resemblance to what would be revealed by a contemporary sociology of less widely used languages. Leibniz was concerned about language-based social stratification within Germany (the learned people spoke French — oft badly — while the common people spoke German). Like Gottsched and others in Germany, he was intensely concerned about the quality of German. He deplored the fact that "few straightforward books are written in Germany" in contrast to the situation in England, France or Italy where "the splendor of wisdom is not reserved to learned men only but has trickled down to the mother tongue".

While the mother tongue, then, was largely defined at national levels and by contrast to whatever languages were used for international communication, today it has to be defined in subnational terms as well. Policy-making and sociolinguistic thought have come a long way, from the programmatic report for Post-Revolutionary France which a radicalised Abbé Grégoire presented in 1794 to the French National Convention under the title *Rapport sur la nécessité et les moyens*

---

5. See Eade (1997).

6. George Amposem is thanked for indicating names of globalisation theorists, and for serving as sounding board to this discussion.

7. See Robertson (1992, 1994) among other works by Roland Robertson.

8. See Coulmas (1988) as well as Leibniz's 1683 admonition to the German People titled *Ermahnung an die Deutschen, ihren Verstand und ihre Sprache besser zu üben, samt beigefügtem Vorschlag einer deutschgesinnten Gesellschaft*.

d'anéantir les patois et d'universaliser l'usage de la langue française,[9] to the view in the 1960s and 1970s that multilingualism (believed to be characteristic of states south of the Atlantic) was a liability because it correlated with poverty, marginalisation, ignorance, political instability, etc.[10] With the emergence of new states around the world and renewed ethno-linguistic self-assertion in existing states, multilingualism has become a fact of life. It is no longer seen as incongruous with the directive principles of state policy or with *thinking globally*. Europe even has a Multilingual Action Plan (MLAP) for creating a Multilingual Information Society (MLIS). Terminology, incidentally, is playing an important role in the MLIS.

Today, one world-wide challenge of language planning (LP) research and terminology scholarship lies in working out the details of how to create specialised discourses for functional (as opposed to mere symbolic or demonstration) purposes. In other words, the concern is one of ensuring that many more languages are able to serve as means for communicating specialised information and knowledge, so crucial to the pursuit of goals on the global agenda, for example, the environment, international public health, empowerment, democratisation and good governance, etc. The world today is one in which timely access to specialised information and knowledge determines what rung of the social, political and economic ladder exclusive speakers of certain languages find themselves.

About this book: Specific motivations and contents

This book derives its broader context from the foregoing discussion. The book seeks to establish the bases for alternative needs analysis, work methodologies as well as modes of theorisation in LP, specifically planning in respect of terminology. Africa, an important source of impetus for the formalisation of LP as a branch of sociolinguistics in the 1960s, serves to illustrate the discussion. With respect to its more specific African context, the book suggests that (1) there often

---

9. An English translation by Antia & Brann has been published as *Report on the Necessity and Means of Suppressing Local Dialects and of Generalising the use of the French Language (in France)* as an appendix to Brann (1991). According to Brann, Abbé Grégoire, a representative of the clergy in the National Assembly, appears to have been receptive to the idea of other languages co-existing with French at the time (1792) he sent out his questionnaire on language use in France. This attitude changed when it was obvious that reactionary forces to the French Revolution rallied in the other languages. Barère's language report of 1794, the same year as Grégoire's, is instructive in this regard.

10. See, for instance, the essay by Joshua Fishman on "Some Contrasts between Linguistically Homogenous and Linguistically Heterogenous Polities". In: Fishman *et al.*, eds. (1968: 53–68).

is a gap between the stated goals of work on terminology planning and the resulting products; (2) an inadequate, if not *austere*, theoretical framework is employed in conceptualising the goals and challenges of terminology planning as well as in evaluating resulting products; (3) there is insufficient appreciation of: (a) the nature of specialist language (in particular from science theory perspectives, syntagmatic dimensions, etc.), (b) the mission of specialist language, and (c) the place of terminology in this agenda.

The corollary of inadequacies of theory and practice is that constitutional and other policy provisions on the use of indigenous languages[11] are not being implemented at all, or haphazardly so. Language continues to be an instrument of exclusion. In spite of this, sound development thinking continues to accord indigenous languages more, not fewer, new roles. The following are but a few examples taken from the domain of legislative or parliamentary procedure. South Africa is currently faced with the task of developing nine indigenous languages on which the post-Apartheid constitution has conferred co-official status with English and Afrikaans (the two official languages under Apartheid). It is the expectation that any of these languages can be used to address Parliament. In Zimbabwe's Parliament provision exists for the use of English and two indigenous languages. Nigeria's abrogated constitutions (1979 and 1989) explicitly provided for the use of three indigenous languages in addition to English at the National Assembly, and an indefinite number in state legislatures. Now, in much of Africa, official languages of European origins are spoken by about 30% of national populations. The measures in the examples cited above reflect awareness of the fact that erstwhile colonial languages cannot continue to be the sole media of discourse if the sector of recruitment for representative political leadership is not to be narrowly defined in linguistic terms. The local and global implications of stable, participatory democracy are such that this streak of successes in policy formulation needs to be urgently backed up by new approaches to corpus enrichment (specifically, expanding terminology). This would also be one way of ensuring that the conditionality or practicability provisions in the policy measures cited earlier are not used as escape clauses for maintaining the *status quo ante*.[12]

---

11. In this book, the use of the term *indigenous language* does not carry with it any value judgement, and invites none. Indigenous simply means endogenous.

12. Section 6(3) of the 1996 Constitution of the Republic of South Africa says, *inter alia*, that "National and provincial governments may use particular official languages for the purposes of government, taking into account usage, *practicality*, [...]" (my italics). The abrogated 1979 Constitution of the Federal Republic of Nigeria stipulates at Chapter 5(51) that "The business of the National Assembly shall be conducted in English, and in Hausa, Igbo and Yoruba *when adequate*

Using process analysis studies in translation and approaches to knowledge processing in text linguistics, the book evaluates a legislative terminology resource, and uses the findings to discuss elements of an alternative framework for LP-oriented terminology.

The first three chapters of the book give a detailed account of terminology as an issue in social and language planning. Chapter 1 reviews some of the literature on language planning and situates terminology within the language planning paradigm. Taking several parts of Africa as case study, Chapter 2 examines the discourse on, and practice of, terminology within the classical language planning framework. Chapter 3 uses experiments on translation and knowledge processing, among other criteria, to critically review a terminology resource produced within the classical language planning tradition.

With the problems observed in the experiments in view, the three chapters that follow present theoretical positions in terminology as they contrast with, draw from, or extend work in semantics, lexicology, philosophy of science and documentation science. The goal here is to develop a framework for understanding the problems and challenges raised by the translation and knowledge experiments reported in Chapter 3. Thus, Chapter 4 discusses concept theory in terminology. It shows, among others, that traditional accounts of the linguistic sign in general language, because of the epistemological positions that underpin them, are inadequate to deal with the sign in specialised language. It is suggested that a number of problems observed in the experiments result from the implications of the distinction between these two sign models or model constellations not being fully realised. With the experiments still in retrospect, Chapter 5 discusses collocations and communication in specialised languages. It describes the importance of, as well as approaches to, the syntagmatic dimension of terms and discoursing in specialised languages. Chapter 6 examines issues of concept and term representation as they impact on questions of knowledge. Models in thematic lexicography and documentation science are examined.

The premise of Chapter 7 is that terminology is currently in a phase of rapid evolution, and that pathways offered in Chapters 4–6 to problems raised in Chapter 3 would have to be integrated in a number of other frameworks for enhanced results of terminology planning. Chapter 7 therefore examines the relevance of the following to work on terminology: special language text linguistics, corpus linguistics, artificial intelligence, and language engineering

---

arrangements have been made therefor" (my italics). There could of course be other reasons for seeking to maintain the *status quo*. A discussion of the politics of language in Nigeria's Second Republic National Assembly can be found in Antia & Haruna (1997).

technologies. Chapter 8 describes the creation of a model terminology resource that employs insights and tools offered by preceding chapters.

Among other issues which it addresses, the conclusion proposes the concepts of *optimisation* and *reengineering* of terminology resources, and suggests how some of the evaluation methods discussed in earlier sections of the book might facilitate the implementation of these concepts.

CHAPTER 1

Terminology in Language Planning Theory

Although intervention in the form and function of languages has long been practised and described, its study (and the process of its formalisation as a discipline) acquired greater impetus in the 1960s, which incidentally was the African decade of independence. The newly emergent states had a need for languages that were sufficiently equipped to function in new roles: administration, education, mass communication, etc. The urgency of the need meant condensing the span of centuries over which the languages in question would have naturally adapted themselves to those functions previously taken on by colonial languages. The linguistic implications of political restructuring in these states and elsewhere in the developing world are documented in *Language Problems of Developing Nations*,[1] the product of a 1966 conference.

1.1 Models of Language Planning

Concomitant with the description of problems was theorisation. Models of language development began to appear in great numbers, the pioneer schemes of Garvin, Ferguson and Haugen being modified by their developers and by others (see Garvin 1973, a development of work done previously; Ferguson 1968, an extension of a 1962 model; Haugen 1983, a clarification of previous models). The model proposed by Haugen, who indeed launched the term *language planning*, has been quite influential (Fishman 1974: 15f). It was developed within the context of Haugen's work on the language situation in Norway.

In its classical version, Haugen's scheme of language development or planning comprises four dimensions forming a two-by-two matrix. Language is viewed in terms of *norm* and *function*, then the object of the planning is seen in terms of *society* and *language*. A norm is selected (selection being social in nature),

---

1. See Fishman, Ferguson & Das Gupta (eds.) 1968.

then codified by being given an orthography, grammar, lexica — these being actions on the language. At the level of function, the selected and codified form needs to be implemented or used (implementation being a social exercise) and elaborated — elaboration being a language task resulting in increased sophistication of the chosen code. The drive for sophistication is occasioned by the need to meet new usage challenges. Many latter models of language planning have sought to modify Haugen's scheme, although Haugen has found some of them quite superfluous (see Haugen 1983). Table 1.1 below presents some of the varying conceptualisations of, and designations for, language planning.

In their barest essentials, many issues in language planning theory have arisen from a ventilation of one or the other subdivision of language planning (as seen in Table 1.1), or of the entire process. Issues that have been quite prominent in the literature include: the auspices of, or authorisation for, language planning, degree of preparation for the process (as witnessed by, among others, cost-benefit valuations), the sequence of planning stages, the agents of planning, its ideological nexus or the particularistic directions in which it is pulled, the different environments in which it is conducted, the nature of the products, evaluation, etc. Indeed on the basis of a number of points in the above listing, two schools or model-constellations may have emerged, especially in the 1980s. The first has been referred to as the *rational model* (Rubin 1983, 1973:7), and by its critics as the *canonical model* (Bamgbose 1987), *ideal planning model* (Chumbow 1987). The second current of opinion might be called the *alternative model*, and has elicited a variety of labels from adherents of the other view. Gorman (see Table 1.1) speaks of *language allocation* for the policy aspect of this practice; Jernudd & Das Gupta (1971:199) implicitly suggest *(language) happening*; Neustupný (1983) suggests *language treatment*, in the specific acceptation (see Table 1.1).

Among other scholars (from the developing world particularly but not exclusively), Bamgbose (1987, 1989, 1992) has argued that an adequate model of language planning must account (in non-handicap terms) for practices that do not conform to the canonical model's *credo* as set out particularly in the volume *Can Language be Planned?*[2] A foundation of the canonical model thinking is embodied in the following ideal view of planning:

> The broadest authorization for planning is obtained from the politicians. A body of experts is then specifically delegated the task of preparing a plan. In preparing this, the experts ideally estimate existing resources and forecast potential utilization of such resources in terms of developmental targets. Once

---

2. See Rubin & Jernudd (eds.) 1971.

targets are agreed upon, a strategy of action is elaborated. These are authorized by the legislature and are implemented by the organizational set-up, authorized in its turn by the planning executive. The implementation of the tasks may be evaluated periodically by the planners (Jernudd & Das Gupta 1971: 196).

In Alisjahbana (1971), Karam (1974), Okonkwo (1977), Brann (1983), Khubchandani (1984) and Bamgbose (1987, 1989, 1991), it is implied or forcefully argued that an adequate model of language planning should accommodate: (1) several types/levels of governmental or non-governmental decision-making and implementation; and (2) several planning mechanisms. While conceding to the ideal model the fact that the choice of a national/official language is properly a government decision, the alternative model takes issue with the rigid requirement of governmental sanctioning for all other aspects of language planning. It also quarrels with the expectation that the only level from which authorisation can be derived is *per force* the central or federal government. On authorisation, Alisjahbana (1971: 186) and Okonkwo (1977: 56; 107) specifically, and Karam (1974: 111) more generally, argue that besides government, working through such agencies as the Education and Information Ministries, Language Planning Agencies, etc., "there are less organised and less coordinated sources of change" (Alisjahbana 1971: 186). The list of sources includes: prominent social figures or language enthusiasts not affiliated to government, the press and electronic media, missionaries, etc. These groups do not simply implement government initiatives. Without express government permission, they also take initiatives of their own the results of which become so generalised as to make (subsequent) government action or endorsement mere formality.

A nascent direction or shift in the theorisation on language planning is observable in work by Jernudd and Neustupný (see Jernudd & Neustupný 1987, 1991; Jernudd 1993, 1997). In proposing the construct of *language management*, they independently arrive at the same conclusion as Jean-Claude Corbeil (1980: 9) and William Mackey (1994: 61) who find that the French la *planification linguistique* has a state-dictatorial, authoritarian and (pseudo) technocratic ring to it. But Jernudd and Neustupný's premises are different (they are not primarily connotative). Thus, while Corbeil finds that his (Corbeil's) proposal, *aménagment linguistique*, makes it possible to derive more transparent and acceptable equivalents for (English) *language status planning* and *language corpus planning*, Jernudd (1993: 134) writes that the "shift of focus [i.e. from the planning to the management model] is an academic response to people power in reaction against central imposition and it recognises the multitude of competing interests".

Table 1.1: *Conceptual and terminological variability in language planning (LP) typology**

Author	Generic term for intervention	Basic subdivisions a	b	c	Acceptation/Comments
Haugen (1966)	Language Planning	Norm selection and codification	Function implementation and elaboration	—	*a*: at society & language levels respectively, identification of a standard or lang., and explicit statement of its forms (phonology, grammar, vocabulary); *b*: at soc. & lang. levels respectively, adoption of the norm, and its continued enrichment
Garvin (1973)	Language Planning	Choice of language	Language development	—	While a folk lang. (defined as one not affected by LP) would manifest some of the structural properties of a standard lang. (one affected by LP), differences would lie in whether or not the properties are linked to formal codification. Thus (leaving beside the self-explanatory *a*), *b* is characterised by deliberate efforts to achieve higher degrees of literacy, flexible stability and intellectualization — these being the properties of a standard lang.
Ferguson (1968)	Language development	Graphization	Standardization	Modernization	*a*: provision of an orthography *b*: establishment of a transcending norm *c*: creation of new vocabularies and discourse styles/forms
Kloss (1969)	Language planning	Status planning	Corpus planning	NN but by Karam (1974) called Planning for Language Planning	*a*: decisions on the social position of a lang. in relation to other languages or as seen by a government. *b*: actions on the body of the lang., including creation of new terms, orthographic or script reforms, etc. *c*: economic aspects of language planning.
Neustupný (1970 in (1974)); (1983)	Linguistic treatment**	Policy approach *Synonyms: sociological/ macroscopic approach*	Cultivation approach *Synonyms: anthropological/ microscopic approach*	—	*a*: actions on choice & form of lang. as taken typically in least advanced & developed communities; covers selection of lang., standardization, orthography, repertoire of code varieties, etc. *b*: typically associated with advanced communities; iteration of many of the above processes as a result of concerns for correctness, efficiency, etc. occasioned by increased specialised use.

	Generic term	Basic subdivisions		
Author	for intervention	a	b	c	Acceptance/Comments
Fishman, Das Gupta, Jernudd, Rubin (1971)	Language planning	Policy formulation	(i) Codification & (ii) Elaboration	Implementation	a: decisions on allocation of codes b(i): standardisation of variation in usage via dictionaries, grammars, etc. b(ii): development, via word lists, etc., of inter-translatability with langs. used for technical purposes c: efforts to gain acceptance for policies and products of language planning
Gorman (1973)	Language Regulation	Language Allocation	Language planning	–	a: restricted to language choice, but this choice is characterised by arbitrariness b: systematic or co-ordinated decisions on codification, elaboration etc. of language chosen.
Jernudd (1973)	Language Planning	Language determination	Language Development	Language implementation	Terminological modification of Fishman et al. a: decisions on functional distribution of langs. in a community as well as on variety to be used for specific purposes; b: standardisation & unification of lang. via grammars, spelling manuals, word lists, etc. c: influencing of lang. use through propagation of results of a & b
Karam (1974)	Language planning	Planning	Implementation	Evaluation	a: preliminary (socio)linguistic surveys, data collection, feasibility plans, decision-making & formulation of strategy on lang. selection b: execution of the plan and needed development work & dissemination c: monitoring & assessing results of a & b, and obtaining feedback

	Generic term	Basic subdivisions			
Author	for intervention	a	b	c	Acceptation/Comments
Okonkwo (1977)	Language planning	Language decision making	Decision implementation	–	Policy formulation is not used for *a* in order to stress that LP is not seen as limited to high-level, administrative policy-making activity *a*: involves problem recognition; identification of goals, values and alternative solutions; problem solving model; prognosis; decision on lang. status or corpus. *b*: execution of decision on status of code or on corpus (codification, elaboration), dissemination
Rubin (1983)	Language planning	Allocation of use	Corpus planning	–	*a*: renaming & reinterpretation of Kloss' status planning. Stems from perceived restriction of Kloss' concept, the context of which makes it refer to minority reactions to language domination. Because not all lang. selection decisions are of this nature, status planning is preferably seen as a subtype of language allocation *b*: sensu Kloss, Haugen
Brann (1983)	–	Language policy	Language planning	Language management	Personal communication (16/1/93), cf. also commentary on flow chart in Brann (1983) *a*: consultation, survey, choice of lang. (cf. boxes 3 & 4 of chart in Brann, 1983) *b*: corpus planning, sensu Kloss (cf. box 5 of chart) *c*: costing, resource allocation, implementation & evaluation (boxes 6–8)

Author	Generic term for intervention	Basic subdivisions a	b	c	Acceptation/Comments
Paulston (1984)	Language planning	Language policy	Language cultivation	–	The three divisions in Jernudd (1973) are seen as occurring in two posited foci of LP: policy & cultivation. The former deals with questions of society & nation, while the latter deals with lang. proper, and is the domain of the lang. specialist. Examples below are not strictly Paulston's. *a*: (i) determination, e.g. decision on lang. choice, (ii) development, e.g. resource allocation, personnel training, directives, (iii) sales, campaigns, enforcement *b*: (i) determination, e.g. decisions on how to develop chosen lang., (ii) development, e.g. preparation of spelling manuals, grammars, wordlists, texts, (iii) implementation, e.g. advisory roles on usage
Chumbow (1987)	Language planning	Policy formulation	Policy implementation	–	*a*: has a broad scope including fact-finding, actual policy, implementation goals & processes, allocation of resources *b*: divides into (i) standardisation, covering choice of lang., lang. engineering (sensu corpus planning) & reforms of corpus planning; (ii) dissemination, covering diffusion of policy and outcomes of planning, development of personnel, etc.

* The term *language engineering*, by which many language planners have long described their trade, is also now used in the so-called language industries to describe preoccupation with the development of computer applications for natural language processing (see Chapter 7).

** This term covers communication problems of which those typically addressed by LP are but an instance. Also designates problems not addressed with the rigour & systemicity reserved for, and characteristic of, LP.

In what initially appears as an apparent abandonment of the language treatment terminology (see Table 1.1) and of the government-initiated/agency-focused responses to language problems (see canonical model), Jernudd and Neustupný view discourse as the centre of language management. The "engine of authority" for language planning (as a search for solutions to language problems) is discourse. If the definition of language management below is only arguably a reversal of the classical view of planning, it indisputably removes the strictures of this classical view (in its application to language), thus addressing some of the concerns raised by Bamgbose, Khubchandani (1984), Chumbow (see Table 1.1) and other language planning scholars from the developing world. Jernudd defines language management as:

> a process through which particular people are given the authority to find and suggest systematic and rigorous solutions to problems of language potentially or actually encountered by members of their community. Note that this formulation does not presuppose a democratic or any other particular institutional process of authorization; but it does require identification of the language problem in discourse. Such identification should be rigorous and extensive, although in historical language planning it often remains undeveloped (Jernudd 1991: 134).

With its grassroots or bottom-up orientation, language management seeks to employ data from the way individuals cope or fail to cope with communication challenges as basis for community-wide actions. The *raison d'être* of the management effort is problem encountered or anticipated in language use. This is evident in the requirements of: language feature noting, evaluation as to appositeness or conformity to norm, and of adjustment (see Jernudd 1997; Jernudd & Neustupný 1991: 32). The importance of this approach is better appreciated when it is known that, with traditional approaches to language (corpus) planning, so-called language problems could simply be a façade for the attainment of non-linguistic goals. With the management framework, only problems that are demonstrably present in discourse receive attention.

But the foregoing optimism (felicitousness of the term *management*, and flexibility in the conception of planning auspices) requires moderation. This is because language management, like the presumably obsolescent language treatment (see Table 1.1), is a framework into which language planning figures as type, although the relationship is not always clear.[3] When, in Jernudd (1997)

---

3. Jernudd (1993: 140) writes that "Language management's focus on discourse [...] provides a basis on which to relate language planning to other language management systems such as language

and elsewhere, language planning is described as a type of language management, a generic term that also has a management approach to language planning as subtype, one is inclined to conclude that language planning is still being maintained in its historical formulation (i.e. still held to meet the classic requirements). If that were the case, and non-conforming but discourse-centred practices elicited the term language management, then the inference would be that the historical language planning norm (government/agency-focus) was not being reformed; rather, a parallel framework was being created that more accurately reflected the prevailing people-centred ideology as well as real statistics.

From two papers (Jernudd 1993: 140; Jernudd & Neustupný 1991: 31; 35), it is evident that it is only by subscribing to a language management framework that language planning is able to reflect the relationship between individuals and discourse, or have problems in discourse validate the planning exercise.

But surely, historical language planning can also be re-conceptualised so that planning in this mould ceases to be seen exclusively as the correlate of a command economy, which the contemporary mood of free enterprise frowns upon. Indeed, in parts of the developing world, community level or grass-roots level language planning has been taking place for some time now, and has recently started to be theorised upon in non-handicap terms. This is seen in Khubchandani's concept of situation-bound language planning (Khubchandani 1984), in Emenanjo (1991), and it is suggested by the title of a 1985 publication by Kozelka: *Community-Based Language Planning. A Movement Needed and Starting in West Africa* (University of Laval/former ICRB). A focus on discourse, to reflect another contemporary trend which Jernudd (1993: 140) rightly refers to as "discourse-based discoursing" would be in order. This would also address another requirement of the management model.

Let us now examine the place of terminology in this extremely abbreviated overview of language planning theory.

1.2 Terminology in Language Planning Theory

A number of the models presented in Table 1.1 do not only account for the lexical dimension of language, but actually go ahead to distinguish between two levels — a general lexicon and a specialised lexicon. The latter is of interest here. Terminology is part of elaboration in Haugen's model; an aspect of

---

cultivation, terminology, language teaching, among others".

intellectualisation in Garvin's language development; a part of modernisation in Ferguson's scheme; a component in Neustupný's cultivation approach, etc. Work on terminology is typically the result of challenges associated with (the continuing) implementation or use of the chosen code. But from the point of view of alternative or more flexible models, terminology, like other aspects of corpus planning, can be the reason for choosing a code. In several post colonial settings, language determination or language policy formulation at independence was generally informed by the results of corpus planning initiatives implemented decades earlier by missionary-linguists.

1.2.1 Who plans terminology?

The governmental focus of what was called the ideal model of language planning is also evident in the perception of the agents of terminology planning. This view is confirmed by some premises of the International Research Project on Language Planning Processes (IRPLPP). Jernudd, a member of the team, notes as follows:

> The project emphasized one kind of organization of language planning by selecting to study and therefore assuming the importance of agencies that have been established to manage and prepare language development, namely 'language planning agencies' sponsored by government (Jernudd 1973: 17).

Jernudd (1973), while admitting of the possibility of private and non-governmental initiatives, chooses to refer to the latter as instances of language treatment, reserving language planning for government/agency implementation. It is perhaps a measure of the restrictedness or elusiveness of the Government/agency-centred ideal model that Jernudd & Das Gupta (1971: 210) note that work on terminology can be taken on by individuals and professional associations, groups which empirical studies have shown to "create and disseminate vocabulary with far greater success than government agencies". In an apparent self-reversal, occasioned by the language management construct, Jernudd (and his co-author, see Jernudd & Neustupný 1991: 30f) regrets the focus enjoyed by agencies in the IRPLPP. This acknowledgement is instructive, even though the thrust in the above paper is the relation between language problems of individuals in specific discourse situations and agency solutions. As this thrust has a broader interest, a brief digression into evaluation is perhaps justified. Jernudd & Neustupný (1991: 31) note that:

> It [the IRPLPP] gathered language data only as deemed relevant to evaluating agency influence on language use. Because of this particular interest, the project did not consider, for example, the processes of term evaluation in

various situations of discourse (i.e. in editing, lecturing, writing of manuals, industrial training, laboratory report writing, advertising, etc.).

This is a task that the proposed language management framework could not have missed out. To whatever extent the above pattern has been followed, the critique suggests the kinds of feedback that have been obtained from the much talked-about evaluations of language planning (as far as terminology is concerned).

The prospects of non-institutional or individual language planners becoming objects of scholarly interest may yet be bright. In his conference comments at the end of the Ottawa Language Planning Colloquium (see Laforge 1987), Fishman describes this issue as one of several overlooked or neglected topics. He notes:

> The role of individual language planners has also been slighted in our deliberations. Many languages have benefited from the contributions of particularly charismatic and authoritative advocates, innovators and normifiers. We really know all too little about more than a mere handful of them, and as a result, we really lack any theoretical approach to their successes and failures. [...]. This is definitely an area for fruitful exploration [...] (Fishman 1987: 423–7).

1.2.2 Modelling rationales for success in terminology

Taking a point around the 1960s as the beginning of contemporary, internationally co-ordinated, scholarship on language planning, Ray (1963) and Tauli (1968) may be seen as two early attempts at specifying the bases for success in terminology planning (and language planning in general). Taking a *tool* view of language, both authors set up their postulates of the *ideal language*. Ray postulates *efficiency, rationality, commonality*, while Tauli puts forward *clarity, economy, beauty*. Applied to the lexicon, Ray's efficiency would stipulate, for instance, (1) that frequent words be short; (2) that such words, because of the associations they pick up in various contexts, be least favoured as labels for technical concepts, etc. Tauli's more controversial postulates would require (1) a term to convey to the listener the meaning intended by its creator, and quickly too; (2) be as short as possible (shortness being quantifiable in syllables, etc.); (3) be euphonious, etc.

Less idealistic models which have similarly focused on the language corpus stress empirical and structural rationales for the *good term*. Such a term, in other words, must conform to established term formation or borrowing patterns in a particular language. Countless publications deal with this kind of justification. Fishman sees aspects of this linguistic emphasis as creating a spurious recipe for success in terminology planning. He notes that:

> The tendency to view 'corpus planning' as nothing special, as just one more technical skill that a linguist should be able to pull out of his bag of tricks, is triply mistaken. It reveals a misunderstanding of lexicons per se, of corpus planning as a whole, and of the societal nexus of language planning more generally (Fishman 1983: 2).

Two of these errors, the first and the third, are of interest here. A common view of terminology/corpus planning, according to Fishman, is that it is no more than a "simple, technical, linguistic exercise". Lexicons tend to be seen as "interchangeable, dry and dreary 'nuts' and 'bolts'". Fishman counters this downgrading of lexicons, noting that lexicons "are not endless laundry lists, without rhyme and reason, without order or pattern, without systematic links to each other and to all other facets of language". Fishman leaves the reader to find his recommended panacea to this downgrading of the lexicon in two statements: (1) the "socio-cultural and political sensitivities" required for successful terminology planning are of the kind "most linguists neither possess nor imagine"; and (2) the downgrading "reveals a profound ignorance" of language.

Fishman's interest in alerting the language planning community to the societal auspices of their work comes through quite clearly in the discussion of the third error, that is, the societal nexus of the lexicon/corpus planning. He writes:

> Most serious of all, however, is the lack of recognition revealed by the 'merely lexicon' view of (a) the delicate and complex social context that commonly surrounds corpus planning and of (b) the need for professional expertise with respect to that context if corpus planning is to succeed. It is a devastating mistake to assume that corpus planning merely requires the interplay and coordination of linguistic expertise and technological expertise, devastating certainly if one's goal is not merely to do corpus planning (i.e., not merely to create a nomenclature in chemistry, or in some other modern technological area) but to have it accepted (i.e., to have it liked, learned and used). If the latter is our goal (and anything less strikes me as a travesty), then cultural expertise in all its ramifications is called for as well (Fishman 1983: 3).

The 'sociological argument' would seem to have drowned out the argument associated with the discussion of the first error. That is, in Fishman's essay and in works by others following his lead. In the latter category, the amplification of sociology is such that the equilibrium which Fishman presumably sought to introduce in the scales of rationales for success has been lost. The following view expressed by Seyoum (1985) precedes a quotation from Fishman concerning "the tremendously complicated socio-cultural-political sensitivities" that are required in language planning, but that elude most linguists:

> In Ethiopia, the subject of language planning is usually narrowly perceived. Mostly it is seen only as a simple problem of terminology. [...] [T]he solutions are also believed to be accordingly simple and limited, rarely exceeding the limits of the lexicon (Seyoum 1985: 434).

Complexity is increasingly viewed and probed less from the standpoint of language-related challenges posed by the object of the planning effort (particularly, terminology), but more from the standpoint of socio-cultural factors.

The corollary of language scholars increasingly being less of linguists and more of sociologists and politicians is that language planning processes and products run the risk of being adversely affected by issues like what languages/ cultures words are to be borrowed from, or were borrowed from, and how this is expected to affect acceptability — issues about which the ordinary language user may not have cared if persons (language planners) who may stand to benefit from highlighting divisions had not assigned these issues spurious importance. Indeed, in a few of the language planning agencies known to this writer, the task (often sociologically-oriented) of establishing and ranking sources of borrowing is vital, almost etched in stone, irrespective of, and in advance of, specific language problems. Such is the criticality of sources that, if not adhered to, even the other commonly laid-down principle (conformity to the structure of the language being enriched) counts for nothing as far as acceptability or success of the planning process is concerned.

It certainly would be interesting to find out how technical weaknesses in a terminology, such as arising from the first error identified by Fishman, contribute to societal (non) acceptability. Seen differently, can (publicised) technical considerations be employed to canvass support for a language planning product? How can the need to create terms for a series of related concepts in a given field momentarily invalidate sociologically validated preferences as far as borrowing languages is concerned? How can the use in language x of graphemes associated with language y (speakers of which are put off by community x, and vice versa) be justified in terms of the need to have graphemes that are accommodated in, or supported by, available (computer) character sets? How can other kinds of decision-making on terms be explained by concerns of text production? This latter point on text production is amplified below because of the implications it has for the methodology and evaluation of the current work.

Jernudd's view of the International Research Project on Language Planning Processes (IRPLPP) was cited in Section 1.2.1. Indeed, preoccupied as many of its members have been by sociological matters, the language planning community has failed to draw discourse implications from the data in target-audience evaluations of terms proposed by language academies. The data in studies such as Alloni-Fainberg (1974), Rubin (1977), Kummer (1983), etc. show that the percentage of respondents claiming to use academy proposed terms (in their professions) is consistently lower than the percentage of those who claim to know these terms. Rubin's study is of particular interest, firstly because it is an IRPLPP report, and secondly because its title, "Textbook writers and Language Planning", suggests preoccupation with specific discourse issues. Alas, but not surprisingly in the light of Jernudd's comments, Rubin's study was "designed to elicit information about LPAs [language planning agencies] and not about the language problems which textbook writers face". In the study's two sites, Rubin notes that "stated usage of LPA terminologies was relatively low". Information about LPA terminologies from two sets of textbook writers is presented as Table 1.2.

Table 1.2: *Knowledge and use of academy terms (from Rubin 1977)*

	Indonesia	Israel
LPA Chemistry terminology		
Number of Chemistry writers	24	7
1. Knows of terminology	8	3
2. Uses	5	1
3. Help create	4	2
LPA Grammar terminology		
Number of Grammar writers	16	5
1. Knows of terminology	9	3
2. Uses	8	2
3. Help create	3	0

Surprisingly, one of those who helped to create the Chemistry terminology in Israel does not use this terminology.[4] Rubin then proceeds to determine where these textbook writers obtain their terms. Rubin does this by asking questions on the position of LPAs in relation to other (stated) sources of terms. Findings are presented in Table 1.3.

The poor rating of LPAs leads Rubin to conclude that if these LPAs wish to be more relevant, they "should set about finding what the language problems of authors are and attempt to prepare some materials which might answer these needs".

---

4. Now, it is obvious that results obtained from self-reporting (in respect of both use and non-use) must be taken with caution when they cannot be verified.

Table 1.3: *Textbook writers' use of sources of terminology (from Rubin 1977)*

	Indonesia	Israel
Reference work (existing textbooks, dictionaries, journals)	34	30
Own self or friends	13	15
Agency [LPA]	4	5

One might hypothesise that the problems of the writers could have been of a discourse kind, that is, the integration of terms in discourse. It would have been interesting to analyse what kinds of information textbook writers actually obtained from existing books, journals, friends, etc. Besides views of LPA terms couched in comments like "not exact" (Israel) and "not commonly known" (Indonesia), discourse production considerations may have been revealed by a different evaluation procedure (different from self-reporting based on presented term lists). This is what evidence in subsequent parts of this work will be suggesting. But even if one was wrong about the specifics of the hypothesis, sociology would be a dubious explanation for the non-use of academy terms.

The foregoing does not seek to scuttle sociology. The point rather is that there are rationales for the *good term* that are rooted in sources other than sociology. Language planners would do well to (re)assert these other sources so as to (re)establish a balance in the modelling of rationales for the success of language or terminology planning.

1.2.3   *Where is what done on terminology?*

Neustupný (see Table 1.1) suggests that language planning in developing and developed countries (or speech communities) could be distinguished on the basis of approach. The former societies are characterised by what is called the policy approach, and the latter by the cultivation approach. In Jernudd (1983: 366ff), approaches to terminology in both societies are quite clearly stated. In developed countries or speech communities, the emphasis is said to lie in term systematicity, definitions, and harmonisation achieved typically through the "careful preparation of highly specialised reference works, often containing only a modest number of highly elaborated term entries". In developing countries or speech communities, "a demonstration effect through publication of volumes of lists and perhaps texts (maybe critically selected for impact) should be the goal" (Jernudd 1983: 366).

While this difference just might have stemmed from observation, explained in turn by the different starting points of LP and terminology as disciplines,

Jernudd appears to validate and recommend the thrust in the developing world, quite unlike another author cited by him (Noss) who "dismisses 'gazetting discipline vocabulary' as a means to 'establish discipline vocabulary' in Southeast Asian languages". Rationalisation for the thrust in the developed world is variation in terminology usage, while in the developing world it would appear to be a public relations event, attempting to prove that concepts and discourse of a certain kind can be linguistically indigenised (see Jernudd 1983). It is not clear what course work on terminology is to take after the PR blitz and before proliferation of terms becomes an issue. If what appears as the prescribed thrust of terminology in the developing world has been followed, the findings of the next chapter would appear to have already been outlined. The next chapter examines the discourse on, and practice of, terminology in Africa.

CHAPTER 2

Terminology Discourse and Practice in Africa
Issues, Players and Arenas

This chapter attempts an overview of LP-oriented terminology in parts of sub-Saharan Africa. It sets LP in the broader context of preoccupation with social planning. Using a number of countries and a linguistic bloc as case studies, the chapter describes African terminological practices in terms of motivations, agents, domains, public relations challenges and methods. Also, the theory underlying practice is reconstructed from tendencies in the related metadiscourse. The ultimate goal of this chapter, and of the next, is to investigate if there exist grounds for alternative or complementary modes of practice and discourse.

2.1 Motivation, Players and Arenas: Case Studies

The cases examined here are Somalia, Tanzania, Nigeria, Ethiopia and countries that were formerly under French colonisation.

2.1.1 *Somalia*

1960 saw the amalgamation of the British Somaliland Protectorate and the Italian United Nations Trusteeship territory of Somalia. With this development, colonial presence in Somali formally came to an end. The newly independent state inherited two foreign official languages (English in the North and Italian in the South) both used by a minority, and two systems of education (Caney 1980).

Arabic and Somali had national spread but neither could immediately replace the foreign languages. Knowledge of the former was rudimentary, and the latter had neither a standard orthography nor a single script. Latin and Arabic scripts were in competition (Andrzejewski 1983; Caney 1980). Neither language could therefore support the *paper bureaucracy* of a modern state! The written foreign languages (English and Italian) offered no ideal solution either in the now unified country: only very few civil servants knew both languages. The problems of administration and education in the new state are well captured by a United Nations official sent to study the situation:

> ... the continued language problem is impeding the development of the Somali state. Students are discouraged from attending school because they must struggle with the essentials of a foreign tongue before they can master the substantive courses. All available literature remains the preserve of a privileged few. Laws that define the rights and obligations must be interpreted, often falteringly, to the people. Finally, the absence of a nationally accepted written language inhibits further development of a virile consciousness (quoted in Caney 1980: 29).

To round off this catalogue of problems, mention ought to be made of an ideological issue. Somalis have repeatedly been described as extremely proud of their language, Somali. So great is the emotional investment in the Somali language that Somalis may have been dissatisfied with English or Italian, had either been the only linguistic legacy of foreign presence in their country. According to Andrzejewski, for many Somali intellectuals it was important to battle the concept of *Gumeysi maskaxeed* (colonisation of the brain) by which they mean the "excessive admiration of foreign languages and cultures, even leading sometimes to a belief that African languages are not adequate to meet the challenges of the modern world" (Andrzejewski 1983: 69).

With this background of sentimental attachment, it is perhaps no surprise that when the decision was eventually taken to seriously tackle the language (and terminology) problem, the success obtained was phenomenal in its rapidity. Within a few years of its ascent to power in 1969, the self-styled Revolutionary Government of Siad Biarre had been able to achieve a number of feats: Somali had been declared the sole official language; the Latin script had been adopted; Somali had been introduced as the sole medium of instruction in the lower levels of primary instruction; terminologies and school textbooks had begun to be produced in great numbers; literacy in Somali had become widespread among civil servants, etc. Indeed, by 1983, Somali school books had become available for the entire spectrum of pre-university education.

Terminology was clearly one of several important foci in this transformation of Somali over a period of ten odd years. It is a moot point whether the decisions of the Revolutionary Government were affected by the work of previous administrations (compare Bamgbose 1991: 15 with Caney 1980: 17). But it is noteworthy that before the advent of the Revolutionary Government of Siad Biarre, members of the Somali Language Commission had been sent to the then Soviet Union, China, the Arab states, etc. to study methods of vocabulary expansion (Caney 1980: 17). It is Caney's view that although its foundations had been laid in the 1940s, with the advent of broadcasting, Somali lexical modernisation officially took off in 1972. This must be particularly true of terminology associated with school subjects.

The task of creating terminologies for school books initially fell to the Somali Language Commission, and subsequently to the Department of Curriculum of the Ministry of Education and Youth Training. For vocabulary of a general *cum* political nature, the responsibility was shared primarily between the Ministry of Information and the radio service. Broadcasting was introduced into Somalia during the Second World War. Concepts of the day that were alien to the traditional conceptual universe of the Somalis somehow had to be communicated *via* translation to Somali audiences. The role of the mass media as a language (terminology) planning agency has been described elsewhere (Antia 1991, 1992). In filling this tall order, made all the more difficult by an audience with strong views on language, translators had to collaborate closely with poets. Because of what may be called their 'wordsmithery' poets are respected in traditional Somali society.

Besides vocabulary of a general *cum* political nature, many other domains were covered. To illustrate his discussion, Caney obtains terms from a variety of sources and arranges them in twenty fields of discourse. In spite of the acknowledged difficulty of determining whether specific terms in these fields are the result of conscious planning or of unplanned development, it seems safe to assume that much of the terminology in the school-type subject fields originated from the planned activities of the Language Commission and the Education Ministry. The fields of discourse listed are: Agriculture, the Armed Forces, Banking and Finance, Chemistry, Commerce and Industry, Communications, Education, Geography, Language, Law, Mathematics, Medicine, Office equipment, Physics, Politics and Public Affairs, Printing and Publishing, Sport, Town and Facilities, Vehicle and Vehicle Parts, and Work.

2.1.2   *Tanzania*

In Tanzania, Swahili played an important role in the struggle for independence from Britain. The nationalist movement, the Tangayinka African National Union (TANU), just like its predecessor, mobilised the masses in Swahili, and generally conducted its affairs in this language. As J. O'Barr (1976: 70) notes, "Swahili became a medium of developing a political consciousness". With the attainment of independence in 1961, the language was again to be called to duty by a grateful leadership as it came to terms with the manifold task of nation-building.

In 1962 when Tanzania became a Republic, the President of the newly independent state, Julius Nyerere, signalled the role Swahili was to play in the new dispensation by making his speech to the nation on Republic Day in Swahili. This date and event are generally taken to indicate the endowment of national status on Swahili.[1]

Beginning from this same year (1962), the requirement that aspirants to the National Assembly be proficient in English was dropped (J. O'Barr 1976: 77). According to J. O'Barr, while the Constitution of 1965 did not establish a linguistic requirement for membership of the Assembly, it had provisions requiring that electoral campaigns be conducted in Swahili. The import of these provisions on the competence of legislators in Swahili is obvious. In the area of the law, Swahili was given official and co-official status in primary courts and high courts respectively in 1964 (DuBow 1976: 87).

In 1964, the position of Promoter of Swahili was created by government (Polomé 1983/4: 65), and in 1967 Swahili was declared an official language. The educational sector was to be one of the key arenas for implementing this policy. Although Swahili was already being used in primary schools, it was to be extended to the secondary tier as medium of instruction, and not just as a subject. In the phased programme of transiting from English to Swahili which educational authorities drew up, 1971 was projected as commencement date for teaching the following subjects in Swahili: History, Geography, Political Education, Mathematics, Agronomy and Biology (Kummer 1983).

In 1974, government restated its commitment to implementing the swahilisation process when the Vice-President declared that "from August 1st, all correspondence, forms and sign posts in all parastatal and public organizations must be in Swahili" (Polomé 1983/84: 65).

These measures were consistent with the directive principles of state policy which actively sought to enhance popular participation in institutions of state. In this particular instance, English was the hurdle to be removed. It is irresistible to quote the eminent scholar, Ali Mazrui, who, writing in 1967, contrasts the level of mass participation in Tanzania with other parts of Africa:

> In a country such as Tanzania, national leadership can be recruited from a wider sector of the society. First Vice-President Abeid Karume has no com-

---

1. In Africa it is important to note that a difference is sometimes made or intended between *national language* and *official language*. See discussions in Antia *(forthcoming)*, Bamgbose (1991) and Brann (1989). In Antia *(forthcoming)*, it is suggested that in the Tanzanian case the *national language* serves ceremonial or symbolic purposes, whereas the *official language* is understood more in the sense of working language.

mand of English, and there are many important TANU figures who hold high office without the credentials of fluency in the English language. It used to be said that 'every American is a potential millionaire'. This was always a gross exaggeration, but it was a useful way of portraying the United States as a land of capitalistic opportunity. Today it can be rhetorically claimed that 'every Tanzanian is a potential TANU leader'. This too is a gross exaggeration, but it indicates the range of egalitarian opportunities in Tanzania. And the sector of political recruitment is larger and more varied than in the neighbouring states partly because the national language, Swahili, is not an elite language (quoted by J. O'Barr 1976: 76).

The motivation for work on terminology in Swahili in Tanzania came precisely from the place accorded this language in the socialist vision (*ujamaa*) of the country's leaders.

The task of creating terminologies fell to a number of bodies co-ordinated by the Swahili National Council (BAKITA) which was established in 1967, the year Swahili became an official language. One of the functions of this apex regulatory body was "to co-operate with the authorities concerned in establishing standard Swahili translations of technical terms" (Polomé 1983/84: 64). Other players include such units of the University of Dar es Salaam as the Institute of Education, which is concerned with terms for school books, and the Institute of Kiswahili Research, concerned with a more general terminological enrichment of the language (Khamisi 1991: 215ff). Individuals in other academic units, such as Professor Weston of the Law Faculty, have been associated with specific projects. There are also players outside of the ivory tower, among them the Tanzania Episcopal Conference, and the mass media.

Terminologies have been created for a variety of domains. The information presented below is based on inspected term lists, some of which date back to the 1970s. *Tafsiri Sanifu* is a BAKITA organ for publishing approved terms. The second issue for 1976 contains term lists in the following fields: Commerce and Economics (438 terms), National Assembly/Parliament (274 terms), Mathematics (132), Geography (184 terms), Library and Bindery (122 terms), Post Office (63 terms), Science (145 terms), Language Science (185 terms), Educational Research and Evaluation (62 terms), and Ministries, Institutions, Departments, Posts Held, etc. (975 terms). A 1985 issue of the same publication (no.5) lists the following: Administration/Management (68 terms), Agricultural Engineering (324 terms), Agronomy and Animal Husbandry (549 terms), Mathematics (72 terms), Motor Mechanics (124 terms), Photography (72 terms), Physics (37 terms), Plant/Animal Diseases and Pests (134 terms), Psychology (251 terms), Punctuation marks (14 terms). These domains, in addition to some others like University units and positions, are also reflected in older lists published in another BAKITA journal, *LughaYetu*. Lists of anywhere between 20 and 100 hundred terms are to be seen in this latter outlet. *Kiswahili*, the journal of the Institute of Kiswahili Research of the University of Dar es Salaam, has also published term lists in several of its issues. While up-to-date information could not be obtained, it appears that some domains for which few terms were created in the 1970s have received more comprehensive treatment. In these cases, as in the linguistic and literary terminology, whole publications are dedicated to the particular domain. The linguistic terminology, which appeared in 1990 as *Kamusi Sanifu ya Isimu na Lugha*, contains 1,439 terms, with definitions. The inclusion of definitions is quite exceptional.

2.1.3   Nigeria

Although in the run-up to Nigeria's independence in 1960, and immediately thereafter, calls for the replacement of English as official language by an indigenous language were common, these were seen in certain quarters as being more self-serving than altruistic (Antia & Haruna 1997). Pre-independence rivalry and suspicion between the country's major ethnic groups, the absence of a single language with a nationally strong speaker base, vocal minorities, a government unprepared to upset the applecart — all of these meant that a decision on official status for one or a few of the country's 400 languages was an issue that was too hot to handle.

The taciturnity of political authorities on the subject meant that pre-independence linguistic practices were largely to be continued. Thus, in the legislatures, offices and schools of the three post-independence regional administrations (and of later administrative units), English or Nigerian languages, or admixtures of both, simply continued to be used. To give an example, in public primary schools, use of the mother tongue in initial classes was maintained, a practice that had been more or less followed in British West Africa since the Phelps-Stoke Commission recommendations of 1922 (Bamgbose 1976: 10). In reality, mother tongue education often meant code-mixing. A typical language behaviour in a mathematics class taught in the mother tongue (Yoruba) in some areas of South Western Nigeria is given by Oredugba (1977). In stating the task represented by 24 + 43 = ?, the teacher says *Kini twenty-four plus forty-three?* And by way of answer: *three plus four je seven; four plus two je six; ansa je sixty-seven.*

A significant, but short-lived, exception to the pattern of initial mother tongue education was in Northern Nigeria where a *Straight-for-English* policy was adopted at independence, a policy which sought to introduce English as early as possible into the educational system. The six states created in 1967 to replace the former Northern Regional Government reverted to variants of the old policy (Bamgbose 1976: 18). To remain with Northern Nigeria, that region's post independence legislature maintained the tradition of its predecessor by granting Hausa co-official status with English, even though the latter was to prevail in cases of conflict in records. And as noted elsewhere (Antia 1996b) code-switching/mixing (Hausa-English) was a feature of deliberations of that legislature, albeit one that was frowned upon.

These default language policies provided the motivation for whatever little work was done on terminology, until (1) the series of events leading up to, and including, the formulation of a National Policy on Education (1977), and (2) the promulgation of the 1979 Federal Constitution. Both documents have explicit language provisions. Let us take each of these two points in turn.

In 1970, the Institute of Education at the then University of Ife began a project called the Six Year Primary Project. According to Bamgbose (1991: 85), the "objective of the Six Year Primary Project was to compare the traditional mixed media with a new system in which Yoruba was used as a medium of instruction for the full six years of primary education". Evaluations, which began in 1976, showed consistently that the experimental group that was taught in Yoruba performed better than the control group that was taught in the traditional fashion.

In 1974, the Federal Government of Nigeria, while making its views known on the report of a Federal Civil Service Review Commission, noted as follows:

> Although the adoption of a lingua franca in Nigeria is a task which cannot be achieved overnight, Government is of the view that a beginning should be made as soon as possible and considers it to be in the interest of national unity that each child should be encouraged to learn one of the three major languages in Nigeria other than his vernacular (quoted by Ojerinde 1978: 15).

For the take-off of its Universal Primary Education Programme, billed to start in September 1976, government announced in 1975 that it was ready to support the preparation of teaching materials in seven languages, *viz.*: Edo, Efik, Fulfulde, Hausa, Igbo, Kanuri and Yoruba. In that same year (1975), government created the National Language Centre as a service arm of the Federal Ministry of Education. In 1977, the National Policy on Education was promulgated (amended 1981). The policy provides for the use of the mother tongue from pre-primary education to some point in primary school at which a switch to English is effected. It also provides for the teaching of two Nigerian languages in Junior Secondary School, and one in Senior Secondary School. The language in the latter tier had to be one of Hausa, Igbo and Yoruba, these being the major languages identified by the policy.

These series of events provided the impetus for two milestone projects in the Nigerian history of terminology. In October/November 1978, government, through its Education Ministry (National Language Centre), sponsored a Terminology Workshop at the Faculty of Education of the then University of Ife (renamed Obafemi Awolowo University). The aim, as stated in the workshop programme, was "to compile an official standardized glossary of technical and scientific terminologies for the primary school curriculum in the following nine (9) Nigerian Languages: Edo, Efik, Fulfulde, Hausa, Igbo, Ijo, Kanuri, Yoruba and Tiv". These projects have since appeared, in three volumes (3 languages per volume), as a *A Vocabulary of Primary Science and Mathematics*. On average each language has over a thousand entries. There are no definitions.

In 1981, another Federal Government parastatal, the Nigeria Educational Research Council (NERC) — which was to be merged in 1988 with the National Language Centre — set about implementing the provision on the teaching of indigenous languages. That year, the NERC provided financial support for a Yoruba Metalanguage which had been in gestation for some seven years, having been discussed at the 1974 Annual General Meeting of the YSAN, the Yoruba Studies Association of Nigeria (Bamgbose 1990: v). Similar initiatives from the Society for Promoting Igbo Language and Culture (SPILC) and the Hausa Studies Association (HSA), were now to become part of NERC's supported Metalanguage Projects. These projects have since appeared as *Hausa Metalanguage*, *Igbo Metalanguage* and *Yorùbá Metalanguage*. The average number of terms for each language is two thousand. Terms are not accompanied by definitions.

The other policy event that served as catalyst to another significant project was the promulgation of the 1979 Constitution of the Federal Republic of Nigeria. Section 51(1) of that Constitution provides that "The business of the National Assembly shall be conducted in English and in Hausa, Igbo and Yoruba when adequate arrangements have been made therefor". At the level of state legislatures, the same document stipulates that "The business of the House of Assembly shall be conducted in English, but the House may in addition conduct the business of the House in one or more languages spoken by the state as the House may by resolution approve". In 1980, the National Assembly commissioned the National Language Centre to develop terms in Hausa, Igbo and Yoruba, so as to enhance the prospects of the use of these languages for legislative business as envisioned by the Constitution. The termination of the Second Republic delayed work on the project, which however eventually appeared in 1991 as the *Quadrilingual Glossary of Legislative Terms (English, Hausa, Igbo and Yoruba)*. This work has 18,000 entries. There are no definitions.

Besides the mathematics/science, metalanguage and legislative terminologies produced by the respective agencies, there are other efforts under different auspices: terms evolved in the course of writing primers in indigenous languages, produced at university research centres, or by the mass media, but these are regrettably not always publicised or compiled. With respect to the mass media, a notable exception is, as noted elsewhere (Antia 1995a), the publication by McIntyre and Meyer-Bahlberg, *Hausa in the Media: A Lexical Guide*, which is a collection based on words gathered from a Hausa language newspaper in Nigeria, together with translations done by the Hausa Service of *Deutsche Welle*, the international service of German Radio.

2.1.4 *Ethiopia*

With the exception of the legendary conquest by Moses put at about 1300 BC, and a five-year (1936–1941) Italian occupation, Ethiopia has the distinction of not having been colonised (Edmonds 1975: 12). Amharic, the most widely spoken of the country's seventy languages, has enjoyed a high social profile since the thirteenth century, beginning with the fall of the Aksum empire and the concomitant replacement of Geez as the *Lisane Nigus*, or King's tongue (Seyoum 1988). Seyoum cites a number of reasons why the spread and development of Amharic fall short of expectations spawned by the language's 700-year history of societal prestige — underpinned, albeit, by a mutation of declared *de jure* statuses.[2] Seyoum also notes that modern education, with the varied, systematic and novel communication challenges it poses, has been the greatest catalyst for the development of Amharic in recent times. One effect of the officialisation of Amharic in 1955 was its introduction, in 1964, as medium of instruction in primary schools. Amharic textbooks and teaching materials had to be developed. By developing terminologies to facilitate translation of school texts, the Academy of Ethiopian Languages was an important ally in the linguistic indigenisation of the school curriculum.

Since Ethiopia's modernisation drive was not conceived as exclusively linked to formal education, inability to carry through the amharicisation process to higher tiers of the educational spectrum did not mean a halt of terminological activities. Terminology was indeed a component of a 1991 project involving the Ethiopian Government and the United Nations Interim Fund for Science and Technology for

---

2. A revised Constitution promulgated in 1955 accorded Amharic official status. A National Democratic Revolution Programme (1976) changed this *de jure* status, and considered all languages to be socially equal. A draft Constitution (1986) recognised Amharic as the working language of government.

Development (UNIFFSTD). The project, titled *Development of National Capacity of Popularization and Training in Science and Technology through Language and Demonstration*, had the following premise which I quote *in extenso*:

> Parallel to the growth of science education at the university, one also witnesses the development of an insatiable interest among the population at large to learn, understand and apply scientific and technological concepts. This general shift of interest towards science and technology has far reaching implications and consequences on the total population of the country, now estimated at 45 million, a great majority i.e. over 95% of which neither speaks nor understands English or any of the major European languages (Dagne/Gemeda as reported by Stoberski 1987: 3).

Recognition of the place of terminology in making Amharic serve this goal of popularisation was reflected in the creation of a sub-project, *Development of Scientific and Technological Terminology in Amharic*, widely referred to as the Science Technology Terms Translation Project (STTP). An agreement between the Ethiopian Science and Technology Commission and the Academy of Ethiopian Languages saw the Academy take up this part of the project (Stoberski 1987). The report on that project shows terms were created in the following fields: Agriculture (894 terms), Botany (1,054), Zoology (1,140), Chemistry (1,335), Geology (1,204), Geography (1,715), Mathematics (1,038), Medicine (1,415), Nutrition (439), Physics (2,154), Statistics (581), Electro-Mechanics (1,182), Building-Construction (939).

Next, I consider countries that were under French colonial rule. The country profiles do not extend to ex-Portuguese and Spanish colonies. The international institutional framework within which a number of terminology projects have been carried out in Francophone countries justifies a collective treatment.

2.1.5 *Francophone Africa*

Unlike its British counterpart, French colonial policy in Africa (conveniently summed up by the concept of *assimilation*) had very little role for, or recognition of, African languages. In the area of education, for instance, Bamgbose (1976: 10) notes that French and Portuguese colonial policy aimed at "assimilating Africans into the civilization of the metropolitan power", as a result of which "the use of the mother tongue in education was prohibited". Only the relevant European language was permitted. Relating the experience of Senegal, a former French colony, Ka (1993: 306) points out that "the rare attempts that were made to introduce [Senegalese languages] in the school system were promptly discouraged […]. The only medium of education was French, the 'civilizing' language".

Given such reasons as the self-serving interest of a local élite that was itself the product of this policy, and presumably the problems of choosing an indigenous official language, this discriminatory attitude continued after 1960, the year many of these countries became politically independent.

Ostensibly to redress this bias, the Francophonie — an association of countries having in common the use of the French language — tried to create, in the 1980s, what it called a *nouvel ordre linguistique* (a new linguistic order) in which African languages and French would be recognised as playing complementary roles in an equation involving language and development.[3] The Agence de Coopération Culturelle et Technique (ACCT), one of the Francophonie's specialised agencies, has had the mandate of implementing this body's programme of linguistic cooperation.

The ACCT's first generation projects included (socio) linguistic atlases as well as lexis-oriented documentation (e.g. the thematic lexica of Central Africa). The second generation projects began in 1984, and include, among others, specialised lexica ('LEXIS'). Without prejudice to nationally or individually-initiated projects (see Section 2.2 below), plans and work associated with these specialist lexica must have very prominent spots in accounts of terminology planning in former French colonies. In his three-period division of work on terminology in Francophone Africa, Halaoui (1991: 12) indeed assigns these lexica exclusively to the third and current period, a period beginning in 1984. The objective of LEXIS, as stated in the project description, is:

> to more broadly expose African, Creole and Arabic languages to contemporary scientific and technical terminology, in order to introduce them into, or improve their use in, professional activities, different kinds of training programmes, as well as to give them standardised equivalents of scientific vocabulary in French, English, etc. The LEXIS projects should also address the needs of participating countries in the areas of information, communication and popularization of knowledge (my translation from the French).[4]

The African part of the project involves some sixteen countries belonging to the three working zones of West Africa, Central Africa and East Africa/the Indian Ocean. Centres of Applied Linguistics of universities and Language Directorates

---

3. See the mission statement of the ACCT (section titled "Les langues et l'espace mondial de la langue française") in a 1989 ACCT publication by N. Halaoui titled *Questions de méthode en terminologie des langues africaines.*

4. See objective of the LEXIS projects, as stated in *Projet de Lexiques spécialisés (Lexis)* in: André Clas (1985: 29).

in participating countries are the principal bodies entrusted with the actual task of producing the specialist lexica (Halaoui 1990: 20–1).

Besides identifying languages to be worked on, each country identifies a number of fields that are priority areas in its development programmes. From the published proceedings of a 1988 conference on the second generation projects (ACCT 1989), fields such as the following were chosen by participating national teams: Public life, Social life, Health (including Trado-medicine), Agriculture, Pisciculture, Cattle rearing and War. Few countries appear to have chosen what might be regarded as school subjects. Cameroun made such a decision, as the following list shows: History (465 terms), Geography (236), Technology (967), Accounting (180), Biology (742), Grammar (250) and Law (375).

The choice of school-type and non-school type fields can be explained in terms of priorities identified. The choice by Côte d'Ivoire of lagoon fishing as domain for two of that country's languages (Adioukrou and Ebrié) is motivated by a perceived need for more efficient communication strategies in (rural) extension work (Gbery 1993). Previous campaigns aimed at changing certain fishing practices[5] were conducted in French and had limited success. The fishing terminology, therefore, provides extension workers with the requisite communication infrastructure needed to get across to fishing communities. In Niger the introduction, on experimental basis, of indigenous languages into the school system quite naturally called for appropriate terminologies. The opportunity provided by the ACCT's LEXIS projects was used by this country's national team to develop linguistic terminology in Zarma for the success of the experimental school (Issoufi 1993).

The high international profile of these projects must, however, not belie the significance of work by university centres and individuals. These ACCT projects, regrettably, appear to have ground to a halt, going by the personal communication of an Ivorian linguist close to them.

The foregoing, then, is a select account of African terminology planning as seen from the standpoints of motivation, players and products. While the goal in all of the cases reviewed is ultimately the same, the specific motivations were seen to differ. In the next two sections, other pertinent perspectives to African LP-oriented terminology are presented.

---

5. For example, the abandonment of closely meshed nets that catch tiny fish which, besides having no gastronomic and economic value, rapidly deplete the lagoon's fish resources.

2.2 Combating cynicism

In the Somali and Ethiopian case studies, the favourable climate of public opinion to the use of African languages in new domains must be seen as an asset which has not traditionally existed in many language communities and countries across the continent of Africa. Public relations battles have had to be waged in several countries in order to make public opinion receptive to the idea of African languages serving as media of fresh discourse, that is, discourse outside the traditional ethnocentric and liturgical realms. The translation, in the 1960s, of Shakespeare's *Julius Caeser* into Swahili by Tanzania's president, Julius Nyerere, must be seen in this order of ideas. But of greater significance was the work of Cheikh Anta Diop on Wolof, a language spoken in Senegal. The rest of this section is devoted to this important work.

Cheikh Anta Diop's reflections on terminology may be regarded as a watershed in the discourse on terminology in Senegal, but also in other parts of Africa. Diop was from Senegal. He was an unusual historian with a breath-taking range of preoccupations.

In May of 1971, the Senegalese government promulgated decree no. 71–566 which conferred the status of national language on six of the country's languages, including Wolof (Ka 1993). The decree further expressed government plans "to introduce national languages in the Senegalese educational system, from Primary School to the University". Public opinion, according to Mbodj (1994), weighed heavily against the implementation of this mother-tongue education policy. The main argument of the policy's detractors was that indigenous languages could not express educational concepts. This cynicism provided Diop the opportunity to revisit a plea he had made, some two decades earlier, for the development of indigenous languages, such a development being important for scholarly achievement by African children in Western schools. In 1975, Diop published a seminal article titled *Comment enraciner la science en Afrique: Des exemples walafs* (How to implant science in Africa: Examples from Wolof). In this article, he translated into Wolof scientific texts from a variety of subject areas.

Diop's campaign was unique in two senses. Firstly, his method for combating popular cynicism to the use of African languages was rare. Rather than coin, or point to, a few terms designating some artefact of Western technology, Diop opted to translate texts. The sense of domain which comes with translating specialist texts is also evinced in his published term lists. Tables 2.1 and 2.2 present the subject matter of his translations and term lists, as published in Diop (1954[1979]) and (Diop 1975) respectively. In both cases, French was the source language and Wolof the target. Wolof is the language of the largest ethnic group in Senegal.

Table 2.1: *Texts translated by Diop into Wolof from French*

	Subject	Approx. no. of words
1954 (1979)	Principle of relativity (Paul Langevin's works)	2400
	Corneille's *Horace*	198
	La Marseillaise (French anthem)	57
1975	Set theory	4480
	Mathematical and theoretical physics	1120
	Quantum level organisation of matter	6000
	Special and general theory of relativity/ Relativist cosmology	5040
	Quantum chemistry	2800

Table 2.2: *Diop's term lists (French-Wolof)*

	Subject/theme areas	Approx. no. of terms
1954 (1979)	Geometry Trigonometry Equation of the second order	429
	Thermodynamics Electricity General Chemistry Atomic structure Molecular structure	483
1975	Tensor calculus Tensor theory of special relativity	60

A second striking feature of Diop's campaign aimed at proving the amenability of African languages to functional extension is his choice of illustrative examples. Tables 2.1 and 2.2 show a decided preference for what would popularly be considered as abstruse subjects. Besides what may have been a personal flair for such subjects, the choice also had a more objective reason. Concerning set theory, for instance, Diop writes that this being an abstract and difficult branch of mathematics, providing terms in Wolof for concepts in this field should give the lie to claims that African languages are unable to cope with abstraction (Diop 1975: 154). Additionally, Diop was attracted to some of these abstruse subjects in the context of his preoccupation with radiocarbon dating for historical pursuits, within which he sought to establish the temporal precedence of Egyptian and Black civilisations over Greek civilisation. Table 2.3 and Figure 2.1 below present, respectively, a sample each from Diop's term lists and translations. These samples are taken from Diop (1979(1954)) and Diop (1975) respectively.

Table 2.3: *Sample term list: extract from subject heading labelled* General Chemistry

Allotropie	Vûtékbîr	Isométrie de position	Boktenik tib tahavây
Poids atomique et moléculaires	Dissâyu'b harèful, véssôful	Tautométrie	Yaram tenkñâral
Volume moléculaire	Kembâyu'l véssôful	Réfracton moléculaire	Damu'g vésôful
Tonométrie	Nat bes	Polymorphomisme moléculaire	Baribindu'b vésôful
Ebulliométrie	Nat bah	Polarisation rotatoire	Dotal dargandalu
Crytométrie	Nat sèd	Dissymétrie de structure	Dékérlôdi'b bindbîr
Chaleurs spécifiques	Tangâyu bopam	Spectographie de masse	Redhonu'g laf
Isomorphisme	Bokdundâ		
Théorie des ions	Faramfatê harêful		

While aspects of Diop's preoccupation with linguistics (historical reconstruction, transcription of Wolof, etc.) have elicited critical comments, the evidence he adduces in support of the amenability of Wolof to new specialised discourses is unassailable, and might rightly be considered an overkill. As an overkill, it had the desired effect. In the immediate aftermath of Diop's 1975 article, the creation of indigenous language terms became something of a national avocation among Western-trained Senegalese professionals (Mbodj 1994). By the beginning of the school year in 1978, experimental primary school classes in Wolof had started, a development which Mbodj (1994) attributes to the influence of Diop's work on public opinion. The period 1978–1981 saw the commencement of classes in Seereer, Joola and Pulaar (Mbodj 1994, Ka 1993). Although these

Rappelons que les événements de la mécanique non relativiste se passent dans l'espace euclidien à trois dimensions tandis que, en phase relativiste, on est dans le cadre de l'espace du temps quadridimensionnel.	Nanu fatàli ne xewxew i metkanik gu kajuteefalul ñi ngi'y ame ci jaww gestucakeefal ëlkiidal ju ñatt i xebla waaye bu dee metkanik kajuuteefal ci jaww jamono ñentixeblaal lees di nek.
1° Deux particules de champ, le photon, quantum du champ gravitationnel, diffèrent de toutes les autres particules: tous deux sont stables, sans charge électrique, de spin 1 et se propagent à la vitesse de la lumière.	1) Naar i dogatiit yo'y tool wuute nañu ak yi ci des yép: niki ⟨leeralsi⟩ (fotong), di dogatal u tool ub mbëj lasiyaal, ak ⟨wëgëntesi⟩, wara nek ci les foog, dogatal u tool u wëgënte: ñoom ñaar ñép du ñu yébiku, amu ñu sëf ub mbëj, séén ug ëcc = 1, séén ub gaawaay di bob leer.
2° Vient ensuite la famille des leptons à laquelle appartiennent: a) Les neutrinos: il en existe deux, le neutrino électronique et le neutrino muonique. Ainsi que leurs antiparticules, les anti-neutrinos. Tous sont considérés comme des particules de masse propre nulle, stables, neutres. Ils participent aux interactions faibles pour assurer la conservation du nombre leptonique: le nombre des leptons dans l'univers est un invariant.	2) Dogatiit yi ci tegu ñoo'y njaboot ug ⟨wayaftoyy⟩ yi niki: a) ⟨cëfulsi⟩ (neutrino) yi: yaar i xeet la ñu cëfulsi mbëjfepalal ak cëfulsi ⟨mional⟩; ak séén i safaan-dogatiit, niki safaan-cëfulsi yi. Ñoom nép ñi ngi léén jape ay dogatiit yu séén laf u bop tusal, teg ci du ñu yabiku, te sëfu ñu. Bok ñanu ci dogatiit yi' y jëfënte jëfënte bu néw doole ndax lim ub ⟨wayaftoyyal⟩ bi (leptonique) wara baña toxu: lim ub ⟨wayaftoyy⟩ yi ci mboolemcakeef gi ab toxutil la.opw
b) Les électrons: il en existe deux, l'électron positif, positron, et l' électron négatif. Tous les deux sont stables dans le vide, chargés, de spin 1/2, et participent aux interactions électromagnétiques, ainsi qu'aux interactions faibles. […].	b) mbëjfepal yi: ñaari xeet la ñu ñoomitt; am na mbëjfepal ëptusal ak mbëjfepal yéétusal; ñoom ñaar ñép tojtil la ñu (stable) ci barab bu ne wëgëñ, sëfu nañu, séén ug ëcc di 1/2 (spin = 1/2) ; bok nañu ci jëfënte' y mbëjlasiyaal ak ci jëfënte yu nééw doole. […].

Figure 2.1: *Translation of text on classification of elementary particles (quantum organization of matter)*

experimental classes had to be discontinued, due to lack of adequate preparation on the part of the state, the idea of African languages in formal education as well as in other domains no longer elicited as much hostility as in the past. This was Diop's goal, as may be gleaned from the following assertion:

> With these translations our goal is not so much one of popularisation as it is to demonstrate that scientific discourse is possible in African languages. […]. The translations show that if we elect to (and are prepared to put in a lot of effort)

we can have our languages express scientific thought without this thought losing any of its original worth (my translation from the French; Diop 1975).

2.3 Terminology Planning Process

Insights into the process of terminology planning are perhaps most fruitfully obtained from a variety of general perspectives. Such broad perspectives have the potential of foreshadowing what would narrowly be considered as methodological issues and, through the latter, giving some insight into the success of the planning effort. In this respect, the terminology planning projects may be investigated from a number of perspectives including: the focus of the planning effort (documentation/development), the degree of insertion of the planning effort within other processes, work sessions and collaborators. These perspectives are now discussed as they apply to the case scenarios sketched previously. A complement to this discussion is to be found in Section 2.4.

2.3.1   *Focus of the planning effort*

The choice of domains in the Francophone projects was earlier attributed to national priorities. This choice also reveals what might be considered as the focus (documentation/development) of the planning effort. By 'documentation' is meant the compilation of the terms of an African language as used in a domain that is well known to speakers of that language or practitioners of the related domain activity, but perhaps less well known to an uninitiated audience. The opposite of this description would be 'development'.

2.3.1.1 Development-orientation
Most of the projects reviewed have a development perspective, a point that is obvious from the language(s) of: the source data; sources of terms, particularly loans; and of terms considered as working models. For the Swahili Biology Dictionary Project, specialised English dictionaries of Biology were used as data sources (Kummer 1983: 87). The introduction to the Swahili Linguistic Dictionary also lists specialised English reference works on the subject as sources of terms. The identification of fresh needs for terminology in Somali saw the compilation of term lists in Arabic, English and Italian, all considered as source or reference languages. It can be inferred from Stoberski (1987) that in the production of the Amharic STTP (Science Technology Terms Translation Project), the planners found patterns in two other Semitic languages (Hebrew and

Arabic) useful. In the preparation of the Zarma linguistic terminology, the elicitation list came in part from available descriptions, in the French language, of Zarma (Issoufi 1993). In the Nigerian projects, English was the language of the elicitation list and, with the probable exception of Arabic (for the Hausa glossaries), the only foreign language from which terms were borrowed. Such is the significance of the question of term sourcing in Swahili terminology planning that three schools of thought have crystallised: the Unguja School, which prefers Oriental sources; the Mrima School, which favours European sources; and the Tanga School which gives dialects of Swahili precedence over other languages in the search for terms (Khamisi 1986: 274). The point about these development projects is that they all potentially make it possible to transfer substantial knowledge to speakers of the target languages.

2.3.1.2 *Documentation-orientation*

Let us now turn to the documentation-type projects and the methodological issues they raise. Given the comparative wealth of experience which target communities have in such areas as cattle-rearing or trado-medicine, the reflection of these domains in some of the Francophone projects suggests, although not necessarily, that that the focus is on documentation. The purpose of such documentation could be, as in the lagoon fishing example, to make it possible for non-practitioners to influence change. But the purpose could also be to make the given practice more widely known to a foreign audience.

At all events, with such fields the goal is hardly to create knowledge in the fashion of the development projects. Guidelines established for the Francophone projects required two kinds of spade work: ethnographic research (*enquête ethnographique*) to obtain, by a variety of means, existing indigenous language terms in a given field, and scientific research (*enquête savante*) to obtain French terms in the given field. On the basis of this exercise in comparative terminology, degrees of equivalence can be established and, proceeding from there, gaps in the African language terminology *vis-à-vis* the French are filled, i.e. to the extent that the African environment of the given practice justifies such a remedial measure (Halaoui 1989, 1990; ACCT 1989). The filling of gaps is one sense in which documentation can be incidentally prescriptive or normative.

The ethnographic component of this composite methodology is justifiable even when it might be reasonable to expect either a wholesale transfer of knowledge or to feel that it would be necessary to create masses of terms for unidentified concepts. A telling example of the latter is provided by Maiga (1991) who recalls the experience of a team involved in a botany course in Bambara, a language spoken in Mali:

Most course participants were convinced that beyond equivalents for a few terms like root, stem, flower, leaf, Bambara had no botanical terms. They had no doubt that borrowing [from French] would have to be resorted to. In their minds' eyes, they had already seen *koroli, sepali, etamini, pisitili, overi*, etc. But on visiting Bambara villages, the team realised the villagers already had terms for petals (*feere kala*), corolla (*julakôrôbô*), stamen (*jonbôjonbô*), pistil (*denkala*), and for ovary (*denso*) (Maiga 1991: 16–17; my translation from the French).

With other examples, the question can of course arise as to the extent to which traditional terminology and classification or distinctions can be accommodated within the structure of the source or donor knowledge system.

2.3.2 Integration of the terminology planning effort within other processes

The integration of terminology planning into other processes like text production has important implications for the planning effort. These other processes provide instant feedback on the terminology, besides also determining how such terminology is to be evaluated (see Section 2.5). With respect to Somali terminology planning, sources consulted tend to all indicate that terminology was created *pari passu* with the school book production process, as opposed to being created for some anticipated but uncertain text development activity. Caney reports that when the somalisation of the school curriculum was to be extended to the remaining levels of the primary school cycle, a seminar for teachers was convened in 1973. New needs for terminology were examined, and on the basis of this analysis, term lists were compiled in Arabic, Italian and English. Somali equivalents were discussed, and proposals formed the basis of textbook writing campaigns which began in 1974.

In Tanzania, such an integration can be claimed in respect of those terms created by the Institute of Education which, as might be recalled, has the mandate for developing didactic materials. In Section 2.4 feedback on terminologies produced by this institute is described. The foregoing concurrence or close coordination would also be true of those Yoruba terms coined for the Ife Six Year Primary Project, terms that later became part of the Nigerian *Vocabulary of Primary Science and Mathematics*. Interestingly Issoufi, commenting on the Zarma linguistic terminology in Niger, notes that this terminology's definitive form was arrived at only after it had been used to produce Zarma grammar manuals (Issoufi 1993: 74).

With respect to the other projects, there is little evidence from which to infer a (near) concurrence of terminology planning and text development, of the kind seen above. Of course there might exist evidence of use of terms in oral communication, but this kind of evidence is even harder to document. In any case, the extreme flexibility of orality makes this medium less efficient as a source of feedback for the terminology planner. It might indeed be worthwhile, in some cases at least, to attempt to correlate the *terminology — text* concurrence with the degree of commitment to policy.

2.3.3 The plenary and committee sessions

At least in some of the terminology projects, work was carried out on committee basis, usually after a plenary session had taken place. This was the case with the Nigerian primary science/mathematics and legislative projects. Besides discussing the project mandate, such plenaries typically receive input from subject specialists (in a variety of ways), take decisions on guidelines (e.g. whether to borrow, where, and how) and agree on an elicitation list of terms for which indigenous language equivalents are to be provided. Thus, at the Ife Workshop or plenary for the Nigerian science/mathematics glossary, participants discussed the relevant portions of the National Policy on Education as it affected language in schools, and listened to presentations from science educationists and other professionals on: how children acquire mathematical concepts, how these are taught, numeration and what makes a counting system good, characteristics of science in primary education, linguistic features of the nine project languages, etc. As for working principles, creations *ex nihilo* were to be preferred to the use of existing words capable of leading in the wrong direction of association; when borrowing was inevitable, English was to be favoured as source language; borrowed forms were, however, to conform to the structure of the receiving language. An English elicitation list of terms was also approved. For the Lagos plenary on the legislative glossary, experts were invited from politics and the other fields (health, information, trade, sports, etc) "into which government business is traditionally divided". They were requested to "provide word-lists in their various fields which they thought would be essential in these fields in a national assembly" (see preface to the project).

At the conclusion of these plenaries, committees would normally be formed corresponding to different language groups, as in the two Nigerian cases, or to (sub) specialities, as in the Ethiopian STTP. In this latter example, thirteen committees were formed for the thirteen subject areas defined.

2.3.4 Collaborators

As the discussion on players suggests, the projects are generally organised around teams, the latter being associated with Institutes of Applied Linguistics of universities and Language Directorates. Each of the thirteen fields worked upon during the Ethiopian STTP was handled by a committee that was comprised of a linguist-chairman and two subject specialists (Stoberski 1987). The preface to the Nigerian legislative glossary emphasises the role of linguists and language scholars of various persuasions in the production of that work. After experts from politics and other fields had contributed word-lists deemed essential for the national assembly, the next task was to identify individuals in each of the glossary's target languages who "were versed in the languages and had enough linguistic sophistication to handle translation". To ensure coordination, for example, to see to it that all three groups of translators were rendering the same sense of a headword, translators were engaged "each of whom could speak all the four languages involved".

The place of language scholars is also evident in the ACCT projects. At the 1988 Abidjan ACCT conference, about 70% of participants were linguists, judging by the explicitly stated institutional/unit affiliations on the attendance list. In one overview of these projects, the near insignificant role of subject specialists has been observed (Halaoui 1990: 21).[6] The obvious exception is of course in the area of linguistics where linguists are involved.

Given the above profile, it is reasonable to infer that, in their work, the teams reflected whatever aspects of their linguistic expertise was called for.[7] To give an example with the Nigerian legislative glossary: in describing the challenges posed by this work and how these challenges were met, the editor-in-chief of the glossary notes that "It has truly been said that of all the branches of linguistics, lexicography is the most [tasking]". In the context of the Francophone projects, one finds a (non-patronising) recognition of the need for training complementary to that already possessed by the linguist-collaborators. In 1984, the year in which the Francophone LEXIS projects commenced, a course was held in Bordeaux, France, for teams involved with LEXIS and its sister project on monolingual dictionaries (DIMO). In the years that followed, other courses were organised: 1984 (Bordeaux), 1986 (Montreal/Bordeaux), 1988 (Bordeaux), etc. This is apart from the regional seminars, e.g. Ouagadougou 1987. A look at

---

6. Incidentally, similar findings were reported in the context of the International Research Project on Language Planning Processes. Writing on personnel, Jernudd (1977: 136) notes that "the agency officers in Israel and Indonesia were language specialists, who, on the whole, lacked training in technological fields. Practically everyone had a humanities education, with a specialization in language and literature studies".

7. It will be possible to assess this suggestion in Section 2.4 which, as mentioned earlier, complements the current section.

the 1984 course (from which a 1985 manual edited by André Clas resulted) shows that LEXIS participants were introduced to: domain delimitation, structuring of domains using tree formats, concepts and concept relations, term identification, definition, corpus approaches, terminological systems, term record files, collaboration with domain experts etc. These and other questions, particularly computer-based terminography, were further addressed at subsequent courses (see Halaoui 1989; Diki-Kidiri *et al.* 1989). While these notions could have been acquired in a linguistics or some other course, they are easily recognisable as fundamental in the theory of terminology. Thus, while one or the other of the above terminological constructs is reflected in the critical metadiscourse reviewed below, the balance of thrusts in this discourse should be telling evidence of the dominant paradigms in African terminology planning.

2.4 Critical Metadiscourse

This section is a complement to the previous one on the terminology planning process. Here, it is attempted to identify where the greater emphases lie in critiques or appraisals of terminology projects. The goal is to use discourse related to work on terminology as basis for reconstructing the theory underlying practice. *A priori* and *a posteriori* (on the basis of available literature), a number of thrusts, including the following, might be expected in a critical metadiscourse on terminology: a linguistic approach (strategies used), a terminological systems approach (how groups of terms reflect the relationship in the corresponding sets of concepts), a communicative approach (the usability of the terminology in discourse), knowledge approach (the effectiveness and efficiency of the terminology project as a means of imparting knowledge), and a sociological approach (societal validation of the terminology planning effort as evidenced by knowledge of, and attitudes towards, the terms).

This categorisation represents an *ideale Konstruktion*, not in the least because each of the thrusts can be severally interpreted. Besides strategies used, a linguistic approach may also incorporate analyses of how new terms stand in relation to the structure of the language in which it is being introduced. Apart from usability, the communicative approach could also refer to the adequacy or coverage of the proposed terminological infrastructure. In addition to the foregoing issue of multiplicity of strands, there is the question of frontiers. At some point, the knowledge and terminological system approaches overlap, given their concern with conceptual systems. Not infrequently, linguistic analyses also involve some form of conceptual analysis, the basis for the other two approaches.

This form of concept analysis is often *ad hoc* in nature, as opposed to systematic.[8] Some illustrations.

While the conceptual analysis which is so indispensable for the knowledge approach is also present in the terminological system approach, the influence of this analysis may not necessarily be reflected in the organisation or presentation of the final terminology product. This presentation is important to the product's knowledge-mediating potentials. But besides presentation, the issue of domain is crucial to the knowledge approach. By this is meant the subject relevance or relatedness of entries in a terminology product. On the relationship between the linguistic approach and the other concept-based approaches, it might be said that discussions of the semantic transfer strategy, for instance, imply that some thought has been given to the features of a new concept to be designated as well as to those of a pre-existing and analogous concept for which a designation obviously exists. There is therefore room for some eclecticism.

2.4.1   *Linguistic strategy*

The thrust that appears to be most prevalent is the one on linguistic strategy (alone or in combination with *ad hoc* concept analysis). Caney (1980) is mainly devoted to a discussion of Somali lexical modernisation strategies — as a specific manifestation of a universal phenomenon. In some two hundred pages, the author discusses the use made in several discourse fields of the following strategies: semantic shift or transfer, borrowing, derivation, compounding and phrase grouping. A comparable approach is also taken by Andrzejewski in his study of lexical modernisation in Somali. Examples of semantic shift cited by Andrzejewski (1983: 80–1) in the field of chemistry include:

(1)   *summad*
      mark, mark that is branded on a domestic animal to show ownership
      'chemical symbol'

(2)   *dhun   hubsasho*
      pipe/reed making sure/ascertaining
      'test tube'

---

8. As employed here, the term *ad hoc* is not pejorative. It only seeks to convey the idea that the corresponding concept analysis is isolated; its results reflect only one or a few out of a presumably larger number of related or relatable concepts.

From the standpoint of systematic concept analysis, it would be interesting to know if the Somali chemistry list also has a term for *beaker*, and if not, how the need to designate this concept might have affected the solution arrived at for, say, *test tube*.

In their discussion of "Terminography in African languages in South Africa" Mtintsilana and Morris (1988) focus on the processes of semantic transfer, paraphrase, compounding, deideophonisation and borrowing as applied to Zulu, Ndebele, Sotho and Xhosa. With deideophonisation, a prefix (*isi*) is added to a prototypical perception of the sound made by an object. An example from Xhosa and Zulu:

(3)   *isithuthuthu*
        PREF.IDEOPHONE
        'motorcycle'

The motorcycle's running engine is perceived as *thuthuthu*. In these as in the Somali examples, evidence of some concept analysis is evident in the choice of linguistic strategies.

Similar analyses are to be found in many of the contributions on African languages in the volumes (*Language Reform*) edited by Fodor & Hagège, in papers in several issues of *Kiswahili, Terminologies nouvelles*, and in other collections.[9] This thrust is to be seen in many introductions to compiled terminologies (e.g. Bamgbose 1984 [1992]). A good many criticisms of terminology projects are based on the linguistic strand, alone or in combination with *ad hoc* concept analysis. Thus, Mdee (1983) notes inconsistencies in the adaptation of affixes and of dipthongised vowels in terminology projects of the Swahili National Council. Some of his examples:

(4)   *aluminiamu* (from English: alumin**ium**), *kalisiamu* (from: calc**ium**), *potasiamu* (from: potass**ium**), but *amonia* (from: amon**ium**), *trapeza* (from: trapez**ium**), *hebani* (from: herban**ium**).

(5)   *maikro* (from: m**i**cro), *kloraidi* (from: chloride), but *fomeka* (from: formica), *virasi* (from: virus).

Kummer's paper (1983), which actually situates at the intersection of several thrusts, is perhaps the best example of a criticism that is done explicitly from the linguistic strategy and *ad hoc* concept analysis standpoints. As term formation

---

9. The journal, *Terminologies nouvelles*, has provided a forum for participants in the Francophone LEXIS projects to report on their work.

processes employed in the Swahili Dictionary of Biology which he evaluates, Kummer identifies borrowing (with phonological adaptation), quasi-definition,[10] morphological derivation from existing roots, and semantic shift/terminologization, the latter three being more significant. Each of these more significant processes is discussed from the standpoint of several problems. Quasi-definition is discussed in terms of, among others, (a) the choice of concept characteristics, and (b) the semantic shift that is made to take place in order to express a concept characteristic.

Indeed, criterion (a) is an issue in all the other significant processes. In many instances, Kummer finds the concept characteristics chosen for term formation as non-essential, when they are not outright misleading. Commenting on, among others, the Kiswahili terms created through quasi-definition for (1) *carbohydrate*, (2) *chlorophyll* and (3) *nucleoplasm*, Kummer says of (1) that referring to it by a term that is glossed as *thick dough* is to ignore its chemical composition; of (2) which glosses as *leaf maker*, he says the suggestion is that the substance is responsible for growth of leaves, a suggestion which is at variance with its real pigmentary function; and of (3) which translates as *sticky liquid*, he says it misses the important point about location in the nucleus. This discussion in effect evinces concern for concept analysis within a framework of strategies of term formation. But the point remains that the conceptual analysis does not, in each case, extend beyond one concept, with the implication that (sub)system-related issues are not taken into account.

2.4.2 *Terminological system approach*

Some discourse also exists on the terminological system approach which, as described earlier, is concerned with concept inter-relatedness as basis for consistency in a given terminological infrastructure. MacWilliam (1985) uses term proposals for the Swahili Biology Dictionary Project to examine prefixes and the conceptual/terminological systems that they suggest. She finds inconsistencies in the rendering of Greco-Latin affixes/formants, with the result that the overt marking of the underlying relationship obtaining between groups of concepts is lost. The prefixes (1) *endo-*, (2) *ecto-*, (3) *epi-*, (4) *meso-* and (5) *peri-* are consistently applicable in English to the formant *derm(is)* to yield a

---

10. Kummer uses this term (in German) for a semantic coinage strategy requiring the use of words pre-existing in a language (for a concept's characteristics) to designate a concept. This can be through composition or (semantic) shift.

series. This uniformity is lacking in the Swahili proposals queried by Mac-William. The composite in (1) above is *tabaka ndani* or *endodemu*; in (2) *uwamkiini*; in (3) *tabaka nje*; in (4) *maji ya chembe misuli*; and in (5) *utanda koki*. Tumbo (1982) is another study which uses Swahili examples to make comparable points.

A similar concern is to be found in Oyelaran's introduction to the Yoruba section of the Nigerian Primary Science and Mathematics Vocabularies (the prepublication version). In discussing the linguistic strategy of borrowing, he notes that it is ill-advised to borrow in isolation a form that "belongs to a paradigm or is a member of a morphological series". It is senseless to borrow *dividend* into Yoruba when *divide, division, divisor*, and *quotient* have respectively been rendered as *pín, pípín, apín,* and *ìpín*. He notes, interestingly, that an inconsistent pattern can pose problems of learning.

2.4.3 Sociological approach

Also prevalent in the metacritical discourse are sociological analyses of sets of proposed terms. A 1994 M.A. thesis by Maryam Askira at the University of Maiduguri in Nigeria is one such analysis.[11] It focuses on the mass media. Askira investigates how English terms (and other expressions) drawn from several fields are understood in news translations from English into Hausa and Kanuri by her respondents. In the questionnaires, respondents have to rank several English alternatives for a given Kanuri or Hausa term. Only one of these English alternatives is correct as to specific form or referent, the others having been made up by the researcher. Responses enable her to determine the degree of accuracy, acceptance and standardisation of the terms.

Consider the following Hausa example in which the term picked from the media is *Rijiyar Burtsatsi*. Respondents have to back-translate into English, in order to identify the intended English term. They have to rank (1) 'pumping well', (2) 'bore hole' and (3) 'manual water pump' according to the following criteria: (a) not accurate, (b) satisfactory, and (c) very accurate. The alternative in (1) scores 66.67%; (2) which is the intended concept and term scores 100%, while (3) scores 33.33%. *Rijiyar Burtsatsi* is therefore considered an accurate, accepted and standardised version of *borehole*.

---

11. Regrettably, I was unsuccessful in obtaining the 1980 M.A. thesis of James Mdee titled *The Degree of Acceptability of New Swahili Terms: Speakers' Response Analysis*, submitted to the University of Dar es Salaam.

Although structured differently, Kummer's sociological evaluation (Kummer 1983) also deserves mention. Besides its relevance here, this study should also enable me to venture some thoughts on sociological evaluations of proposed terminologies. Kummer uses respondents to investigate knowledge (*sensu* familiarity with), translatability into English, and usage of Swahili terms created in six fields, *viz.*: National Assembly/Parliament, Commerce and Economics, Science, Library and Bindery, Geography and Language Science. Thirty respondents are polled, five for each field. Respondents in each field are university students or university teachers in that field or in closely related subjects. Answers are then solicited on questions dealing with knowledge, translatability and usage of experimental terms. Table 2.4 below presents recomputations of some of Kummer's results.[12]

Table 2.4: *Kummer's findings*

	Do you know this word?	Can you translate this word into English?	Do you use this word?	Mean deviation on all three questions
Nat. Assembly No. of words: 274	98.59%	98.23%	97.51%	0.41%
Commerce/Economics No. of words: 438	95.57%	94.65%	93.78%	0.38%
Science No. of words: 96	83.54%	80.41%	78.54%	1.41%
Library & Bindery No. of words: 122	93.77%	91.64%	90.32%	0.87%
Geography No. of words: 179	85.81%	84.46%	82.90%	1.04%
Language Science No. of words: 184	57.17%	42.28%	31.95%	2.85%

All the figures represent averages of responses by informants in each field. The last column shows the average variation among the five members of each group on all three questions posed.

Kummer's inferences and rationalisations *vis-à-vis* these results are sociological in nature. The high figures in the first two domains are seen in the light of Swahili's role in independence struggles and post-independence nation-building

---

12. Sophia Oteng is thanked for the recomputation.

(causes in which political and economic discourse was prominent). Dissemination of these terms by the mass media is another factor. The lower figures for language science are seen from the standpoint of the novelty of the terms, the dominance of linguistic literature in English, dissemination channels, and the significance of Arabic as source of many of the terms in this field. Most of the unknown terms were of Arabic origin, but the differential in figures between *knowledge* and *usage* suggests that even those Arabic terms that were known were not used. The most important inference which Kummer draws from these results is that formal and institutional state channels of dissemination are not as effective as informal means. Incidentally, the issue of dissemination forms part of the conclusion of Samsom's sociological appraisal of another terminology planning effort in Swahili. See Samson (1991).

2.4.4 Communication approach

Samson's study also draws attention to another perspective, the communicative thrust, albeit in passing. Samsom's emphasis here is on the extent to which proposed terms cover the pertinent field. It is noted that Swahili terms proposed for the field of car engineering are numerically inadequate for a sustained discussion in that field. Writing in the context of terminology planning in Yoruba, a Nigerian language, Awobuluyi (1994: 40) observes that "not only is the estimated number of terms so far created considerably short of what is required, the terms themselves would also appear to be restricted in coverage". Writing on Kiswahili, Mdee (1981) has deplored the situation where "the desire of science writers to disseminate popular science to the Swahili community" has been frustrated by insufficient terminology. In spite of the foregoing, it might help to distinguish between restricted coverage that arises from imposed limitations and one that stems from methodological inadequacies.

Another strand of the communicative approach (usability of terms) is highlighted by Kummer. The difficulties of translators and writers who have to produce didactic materials on the basis of terms produced by the Institute of Kiswahili Research are expressed thus by Kummer:

> In the translation or production of didactic materials, problems are to be observed in the incorporation of these standardised terminologies; in and of themselves, the terms are insufficient for transposing texts into Swahili, a point about which translators in particular complain. (Kummer 1983; my translation from the German).

Although the exact nature of the problem is not discussed in the text of the paper, Kummer, in a personal communication, informs me that collocations were a big part of the translators' problems.

2.4.5 Knowledge approach

True, the knowledge approach is hinted at in the preceding two paragraphs, but it is in the very restricted sense of terminology serving as an ancillary to other activities (translating, writing) in their knowledge-mediating goals. But even in this marginal perspective, the verdict does not appear to be good. Apart from Tumbo (1982), very little else presumably exists that evinces any of the strands of the knowledge approach as this approach was defined earlier. Commenting on the standardised Swahili Commerce Terminology, Tumbo conjectures that "there were a lot of difficulties in deciding what concepts really belong to commerce". Among other kinds of evidence adduced, there are the terms *logarithm* and *quadratic equation*. Clearly, and irrespective of other factors, the goal of knowledge transfer is hardly met in a terminology resource that fails to define its domain of coverage. Against this background, it becomes quite tempting to suggest that at times the problem of inadequate coverage (discussed in the context of communication) may be the outcome of a methodological shortcoming.

It is in the negative sense of Tumbo's observation that the knowledge perspective might be said to exist in the discourse associated with the LEXIS projects. In an evaluation of these projects, covering the period 1984–1988, the ACCT lamented that, in spite of the methodological courses, some teams appeared "not to have entirely adopted procedures recommended, preferring term for term *translation* to methods requiring corpora and hierarchies" (ACCT 1989: 21; my translation from the French). Indirect evidence for part of this evaluation may be gleaned from the fact that in accounts of these projects published in *Terminologies nouvelles*, there is hardly any concern with structuring concepts/terms in the chosen domain. This dearth contrasts with the recurring preoccupation with descriptions of linguistic strategies adopted in the creation of terms.

To return to Tumbo, she recommends to Swahili terminology planners the use of bibliographical classification systems like the United Decimal Classification (UDC) as aids in the definition of domain and in term representation.

These, then, are the thrusts of the discourse on terminology planning. The varying salience of these thrusts has been shown, and this might be taken as indicating the kinds of theories underlying practice. It is hypothesised that the relative dearth of discourse in the areas of communication (usability of terms) and knowledge impacts on the ability of terminology resources to meet the expectations of the policies that motivated their creation. This would be particularly true of standalone projects (as opposed to those integrated into a text development process). Should this hypothesis be shown to have some merit, the case would have been made for raising the profile of communication and knowledge transfer in the theoretical discourse on terminology planning in Africa. The main task in Chapter 3 will be to investigate this hypothesis. However, in the remaining part of this chapter, it is intended to revisit the issue of sociological evaluations of products of terminology planning.

2.5 Sociological validations of terminology resources: A critique

The fate of a terminology resource may be determined by the design of evaluation studies, and by the importance attached to the findings of these studies. Evaluation that seeks to determine knowledge, usage, accuracy, acceptance, etc. of proposed terms must be targeted at specialised audiences, in the same way as the creation of such terminologies should normally have called for some degree of domain-specific competence. There exists the danger that well thought-out terminologies could very well not be put to use because of responses from persons who lack what it takes to appreciate what such tasks involve.

Askira, whose 1994 work was discussed in Section 2.4.3, rightly notes that some proposals offered by translators of news bulletins (from English into the northern Nigerian languages of Hausa and Kanuri) may be explained by certain constraints, for example "how the version fits into a given text". This contrasts with the discrete or single-unit evidence normally presented to research respondents. The point may be illustrated further, and to do this I choose my examples from those parts of Askira's data dealing with medicine. In Askira's questionnaire, the Kanuri *foto gotə* has the following as candidate English translation equivalents: (a) snapping of photograph; (b) X-ray; and (c) photography. The Hausa *Daukar hoton kirji* also has the same candidate English equivalents. Responses to the Kanuri term are as follows: the alternative in (a) scores 83.33%; (b) which is the intended concept scores 50%; and (c) scores 66.67%. Responses to the Hausa term are as follows: the option in (a) scores 66.67%; (b) scores 100%; and (c) scores 33.3%. The fact of Kanuri respondents scoring (a) highest in the back-translation is rightly interpreted as meaning that the concept intended (X-ray) was not correctly rendered into Kanuri by the news media. However, the Hausa term *Daukar hoton kirji* which evokes the intended concept (X-ray), thus validated by respondents, can be invalidated on technical grounds. Like Askira herself notes, X-ray does not "involve the chest alone" as the Hausa term suggests. While I admit that a term's motivation can convey the very opposite idea of what the corresponding concept is (e.g. atom), and that metonymy and synecdoche have a place in terminology, the point remains that the Hausa term, which can be invalidated on technical grounds, has been declared "accurate, accepted and standardized" by respondents. In the next example, the English term expected from respondents' back-translation is *Gastro-enteritis*.

The given Kanuri term is *kosuwa ngəwu Alabarga səkkə/kosuwa suro kəritəbə* and candidate English equivalents are: (a) stomach ache/many diseases; (b) gastro-enteritis; (c) applicable to any disease. Results of the ranking are as follows: (a) scores 91.67%; (b) scores 75%; and (c) scores 33.33%. The corresponding Hausa term is *Annobar amai da zawo/cuta dangin kolera*. Candidate English equivalents proposed are: (a) gastro-enteritis; (b) cholera; and (c) vomiting and diarrhoea-epidemic/cholera-related disease. Results of the ranking are as follows: (a) scores 33.33%; (b) scores 66.67%; and (c) scores 100%. There could hardly be better proof of the need for specialist respondents than Askira's speculation that the fact of gastro-enteritis *not* being rated highest in both languages may reflect respondents' unfamiliarity with this English term.[13]

It is against this background that Kummer's decisions on choice of specialist respondents and, more importantly, on interpretation of results obtained commend themselves to evaluators. The very high figures on the three variables (knowledge, ability to translate and usage) would, with the probable exception of political terms, most certainly not have been obtained had Kummer's respondents not been domain specialists.

Kummer's study makes it evident that utmost prudence is called for in the metalanguage used to describe results of such evaluations. The commonly used term, *acceptability*, ignores the fact that there is not one, but several possible acceptability variables. Although Kummer, like many others, uses the (German) description *Grad des Akzeptierens* (degree of acceptability), his analysis makes it possible to see what specific acceptability variable is meant. Recall, for instance, that the figure for usage of proposed terms in the field on language science was 31.95%, but the one for knowledge was some 20 percentage points higher. It is this non-differentiation of acceptability variables that puts Askira in the difficult position of being compelled by her figures to declare a term as standardised, accurate and accepted, even when she is clearly not at ease with it, and rightly so. A need therefore exists to distinguish between different types of

---

13. From one brief review of the unavailable thesis by Mdee, it appears my reservations might also be applicable to that study. Samson (1991) notes that one instance where Mdee's respondents did not accept newly proposed terms was when they did not "adequately understand the concept".

acceptability, in analogy perhaps to some of the thrusts and strands reviewed in the critical metadiscourse. It would also be important to classify forms of acceptability according to what categories of respondents can make judgements on them, and at what time in the life of a terminology product these judgements are to be solicited.

The next chapter creates a set of conditions in which one product of terminology planning is evaluated. The evaluation will seek to establish what impact the terminology discourse environment reviewed in this chapter might be having on terminology products.

CHAPTER 3

Evaluation of a Terminology Resource

The previous chapter showed the relative salience of five approaches in the critical metadiscourse on LP-oriented terminology management. The current chapter attempts a critique of a terminology resource produced under the discourse climate that emerged from the two preceding chapters. The evaluation will serve to establish the need or otherwise for complementary premises, methods and quality standards in terminology planning. Justification for a shift in, or extension of, the discourse framework as presented in Chapters 1 and 2 will of course be predicated on how the resource appraised performs *vis-à-vis* the test criteria.

The resource evaluated is the Nigerian project entitled *Quadrilingual Glossary of Legislative Terms* (see Chapter 2.1.3 for a background to this project). The test criteria are communication and knowledge (transfer). These criteria would seem quite appropriate given the suggestion in Chapter 2 of a relative dearth of discourse in these two areas, and mindful of the goal of determining whether a need exists for an extended framework of terminology discourse in LP. Further justification comes from the preface to the glossary which discusses the work's *raison d'être* in terms of the communication and/or training needs of legislators, administrative and secretarial staff, and of translators and interpreters — needs occasioned by the corresponding policy. There is as well theoretical validation of the criteria in the literature on terminology and on the sociology of dictionary use respectively. Writing from the terminological standpoint, Cabré (1996) assigns two functions to terminology: representation of knowledge in an organised way to facilitate structured mediation, and communication of specialised knowledge, as between subject specialists or as practised by translators, broadcasters, technical writers, etc. From the sociology of dictionary standpoint, dictionaries have been classified by Kühn (1989) according to usage goals: as a reference work (for verification, text reception, *text production*, *translating*, specialist language tasks, linguistic research) or as a textbook (for *instruction/enlightenment* and language learning). Admitting that there are overlaps, the usage goals in italics would be most directly related to the evaluation criteria selected.

In the two major sections that follow (3.1 and 3.2), I describe experiments that were aimed at investigating the degree to which the *Quadrilingual Glossary of Legislative Terms* is able to support translating (as an instance of communication) and knowledge (acquisition and transfer). The communication activity of translating is chosen because it is quite consistent with the typical terminology planning goal of capturing in a given target language some of the experience that is recorded in one or several reference languages.

3.1 Translation experiments

Two experiments were designed to obtain data in a context that required subjects to produce a written translation of a text on legislative procedure while verbalising their thoughts. On the qualified assumption that it would give insight into the minds of the subjects, the on-line introspective data was analysed for clues on the degree of adequacy of the glossary for translating a text, one that treats a subject within the purview of the glossary. The experiments were clearly set within the framework of process studies in translation

For purposes of triangulation, two teams of translating subjects were formed. In one, a single subject who is a university assistant lecturer of the target language (Hausa) verbalises and translates all by himself. The protocol of his video-taped and transcribed monologue is identified henceforth as the *individual Think-Aloud Protocol* (iTAP). In the other team, two colleagues of the iTAP subject as well as an assistant law lecturer worked together on the same translation task. The protocol generated by this team will be referred to as the *dialogue Think-Aloud Protocol* (dTAP).

The lawyer in the dTAP team was expected to provide factual knowledge in order to complement the linguistic knowledge of the language teachers. See Wilss (1993) for different kinds of knowledge in translating. Although the language teachers in both teams teach the so-called pedagogical translation, none of them is a trained translator (no such training exists in the target language). A degree of concern about the quality of procedural knowledge led to some remedial measures being taken. Subjects were given talks on certain aspects of procedural knowledge. In spite of the foregoing, there was no undue concern about the effects of the presumed deficit in procedural knowledge, given that the goal was to establish *intersubjectively verifiable* problem areas, rather than to investigate resourcefulness or creativity. The deficit was therefore not seen as one that could invalidate the main conclusions that could be drawn from conducting the experiment. There is no doubt that problem identification can also be a matter of resourcefulness, but this is a question that confronts trained translation professionals as well, as evidenced by the rationale of work by Gerzymisch-Arbogast (1994, 1996).

In situating my experiments within translation process studies, it might be said that although such studies discuss dictionaries or compute them into the system of weighted indicators, it rarely is the case that the dictionary drives the collection or analysis of process data. Although dictionaries typically come in for bashing, the real raw deal they get, in my opinion, lies in the absence of systematic reflection by analysts on how they (the dictionaries) might have been better translation aids. Krings' (1986) pioneering process study is quite extensive in its treatment of dictionaries in the translation process, particularly from a descriptive standpoint: frequency of use; type of dictionary used (bi- or monolingual); correlation of dictionary type to problem category (reception, production) or translation direction (into and out of L_1), etc. However, from the standpoint of evaluation where the notion of success becomes quite central, Krings avoids taking what would have been a useful stance on the adequacy of dictionaries used by his subjects. Consistent with his view of success as a process category rather than as a normative construct, Krings, like Lörscher (1991), defines success of consultation in relation to subject-exhibited evidence, and not by reference to some external or interindividual standard. In my study where a reference tool is the unique centre-piece, I will quite naturally be interested in process data upon which to base recommendations for improvements in the reference tool, if such a need is established. Given the nature of specialist knowledge and texts, any such recommendations will have to be made with reference to some notions of standard for which intersubjective agreement exists. I will therefore differ from the definition of translation success as adopted by Krings and Lörscher.

3.1.1 *Experimental text, Pre-analysis & Research questions*

The text to be translated (from English into Hausa) with the help of the legislative glossary was taken from the Standing Orders of a State House of Assembly (Sokoto). The text was prepared in accordance with Nigeria's 1979 Constitution, which incidentally was the document that motivated the creation of the glossary. The text is reproduced below.

Relevancy in debate

29. (1) Debate upon any motion, bill or amendment shall be relevant to such motion, bill or amendment, except in the case of a substantive motion for the adjournment of the House.

(2) When a motion is made for the adjournment of a debate or the House during any debate, or that the chairman do report progress or do leave the chair, the debate upon such a motion shall be confined to the matter of such motion; and a Member who has made or seconded such a motion shall not be entitled to move or second any similar motion during the same debate.

(3) When an amendment proposes to leave out words and insert other words instead of them, debate upon the first question proposed on the amendment may include both the words proposed to be left out and those proposed to be inserted.

(4) On an amendment proposing to leave out words or to insert words debate shall be confined to the omission or insertion of such words respectively.

From the standpoint of acceptation in legislative discourse, this source language (SL) text contains a number of terms, the exact shape and number of which may vary depending on how certain multi-unit terms are identified. A paragraph-by-paragraph listing of terms could look like the following. (The list does not repeat terms, and it presents terms in what would be their canonical form):

§1: *debate, motion, bill, amendment, substantive motion for the adjournment of the House.*

§2: *make motion, adjournment of debate* (or *motion for the adjournment of debate*), *motion that the chairman do report progress* (or *that the chairman do report progress*), *motion that the chairman do leave the chair* (or *that the chairman do leave the chair*), *Member*; in the following two examples, the first elements (*second* and *move*) may be taken as terms; alternatively, the entire compounds of which they are constituents would be the terms, that is, *second motion, move motion* (the latter as a synonym of *make motion*).

§3: *amendment to leave out words and to insert words* (or *leave out words and insert words*), *propose question.*

§4: *amendment to leave out words, amendment to insert words, omit words.*

There are other compound forms that look like *propose question, move motion*, etc. in the above list. Examples are: *relevant debate* (§1), *confine debate* (§2, §4) and *amendment proposes/words proposed to be ...* (§3, §4). These forms have an element (*relevant, confine, propose*) whose acceptation, either as a standalone or in combination with the second element, is clearly not specialised. Note that *propose* in the context of *question* is not the same as in the proximity of *amendment*.

It is to be noticed in respect of the multi-unit terms that, whereas in some, the constituents occur in proximity (e.g. §1: *substantive motion for the adjournment of the House*), in many others this is not the case. Thus, in §3, *proposes* comes between constituents of the particular type of amendment described. It is also instructive to note that, whereas in some cases what might be called the integrity of the terms is maintained, in others, the need presumably felt by the author(s) of the SL text to avoid repetition meant that certain terms had to lose their formal integrity. Thus, in §2, two terms which out of context would appear as *(motion for) adjournment of debate* and *(motion for) adjournment of the House* undergo a deletion transformation in the construction "When a motion is made for the adjournment of a debate or the House [...]". The same holds true for "(motion) that the chairman do report progress" and "(motion) that the chairman do leave the chair", and (in §4) for "amendment to leave out words" and "amendment to insert words". These two kinds of amendment must not be confused with their conjunctive variant, "amendment to leave out words and to insert words" in §3.

Two research questions will guide the reporting and analysis of findings. The questions are:
1. Did the glossary help to identify and correctly render multi-unit terms?
2. What kinds of processing were glossary solutions subjected to?

Answers are discussed in terms of factual accuracy, speed of production, readability, and adoption and non-adoption of glossary solutions. For now, the reader's attention is drawn to Figure 3.1 (on page 69) which is part of a sample page of the Nigerian glossary.

3.1.2 *Findings*

Let us begin with a few general remarks. Differences were observed in the protocols generated by the two teams of translators. Compared to the dTAP team, the iTAP subject verbalised fewer problems, analysed the text better, dwelt less extensively on verbalised problems and made fewer glossary searches. So while my decision to adopt the approach of multiple triangulation (i.e. between-person and between-method strategies) led to the identification of a core of problems common to the two teams, the data-yield corresponding to these problems was not always comparable. As an aside that is relevant to experimental translation scholarship, I do not see this as unqualified proof that group think-alouds are better suited for pedagogical purposes as has been claimed. In order to cover a broader variety of issues in the findings, I will only occasionally dwell on one problem from the two protocols. I might note that between the two teams the most coincidences in problems verbalised and data-yield (from interaction with glossary as well as from processing patterns) were recorded in respect of single-unit terms. Each team consulted the glossary for six of the seven pre-identified terms, with one term differing for each team. The glossary provided adequate solutions to these pre-identified terms. The solution to *motion* raised some eyebrows in both teams, though this solution was eventually used. The implication of this is analysed in the answer to the second of the two research questions. Let us now turn to the research questions.

3.1.2.1 *Research question 1*

To address this question on multi-unit terms, the protocols are examined from the three interrelated standpoints of *term identification, term parsing* and *term collocates*. For reasons of space, only English glosses of extracts from the protocols are presented. Much of the subjects' verbalisation was in Hausa, the TL. Underlined words are searches announced by subjects, or finds in the glossary some of which are merely entries occurring in the neighbourhood of terms being searched (as in *leave of absence* below). Comments in square brackets are mainly mine. In the extracts, subjects are identified by their initials.

To illustrate the problem of term identification, let us consider extract 1 below from the dTAP. The extract concerns the non-contiguous term, *(motion) that the chairman ... do leave the chair.*

Extract 1.

J: Le.., let us check le.. (leave) [...] here it is, ... A: Found, right? S: right, leave of absence, then also bill introduced [leave to introduce bill] J: bill introduced, ... ok, it should be a bit, ... [*deep sigh*] A: this one is leave the chair..S: [sigh] J: [laughter] A: he left the chair... J: agreed, ok,... S: leave, leave the chair... hey! Let's check chair and see .... J/A: ok... A: leave the chair,...S: Mm... [...] chair...man?.... chairmanship, chair... at this point we should check [*find is probably meant as S sees chairman, etc in glossary*] chair ..mmm..what! None [*§2 reread*] [....] Hey, in yours (profession) what does it mean? J: But my view is like it [...] S: surely, it can't be leaving chair J: join the members of the floor S: Mhn.... J: maybe join the members of the floor [...] A: or, or, if it turns out he isn't around...

[*After nine minutes during which time other terms have been looked up, a fresh attempt at translating the paragraph is underway, and the issue of leave the chair again arises*].

S: or it turns out... A: ok S: he isn't around.. A: or S: or he has given the go-ahead A: or he ... S: or it happens he's not around J: mmm A: or ... S: he has given the go-ahead... A: or .. he has given the .. S: go-ahead .. A: go-ahead? S: yes ...

In this extract, the subjects should have been looking for any of [*motion* [*that the chairman do leave the chair*]]. The glossary, admittedly, does not enter either variant. Even if it did, the subjects might not have found it, except there had been in place a strategy for guiding the subjects from their truncated searches, that is, searches on parts of this term (*leave*, etc.), to the full term. In the extract, we see the subjects wrongly identify, in successive steps, what should have been the correct search unit. The motion that the chairman do leave the chair, if carried, is an adverse disposal of a matter before the committee of the whole House. In the final translation handed in by the dTAP team, the solution proposed reads (in back-translation) as *he is not around or he has given the go-ahead*. It took the subjects ten minutes to get it wrong. The iTAP subject proceeds quite quickly here, and does not even bother to look up the glossary. The two alternatives he monitors (in back-translation: *he stands up* and *he leaves*) show his solution is also wrong, although this cannot be attributed to the glossary. A possible conjecture for why the subject does not dwell on this term is problem-fatigue arising from an intensive ten-minute preoccupation with the preceding term, *that the chairman do report progress*. (Part description below.) The way the iTAP subject processes this term is quite similar to the description given above of the dTAP team. He successively identifies parts of this term (beginning with *chairman*) as his search and translation unit.

In the next extract, a *phantom-term* is identified due to the lexicalisation of a grammatical construction. The principal clause of §3 (*debate upon the first question proposed on the amendment may include ...*) contains a multi-unit term whose canonic or citation form is *propose question*. The term designates the action of the presiding officer in inviting discussion on any matter. Without the presiding officer proposing the question on a motion, amendment, etc. that has been introduced, floor discussion cannot take place. Now, consider the following protocol in extract 2.

Extract 2.

S: Hey, what's meant by first question? When first question is mentioned ... J: question ... I think what is meant here ... S: Mmm J:... when the proposals are many .... [...] A: first question .... of advices* [*glossary for proposal: shawara*] for amendment A: I was only trying to see if we could construct something J: ok S: debate on first question

Not finding *question* (in the glossary) in a syntagma that includes *propose*, or as a standalone, and having found a word for *proposal* (that back-translates as *advice*), the dTAP subjects proceed to render the principal clause of §3. From the protocol in extract 2 above, it is clear that their identification is wrong. By believing that *first question* is the translation unit, A and S appear to lexicalise what is otherwise a grammatical construction. They also ignore J's incomplete but correct explanation when he (J) talks about what happens when there are many proposals. J is the lawyer. Besides the issue of lexicalisation, *question* is shown by some other part of the protocol to be understood as interrogation. The idea intended in the English *first question proposed* is of course that of placing before the House, for discussion, the first of several proposals to amend an item through a type of amendment that at once deletes and adds words in the item's original formulation. Perhaps this wrong interpretation would have been averted if the glossary had entered *propose question*.

Let us now turn to the issue of term parsing, introduced already by the preceding example on wrong lexicalisation. In §1 of the source-text, there is the multi-unit term *substantive motion for the adjournment of the House* whose sense is not derivable by a conjunction of its apparent principal components, namely, *substantive motion* and *adjournment of the House*. The motion in question enables the House to discuss an issue without taking a binding decision. The motion has nothing to do with when the House *closes*. Now, consider extract 3 below.

Extract 3.

J: it's substantive motion we have to look up, substantive motion S: substantive J: yes... S: sub..stan..tive A: ok, they obviously have it S: gundarun batu A: ok, gundarun batu, it's ok. [...] the adjournment of the house... S: what? J: adjournment ... adjournment is what is to be looked up [...] J: or can adjournment of the House be found? S: well, let me check first A: or adjournment alone S: adjournment alone? [*reads out the 2 equivalents in glossary*] dagawa or dakatarwa ... A: ok, dagawa ... J: what else? S: [*reads some other entries, then*] here is adjournment motion A: ok S: is it the one we are looking for? A: it says [*reads SL text*]... for the adjournment of the House ...S: there is adjournment of the House... A: it exists... separately apparently... S: yes J:[*reads out*] dakatarwar ... dakatarwar majalisa...

[*The protocol/final translation of the last clause in §1 before subjects proceed to §2 reads thus in backtranslation*]

A: except as a result of presenting substantive motion because of [rising of sitting of assembly] J: ok S: perfect, ok.

Either because they are consistent with what was earlier referred to as their truncated search instinct, or because they have been forced by previous experiences to moderate their expectations, the subjects at certain points convey the impression they would be quite content to find *substantive* and *adjournment* respectively. They are pleasantly surprised to find in the glossary the segments, *substantive motion* and *adjournment of the House*. They possibly avoid errors as a result. However the error of parsing evident in the translation of *substantive motion for the adjournment of the House* stems precisely from the glossary not entering this multi-unit term. The subjects render this term in the TL in a way that makes *for* (translated as *domin* = *because of*) express cause/consequence, rather than the genetive sense (*aka* or *na* = of). In other words, in the Hausa TL text, substantive motion is seen as the cause of adjournment of the House; conversely, adjournment of the House is seen as the consequence of substantive motion. This is of course wrong.

Because the translators easily call back to memory solutions reached at different points in the text, and occasionally reuse such solutions when there are fuzzy matches, their error of parsing rubs off on the translation of line 1 of §2. The source-text reads "When a motion is made for the adjournment of a debate or the House [...]". The corresponding portion of the TL text, when glossed back into English, reads: "When a motion is made because of [...]". For stylistic reasons, presumably, the authors of the source-text let the head adverbial phrase "When a motion is made" control the four distinct motions mentioned in §2 (*adjourn debate, adjourn House, that the chairman do report progress, that the chairman do leave the chair*), in addition to effecting other required deletion transformations. The consequence for discourse of this parsing problem is discussed along with other issues below in Section 3.1.3.

Let us now consider the collocates or environment of terms, as a final issue under research question 1. In §2 of the source-text there is the non-contiguous term, *(motion) that the chairman do report progress*, an informal synonym of which would be *report progress*. This is a motion that allows a committee of the whole House to, for instance, bring to an end its deliberations for a given day (adjournments are out of order in committee), while allowing for the resumption of the particular committee business on a future date. In this sense, the motion is analogous to adjournment of debate when the House is not meeting as a committee; as a dilatory or time-wasting motion, it is analogous to adjournment of the House. Now, when the iTAP subject, like the dTAP team, finds nothing in the glossary for the verb phrase, *report progress*, he changes search strategy. He looks for *progress*, and is quite pleased to in fact find the noun phrase, *progress report*. A legitimate question can be posed as to whether the noun phrase has the legislative acceptation of the verb phrase, but that need not preoccupy us here. The transposition of grammatical categories (verb phrase to noun phrase) creates a problem for the iTAP subject who generally appears to be sensitive to certain details. Because the glossary does not have collocates of terms, the iTAP subject has to struggle to find an appropriate verb to use with *progress report*. Extract 4 captures some of his deliberations:

Extract 4.

Great! Here's progress report ... now that I've found progress report, *rahoton ci gaba*, rahoton ci gaba. Let me see [*1st attempt at translating §2 upto progress report*]: *Idan an gabatar da batu kan* (when a motion is presented on ...)... or on the chairman's reading of progress report, chairman's reading of progress report, or on chairman's reading of report on what was discussed concerning progress. What is said? Read what was discussed? [...] Or on chairman's reading, reading, reading ...[*subject reads source text: or that the chairman do report progress or do leave the chair, the debate upon...*]. [*2nd attempt at translating §2 upto progress report*]: *Idan an gabatar da batu kan* ...on chairman's writing of progress report, writing progress report, he wrote a report on ... I think I'll say: or the chairman's writing, writing a report of what was discussed, writing a report of what was discussed, writing a report of what was discussed. [*3rd attempt at translating §2*]: *Idan an gabatar da batu kan*....on chairman's writing a report of what was discussed, report of what was discussed, or leaving of the chair. Why have I written report of what was discussed? I think I should put: report progress [...]. It's not everything that was discussed that should be ... Let me take: report progress. [*4th attempt at translating §2*]: *Idan an gabatar da batu kan* ... on assembly chairman's writing, or giving report. He gave a report of what was discussed. I think that's how it should be. He gave, let me take out: he wrote. He gave a report of what was discussed [...].

Besides the processing time taken, the important point of this extract is that it suggests how an issue of collocation could correlate with a decision on whether and how a term proposed by the glossary is actually used. In searching for an appropriate verb for the TL noun phrase beginning with *rahoton* (borrowed from English *report*), the subject works his way through the verbs *read* and *write* before eventually settling for *give*. Each of the first two options is monitored (repeated and pondered over) several times, an observation which in this instance suggests the subject's dissatisfaction with these solutions. It is perhaps noteworthy that concern about an appropriate verb leads to, or is at least concurrent with, a modification of the glossary proposal. In spite of himself, the subject does not use *ci gaba* (progress) in connection with *rahoton* (report), but prefers the phrase *what was discussed*. (This is what appears in the final translation). At any rate, the glossary's *progress report* is only incidentally related to *report progress* as a legislative time management device. The next set of examples show how a problem of collocates impairs the readability of the translation produced by both teams.

It would be recalled from the analysis of the source-text that there were word combinations like *confine debate, amendment proposes,* etc. which had verbs (*confine, proposes*) that were not specialised, either as a standalone or in combination with the second element. These combinations were contrasted with combinations like *move motion, second motion,* etc. where the verb was specialised. Now this view, particularly as it relates to the former set of word combinations, would seem to require modification in the light of the diverse subject areas covered by the glossary (thus, the enhanced prospects of polysemy). The verbs in both the former and latter sets of combinations are not entered in the glossary. Rather, nouns are entered from which verbs are easily derived by the translators. While the derivations from *mover* and *seconder* are semantically adequate in the environment of *motion*, the same cannot be said of the verbs derived from *confinement* and *proposal* (in post-position to *amendment*). The TL acceptation of *confinement* in the glossary suggests *shield, protection* (in a concrete, rather than, abstract sense), while the acceptation for *proposal* translates as *advice, counsel or idea*. In all likelihood, the producers of the glossary would have had alternative equivalents for *confine(ment)* and *propose/proposal* if they had thought of them as collocates of *debate* and *amendment* (pre-posed) respectively. Both groups of translators err by using the glossary entries as sources of their collocates.

To answer research question 1, then, the foregoing examples point clearly to a problem of identifying word combinations that are more or less specialised. Not being specialists in the field, experimental subjects typically formulated searches in truncated form, mainly as search hypotheses. On occasion, interaction with the reference glossary invalidated such hypotheses, and pointed subjects in the right direction of segmentation, that is, identifying the correct translation units. But such occasions were few and far between. There are two paradoxes here: (1) the glossary regularly entered word combinations; (2) multi-unit terms proposed by the glossary were often not used. Mindful of the first point, it clearly would be simplistic to say that the errors observed in the protocols would have been avoided if the glossary had entered multi-unit terms. Chapter 5 should throw some light into the complexities of this first paradox. The second paradox is taken up as an issue under research question 2.

3.1.2.2 Research question 2
The emphasis here is not on what terms are missing in the glossary, but on what happens to TL terms which subjects actually find in the glossary, that is, after having verbalised the corresponding SL terms as problems. Two sets of processing scenarios are discussed. In the first, the ultimate outcome of the processing is adoption of glossary solutions. In the second set, processing leads to a partial or total non-adoption of glossary solutions.

A short example will illustrate the first. For *motion*, the TL equivalent proposed in the glossary is *batu* (which, when back-translated, means *talk*).

Extract 5 below documents the reaction of the dTAP team to what they find in the glossary on searching for *motion*.

Extract 5.

J: there is motion ... S: yes.. it's motion.. J: [...] batu ... S: What!.. A: isn't... is it the only meaning [equivalent] because it can't be ... J: batu

[*The looking up of terms is followed by an attempt to translate §1. The translation is interrupted at the point where motion occurs*]

S: any ... raw [word for "substantive"] ... A: ok S: on any substantive talk [motion] right? A: on ... is motion really talk? J: it is not it that is motion S: look at motion here, talk, right?

Incidentally, the reaction of the iTAP subject is quite comparable. He in fact looks up a general language Hausa dictionary (Skinner's), and finds the same equivalent. As a commentary on the glossary, much must not be made of this reaction to an equivalent for motion that translates as *talk*. All that this processing says is that translators are not aware that the general language word, talk, has been given terminological status in the legislative field where it represents the concept known as motion in English. Perhaps this *new* acceptation would have been promptly accepted if the glossary had provided a definition. But the fact that it is used in the final translation can be taken to mean that whatever processing time was spent on it counts for something.

Let us now look at the second scenario, with which more complex forms of processing are associated. For the term *adjournment* as a standalone, the glossary provides two entries in the TL: *dakatarwa*, which glosses roughly as *halt, stop*; and *dagawa*, which translates as *lift, rise, postpone*. The former forms part of the compound term proposed in the glossary as TL equivalent for *adjournment of House* (*dakatarwar majalisa*), while the latter goes into the term for *adjournment of debate* (*daga muhawara*). In protocol extract 6 below, *adjournment of the House* is being translated by the dTAP team, but in doing this, the subjects are focusing on the two entries under adjournment as a standalone.

Extract 6.

S: because of... A: what? S: rising of... sitting of assembly...or rising [...] A: or... or stopping.... emm or [...] because of stopping of assembly, right? J: yes A: stopping of assembly J: why can't one say rising instead of stopping S: yes, rising ... J: yes, rise/lift sitting of assembly ...rising... S: yes, stopping of ... this stopping of ... J: yes, it'll be better S: suggests stoppage ... A: yes... rising...S: rising, it suggests the thing has been pushed forward ... J: yes... A: stopping ... S: so, they almost mean the same thing J: yes A: rising — stopping, they appear to mean the same thing ... S: but rising is the one that appeals to me [...] A: alright J: ok, alright [...] to lift/rise shows that there will be another sitting A: exactly

[*A fresh attempt to translate §1 sees other issues coming up, including a definitive decision on adjournment of the House — as seen below*]

S: [...] on substantive... because..em, because ...em ... because..[...] J: stopping of assembly S: stopping... lifting sitting of assembly..A: lifting... S: it'll be better ... J: yes... S: because, personally I prefer rising to stopping J: sitting of assembly, indeed, rising will be better than stopping A: rising... sitting of ... assembly.

Now, let us assume for a moment that the translators were right in considering *adjournment of the House* as the translation unit, and not *substantive motion for the adjournment of the House* in which it actually occurs. An *adjournment of the House*, when carried, spells the end of the business that was being considered, whereas an *adjournment of debate* means that business at hand at the time this motion is adopted can be resumed at a later time. The glossary rightly captures this difference by proposing two entries for *adjournment*, and by using, for the two aforementioned types of *adjournment*, the entries that mean *stop* and *lift/rise* respectively. Apparently, this difference is also mirrored in the discussion in extract 6 above, but only one acceptation of *adjournment* is considered probable (*lifting/rising*). The glossary entries in the TL for *adjournment* are presumably seen as free variants, a point that might explain the rather strange flow of discussion, or consensus-building pattern, seen in extract 6.

Once the translators' minds are made up that lifting/rising and halt/stop are free variants, it no longer matters that the glossary has different TL words in its equivalents for the initial word in the SL *adjournment of the House* and *adjournment of debate*. Not surprisingly, then, the entry for *adjournment* that is considered most probable is generalised. This was almost inevitable given that the glossary provided no definitions which would have served to check impressionistic statements or verify hunches on the relationship between the two adjournment types. The result of the generalisation is that the original distinction presented above becomes obliterated. But unfortunately, the acceptation of *adjournment* in §1 of the SL text is precisely the one that was not considered probable by the translators, that is, *stopping* — implying the death of whatever business that had not been completed.

So, the error in translation here stems not from the glossary's failure to enter a particular multi-unit term (or part thereof), but from the absence of information to guide translators' thought processes, as they work their way from the single term, *adjournment*, to its expansions, *adjournment of the House* and *adjournment of debate*. The absence of definitions, in other words, led to the activation of non-text and non-domain pertinent knowledge bases or intuitions. In parentheses, the dTAP protocol is silent on why *zaman* (= *sitting of*) was introduced (see *lifting/rising of sitting of Assembly*), but it would seem to reinforce and explicate *lifting/rising* — in other words, members who had been seated deliberating matters have now come to the end of proceedings, and rise.

Let us see how the iTAP subject deals with this same problem of *adjournment of the House* and *adjournment of debate*. The context is the same as in the dTAP (that is, *substantive motion for the adjournment of the House* in §1 of the SL text). The spatial proximity of the House and debate adjournment terms in the glossary sees the iTAP subject processing both simultaneously. In extract 7 below, the iTAP subject's own back-translated English glosses are used in respect of *adjournment* terms, and these are underlined.

Extract 7.

For me what is really worrisome here is the way adjournment [*of debate*] is stated [*in glossary*]: suspension of debate, suspension of debate. Adjournment of the House, halting of assembly, it cannot be halting of assembly [...] it is not halting they are doing. Close is what they are doing [*Reads out his translation*]: but with exception of substantive motion of closure of assembly. But with exception of subst. motion of closure of assembly. I think it's close they did. I think halting ought not to have been written here.

[*Elsewhere the subject focuses some more on adjournment of debate. Below the subject is translating §2, line 1*].

If then one presents a motion on suspension of debate or otherwise for suspending debate. One halts debate. Inside this dictionary it is said suspension of debate.

The subject has difficulties accepting, on the one hand, the association between *dakatarwar* (=*halt, stop*) and *majalisar* (=*Assembly, House*), and on the other, the co-occurrence of *dagawar* (=*suspend, lift*) and *muhawara* (=*debate*). Within the knowledge system which the subject sets up, and within which the glossary equivalents are evaluated, we observe three lines of reasoning. Firstly, the glossary equivalent for *adjournment of the House* (=*dakatarwar majalisar*) is seen as meaning a more substantive kind of termination as opposed to, say, a daily or an intra-diurnal break. Secondly, *adjournment of the House* in the SL text is seen as referring only to a halt or break in proceedings, these being capable of resumption — a point that is taken to disqualify the glossary solution. Note here that the subject says *closing is what they are doing*. The Hausa verb *tashi* means *rise*, and in the context of meetings it means *close*. The translator thus employs this word in his term for *adjournment of the House*, rather than use the glossary suggestion. A third issue relates more to the choice of a combining word. For the translator, *muhawara* (=*debate*) should co-occur with *dakatar* (=*halt*) and not, as the glossary says, with *daga* (=*suspend*). Because the glossary does not provide definitions, the subject uses the first two lines of reasoning as basis for providing what is felt to be the more adequate equivalent for *adjournment of the House*, that is, *tashin majalisa* (close of the assembly, with *close* understood as temporary break). And presumably because the third issue above is seen as a minor one, the subject defers, resignedly, to the glossary in the final translation.

Taken in isolation, the subject's *tashin majalisa* can hardly be faulted. But the logic of the second inference above invalidates this solution. As seen in the analysis of the dTAP, the effect which a carried motion to adjourn the House has on business is that such business cannot be resumed. Findings from the knowledge experiment reported later in this chapter allow for the conjecture that if the glossary had not been alphabetically ordered, and if all concepts and terms dealing with a conceptual primitive like *end* had been entered in proximity of one another, the glossary may have stood a better chance of influencing the knowledge system set up by the iTAP subject.

To answer research question 2, then, the foregoing suggests that much of the processing that accompanied glossary solutions had to do with a conflict between the subjects' pre-knowledge or expectations and what they found in the glossary. Now, because the glossary provided no concept descriptions or definitions, and arranged its entries alphabetically, it stood very little chance of influencing knowledge systems or bases which subjects brought to bear on the task. This regularly entailed the setting aside of glossary solutions.

3.1.3 Conclusion to translation experiment

Protocol extracts have been presented and analysed with the goal of determining the extent of support provided by the glossary in an experimental but ecologically valid situation of interlingual communication. In spite of whatever differences there might be in the competence and in the psychological make-up of the two sets of translators, their protocols reveal a common set of terminological problems. A recurring problem was in the area of more or less special word combinations (combinations that are clearly multi-unit terms and those that are less clearly so). From the interaction of both groups of translators with the glossary, it emerged that (1) the glossary did not always enter these multi-unit terms or special word combinations; and (2) when word combinations were entered, the glossary failed to justify to the users why solutions proposed ought to be favourably considered.

The consequences of the foregoing are varied. In the dTAP, point (1) above was a factor in the wrong identification of terms. For both groups of translators, point (1) above meant that certain multi-unit terms in the SL text were wrongly translated. Because the wrong solutions were not always arrived at immediately after the glossary had been consulted, more or less lengthy time periods went into their processing. The latter point can also be made in respect of the observation in (2) above. Point (2) was also a factor in the setting aside of glossary solutions for subjects' own solutions. These solutions were often time-consuming, and were not always correct.

One further consequence worth mentioning is that these errors went beyond the level of lexis, and affected the texture of the translation. Given the experimental text, this is not surprising. On the basis of term tokens (as opposed to term types), about one-fifth of the experimental text is made up of terms, many of which are multi-unit. The significance of this proportion is better appreciated when it is realised that closed class words (articles, prepositions, conjunctions, etc.) that are not part of terms account for much of the remainder of the text. With these statistics, it seemed plausible that problems of terminology would have an impact on the texture of the translation, specifically in the area of cohesion (syntactic and lexical) as this is understood within the Hallidayan framework (see Halliday 1994; Halliday & Hasan 1976). The iTAP subject for instance conflates two different amendment terms in §4 (*leave out words* and *insert words*) with their conjunctive cognate in §3 (*amendment to leave out words and insert words*). Couched in the discourse of Hallidayan cohesion, it might be said that the subject created continuity, or saw ties, between the two paragraphs on the basis of wrong lexical premises. In the example cited on parsing, it was seen how a terminological problem in §1 of the SL text led the dTAP team to introduce a cohesive marker (*because*), which in that context produced a factually wrong translation. That error, which had to do with the glossary not entering a given multi-unit term, was carried over to the processing of §2 of the SL text, where it created a problem of syntactic cohesion (*reference* or *antecedence*). The subordinate clause and the beginning of the principal clause of §2 of the SL text read as follows: "When a motion is made for the adjournment of a debate or the House during any debate, or that the chairman do report progress or do leave the chair, the debate upon such a motion shall be [...]". As was seen earlier, the SL subordinate clause contains four motions that are expressed as multi-unit terms. These four terms are controlled by, or they all share, the adverbial/head phrase *when a motion is made*. In the TL translation, *motion* ceases to be commonly shared as a result of wrong term parsing. The consequence: the antecedent of "such a motion" in the main clause becomes misunderstood or restricted.

In the next section, a second experiment is reported. It sheds light on the glossary as a means of supporting the mediation or transfer of knowledge.

3.2 Knowledge experiment

An experiment was conducted to assess the extent to which the quadrilingual glossary lends itself to structured knowledge retrieval. The glossary was given to an experimental subject who had to use it to produce a text on the legislative concept, *bill*. The cautious assumption was that the protocol (that is, the text produced) would give some insight into the retrievability of knowledge from the glossary. To have a basis for comparison, a control experiment was put in place. A trilingual glossary, the *Parlamentarische Terminologie*, produced by the Language Service of the German Parliament (Bundestag), was given to an English-German bilingual who was asked to write an essay in English on *bill*, the corresponding German term being *Gesetzentwurf*. For both the main and control tests, subjects had several days to familiarise themselves with the respective resources without however being told the concept upon which they would be asked to write. A pro forma or warm-up test was then conducted on other concepts. Both test subjects are University students of literature and language.

3.2.1 *Theoretical framework: Text, mediation and knowledge*

Several objections may be raised against this test. It could, for instance, be claimed that (1) it is only by means of mediation (*sensu* Beaugrande & Dressler 1994) that text-conveyed information normally becomes appropriated as knowledge, and that (2) the communication of this knowledge normally sees the communicating subject mediating in order for the text thus produced to fit the current communication situation — with the result that this text becomes even more detached from the original input. But I intend to argue that these two forms of mediation, particularly the first form, are actually indicative of the ease of reconstituting and transferring knowledge in the primary or source text.

One of several conclusions reached by Beaugrande & Dressler (1994) from an investigation of text comprehension and recall is that information in text is more easily processed to become knowledge if it is able to activate, or map onto, a global organisation pattern (frame, schema, plan or script). Within such an organisational framework, the text user more easily supplies missing links whenever sense discontinuities are perceived. Beaugrande & Dressler write that "the simple juxtaposition of events and situations in a text will activate operations which recover or create coherence relations". Now, there appear to exist two kinds of coherence patterns. The first could be described as a mental store of abstract coherence expectancies or relations (agent, attribute, part, instrument, cause, motion, etc.). This pattern would explain why a text with unfamiliar subject matter (thus allowing for very slight intertextual mediation) could nonetheless be understandable. The second pattern would be a mental storage of specifically interpreted relations associated with a given concept (launching pad, flame, take-off, etc. associated with a rocket launch). This pattern would explain identical answers given by different respondents in cloze-type tests of text recall.

Now, applying the foregoing to a terminology *sensu* collection, it seems obvious that the data constellation in a terminological collection has to be such as to activate a mental pattern without which the shift from data to knowledge cannot take place. So while it is true that extracted knowledge is the result of cognitive processes, the quality of these processes is affected by the input data.

Evidence for the successful activation of these cognitive processes would be (1) the number of inferences made, and (2) the extent to which these inferences are directly based on the evidence in the glossary. The foregoing two points are also posited as factors for assessing the degree to which knowledge can be retrieved from the glossaries. This is because inferences are attempts at declaring (conceptual) relationships, and it is by such relationships that knowledge is defined. The need to have an evaluation system for knowledge calls for further criteria. Thus, other factors would be (3) the extent to which the data in the glossaries restrict factually incorrect inferences, and (4) the perception of the reconstituted knowledge by the subjects. In other words, does the language of the reconstituted knowledge betray the degree of the subject's commitment to the knowledge thus reconstituted? A glossary with strong knowledge reconstitution credentials will rate highly on the first three criteria, whereas one with weak credentials will rate poorly. With respect to the fourth criterion, a salience of epistemic modality markers will be taken as indicating weak credentials, even though this evidence is of itself inconclusive. Indeed, the criteria must be seen as interlinked.

3.2.2 Findings

The texts or knowledge protocols of the two subjects are given below. H. G. is the Nigerian subject, while N. S. is the German subject. Errors in the protocols are left intact. Standards of textuality used in the analysis are italicised. Chapter 7 (Section 2) discusses these standards.

H. G.'s text, produced in 18 minutes, has 165 words and appears to have -

H. G.'s knowledge protocol

The Legislative Concept Bill

1 *Bill* [1] is a word which could be used to connote different meanings in different context for example:you
2 can have such suffixes as board (*bill board*) [2], *bill of aids* [3], *bill broker* [4], *bill of credit* [5], *bill of*
3 *entry* [6], *bill of exchange* [7], *bill of goods*[8], *bill of lading* [9], *bill of rights*[*10*], *bill of sale* [11], *bill*
4 *of trade and supplies* [12], *bills payable* [13], *bills receivable* [14] etc etc. However when used
5 legislatively the phrase appears as '*bill before the house*' [15]. Here the immediate denotation is a kind
6 of degree which is waiting passed to be passed into law either at the house of assembly, house of
7 representative or house of senate. Once a bill gets to the house of senate then whatever decision is
8 taken on it there is the final decision.
9 A bill is used in the legislative context to refer to any kind of procedure involved in passing a decree
10 into law either at the house of assembly, house of representative or house of senate.

N. S.'s knowledge protocol

1 There are several institutions which can introduce a *bill* [1] in the German legislative
2 system: For First, the members of the Bundestag (we then speak of a *Bundestag-*
3 *iniated bill*) [2]; second, the Federal Government can introduce a bill (a so-called
4 *Federal Government bill*) [3]; and as the third and last possibility: the *bill of the*
5 *Bundesrat* [4]. These rights are stated in article 76 of the Grundgesetz, which is
6 the *German Basic Law* [5].
7 When one of these institutions introduces a bill, it can be dealt with in several ways:
8 There can be *consideration of the bill* [6], in which it will be *debated* [7] . It might If
9 there is a controversy about the bill in Parliament, it will probably be *referred to a*
10 *committee* [8]. In the discussion there, *objections against the bill* [9] will be formulate
11 brought forth and *amendments of the bill* [10] will be made on the basis X of
12 compromises.
13 The bill will then again be tried to be brought through Parliament. If the *adoption of*
14 *the bill* [11] takes place, it becomes a *law* [12]. If it is *rejected* [13], it will be *referred*
15 *back to the committee* [14]. In this way, a *bill can be pigeon-holed* [15] or *watered*
16 *down* [16] by continu the continuing search for compromises. Eventually, the *bill may*
17 *also be killed off* [17] this way. We then speak of the *defeat of the bill* [18].

. . . .

18 If the bill had been *given final consideration* [19] and had been adopted, it is
19 possible to *veto a bill* [20] and thus cause its defeat. If it is *an urgent bill (as*
20 *regulated by article 81 of the Grundgesetz)* [21] there will probably be no
21 possibility to pigeon-hole it. The Its *scrutiny* [22] will have to take place soon to
22 be able to *pilot it through Parliament* [23] quickly, after amendments of the bill
23 have possibly taken place. The *deliberation* [cf. 6] of it will probably have to take
24 place within a certain space of time.

Legend: The numbers in square brackets [ ] refer to the terms and expressions I suspect the subjects used. Some of these are reflected in the sample pages presented as Figures 3.1 and 3.2. The italics indicate the extent or boundaries of terms and expressions. An underlined form in N. S.'s protocol is a form the subject had written, but cancelled. An X is also a cancelled form, but one which I could not decipher. In N. S.'s protocol, the part above the dotted line corresponds to the green ink used by the subject in the first segment (20 minutes), while the part below corresponds to the section of the protocol written in black ink. Ink colours were intended to correlate with 20-minute segments.

two major parts. The first part (lines 1–4) is a general introduction, while the second (lines 4–10) attempts to specifically treat the topic of the essay. Information in the first part is conceptually incoherent with the topic of the essay. The effect of this sense discontinuity is, however, cushioned by the first sentence which is the only inference in this part, the other sentence being merely an enumeration. This first sentence is apparently motivated by the subject's concern to give the text communicated some coherence, but also by the constellation of the data in the glossary. This cushioning notwithstanding, it is arguable that the information in this sentence will be described as *acceptable* by anyone who is interested in the legislative concept, 'bill', particularly in the light of the whole essay. In effect, what the first part exemplifies is the semasiological or lexicography-type relationship. Nothing other than alphabetical happenstance or a common component in designation explains the bringing together of *bill board*, *bill of rights*, *bill of credit*, etc.

From the standpoint of conceptual relationships, the second part of the essay is obviously more interesting. This part shows at least three conceptual relationships in interaction: a logical (kind of decree in line 6/7, kind of procedure in line 9); sequential (*sensu* developmental: lines 6, 9/10; *sensu* cause-effect: lines 7/8), and a locative (notice mentions of legislative chambers). This second part obviously contains more inferences, given that each conceptual relationship established is an instance of mediation. But the substantially tautological nature of the last paragraph (lines 9/10) may be taken as an index of a problem of cognitive activity or processing. Beaugrande (1984: 142) views tautologies in these terms: "*Tautologies* suggest a partial or contaminated conceptual development that has not yet recovered enough material to make a worthwhile statement". Contamination, of which redundancy is a type, is a processing problem that disrupts one or the other textuality feature.

Let us now examine the factual correctness of the inferences. The inference on the bill requiring passage in order to become law is correct; but it is not correct to subordinate it to decree (misspelt "degree") which refers to law made by the military in Nigerian jurisprudence. Bearing in mind (1) that the two chambers in a bicameral legislature have means (conferences, joint sittings, communications) for resolving disagreements over their different versions of bills, and (2) that the head of the executive arm of government may be able to exercise the power of veto, the inference in lines 7/8 is not quite correct. A bill is of course not a kind of procedure as line 9 claims. In relating the number and quality of inferences to the glossary, it is worth mentioning that in the course of this exercise the test subject opened the 294-page glossary only once, to the page where 'bill' is entered. See Figure 3.1.

It is obvious that part two of the essay is significantly mediated, that is, based less on the evidence in the glossary, and more on the subject's beliefs. When it is recalled that the subject claimed not to be particularly knowledgeable in this field, it is not surprising why, with such little input, many of the subject's inferences were wrong. If it were possible to discountenance the previous remark on "decree", line 5/6 would be the only knowledge inference in the essay that at once satisfied the textuality criteria of *coherence, informativity* and *acceptability*. This inference is incidentally less mediated compared to the others. By the subject's own admission, the motivated equivalents in Hausa and Yoruba of the relevant acceptation of 'bill' prompted the description of this concept as sequentially preceding *law*.

Let us now turn to the control experiment. The text produced by the control subject in 28 minutes contains 311 words. 60% of this text was produced within the first 20-minute segment. Two major parts are discernible in the protocol: the first part (lines 1–6) deals with sources, or the introduction, of bills, while the second part (lines 7–24) attempts to describe the processing, or stages, of a bill.

ENGLISH	HAUSA	IGBO	YORUBA
bilateral trade:	cu..kin kasashe biyu	àrumahia mbà àbụọ̀	òwò láàrin (orílẹ̀-èdè) méjì
bilingual: n.	wanda ya iya harsuna biyu, maji harshe biyu	ọ̀sụ asụ̀sụ àbụọ̀	gbédègbéyọ̀
[1] bill: n.	takardar kuɗi. shirin doka	bülı	àbá-ẹ̀fín/būll; owó-iṣẹ́/ọjà
[15] bill before the house:	shirin doka gaban majalisa	bülı chère ogbakò	àbá-ẹ̀fín tó wà níwájú àwọn aṣòfin
[2] billboard: n.	allon sanarwa	bülbọ̀ọ̀dụ̀	pátákó ìpolówó-ọjà
[3] bill of aids			
[4] bill broker:	dillalin huɗa	òreë bülı	alárinà bülı/òwó
[5] bill of credit:	takardar kuɗi na jiya	büli kèkredút	iwé-ìdániilójú owó-àsansiẹ
[6] bill of entry:	takardar shigar kaya	büli kèmbàta	iwé-àṣẹ àtiwọlé-erù
[7] bill of exchange:	garantin biya	büli kènzụkọ̀rịta	iwé-ìfowóránṣẹ́ láti ilé òkèèrè
[8] bill of goods:	takardar kayayyaki	büli kèngwa ahịa	àkọsílẹ̀ iye-ọjà
[9] bill of lading:	takardar lodi	büli kènzipụ̀	àkọsílẹ̀ erù-akósòkò
[10] bill of rights:	takardar 'yanci	büli kèörùrù mma-iù	àkọsílẹ̀ ònìrúurú ẹtọ́
[11] bill of sale:	takardar sayarwa	büli kèörire	àkọsílẹ̀ ọjà-títà
[12] bill of trade:	takardar kasuwanci	büli kèàsụmahia	àkọsílẹ̀ òwò
and supplies:	takardar taimako aa kuma kayayyaki	büli kèmbunye ngwa ahịa	àkọsílẹ̀ ohun-elò àti ohun-àmúlò
[13] bills payable:	takardun lamuni	büli kèakwuàkwù	àkọsílẹ̀ owó tó yẹ ní sísan
[14] bills receivable:	garantin da aka ki ba	büli kènnabàta	àkọsílẹ̀ owó tó yẹ ní gbígbà
bimetallism: n.	tagwan kuɗi	taimètalisìm	ìlànà owó amú-...

Figure 3.1: *Extract from Quadrilingual Glossary*

In effect, there is some diversity in the type of concept relations used in the essay. For a subject who claimed not to be particularly interested or knowledgeable in the subject matter, this broad coherence of the essay is evidence of the successful activation of what was referred to earlier as abstract coherence expectancies.

This protocol abounds with inferences. In the first major part of the essay, the subject's inferences are to be found in lines 1 and 4. The latter is particularly interesting because of its very definitive nature: "third and last possibility". Further evidence for inferencing, and, *ipso facto* for the successful activation of an organisational pattern, can be gleaned from the number of if-clauses (lines 8/9, 14/15, 18/19, and 19/21). The sequential relation instantiated in these clauses is also evident elsewhere where it is differently announced (see line 16/17 "eventually", line 22/23 "after amendments have possibly taken place"). There is clearly an attempt to relate the various concepts found in the resource.

Since *coherence* is not coterminous with factual correctness, let us now examine the validity of some of the inferences. The very categorical inference in line 4/5 is correct,[1] and I shall be speculating later on the source of this as well other inferences. Much of the inference in line 10/11 on objecting to, and amending, a bill during committee is right. The relationship between bill and law in line 13/14 is also correct, as are the inferences in lines 18/19, 19/21, among others. This is not quite the case with the inference in line 8/10 (relationship between controversial nature of bill and its referral).[2] The set of consequences in line 15/16 is also questionable. At a different level of analysis, the subject does not appear to clearly appreciate what (synonymous) relationship there exists between certain concepts, for example, "reject a bill" (line 14) and "defeat a bill" (lines 17 and 18/19).[3]

It is instructive that many of the German subject's inferences or declared conceptual relationships are moderated or hedged. Epistemic modality is introduced into many of the if-clauses. Thus, there is "probably" in lines 8/9 and 19/21.

---

1. This is confirmed by a poster describing the path of a piece of legislation ('Der Weg eines Gesetzes') in the German Federal Legislature (Bundestag). It reads in part: *Nach dem Grundgesetz beginnt das Gesetzgebungsverfahren mit der Einbringung des Gesetzentwurfs im Bundestag durch die Bundesregierung, den Bundestag oder den Bundesrat.*

2. A bill need not be controversial *ab initio* to be referred to a committee. Rule 80 of the procedure in the German Bundestag governs committee referral.

3. In a written response to some of my questions, a source at the Language Division of the German Federal Legislature says that the corresponding German terms are "synonyms at the conceptual, but not at the surface linguistic, level" (my translation from the German).

Even in other constructions expressing sequential relations, just like the if-clauses, one also encounters modal expressions suggesting uncertainty. In line 16/17, there is "may", in line 18/19 "it is possible", in line 23 "possibly" and "probably". The analysis of modality in this protocol is in a sense made difficult, not so much because N. S., its author, is a non-L_1 user of English (although this should be kept in view) but because of the occasional ambivalence of the English language *vis-à-vis* the expression of different kinds of modality. The modal auxiliaries and expressions in lines 7("can"), 8 ("can"), 15 ("can"), 16 ("may"), 18 ("it is possible") can be epistemic or deontic. As deontic modality, they would specifically express factual equipossibility, as opposed to N. S.'s uncertainty.

The observation has been made that in written academic discourse, hedging of this kind with modal words could be a ploy for "strengthening the argument by weakening the claim" (Meyer 1997). For the merely descriptive task in this experiment, it should be safe to rule out this particular strategic use of hedging. Absolution from responsibility, in the event of error, is the strategic goal here.

In comparison to the main experimental protocol, the control text is more *coherent* and has more inferences. In relating the number and quality of inferences to the glossary, it might be noted that all the terms in the control protocol are taken from just two consecutive pages of the 188-page resource. Figure 3.2 below is the first of the two pages consulted.

It is safe to assert that the concentration of terms related to *Gesetzentwurf* (bill) in these pages is a factor in the speed with which the subject was able to develop a broad and coherent pattern. This proximity, more or less, of conceptually related terms appears to account for some of the correct inferences made by the German subject. Take for example the three sources of bills (lines 1–5 of protocol). The relevant terms — [2], [3], [4] in the protocol — appear as numbers [5], [7], [8] in the section of the resource consulted (see Figure 3.2). My conjecture is that, having seen these three terms in some close proximity, and presumably not having seen any others within the two pages consulted, the subject felt comfortable enough to categorically assert that the Bundesrat was the "third and last possibility" — after listing members of the Bundestag and the Federal Government.

But it can also be argued that, in many cases, incorrect inferencing or wrong mediation is ultimately attributable to the resource. This is certainly the case with the questionable knowledge of the (synonymous) relationship between "reject a bill " and "defeat a bill " (lines 17 & 18/19). The same attribution is defensible in respect of many of the epistemic modal words. The evidence we find for these assertions is that although many of the entries are phrasal in nature (bill + collocate) they do not have definitions. There are no cross-reference indications (at least not in the pages

E law amending the Constitution (the Basic Law)

F loi f de révision constitutionnelle
 loi f portant révision de la constitution

Gesetz-: Verfassungsmäßigkeit eines Gesetzes

E constitutionality of a law

F constitutionnalité f d'une loi

Gesetz-: verfassungswidriges Gesetz

E unconstitutional law

F loi f anticonstitutionnelle

Gesetz-: Verfassungswidrigkeit eines Gesetzes

E unconstitutionality of a law

F inconstitutionnalité f d'une loi

Gesetz-: von Gesetzes wegen

E by virtue of the law
 on the strength of the law
 under the law

F de plein droit

Gesetz-: zum Gesetz werden

E to become law
 to pass into law

F passer en force de loi

Gesetz-: zustimmungsbedürftiges Gesetz
(GG Art. 77 Abs. 1)

E bill requiring Bundesrat approval

F loi f requérant l'approbation du Bundesrat

Gesetzblatt
 s.a. Bundesgesetzblatt

E law gazette

F Journal m officiel

[1] Gesetzentwurf

E bill

F projet m de loi (émane du gouvernement)
 proposition f de loi (émane du Bundestag ou du Bundesrat)

[13] Gesetzentwurf-: Ablehnung eines Gesetzentwurfes

E rejection of a bill

F rejet m d'un projet ou d'une proposition de loi

Gesetzentwurf-: Änderung eines Gesetzentwurfes [10]

E amendment of a bill

F amendement m d'un projet ou d'une proposition de loi

Gesetzentwurf-: Annahme eines Gesetzentwurfes [11]

E adoption of a bill
 passing of a bill

F adoption f d'un projet ou d'une proposition de loi

Gesetzentwurf aus der Mitte des Bundestages [2]
(GG Art. 76 Abs. 1; GOBT § 76)

E bill introduced by Members of the Bundestag
 Bundestag-initiated bill

F proposition f de loi présentée par des membres du Bundestag

Gesetzentwurf-: Beratung eines Gesetzentwurfes [6]

E consideration of a bill
 deliberation of a bill
 discussion of a bill

F délibération f sur un projet ou une proposition de loi
 discussion f d'un projet ou d'une proposition de loi

Gesetzentwurf der Bundesregierung [3]
(GG Art. 76)

E bill of the Federal Government
 Federal Government bill

F projet m de loi du Gouvernement fédéral

Gesetzentwurf des Bundesrates [4]
(GG Art. 76)

E bill of the Bundesrat

F proposition f de loi du Bundesrat

Gesetzentwurf-: die Behandlung eines Gesetzentwurfes verschleppen [15]

E to pigeon-hole a bill

F laisser traîner en longueur un projet ou une proposition de loi

Gesetzentwurf-: dringlicher Gesetzentwurf [21]
(GG Art. 81; GOBT § 99)

E urgent bill

F projet m de loi déclaré urgent

Gesetzentwurf-: einen Gesetzentwurf abschließend beraten [19]

E to give final consideration

Figure 3.2: *Sample page from Parlemantarischer Glossar*

consulted by the subject). Other than spatial or physical proximity of terms, no other means exist for representing the relationships among terms entered.

3.2.3 Conclusion to knowledge experiment

The heuristic value of the experiment conducted would seem to have been confirmed. There is an interesting set of correlations: on the one hand, between N. S.'s richer knowledge protocol and the macrostructure of the (German) reference glossary, and, on the other, between H. G.'s poorer protocol and the Nigerian glossary. The former glossary represented its entries to some extent conceptually, while the latter adopted an alphabetical ordering system. Undoubtedly, the correlations could be explained by different degrees of exposure to parliamentary democracy (more for N. S., and less for H. G.); in other words, by various degrees of mediation all of which are detached from the primary evidence (the glossary).

However, the significance of the glossary-protocol correlations suggests the overriding importance of facts in the glossaries, specifically the way entries are organised. A *coherent* data constellation was to be found in the German glossary, but not in the Nigerian one. It is instructive that in both glossaries, but particularly the Nigerian one, there was a lot of bill-related information at other locations. Information concerning the reading of bills, types of bills, committal of bills etc. was not retrieved because these concepts did not form part of the constellation found in the bill page. No subject who did not already know these concepts could retrieve them in any systematic and time efficient way. Interestingly, these results remind of studies intended to compare performance of subjects reading paper documents with that of subjects reading hypertext documents. The 1989 study by Egan *et al.* (cited by McKnight *et al.* 1991) showed that "students using Superbook [a hypertext implementation] answered more search questions correctly, wrote higher quality [...] essays, and recalled certain incidental information better than students using conventional texts". It can therefore be concluded that the degree to which a glossary is able to meet certain knowledge-mediation goals is very much related to the way its entries are organised. Chapter 6 takes up this issue.

3.3 Miscellaneous

Communication and knowledge (in the sense of the preceding sections) are not the only arenas for critiquing the quadrilingual glossary. This resource can indeed be reviewed from the standpoint of the more common critical discourses identified in Chapter 2 (Section 2.4). A brief consideration of issues from these other standpoints is important in determining how holistic and extensive an alternative framework of terminology discourse and practice would have to be. The discussion below is, unlike the one in the preceding sections, not restricted to Hausa. Rather it covers the two other target-languages (Igbo and Yoruba) of the quadrilingual glossary (English is the source-language). Labelling conventions adopted are as follows: H (Hausa), I (Igbo) and Y (Yoruba). Glosses in English are provided under each example.[4]

3.3.1 Adequacy of term motivations

A term can, admittedly, suggest the opposite of what the concept it designates stands for (e.g. *atom*). Thus motivation, viewed superlatively, is an ideal in terminology planning that is not always met. This underscores the role of definitions in leading in the right or intended direction of association. The absence of definitions, as is the case in the glossary, makes interest in the motivation of terms quite compelling. On the basis of the examples that follow, two conjectures suggest themselves: the glossary-makers did not work with definitions, and therefore relied on general knowledge of English and of the world, rather than on the specialised knowledge of legislative practice; if they did work with definitions, they had difficulties determining what characteristics of concepts needed to be reflected in the corresponding terms which they had to create. Consider Table 3.1 below.

Table 3.1

	H	I	Y
casting vote	*jefa ƙuri'a* throwing of vote	*voòtù onye isi ochē* chairman's vote	*ìbò ala-ọ̀mì* tie-breaker vote

Conceptually, the Hausa equivalent is poorly motivated in comparison with the Igbo and Yoruba equivalents. The Speaker (or presiding officer) of a legislative body normally does not vote. S/he does so only in the event of a tie. The speaker's vote which seeks to break the tie is what is called casting vote.

---

4. For providing English glosses of terms in the glossary's target languages, the following are thanked: Mal. Bello Bala Usman & Dr. Andrew Haruna (Hausa), Ms. Ifeyinwa Uzuegbu & Dr. Augustin Okereke (Igbo) and Professor Rotimi Badejo (Yoruba).

The *Bar* is a term used traditionally in a number of contexts to designate a partition that separates an area occupied by professionals or persons with special privileges from the area occupied by non-professionals, etc. The former could be clergy/choristers, presiding judge, legislators, etc. In legislative assemblies only legislators and legislative staff may go beyond the Bar. Only on invitation are other categories of persons allowed to go beyond this point. Now, consider the entries in Table 3.2 ((a) and (b)) below.

Table 3.2

	H	I	Y
a. Bar of the House of Representatives	6angaren lauyoyi na majalisar wakilai ta kasa section of lawyers in House of Reps.	baà ǹkè u̱lō ǹǹo̱chitere (sic) bar (loan) of the House of representatives	ibi ìjókó àwo̱n lo̱yà nínu ile àwo̱n aṣofin sitting place of lawyers in House of Reps
b. Bar of the Senate	6angaren lauyoyi a majalisar dattijai section of lawyers in Senate	baà ǹkè seneētì bar (loan) of Senate (loan)	ibi ìjókó àwo̱n lo̱yà nínu ilé àwo̱n aṣofin àgbà sitting place of lawyers in Senate
c. private act	aikin sa kai individual work	aaki̱ti̱keoñwe act (loan) out of one's personal strength	ìṣe-tara-e̱ni lábe̱ òfin individual work done discreetly/behind the law

Lawyers do not have a place specially reserved for them in legislative assemblies. While the situation in Nigeria could very well have been different, persons connected to one Second Republic legislature have no recollection of such a sitting arrangement. Since terminology planners in Igbo opted for the loan *baà* it is not immediately apparent if they similarly had lawyers in mind while processing (a) and (b) in Table 3.2. Suggestive, but inconclusive, evidence is provided by the two equivalents proposed for *bar* (as a standalone), which is the term that immediately precedes entry a in the above Table. Planners propose the loan *baà* and *òtu ndi̱ ōka īwu* (association of lawyers). Now, but for the loan, Igbo would presumably have been seen to err by using, in the parliamentary context, the legal interpretation of 'Bar' (law profession/practising members).[5]

---

5. The confusion is reminiscent of the one associated with a character in a novel by the Nigerian author, Cyprian Ekwensi. The character wonders why people (i.e. Nigerians) have to go all the way to England to be called to the Bar when there were good bars across the street! England was for a long time the place of choice for Nigerians seeking legal education.

Entry (c) in Table 3.2 (that is, *private act*) is perhaps the loudest statement of the importance of definitions in terminology planning. In legislative discourse (which is what the glossary should be about, primarily) a *private act* is a kind of *act*, the latter occasionally used synonymously with *law*.

3.3.2 Inter(target)language variation

The fact of creating terms in three target languages apparently posed a challenge of coordination. The preface to the glossary describes this challenge as follows:

> We then entered the most crucial phase of the project. It was not enough for each of the three groups of translators to do an excellent job; the three groups had to be very carefully coordinated so that they were translating the same sense of each headword. This stage of the project inevitably took a very long time, and even then, it can hardly be claimed that a perfect stage of coordination was reached before going to press. Scores of hours of meetings have resulted in a reasonable degree of coordination. To achieve a perfect coordination, we had to engage translators each of whom could speak all the four languages involved. Further revisions would no doubt result in greater refinement (p. vii).

Scholars of hedging in academic discourse should find this passage interesting, if not intriguing. Table 3.3 below offers some evidence for what is believed to be the problem, one which should not have arisen if concept definitions or descriptions had played a more important role.

The Hausa term in a apparently refers to a concept that is different from the

Table 3.3

	H	I	Y
a. original bill	*Takardun biya na asali* Original papers of payment	*Bûlù gboo* Old bill (bill, loan from English)	*àbá-òfin àpilẹ̀ṣe* motion for new legislation
b. speaker	*mai jawabi* the one speaking	*Spikà* Speaker (loan from English)	*alága ilé ìgbìmọ̀ṣọ̀fin; aṣafò* chairperson of legislative house

---

long time the place of choice for Nigerians seeking legal education.

one designated by the Yoruba term. Igbo, again, borrows from English. With respect to (b), the Hausa term is rather intriguing. Igbo again borrows. Only in the Yoruba is there certainty concerning the legislative acceptation of 'speaker'. In subsequent entries (*speaker of house of assembly, speaker-elect* etc.), Hausa reflects the intended acceptation of presiding officer. Now, even if part of the penultimate sentence of the preface quoted earlier had read "we would have had to engage quadrilingual translators", it is doubtful that the goal of perfect coordination would have been achieved.

3.3.3 Selection policy and coverage

It is clearly a daunting task to provide (in one fell swoop) an adequate terminological infrastructure in support of law-making in languages that do not have a long tradition of use in Western-type legislative assemblies. The challenges that confronted the makers of the quadrilingual glossary are expressed thus in the preface:

> The first and most crucial task was to agree on the size and range of English headwords to be glossed into the three major Nigerian languages. In theory, any field of discourse under the sun is potential subject for debate at a National Assembly; but at the same time, it is reasonable to assume that there is a distinct register of legislative discourse.
>
> This was no mean task. Experts in the various relevant fields had to be assembled and they represented not just the obvious fields of politics and economics, but also all the other fields into which government is traditionally divided — health, information, industry, trade, education, social development, sports, etc. Experts from these fields, drawn from the universities, were brought together and invited to provide word-lists in their various fields which they thought would be essential in operating in these fields in a national assembly (p. vii).

The ambitiousness of the plan as well as the underlying methodology explain some of the glossary's shortcomings in respect of scope. It fails to enter such relevant legislative terms and collocations as: *negative (a motion), recommit (a bill), voice vote/collect voices*. Yet, it has space for: *aspirin, basic travelling allowance, depressect, paleoanthropology, sonic boom, tattoo, vegetative propagation, wire wound resistor,* and *zoom lens*.

The apparent problem of defining the glossary's scope creates interesting situations of polysemy and disambiguation. Several polysemous SL terms in the glossary are given TL equivalents whose frames of reference lie outside the discourse of parliamentary procedure. But in entries where these terms collocate with other elements, the legislative acceptation is provided in the TLs. Cases in point are the glossary entries for *division* and *division bell* as well as for *teller* and *teller for noes*. Whereas for *division* equivalents proposed in the TLs translate as 'cut', 'half', and 'local administrative unit', it is with *division bell* that the idea of voting becomes explicit. One item each in the Yoruba and Igbo entries for *teller* is associated with voting. Hausa has just one item, a form borrowed from English. This borrowed form, like the remaining items in Yoruba and Igbo, are associated with the banking context. With *teller for noes*, Hausa drops the borrowed form, and proposes a term that translates as 'the representative of the no people'. A *division* is a voting procedure resorted to after another procedure (voice vote) has been challenged. A bell (*division bell*) is rung to alert all members in the vicinity of the House to the imminence of such a voting exercise. Should the voting actually take place, the presiding officer would normally appoint tellers for each side of the question being decided. The tellers then count the number of members voting on each side (yes and no).

The above examples support the claim made in the analysis of the translation protocols that *confine(ment)* and *proposal/propose* would have been given different equivalents in Hausa if the glossary producers had anticipated their occurring with *debate* and *amendment* respectively.

3.4 Consolidated summary

When seen in the light of parts of Chapter 1 and of areas of discourse emphasis presented in Chapter 2, the issues raised in this chapter, particularly those relating to communication and knowledge, are taken to justify the need for an extension of the framework of terminology practice and discourse in Nigeria and in other parts of Africa. Many of the projects reviewed in Chapter 2 are similar in many respects to the Nigerian glossary evaluated here. Chapter 2 (Section 2.4.4) also showed that it was more in the negative sense that communication could be said to be a concern of, or present in, the critical metadiscourse on terminology. The translators in Tanzania interviewed by Kummer described problems of text production indicative of inattention by terminology planners to the syntagmatic dimension of language for special purposes. There is perhaps a little more than fortuitousness between these comments and some of the problems of word combinations seen in the current chapter. In expressing the opinion below, Paepcke just might have been speaking on behalf of the translators in this chapter as well as in the Kummer study:

It is not enough to simply draw up lists of technical terms without determining their function in sentences as well as in texts, and without taking cognisance of their links to other words and phrases (Paepcke 1985: 8; my translation from the French).

As for knowledge transfer, there is perhaps more than just coincidence in the correlation between the dearth of knowledge concerns in the critical meta-discourse and the comparatively poor knowledge-mediating potentials of the Nigerian glossary evaluated in this chapter. This is quite consistent with the view quoted in Chapter 1 according to which language planning theory has traditionally failed to consider the "process of term evaluation in various situations of discourse (i.e. in editing, lecturing, writing of manuals, industrial training, laboratory report writing, etc." (Jernudd & Neustupný 1991: 31).

In the chapters that follow, I provide theoretical frameworks that serve the twin purpose of accounting for the problems raised in this chapter, and defining the outlines of alternative directions of terminology discourse and practice within the context of African and general language planning.

CHAPTER 4

Concept Theory in Terminology

A useful way of broaching the field of terminology studies is through considering the notion, *concept*. The concept is very central to the discourse and practice of terminology. A pioneer scholar, Wüster, writes that work on terminology takes the concept as its point of departure (Wüster 1974: 67). Picht & Draskau (1985: 36) observe that in "the theory of terminology there is widespread agreement that the concept occupies a central position".

A theoretical account of the concept in terminology is however not quite as simple or straightforward as this consensus would suggest. The challenge would seem to stem from two sources. First, there is the point about the eclecticism of terminology as a discipline, that is, the fact of its drawing from several disciplines some of which have a long and diverse history of preoccupation with concepts. For instance, in philosophy, linguistics, psychology, knowledge engineering, etc. there is, or has been, a concern with concepts in the context of one or a combination of the following *actions* on *reality*: perceiving it, (re)creating it, stabilising it, organising it, and communicating it. Second, terminology is a phenomenon of specialised subject areas. This means that accounts of the concept would have to recognise that specialised subject areas work with different ontologies and are underpinned by different epistemological positions — a diversity that can be expected to affect how concept creation and description is viewed.

What is called for, then, is a polycentric and flexible terminological concept model which must not however make claims of universal explanatory adequacy. The point of departure of any such model is of course specialised subject matter and expression. The goal of the following presentation of a concept theory in terminology is to provide a framework for viewing some of the issues that arose from the evaluation in Chapter 3, and simultaneously to introduce components of an alternative framework of discourse and practice for LP-oriented terminology. The theoretical presentation is rather extensive. Readers whose background is more in language planning than in terminology, and who wish to get a sense of where this presentation could lead, may well find it worthwhile going first to the concluding section (4.9) of this chapter.

4.1 Parameters for a concept theory[1]

Mainstream literature on terminology is replete with definitions of the concept, as can be confirmed by a reference to textbooks (Wüster 1991; Felber 1984; Felber & Budin 1989; Picht & Draskau 1985; Sager 1990, etc.), articles (Hohnhold 1982; Dalberg 1976, etc.) and to standards, both national and international (Austrian–Önorm; German–DIN; international–ISO). Sager (1990: 23) notes that from the "great diversity of definitions [of the concept] formulated with the same intention and purpose it is obvious that there is considerable divergence of opinion on the matter". Recent work by Picht also makes this point (see Picht 1997, and one of the chapters by him in Laurén, Myking & Picht 1998). This work has influenced the following discussion. Rather than list the various definitions that have been proposed I elect to proceed differently. Taking a unifying view of the diverse and oft contradictory definitions, I offer the following parametric view of the concept. The concept is a unit of thought, knowledge or cognition which:

1. though dependent on language (see 5 below) is *independent of a given language*; it can however be influenced by a variety of socio-cultural factors that correspond to linguistic boundaries;
2. is a mental representation, reduction or (re)interpretation of reality that is perceptible, imperceptible or that was previously non-existent;
3. is comprised of characteristics that are (at some point, at least) negotiated within a specialised knowledge community;
4. typically enters into some (organic or logical) relationship with other concepts;
5. can exist without symbols (whether linguistic or non-linguistic), but requires symbols for purposes of communication.

I will return to this parametric description momentarily.

There has been much discussion as to what exactly the concept is a unit of (see Dahlberg 1976, Felber 1995). Articulating further the attempt by Picht at a reconciliation (thought, knowledge, cognition), approaches may be hypothesised

---

1. The designation *concept theory* is an umbrella one, subsuming for instance what will be described as an *object theory*.

here that are rooted in the following notions: life-cycle, disciplinary interest and typical domain. The 'unit of thought' acceptation might be relevant at the initiation of a concept's life-cycle, when the concept is being constituted and its intension is yet to be fully formed. It would be part of the thought process of an individual who would later be credited with an invention or a discovery. The mental domain here is private, since one would be speaking of an individual or a fairly restricted group. The 'unit of knowledge' acceptation might be relevant when the concept is fully formed and accepted by a specialised knowledge community. The mental domain here is public, since one would be dealing here with a community, a *Denkkollektiv*. This acceptation differs from Felber's account in which the concept is only part of a unit of knowledge — the latter being seen in terms of logical propositions represented by sentences (Felber 1995: 26–7). If cognition were viewed as a process, the 'unit of cognition' acceptation might be relevant when, in a Thomas Khunian period of revolutionary science, a community noticed change in the intension of the concept, and observed that a new concept was being derived or created.

With respect to the criterion of disciplinary interests: the philosophy of science would be particularly interested in the unit of thought and cognition senses. The subject disciplines in which the actual conceptual knowledge (not meta-knowledge) is created would be interested in the unit of knowledge acceptation, as would fields and activities that document knowledge states for a variety of applications like terminology resources, knowledge databases, etc. (see Picht 1997; Laurén, Myking & Picht 1998). Common to all these dimensional views and approaches is the indispensability of concept characteristics.

To return to other aspects of the concept: from the parametric description provided earlier are derived the poles around which much of the discussion in this chapter is organised. Features (1) and (5) provide the basis for examining the relationship between concept and symbol; features (2) and (3) together invite some discussion of an object theory in terminology, of concept formation in specialised fields, and of the relationship between objects (and their properties) and concepts (and their characteristics); feature (4) allows for a discussion of concept systems.

4.2 Relationship of the concept to its symbol

Following Wüster, sections of the terminology community view the concept as independent of its symbol (verbal or non-verbal). In Wüster's 1974 article in the journal, *Linguistics*, we find the following passage:

Every terminological activity takes the CONCEPT as its starting point. Such an activity aims at clearly defining the borders between concepts. In terminology, the realm of concepts is viewed as independent of the realm of designations. This explains why terminologists speak of *concepts*, whereas most linguists speak of *meaning*. For the terminologist, a unit of designation is comprised of a *word*, to which a concept is, by way of meaning, assigned. For most contemporary linguists, however, a word is comprised of two inseparable units, word-form and meaning.

A way of dispensing with the term, *concept*, would be to say that for the terminologist, the meaning of a word is limited to that assigned to it in a subject field, thus subject meaning, which may also be seen as conceptual meaning (Wüster 1974: 67; my translation from the German).

Besides obvious and general cases such as that of an inventor who is still to label the product or process s/he has just invented, the claim of independent realms derives its validity *paradigm-internally* (that is, within terminology), where it enhances the paradigm's work methods and explanatory adequacy *vis-à-vis* its object, *specialised knowledge and expression*. The independence of the realms of concept and symbol gives pre-eminence to the concept, while devaluing, in some sense, the symbol (e.g. term). It only makes sense that the concept, defined in terminology as an entity which is independent of any given language, should not be approached from a standpoint that reflects distinctions which a particular language makes in its vocabulary or in its analysis of reality. *Onomasiology* is the name given to the totality of strategies by which terminological analysis unlocks the ontology of knowledge in specialised knowledge areas in a manner that is independent of a given language, but lets the analyst identify any biases of a given subsection of the knowledge community — whose self-definition may very well coincide significantly with a given language space (Russian, American English, French, etc.). Onomasiological strategies are also useful in those cases where a given specialised knowledge is the exclusive preserve of a given language space. Many of these strategies will be examined in this chapter. The chapter will also show that the epistemological premises of areas of specialised knowledge, although by no means homogenous, differ more or less from the premises underlying general knowledge and expression.

In the quotation above, the recurrence of the word "assigned" can be seen as Wüster's insistence on the point that, in specialised knowledge and discourse communities, the relationship between concept and symbol is one that is consciously (and constantly) transacted or negotiated. But inferences of invariant usage or immutability must not be drawn from this transaction. Transaction refers as much to *fixed* as to *evolving* states.[2]

The separation of the two realms of concept and symbol, the fact of their relation being constantly transacted, and of specialised concepts being imparted in stereotypical form, that is, through (negotiated) definitions, descriptions, etc. — all of these may be offered in contrast to the consubstantiality[3] and to the epistemological position inherent in certain traditional accounts of the linguistic sign. In the quotation above, Wüster's reference to Saussure would have been obvious. But let us look at Ullmann who supports certain Saussurean positions (e.g. Saussure's omission of the object in his dyadic model) in the face of sharp criticisms directed at Saussure by Ogden & Richards (1923[1969]).[4]

In Ullmann's functional analysis of meaning, for instance, "it is vitally important for the understanding of semantic processes that the relation between name and sense is reciprocal and reversible" (Ullmann 1956:13), hence the definition of meaning as "a reciprocal relation between name and sense, which enables them to call up one another" (Ullmann 1957:70). To exaggerate the point, the bond is such that "[n]othing short of the cataclysm, such as the brain lesions studied by the neurologist, will ever sever the link between name and sense" (Ullmann 1956:14). At any rate, even if terminology or specialised knowledge and expression admitted of a link such as posited by Ullmann, but in the pre-controlled environment of consciously negotiated and stereotypically imparted meanings, they (terminology and LSP) would not share the ontological and epistemological premises underpinning Ullmann's bond. Ullmann writes that

---

2. With respect to the so-called fixed states in the concept-symbol relationship, it is important that the inference drawn from the construct of transaction is one of controlled indeterminacy, rather than an invariable, context-insensitive, 1:1, equivalence. The notion of the concept as a sum of characteristics (amplified later) suggests that different configurations of the sum or totality can be focused upon or facilitated. So, the activitated intension of a concept behind an invariable term (for instance) may vary repeatedly according to contexts. See Gerzymisch-Arbogast (1996). The point of associating 'controlled' with indeterminacy is that there exists boundaries beyond which it becomes spurious to claim that one is talking about the same, not different, concepts. One is reminded here of phonemes and allophones.

3. I use *consubstantiality* to describe inseparability of content and form (concept and term). Both are seen as bonded together in a way that suggests that they are of the same matter, and cannot have separate existence. Gerzymisch-Arbogast (1996:9) has suggested that Wüster's writings occasionally contradicted his thesis of concepts and terms belonging to separate realms. For instance, Wüster (1959/60) speaks of a significant degree of reciprocal effect — "hohen Grad von Wechselwirkung" — between concept and term.

4. Of Saussure's dyadic model, Ogden & Richards write that, "unfortunately this theory of signs, by neglecting entirely the things for which signs stand, was from the very beginning cut off any contact with scientific methods of investigation" (p. 6).

"the philologist is in a position to confine himself to one of the three [...] dyadic relations [that is, name and sense] whereas the psychologist, logician and epistemologist have to concern themselves with all three" (1957: 72). He thus takes as a given the process of how reality becomes embodied in language.[5]

Now, disinterest in the process by which reality becomes embodied in language presupposes the uniformity of the embodiment process. This is of course not borne out by the easily verifiable fact that, within a single language, different mental representations of a thing/object are possible — representations correlating, for instance, with idiosyncratic worldviews (in spite of the Whorf-Sapir hypothesis) or with the distinction between popular versus scientific epistemologies. (Notice, for example, that *whale* is considered a fish in German general knowledge and language, but is seen as a mammal in the special language/knowledge of biology; similarly, tomato is a vegetable in general language/knowledge, but a fruit in botany). There are of course also those differences that correlate with different natural languages.

4.3 Relationship of concept to object (an object theory in terminology)

The point in the previous section about disinterest in reality or ontology is made clearly by Ullmann. In collapsing Ogden & Richards' triadic model into a binary one like Saussure's, Ullmann (1956: 13) argues that a tripartite model that includes "thing" offers "too much to the linguist" who is typically "not concerned with the non-linguistic world as such, only with those aspects of it which are relevant to, and embodied in, language".

Be that as it may, there have been some semiotic models in linguistics that have shown slightly less perfunctory interest in the object and in its relationship to the concept. Such models have been keen to describe the possibility of interlanguage phenomena (like translation), and they regularly suggest non-uniformity of the object embodiment process in different languages. Thus, Schifko (1975) presents the model in Figure 4.1, in part as a refinement of Heger's (1965; 1969) which made for the rather problematic identification of semes with noemes.

The inverted triangle is the language-dependent area, whereas the three other

---

5. It is this *given* perception that underlies some, if not much, of the work on prototypes in general language, as well as the scheme proposed by Hallig & Wartburg (1952) for classifying prescientific concepts. Typically such efforts are based on the view of the *average individual* and are often seen as reflecting the epistemological position of naive realism. See Section 4.3.1.

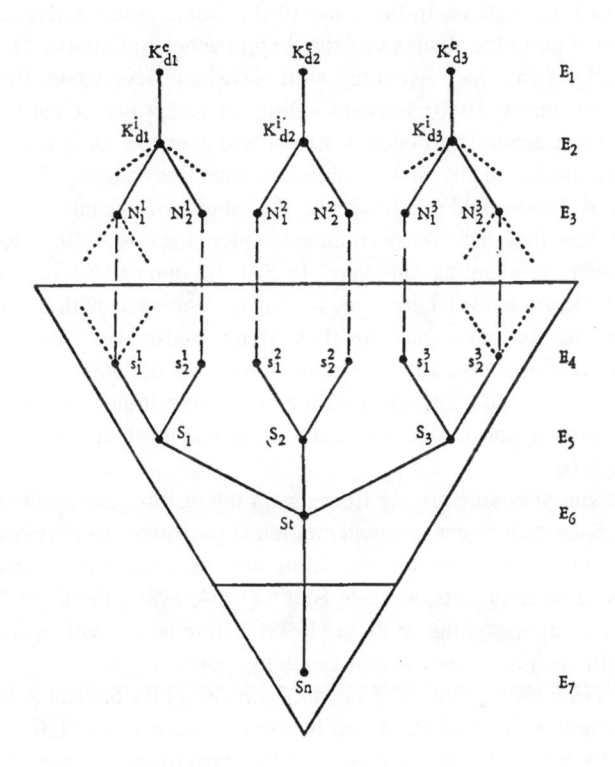

Figure 4.1: *Schifko's sign model*

Legend: E7 = level of signifier, Sn; E6 = level of polysemous signified, St; E5 = level of E6 sememes, $S_{1,2,3}$; E4 = level of E5 semes, s^1_1 etc; E3 = level of noemes, N^1_1 etc; E2 = level of intensionally defined classes of denotata, K^i_{d1} etc; E 1= level of extensionally defined classes of denotata, K^e_{d1}

levels (E_1, E_2, and E_3) are extralinguistic. E_1 is described as the ontological level, E_2 the epistemological level, and E_3 the psychological level. In the sense of the discussion in this chapter, these levels may be seen as corresponding respectively to object, concept and concept characteristics. The (angle-forming) dotted lines that branch out at levels E_2 to E_4 are free valencies suggesting that no one-to-one match is claimed between the entities at the levels being linked. Thus, at E_1, a given node could correspond to more than one entity (concept) at a node of E_2. Similarly, any given language's semes (E_4) will only partially map onto the totality of noemes, these being extralinguistic characteristics of the intensionally defined class of denotata or, in the sense of this book, concept characteristics.

But by and large (no thanks to formal approaches to linguistics), the object is not generally of interest.[6] Although with occasional scepticism, Baldinger, in his book on semantics (1980), appears willing to accept that scientific language requires an object-centred approach to specialised concepts, or in his own words, to "the determination of the mental object in scientific language". In a manner reminiscent of Bloomfield's attitude to the study of meaning in language, Baldinger writes that the "only language which tries to follow (or create?) objective borders is scientific language" (p. 34). He quotes Coserieu who writes that although "science uses language, [...] it is concerned with the designated things themselves, in that it analyses these things and makes a statement about them" (p. 38). It is of course an overstatement to speak of "objective borders". At any rate, it follows quite naturally from the fact of terminology being a phenomenon of specialised knowledge and expression that it should be interested in reality or objects.[7]

The growing literature arising from recent interest in a terminological object theory deals with such issues as epistemological positions *vis-à-vis* reality, types of objects (and implications for the formation of specialised concepts), and relationships between objects, etc. See Budin (1994, 1996); Felber (1992, 1995); Picht (1997); Laurén, Myking & Picht (1998). These issues will be seen to have applications in such areas as concept typology, polysemy, etc.

Wüster (1959/60) defines the object from the philosophical standpoint as whatever thought is directed at, or can be directed at. Budin (1996: 29) sees the goal of a terminological object theory as the provision of bases from which ordering principles can be derived, these principles being central to the construction of concept systems which are in turn fundamental to the creation of

---

6. Kleiber (1990: 40) states the goal of structural semantics as follows: "the European structuralist movement precisely sought to free semes of all association with the referent in order to emphasise their operational or functional side, which is linguistic and nothing else. Even if [...] a referential interpretation is always at the background, it is instructive to note that the goal of structural semantics is to detach from reality in order to describe reality-independent meaning, a goal that it accomplishes by contrasting words [...]" (my translation from the French). Current interest in iconicity in language is according greater importance to ontology in linguistic theorisation.

7. A reading of Budin (1996: 21) suggests that this neglect of ontological issues is actually widespread, that is, in fields other than linguistic ones where there has similarly been contentment with simplistic working models that situate at the extreme poles of Neo-Positivism (naive realism) and Radical Constructivism. The former posits that the world is structured, and perceived cognitively along lines indicated by this structure. The latter claims that the world is no more than our construction of it, denying in effect the existence of an external reality (Budin 1994).

terminological resources. But there is a more specific goal which could be said to be the provision of a basis for investigating how concepts and concept characteristics reflect ontical units (objects) and their properties. This latter goal will be emphasised here.

4.3.1 *Epistemological positions for an object theory in terminology*

It has been argued by Budin (1994) that an epistemological position for a terminological object theory must transcend the naive realism inherent in Neo-Positivism and the solipsism epitomised by Radical Constructivism (see note 7). A number of intermediary positions are deemed to be more appropriate for terminology. Critical Realism posits the existence of a real world which, however, differs sometimes from the way it appears to us. Hypothetical Realism postulates the existence of a real world with structures which are discoverable only to a certain extent.

To give salience to these intermediary positions, or to adopt a broad epistemological outlook, is to subscribe to ontological pluralism, rather than to ontological unity, which in practical terms means that object representations as reflected in disciplines or terminologies are no more than ontological heuristics or hypotheses whose adequacy is determined ultimately by pragmatic considerations. This is at the level of ordering principles. Applied to the level of ontical units, these intermediary positions imply a rejection of qualitative and quantitative consubstantiality between object and concept. This will be obvious in the discussion of formal objects in Section 4.3.2. A pluralist position also has advantages in respect of objects in the social sciences and in the humanities, or in those areas where the lines between object and concept are somewhat difficult to plot. According to Budin (1994: 207), often "the pertinent concepts of social science terminologies are not only hypotheses about social reality, but at the same time hypotheses about the existence *per se* of the object referred to". He describes this as "projective concept formation". This could also be said to illustrate non-abstraction models of concept formation, which are in turn examples of situations where the lines between object (object properties) and concept (concept characteristics) are blurred. See Section 4.3.2 below.

To comment briefly on Schifko's epistemological stance (see Figure 4.1): noemes are seen as having their foundation in a *tertium comparationis* which could be any of a concept system, a thesaurus, a more or less formalised interlanguage, a universal predicate logic/symbolic logic, etc. (Schifko 1975: 56). By implication, a broad epistemological spectrum underlies the intensionally defined class of denotata.

4.3.2 Types of objects

In the literature two broad categories of objects are traditionally identified: concrete/material and abstract/immaterial. The former pair has spatio-temporal dimension while the latter does not. The former is often described as perceived (through the senses directly or indirectly through instruments), and the latter as conceived. An object need not be seen only as a thing. It actually covers a broad spectrum of word classes or grammatical categories, to employ a useful metaphor. Thus an object could be a process, a quality, etc. It is also held to have properties, or to in fact be a set of properties.

What are referred to as formal objects are of interest from the standpoints of the epistemological positions discussed earlier, as well as from the perspective of specialised knowledge and discourse communities, terminology practice, and of the relationship between objects and concepts. Felber & Budin (1989: 2) define a formal object as an *abstract object* as seen from the standpoint of a given subject area (geology, physics, etc.). In Felber (1995) a shift in the superordinate term is noticeable. Felber (1995: 16) writes that one and the same object (*material object*) — "ein und derselbe Gegenstand (Materialgegenstand)" — can be broached from different disciplinary standpoints, each of which is interested in different subsets of the totality of properties which the material object is believed to possess. Thus, object 'coal' is seen as a rock in geology, as a usable mineral in mining, etc. (Felber 1994: 213). The same view is expressed in ISO 704 (1987) which notes that an "individual object can be seen by different disciplines from different points of view which gives rise to the formation of different concepts representing the same individual object" (Arntz & Picht 1989: 58).

From an epistemological standpoint, the formal object construct illustrates the (potential for a) relation of non-consubstantiality (qualitative and quantitative) involving object and concept. This clearly reminds of the position taken in respect of the concept-symbol link. The idea of a formal object underscores the need for flexible positions in descriptions of the concept-object relationship. The formal object construct gives a jolt to Neo-Positivism in its application to a single ontical element. As far as terminology and the subject fields are concerned, the formal object construct underscores why terminology's interest in objects and object properties will on each occasion have to be mediated, contextualised, or restricted by specialised subject fields.

Picht sees no need to posit a formal object since such an entity would be no more than a concept, or at best, be located in the "no man's land" or grey area between object and concept. This is true if, as in the Felber & Budin (1989)

CONCEPT THEORY IN TERMINOLOGY

One object - different formal objects

△ ~ object
△1 ~ formal object 1
△2 ~ formal object 2
⋮
△n ~ formal object n

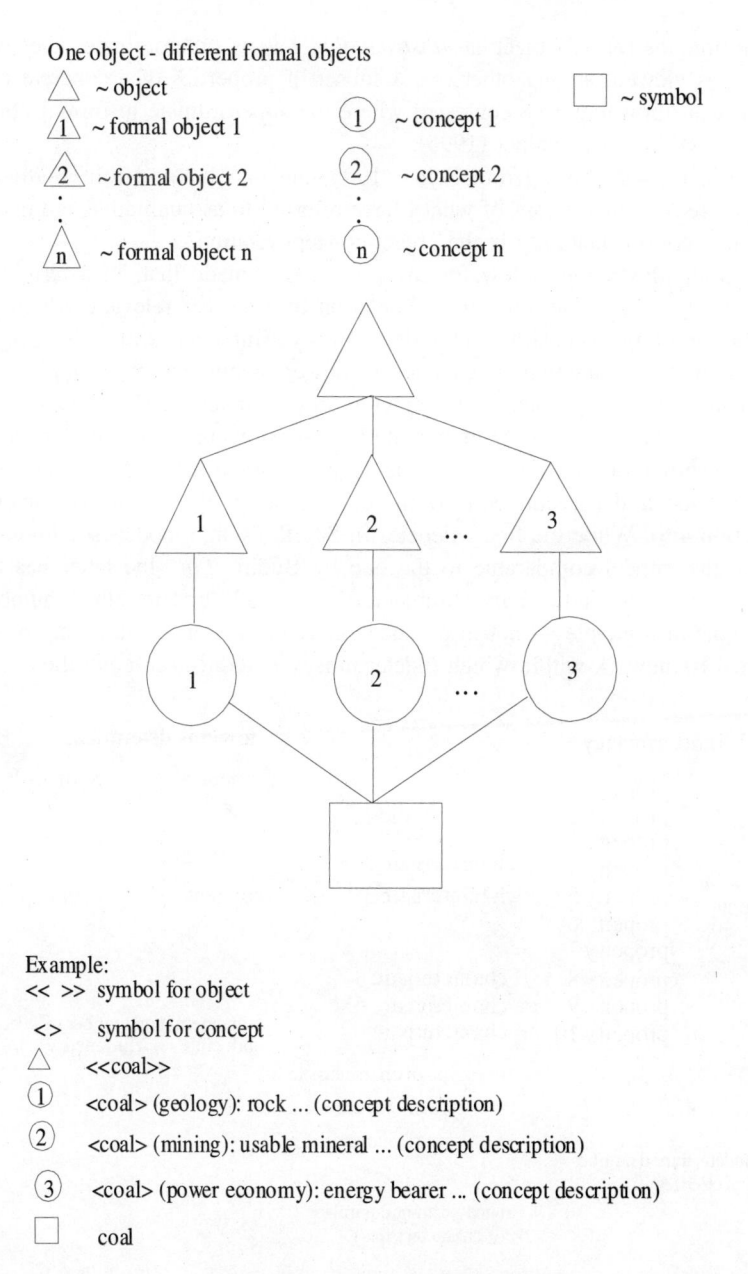

① ~ concept 1
② ~ concept 2
⋮
Ⓝ ~ concept n

☐ ~ symbol

Example:
<< >> symbol for object
< > symbol for concept

△   <<coal>>
①   <coal> (geology): rock ... (concept description)
②   <coal> (mining): usable mineral ... (concept description)
③   <coal> (power economy): energy bearer ... (concept description)
☐   coal

Figure 4.2: *One object – several formal objects (from Felber 1994)*

definition, the formal object has *abstract object* as its superordinate. The abstract object is viewed, among others, as a subset of properties of a concrete object. Picht's position might be contested where the superordinate to formal object is *material object* as in Felber (1995).

Figures 4.2 above (from Felber 1994) and 4.3 below (from Budin *et al.* 1988) are two illustrations of what I have referred to as qualitative and quantitative non-consubstantiality in the object-concept relation.

Both illustrations allow for the point to be made that, in a terminology resource, only a given domain's acceptation of a term is relevant, which is not the same thing as positing total determinacy. But even with this margin of variation, the evaluation in Chapter 3 showed a number of examples where domain-irrelevant acceptation was entered for certain terms. The illustration from Felber (1994) is particularly interesting because it also reveals the other level of relationship (concept-term). The one from Budin *et al.* (1988) prepares the ground for a discussion concerning the typology of concept characteristics (Section 4.5). While the free valencies in Schifko's sign model (see Figure 4.1) make that model comparable to the one by Budin *et al.*, the latter has added advantages. The indications ('Subject A' etc. and 'undetermined number of concepts in principle — not in practice') may be seen as creating an epistemological framework within which indeterminacy is reduced or controlled.

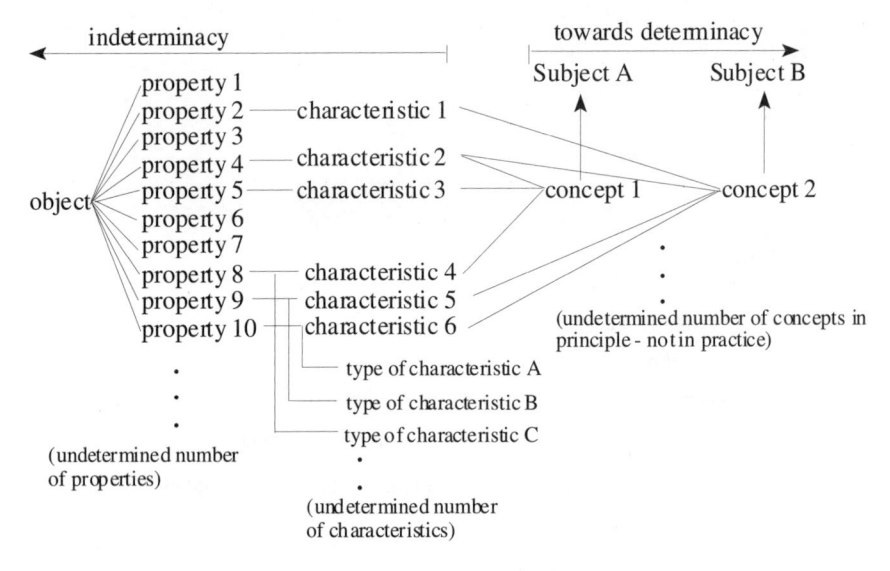

Figure 4.3: *Object–concept relationship (from Budin* et al. *1988)*

4.4 Creation of specialised concepts

Rather than *formation* of concepts, it is elected to speak here of *creation* in order to distinguish what happens in specialised knowledge communities from accounts *à la* Vygotsky dealing with concepts in children. A second distinction may in fact be claimed in the light of what Hallig & Wartburg (1952) appear to understand as concept formation in languages. They see the concept as a clearly circumscribed nucleus which words in certain areas are capable of developing as a consequence of what is referred to as *Arbeit der Sprache* (linguistic processes?). This is supposed to be the linguistic correlate of concept formation in humans. In this process, a concept or nucleus crystallises, and detaches itself from language-conditioned specific meaning. The nucleus, while still related to the word, is no longer fused with it.[8]

The model of concept creation that has probably received the most attention in terminology is the abstraction model, taken over from psychology. Incidentally, the account in Wüster (1959/60) is given from the standpoint of concept acquisition in children, as Gerzymisch-Arbogast (1996) notes in her critique of Wüster's work. Picht (1998) has drawn attention to how widespread the abstraction model is in definitions of the concept as given by several standards.[9] The ISO-Standard 1087 (1990), for instance, sees the concept as being "constituted through abstraction on the basis of properties common to a set of objects". Abstraction is a process of reduction and generalisation that involves the identification, in a set of objects, of commonly shared properties, which then constitute a concept (by being characteristics). The concept as a sum of perceived and common characteristics then serves as a model for subsequent identification and processing. A reading of Gerzymisch-Arbogast (1996) would suggest that the adequacy of the mental model to serve identification and processing depends on how representative the set of objects was defined, and the distribution of properties — not just in terms of presence *versus* absence, but also in terms of variance *versus* invariance (that is, optional *versus* compulsory). But the important shortcomings of the abstraction model for terminology are that it presupposes

---

8. It is however not in all cases that linguistic processes (*Arbeit der Sprache*) lead to the development of concepts from meaning. Hallig & Wartburg write: "There are domains in which the majority of words fossilize, so to speak, in meaning; in such words, linguistic processes fail to develop a nucleus out of meanings" (p. xi; my translation from the German).

9. References will often be made to standards and/or the bodies that produce them. ISO is the International Organisation for Standardization. Its technical committee 37 issues standards for various aspects of terminology. The DIN is the German standardisation body, and has similar concerns.

the materiality of objects and equates the concept with reduction processes exclusively. An account of concept creation intended for a diversity of areas of specialised knowledge must have a pluralist outlook. Picht proposes two models of concept creation that reveal the above weaknesses of the abstraction model.

Consider the following scenario. A biochemist or pharmacologist, for instance, perceives the need for a drug X to be compounded from a, b, c, d, and to be useful for condition Y. If further research confirms the feasibility of the project, a so-called prototype of the drug is manufactured. A successful clinical test run then leads to industrial (mechanical) reproduction of the prototype, possibly by different manufacturers and under different trade names.[10] Admittedly, in referring generically to the several brands of the product one would be abstracting. The point, however, is that the abstraction would be *post hoc*. The properties in the different brands (objects), and which form the basis for this generic reference, would be no different from a, b, c, d with which the biochemist started off. It is difficult to describe the concept characteristics a, b, c, d as the logical correlates of the properties of object or drug X, which could very well have not existed if further research had cast doubts on its feasibility.

Consider another model. There is a need for an institution (which at the end of the concept creation process would be called *ombudsman*). A committee of X number of persons is empanelled each of whom has different combinations and permutations of a, b, c, d, e ... n as the intension of the institution they are to create. In effect, each member has a different concept of the institution. After the panel has interacted a consensus emerges on a subset of the totality of initially proposed features a, b, c, d, e ... n. Thus, a new concept emerges, which cannot be described as an abstraction from the X number of initial concepts. The mandating body may, on receiving the panel's report, have to reach another consensus which has the effect of modifying some characteristics or features in the intension as defined by the panel. This modification sees the emergence of yet another concept, which again is no abstraction. This latter concept is stabilised by its intension being stated (it being defined) and by its being termed *ombudsman*. This model might have been called the consensus model, but such a label would erroneously suggest that the abstraction model, for instance, did not involve consensus.

This latter model is indeed reminiscent of Dahlberg's model of concept construction. In fairly stable accounts (1976, 1978, 1985a, 1985b, 1995) she develops

---

10. In terms used earlier, the clinical test run may be seen as transacting or negotiating the properties of the object.

an analytical concept theory, part of which is illustrated by Figure 4.4 below.

From the world of objects, an item of reference (A) is selected, that is, focused on. This item then becomes an object of thought. Objectivisation of this item in thought requires that it be predicated by correct statements (B) that are verifiable through evidence or intersubjective agreement. This would normally be done by a scholarly community. A label (C), which obviously need not be verbal, is selected to stand for these predications and is used in discourse.

There probably are other models of concept creation. What is common to the three reviewed here is the emphasis on the intension of concepts, that is, their characteristics — irrespective of whether or not these characteristics correlate with the properties of existing objects. These characteristics are not assumed, but

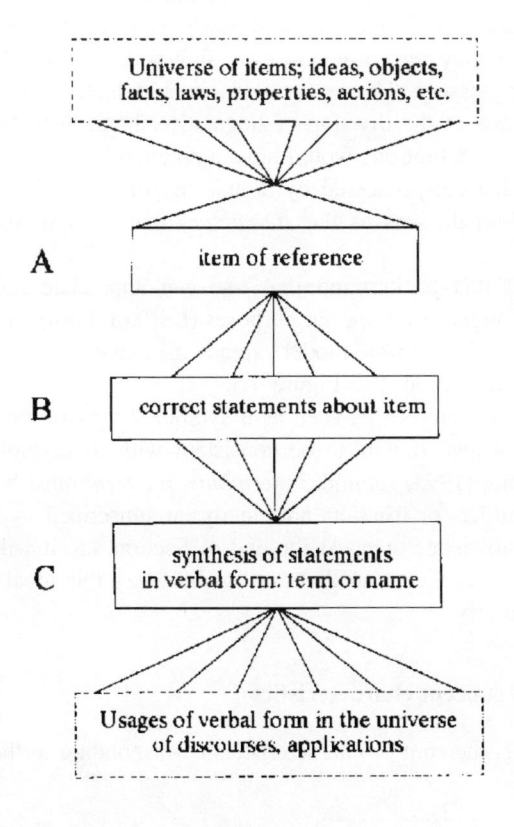

Figure 4.4: *Dahlberg's model of concept construction*

are negotiated (at some point, at least) by the relevant knowledge community. The issue of characteristics is treated in a subsequent section. For now, what emerges from the foregoing, and from the discussion of formal objects in the previous section, is the importance of concept definitions or other descriptive statements concerning a concept's intension in specialised knowledge areas.

The appraisal in Chapter 3 showed that the so-called problem of coordinating the three target language groups in the Nigerian legislative glossary was simply one of the absence of definitions. Had there been definitions describing the intension or characteristics of concepts intended, creators of terms would not have been suggesting different concepts for a term like 'original bill' or 'speaker'. From the user perspective, time-consuming and error-laden deliberations (e.g. in respect of "adjournment") in the translation protocols would have been avoided if the reference glossary had definitions or other concept descriptive statements. In all likelihood, the pre-knowledge of experimental subjects, or knowledge models they set up, would have shown deference to the knowledge mediated by the glossary. The environment would have been reminiscent of Putnam's hypothesis of the division of linguistic labour. Seen from that standpoint, the glossary's definitions would have amounted to those concept predications or criteria that are possessed by domain experts, and that differ more or less from what Putnam sees as the *stereotypes* that are required for ordinary communication.[11]

It is against this background that one can appreciate the relevance to terminology and language for special purposes (LSP) of the sign model proposed by Suonuuti (1997). The simple model extends the classical semiotic triangle by a node meant for definition. See Figure 4.5.

The *term* may therefore be seen as a symbol (linguistic or non-linguistic) that identifies concepts. If it is to be consistent with its etymology which, as Sager & Ndi-Kimbi (1995) remind, is *terminus*, the *term* must be assigned to a concept whose borders or frontiers are clearly circumscribed — in, it might be added, a given knowledge area. At the end of Section 4.8, it will be suggested that in fields where concepts are believed to be fuzzy this ideal definition still has a claim to validity.

4.5 Typology of concept characteristics

While a concept is the sum of characteristics corresponding to the properties of

---

11. Putnam (1974: 14ff); Geeraerts (1985: 29).

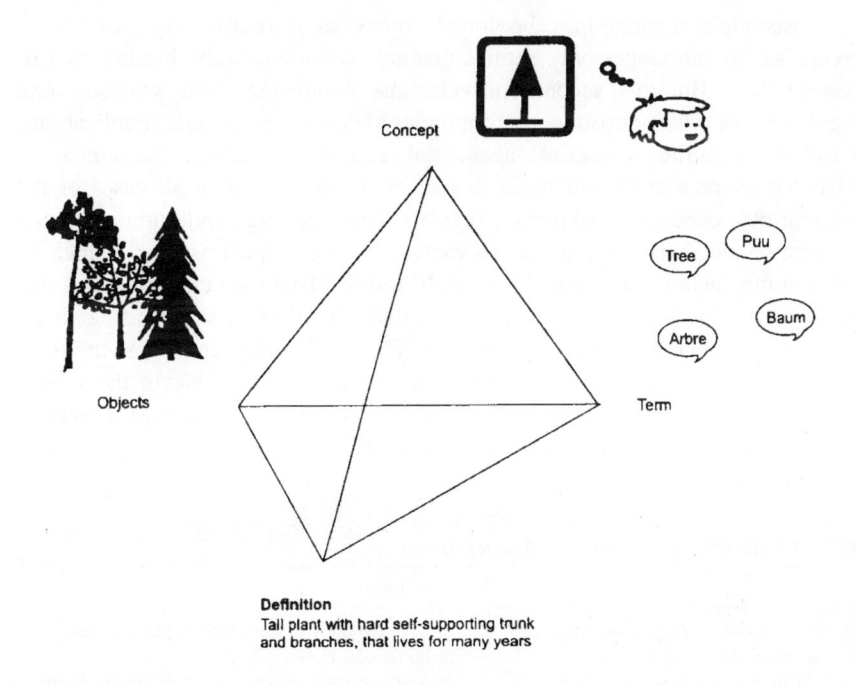

Figure 4.5: *Suonuuti's extended semiotic triangle (cf. Myking 1997)*

a given formal object, it is often the case that for purposes of definition, designation, constructing concept systems, establishment of equivalents, etc., only some of these characteristics will be articulated. Besides, it was seen in the review of discourse thrusts (chapter 2) and in the appraisal (chapter 3) that characteristics motivating certain proposed terms were hardly the most apt. Against the background of the foregoing, and the "type of characteristic" indication in Figure 4.3, a categorisation of concept characteristics should be in order at this point.

Since antiquity philosophers have been concerned with the nature of beings, of what things exist. In Aristotle's ontology, everything that there is is a combination of substance and accident. The substance is a composite of form (the essence of the thing) and matter (the individuating principle). Accidents (nine classes of which are identified by Aristotle) are not intrinsic to a substance; they are "added from without to the combination of matter and essence which is the individual thing" (Grossmann 1992: 16).

Aristotle's account may be found somewhat restrictive: for instance, it recognises as substances only entities that are spatio-temporally located, that is, perceptible.[12] But this account provides the foundation from which several typologies of characteristics in terminology derive. In several publications, Dahlberg identifies essential, accidental and individuating characteristics. Essential characteristics are those that have "to be present in all cases of the referent of a concept" (Dahlberg 1981:19). They are vital, and without them a concept cannot exist. Accidental characteristics are defined as those which "a referent may acquire in one of its specializations". These are characteristics that apply to specific kinds of referents. Individual characteristics apply to a single referent (Dahlberg 1978:145, 1981:19). This trichotomy can be seen to be inspired by Aristotle's form, accident and matter, and relatable to the *genus-species-individum* trichotomy, or the *general concept-special concept-individual concept* classification. See Table 4.1, adapted from Dahlberg 1978, which is applied to the concept, *Man*.

Table 4.1: *Dahlberg's typology of characteristics*

Category	Constituents
Essential (& constituting) characteristics	to have the body of a primate, to have a mind
Accidental characteristics	to be female, male
Individuating characteristics	to have a certain heritage, place & time of birth

The interested reader may also refer to Beaugrande's (1980:71) trichotomy describing relative strengths of conceptual content, *viz.* determinate, typical and accidental.

But the more commonly encountered typologies are the dichotomous ones, opposing characteristics deriving from Aristotle's form to those derived from accidents.

Wüster's (1991:16) division of characteristics into two broad categories — (*Eigenmerkmale*, or intrinsic/inherent, and *Beziehungsmerkmale*, or relational/ extrinsic) — is taken up in a number of other terminological sources: Felber (1985:58); Felber & Budin (1989:70ff), ISO/CD 704.2 etc. In ISO/R 1087 an intrinsic characteristic is defined as "one referring to an object in itself, not in its

---

12. Barnes (1982:46) writes that: "In general, perceptible things — middle-sized, material objects — are the primary furniture of Aristotle's world; and it is significant that he often poses his ontological question by asking if there are any substances apart from perceptible substances".

relation to another".[13] Shape, size, material and colour are some examples cited. An extrinsic characteristic, on the other hand, is one "belonging to an object only in its relations to another". Examples cited include use, origin (discoverer, producer, mode of manufacture), function. Sager (1990: 24) distinguishes between essential and inessential characteristics. He writes: "the sufficient and necessary characteristics for identifying a concept are also called essential in contrast to inessential ones which are observable in the individual object [...]".

It does seem ill advised to treat essential/inherent/intrinsic characteristics on the one hand, and on the other, accidental/extrinsic/relational/inessential characteristics as synonyms. A characteristic inherent in a concept may not always be essential, that is, indispensable for identifying that concept. Often what will be essential will be determined by the context. Indeed as Sager (1990: 24) points out, "inessential characteristics in one scheme of concept creation may, however, become essential for the creation of other concepts". ISO 704 (1987: 2) also observes that "the distinction between essential and inessential characteristics depends on the purpose of the terminology work".[14] In other words, what characteristics are essential for delimiting a given concept can only be defined relative to the knowledge structure into which the concept is entered.

The foregoing characteristics were discussed because of their function in activities such as defining, designating and constructing systems of concepts. A relatively recent function postulated by Picht focuses on characteristics of a different nature (see Picht 1987, 1989, 1990). Picht posits a category of relational characteristics whose purpose is to specify what he calls the "connectability" of one concept to another. Given the concepts *metal, iron, copper, silver, gold,* and *mercury,* a list of characteristics provided for them should include some indication as to whether they are forgeable. *Silver, gold, iron, copper* would have 'forgeable' in their list of characteristics; *metal* would have 'forgeable/not forgeable' (since not all metals are forgeable), while *mercury* would have 'not forgeable'. Picht's concern, as will be seen in Chapter 5, is with specialised language phrases. But there are wider applications of these relational characteristics. Within the philosophy of science, Thagard (1992) describes concepts in a way as to include rules by which one concept is linked to another. Evolution of scientific conceptual knowledge, then, would not only be investigated from the standpoint of concept intension as traditionally understood, but also in terms of relations.

---

13. Quoted in Picht & Draskau (1985: 45).
14. Quoted in Arntz & Picht (1989: 58).

4.6 Knowledge and terminology

Within the knowledge structure from which it derives its characteristics, a concept does not stand in isolation. The field of terminology considers knowledge as representable in systems of concepts. Now, although knowledge or science is not infrequently discussed in terms of propositional as opposed to conceptual logic,[15] descriptions of propositional knowledge in the philosophy of science are generally valid for the terminological view; that is, knowledge as a system of concepts. Thus at least three of VanLaer's seven features of science may be cited in this discussion. They dovetail into one another:

1. a science is concerned with a definite field of knowledge;
2. any body of knowledge labelled science must "constitute a coherent whole of interconnected things and their parts that is appropriately ordered. An enumeration of unrelated facts or data, no matter how much each of them may be worth knowing, does not give rise to a science";
3. logical order is an essential requirement of science. The units of knowledge of a science "may not be enumerated in an arbitrary way" (Van Laer 1963: 8ff).

Against this background, Oeser's definition of *a terminology* is most apt: "an ordered set of concepts of a subject field with terms or linguistic designations assigned to them" (Oeser 1994: 24). This definition is in consonance with Beaugrande's (1994: 11) deprecation of a widespread view of terminology. Beaugrande writes that "the notion of terminology as a list of specialized vocabulary has a long tradition and prevents research on terminology from progressing beyond the fairly elementary stages of issues that can be grasped this way". Albert Einstein and George Orwell must have held similar views of terminology in writing, respectively, that "The substance of our knowledge resides in the detailed terminology of a field" and "Who controls the vocabulary controls the knowledge". At this point, the reader may already be developing a mental framework for the problems discussed in the evaluation in Chapter 3.

Let us now examine the relations through which areas of knowledge are said to be constituted, and which a terminology has to take notice of. The interest is not merely academic. These relations, as will be subsequently seen, have implications for the acquisition, representation and extraction of knowledge.

---

15. The point is well made by Thagard (1992). See also Oeser (1992: 26ff) for a discussion of the philosophy of science of the Vienna circle, etc.

4.6.1 Concept relations

Nuopponen (1994) has done a detailed and illuminating study of concept relations, from which it is obvious that an exhaustive listing of relations, if not of their classification, might be too tall an order to fill.

A common classification of concept relations is the one proposed by Wüster, following Aristotle, which groups relations into two broad categories: logical and ontological. Logical relations (severally referred to as generic relations, genus-species relations, direct concept relations, relations of similarity, hyponymic relations) are based on logical implication or inclusion. Logical implication obtains when a comparison of two concepts shows the intension of one (the superordinate) being included in the intension of the other (subordinate), which in addition has at least one supplementary characteristic. Successive stages of subordination create a vertical series of concepts while a number of subordinates at any given level form a horizontal series.

Ontological relations, unlike logical relations, do not derive from the intension of concepts. An important class of ontological relations is the one concerned with contiguity in space and time. An oft encountered type of relation dealing with contiguity in space is the partitive relation, severally referred to as part-whole relation, and meronymic relation. This relation obtains between a whole (superordinate) and its parts (subordinates) as well as between parts of a whole (Wüster 1974a: 92ff). The possibility of subordination in a partitive relation makes this relation comparable to the logical type. Indeed in Arntz & Picht's account, logical and partitive relations together comprise "hierarchical relations". But because, unlike logical relations, partitive relations are not based on concept intensions, they are of limited transitivity.[16] Partitive relations express HAS-A or IS-PART OF relations while logical relations express IS-A links.[17]

Another type of contiguity relation is the temporal relation, and it refers to chronological sequences (precedence, simultaneity, succession) existing or that can be established between concepts. Some ongoing work by Gampers and Brajaj suggests that temporal relations are a lot more complex than this description

---

16. I have borrowed this concept from lexical semantics. See Lyons (1977: 292, 312) and Cruse (1986: 113ff) for a discussion of transitivity in sense relations.

17. See also Sager (1990: 30, 32); Picht & Draskau (1985: 81). Cruse (1986: 160ff) discusses the inadequacy of 'HAS-A' and 'IS-PART OF' as test frames for meronymic lexical relations. A '-INCLUDES-' frame is proposed.

would suggest.[18]

There is a class of more loosely defined relations. These are called pragmatic (or associative) relations. ISO/CD 704.2:5 gives a number of examples of associative relations: the relation exemplified between 'information' and 'bit' is that of a concept and its unit of measure; between 'painter' and 'brush' it is that of a profession and its tool; between 'coffee' and 'cream' a concept and typical constituent; between 'trade union' and 'strike' a concept and what is perceived as a typical activity; etc.

In two older standards, *viz.* ISO 5964 and ISO 2788, equivalence is identified as a category of concept relations. The latter distinguishes between full and partial synonymous relations, while the former identifies various types of interlingual concept equivalence relations, including exact equivalence, single-to-multiple, non-equivalence, etc.

As mentioned earlier, any number of relations can be declared according to what concepts one is dealing with. The relationships between concepts are more often multilateral rather than unilateral. But as wide as the latitude appears, and as was seen in Chapters 2 and 3, there are terminological collections with entries that are difficult to relate to other entries in the field that the collection purports to cover.

To sum up, a broad categorisation of concept relations could look like Table 4.2.

Table 4.2: *Summary of concept relations*

Class	(Some) types
Equivalence relations	Synonymy (full/partial), one-to-one/multiple equivalence
Hierarchical	Logical, partitive
Non-hierarchical	Associative (pragmatic)

4.6.2 Concept system

It is through relations such as these that knowledge, construed particularly but not exclusively in conceptual terms, is able to fulfil the conditions of interconnectedness and coherence generally imposed on it. As was mentioned earlier,

---

18. The work by Johann Gampers (European Academy, Bozen, Italy) is situated within artificial intelligence, while Bettina Brajaj (University of Surrey, U.K.) approaches the subject from the standpoint of a terminologist with a linguistics background. See their respective talks at the Infoterm Symposium in Vienna, 1998.

knowledge in terminology is seen in terms of concept systems. Concept systems are the outcomes of relations established between concepts. The following descriptions of concept systems are instructive:

1. Arntz & Picht (1989: 76):

> Relationships between the concepts of a special subject area submit to representation in the form of concept systems (my translation from the German).

2. ISO/R 1087:

> System of concepts: A group of concepts connected by logical or ontological relationships. Such a system is constituted by horizontal and vertical series of concepts, or at least by one such series.

3. DIN 2331:

> A concept system is a set of concepts among which relations exist or have been established, and this set represents a coherent whole (my translation from the German).

4. ISO/CD 704.2 (1995: 6):

> A concept system is a set of concepts whose structure reflects the basic relations among the concepts involved and illustrates the unique position of each concept within the system.

In the light of epistemological positions discussed in Section 4.3.1 some measure of scepticism would be in order *vis-à-vis* descriptions that imply a natural ontology.

With respect to significance in the construction of concept systems it is perhaps ill advised to rank concept relations (that is, where such a choice exists). Concepts in a given area of knowledge rarely submit themselves integrally to structuring according to one type of relation. Frequently, systems of concepts will have to be combined to produce mixed systems. Picht & Draskau give the following description of mixed systems:

> Mixed systems are systems of concepts in which two or more types of relations are combined. By this method the flexibility of the system is considerably increased, and many more concepts of various types may be incorporated into the same system. This means in practice that the inventory of concepts of a special subject field can be registered better and more exhaustively (p. 85).

Even at that, the point perhaps need to be stressed, as do Felber & Budin (1989: 167), that a subject field would only rarely submit integrally to representation in concept systems. These systems are more fruitfully elaborated within theme concepts or concept fields. A concept field is defined in ISO/CD 1087–1 as "a set of thematically related concepts".

4.7 Concept system and semantic field

One is perhaps inclined to consider a concept field, but particularly a concept system, and a field in semantics as basically one and the same construct. Strictly speaking, a concept system and a semantic field are only tenuously comparable. To start with, field theory in semantics is not a homogenous construct: more or less very different conceptions have been expounded by Saussure (*rapports associatifs*), Trier (*Wortfeld*), Porzig (*syntaktisches Feld*), Jolles (*Bedeutungsfeld*), Bally (*champs associatifs*), Guiraud (*champs morpho-sémantiques*), Ducháček (*champs linguistiques*), among a host of others.[19] In very general terms, the lexical configurations of Saussure and Guiraud are based on sound and sense associations (that is, formal and semantic criteria), while those of Trier, Bally, etc. derive only from semantic criteria. Trier's fields are of a paradigmatic nature while Porzig's derives from lexical solidarities or essential meaning relations (on a syntagmatic axis). Jolles' (minimal) fields are made up of binary contrasts or correlative pairs, while for Trier the vocabulary of a language breaks down into fields of decreasing sizes. Subjective judgements have an important place in the definition, or constitution, of the Bally field. In contrast to this, clear demarcation is supposed to be one of the hallmarks of the Trier field. With the exception of Jolles' field, Ducháček's superconstruct integrates all of the foregoing fields as subtypes. Given this heterogeneity, a comparison of the field construct with concept systems is obviously more meaningful when done in respect of specific varieties of the former.

Trier's use of terms has elicited criticism.[20] Lyons (1977: 251) notes that "it is uncertain whether 'area' (*Bezirk*) is synonymous with 'field' (*Feld*) and how, if at all, 'lexical field' (*Wortfeld*) is to be distinguished from 'conceptual field'". It is however clear that Trier sees the vocabulary of a language as dividing into fields which fit neatly together without gaps or overlaps. The words in each field similarly fit together, and are reciprocally delimiting. Each (sub)-field covers only a particular *object* area (kinship, intellect, etc.).[21]

A concept system belongs, not to the general vocabulary of a language, but to a specific sphere of knowledge. Although a concept system could correspond to just one particular section of reality (to the extent that the section in question

---

19. For reviews of field theories, see for example Ullmann (1963: 155ff; 309ff), Lyons (1977: 250ff); Ducháček (1960: 15ff); Coserieu & Geckeler (1981: 16ff).
20. See Öhman (1953), Coserieu & Geckeler (1981).
21. The philosophical acceptation of *object* given earlier is intended here.

is comprised in a subject domain), it is not held to meet any such requirement. Data comprising a segment of knowledge which is represented in a concept system do not have to be derived from the same area of reality, or point in the *object spectrum*. In effect, it may or may not reflect postulates on the structure of this *spectrum*. The foregoing is clearly consistent with the epistemological discussion in Section 4.3.1. It would be recalled that naive realism, or an ill-definable world picture of the average person, was said to be the doctrine on which the Hallig-Wartburg scheme was based. This scheme is an example of the application of field theory. Belonging as they do to specific spheres of knowledge, concept systems broadly reflect the epistemological premises, or the non-innately defined consensual positions, of these spheres.

A further or a potential point of difference exists even when a concept system corresponds to the organically related elements of a field. The field *à la Trier* reflects the Humboldtian notion of language as organiser of reality. In other words, the elements in a given field of a given language (or a diachronic state thereof) reflect the distinctions which the language has imposed on the *object spectrum* with its imperceptible gradations. A concept, as was seen, is not dependent on a specific language — even if it may have specific socio-cultural coloring. The same is true of systems of concepts reflecting knowledge structures. In other words, concept systems do not represent language viewpoints. This point is not invalidated by the admission that concept systems may differ across scholarly traditions which may also correspond to language frontiers.

The way I have characterised concept system and semantic field above differs from Ducháček's 1960 distinction. The following is my translation (from French) of the description he gives of the *champ conceptuel* (conceptual field): "The totality of words that express a given concept (centrally or peripherally) form a simple lexical structure which we call conceptual field" (p. 24). With respect to the *champ sémantique* (semantic field), he writes: "semantic fields differ from conceptual fields because their contents are less homogenous, more complex, and have wider spread, e.g. words concerning farming, administration […]".

The point hardly needs to be made that sound or form-oriented lexical fields have nothing in common with concept systems. It is important for our discussion to note that concept systems are flexible or purpose-driven constructs, albeit grounded on consciously imparted consensual positions (no matter how broad). Following Sager (1990: 29, 55), it may be stressed that the terminologist is concerned with concept systems only to the extent that they facilitate the task at hand. The goal is not to create an absolute system, but to have a working frame.

4.8 Critical perspectives on concept theory

The emphasis placed in terminology on concepts, concept characteristics, concept systems, and on specialised knowledge or domains has spawned critical comments. It is therefore important to review these comments before examining the implications which concept theory has for LP-oriented terminology. While a few of these criticisms bear directly on components of the version of concept theory to which this book is committed, other criticisms refer to issues in different accounts of this theory. In this latter respect, some positions held by Wüster have been particularly criticised both in and out of context, and in a way that at times suggests that these positions were inviolable articles of faith of present-day terminology scholars.

A recall of what this book is committed to is in order here. The version of concept theory defended here recognises the importance of concept characteristics; it emphasises concept systems, specialised knowledge domains, and non-consusbtantiality in the relations linking concept to object and to symbol. With respect to these latter relations, the commitment is not to *invariance, determinacy, reversible univocity*, but to the notions of *independence of realms, negotiation of links*, and *controlled indeterminacy*. In addressing criticisms of concept theory, therefore, I will focus more on views that take issue with concept characteristics, concept systems, and specialised knowledge domains. For criticisms relating to invariance, determinacy, etc., see (1) Gerzymisch-Arbogast (1996); (2) Weissenhofer (1995); (3) Laurén, Myking & Picht (1998). The work in (1) is reviewed in Rogers (1997), while (2) and (3) are reviewed respectively in Antia (1997b) and Antia (1999). In what follows, two related criticisms are examined. The adjectives by which they are described, *humanistic* and *prototypicalist*, derive from pleas made by the respective critics.

4.8.1 *A humanistic critique*

Rey (1996) makes a plea for a humanistically-inflected approach to terminology. To understand what is meant, the contrast to a humanistic approach would be the preoccupation with concept characteristics. Rey writes on the need to "[correct] the dominant and overly exclusive analytical trends of the last decade(s): in short, correcting Eugen Wüster. Therein, perhaps, lies the path towards a truly humanistic terminology". The backdrop to this plea is Rey's set of refutations concerning (1) terminology, (2) the putative differences between specialised discourses and, say, the culture-laden language of traditional scriptures, novels, etc., and (3) the translatability of specialised discourses. Key arguments in support of these refutations are expressed as follows by Rey:

> The problems posed by terminologies and those apparently more learned discourses — scientific language in the strict sense of the term or, stricter still, technical languages — are not entirely different from those posed by the major text-codes (the Bible and the Koran, as well as the legal codes), philosophical theories and lastly, the novel form and poetry (Rey 1996: 104).
>
> Terminology can be practised effectively only if we abandon the refining logical-semantic viewpoint which for some people epitomises terminology. We have only to observe the implementation of discourse in a specific language to see the futility of this approach (Rey 1996: 105–6).

If my understanding of the "refining logical-semantic viewpoint" is correct, Rey would seem to be inveighing against two things: (1) the preoccupation with concept boundaries, concept characteristics, and the like; and (2) more broadly, the slighting of social and discourse considerations by terminologists when they broach constructs in (1) above.

Let us begin with the second charge. Its premises would seem to derive from what Cabré (1996) calls a monolithic view of terminology, which here refers to the non-perception of the diverse strands of the discipline; and flowing from this, the drawing and generalisation of inferences of regulation (*sensu* imposition) from work on terminology done in, say, certain industrial environments. The review (chapter 2) of LP-oriented terminology theory in general suggested precisely the opposite of Rey's claim: in certain respects, it was precisely the preoccupation with sociological questions, to the exclusion of subject-field issues, that explained the weaknesses of several terminology resources. It would therefore appear that for that variant of terminology that is concerned with LP, the claim of theoretical insensitivity to social factors can hardly be made. Insensitivity of government language policy-makers is not exactly a reflection of what obtains in scholarship.

With respect to the first charge, it seems that the refining logical-semantic viewpoint should be embraced precisely because learned technical discourses share some of the properties of philosophical or literary texts. The refining logical-semantic viewpoint has heuristic value for discourse problems (see Gerzymisch-Arbogast 1996) and for social or cultural imprints (see Schmitt 1999).

Gerzymisch-Arbogast's method for helping translators to identify conceptual and terminological inconsistency in technical texts involves, among others, the use of concept characteristics, including "relators [of arguments]", which would correspond to the category of relational concept characteristics posited by Picht and by Thagard (see Section 4.5). From the standpoint of dynamism, Thagard's context of evolution of scientific knowledge fits in quite well with Gerzymisch-Arbogast's concerns.

As far as social questions are concerned, it is interesting to note from Schmitt's work just how significant socioculture can be, not just in legal texts, but in technical (e.g. engineering) discourses. Indeed, one of the earlier views cited above from Rey is quite similar to the premise in the work by Schmitt (1999), which is subtitled *Zum Konflikt zwischen Begriffsorientiertheit und Kulturgeprägtheit*, thus expressing the risks associated with an exclusive subject-field orientation to the concept that takes no account of sociocultural imprints. Now, in the analysis of these risks, Schmitt makes use of such criteria as concept hierarchies and concept characteristics. Schmitt's findings related to what constitutes "a middle-sized car" in the USA and in Germany (as defined by governmental authorities, car rentals, etc.), or those related to the differences between American car airbags (known to cause injuries) and German ones, are only arrived at through an *analytical* approach to these concepts — one that examines a broad spectrum of characteristics. The reach of these characteristics, the fact that they are not exclusively defined in intrinsic terms or in the logical terms of functional opposition — these should address other concerns that could be read into Rey's criticisms. The issue of characteristics is discussed below under the prototypicalist critique of concept theory in terminology.

4.8.2 *A prototypicalist critique*

From several preceding sections, it would have been obvious that terminology often views the concept as a bundle of characteristics. It is a goal of terminology to strive to clearly delimit the boundaries of this bundle in order to control indeterminacy and to observe processes of indeterminacy or change. This bundle-view reminds of the stereotypical approach to meaning or to cognitive categories, a point which in turn makes it tempting to pit the terminological view of the concept against another position in linguistic categorisation: prototype theory. Indeed, it has been claimed that reasons for the development of the latter theory to rival stereotype theory are also relevant to terminology — specifically, for the repudiation of concept theory as it is often understood in terminology. This position is forcefully articulated by Zawada & Swanepoel (1994). The significance of this position (and therefore, the need for extensive review) is perhaps better appreciated against the backdrop of what might be called the *prototypical bend* in semantics. Anna Wierzbicka (1996) gives a thoroughgoing critique of what she sums up as the "prototypes save" attitude in semantic theory. My arguments are made from the terminology standpoint, and were developed before I discovered Wierzbicka's. There are occasional coincidences.

Zawada & Swanepoel argue that with the possible exception of safety-critical concepts in the field of technology, scientific concepts exhibit prototypicality effects. This observation would make a prototypical concept theory (henceforth, PCT) empirically more adequate than the classical concept theory (henceforth, CCT) or variants thereof, to which the authors firmly pin down terminological concept theory (henceforth, TCT). PCT holds the following views of the concept or category: (1) perception, interaction and function are important in concept or category identification; (2) membership of a category is based on family resemblance as opposed to the possession of some collectively shared features; (3) categories are organised around a best example; (4) the borders of concepts or categories are fuzzy.

On the other hand, CCT holds that: (1) conditions for belonging to a category are either collectively satisfied or an entity does not qualify to belong (sufficient and necessary conditions); (2) concepts or categories have clear boundaries.

On the basis of their investigation into the characteristics and categorisation of minerals, Zawada & Swanepoel make the claim that TCT is inadequate. The criticism they level against TCT, to the extent that it is identifiable with CCT, is perhaps valid up to the point where the identification of concepts in mineralogy is said to have some degree of individual subjectivity to it, implying that characteristics play a lesser role than holistic gestalts. Other points of criticism, like non-recognition of the role of function, perception, situation, etc. are not only refutable, but also raise questions as to just how identifiable TCT is with CCT.

From the authors' discussion of the epistemological commitments of PCT and CCT, it is evident that TCT is, at worst, more than a variant of CCT, and, at best, tenuously related to CCT. Zawada & Swanepoel see PCT as grounded in the experiential realism thesis, two tenets of which are: (1) "our concepts are not the result of our passively receiving objectively structured impressions from the outside world or of us structuring masses of raw data in terms of innate concepts […]", and (2) existing concepts provide the framework for engaging new experiences and for forming new concepts. As for CCT, it is said to be based on objectivist epistemology which holds that: (1) "concepts (and the conceptual features of which they are made up) are no more than replicas or mirror representations of the objective structure of the world"; (2) "concepts reflect the 'essence' of the entities, relations, processes, etc. that make up the world".

The following two major findings of the Zawada-Swanepoel study closely reflect the antitheses of these CCT positions: (1) "the features used to define a concept [in mineralogy] depend on functional and contextual considerations; 2) features are not independent, but there are complex interrelationships between them and other theories". Another finding of the study, which is intended to double as a criticism of TCT, is stated thus: "the idea that scientific concepts are not based on language and culture is a typical misconception in terminology that is highlighted by this study". In passing, it may be noted that Kleiber would consider the first two findings as misplaced criticisms of CCT.[22]

From the discussion in Section 4.3.1, it is obvious that the epistemology of CCT, as described by Zawada & Swanepoel, corresponds to naive realism, the position on which the Hallig-Wartburg concept system is based. This position differs from the epistemological stance that has been claimed for terminology. As seen in Section 4.3.1, Budin (1994) has argued that between the poles of Neo-Positivism and Radical Constructivism there lie a number of epistemological positions, two of which are deemed to be appropriate for terminology: (1) Critical Realism, positing the existence of a real world which, however, differs sometimes from the way it appears to us; and (2) Hypothetical Realism, postulating the existence of a real world with structures which are only to a certain extent discoverable. It certainly is not as a result of some latter-day paradigmatic shift that terminology recognises:

1. the fact that characteristics used to define a concept can be relational or interactional. We earlier saw characteristics relating to function, etc., and also made relative the notions of intrinsic and extrinsic characteristics;
2. that concept characteristics do not have to be "independent", in the sense of having an existence rooted in objective reality as opposed to one owed to convention (e.g. colour, system of measurement, a theoretical scheme, etc.).

In effect, in TCT, concepts and their characteristics are not passively received. TCT is therefore not completely identifiable with CCT, or the interpretation given to it by Zawada & Swanepoel. But let us for the sake of argument assume the following:

1. TCT is integrally identifiable with CCT and therefore has all the shortcomings of the latter;
2. that data from fields such as mineralogy, etc. present problems for CCT.

Now, it does seem ill advisable to subscribe exclusively to prototypicality. Sowa (1984: 17) supports a compromise between Aristotle (necessary and sufficient conditions) and Wittgenstein (family resemblance/prototype). This middle ground

---

22. Kleiber (1990: 40ff) takes issue with Lakoff in whose view the classical concept theory of categories implies that the criterial traits that define members of a category must be independent and objective. Kleiber counters that categorisation in terms of necessary and sufficient conditions does not mean that the conditions have to be inherent characteristics of the referent. There is no reason, he argues, why the necessary and sufficient conditions cannot also be seen from a pragmatic standpoint (context, etc.) rather than from a strictly objective, inherent and independent standpoint.

is perhaps best formulated by J. S. Mill, quoted thus by Sowa:

> Whatever resembles the genus rose more than it resembles any other genus, does so because it possesses a greater number of the characters of that genus, than of the characters of any other genus. Nor can there be the smallest difficulty in representing, by an enumeration of characters, the nature and degree of the resemblance which is strictly sufficient to include any object in the class. There are always some properties common to all things which are included. Others there often are, to which some things, which are nevertheless included, are exceptions. But the objects which are exceptions to one character are not exceptions to another: the resemblance which fails in some particulars must be made up for in others. The class, therefore, is constituted by the possession of *all* the characters which are universal, and *most* of those which admit of exceptions. (Quoted by Sowa 1984: 16)

The foregoing discussion is not just for the sake of *doing* theory. As will be seen in Section 4.9, viewing concepts in terms of their characteristics or features serves a number of purposes in terminology (designation, definition, construction of concept systems, establishment of equivalents, etc.) — functions for which an exclusively prototypical view would be hard put to take on. The compromise between stereotypes and prototypes which Mills appears to be urging is also found in Weissenhofer (1995). Weissenhofer cites research by Armstrong *et al.* which fundamentally questions widespread understanding of prototypicality. Armstrong *et al.* note that:

> Perhaps the graded judgements and responses have to do with a mentally stored identification function used to make quick sorts of things, scenes, and events in the world. On this formulation, instances of a concept share some rough and ready list of perceptual and functional properties, to varying degrees [...]. For example, grandmothers tend to have grey hair, wrinkles, a twinkle in their eye. Some of these properties may be only loosely, if at all, tied to the criteria for membership in the class (for example, twinkles for grandmotherliness) while others may be tightly, systematically, tied to the criteria for membership (for example, being adult for grandmotherliness). But in addition to this identification function, there will be a mentally stored categorial description of the category that does determine membership in it. For grandmother, this will be mother of a parent. (Weissenhofer 1995: 38f)

I might cite an example here that illustrates this point. On German television, there is a commercial in which a boy asks his school mates what they want to be when they grow up. After each one has named a profession, the enquirer says he would like to be an *Opa* (grandfather). *Opa* does not work, but always has money to give out!

With a revised notion of prototypicality, Weissenhofer argues that this construct can conveniently be integrated into a featural or decompositional framework. He therefore proposes to interpret prototypicality in terminology featurally, in order to account for such baseball concepts as *interference*, *obstruction*, etc. which a referee has to decide upon, often within a split second. Following Armstrong *et al.*, Weissenhofer sees prototypicality as a rapid recognition procedure rather than as a processing model for evaluating categorial membership. With appropriate modifications, such an interpretation might be extended to legal concepts for which no defined borders exist, but on which courts are routinely able to reach consensus decisions.

4.9 Implications of concept theory in terminology

Against the background of much of the foregoing discussion on concept theory, it would appear that the Nigerian reference glossary used by the subjects in the translation and knowledge experiments in Chapter 3 betrayed inadequate concept analysis. Meyer & Mackintosh (1994) understand concept analysis (in the context of a terminologist's work on concepts of a field) as implying that "the concepts' principal attributes and relations (collectively, *characteristics*) are determined, a process which goes hand-in-hand with building up the conceptual structure of the domain, and mapping out links between these systems and those of related domains". A number of these issues will be amplified in the following discussion of the practical applications of concept theory in work on terminology.

4.9.1 *Designation*

Absolute and simultaneous monosemy and mononymy would be said to exist in a language if every unit of knowledge were expressed by a distinct term, and each such term represented only one unit of knowledge. Given, on the one hand, the limitation in the morpheme resources of natural languages and, on the other, the indefinite and ever increasing pool of human knowledge, linguistic innovation could not possibly match innovation in knowledge. The characteristics and relations associated with a concept (some of which would normally have been reflected already in a given natural language) make for a rational use of limited morpheme resources. In other words, because entirely new forms cannot always be created for new concepts, many terms will have to be motivated, that is, attempt to reflect the concept to which they are assigned — again with the *proviso* that designations for their characteristics, or suitable analogies thereof, already exist. This is the idea of secondary or indirect motivation (Baldinger 1980: 11ff). This is the sense in which terminology is often described as drawing from the general language reservoir, of exploiting the socially validated arbitrariness of the general language sign.

The relevance of a concept theory stems from its ability to suggest what concept characteristics, or analogies thereof, are system-relevant and ought to be verbalised in a term. The characteristics may relate to a concept's essence or to its relation to other concepts. In the review of the critical metadiscourse on terminology in Chapter 2, reservations expressed by Kummer on the motivation of concepts were noted. It was seen in Chapter 3 (Section 3.3.1) that the motivations for certain concepts could have been better chosen, in a way that took into consideration system-relevant issues.

But as pointed out earlier, it is not the case that a term will always reflect in its structure the concept it is assigned to. It will not when there are no designations for the concept's characteristics. As a result, a language's existing stock of morpheme resources sometimes has to be supplemented by new ones, generated internally or externally. A concept theory, by presenting the relevant knowledge structure, makes a compelling case for systematic and consistent use of such new designations.

4.9.2 *Definition*

The introduction of a new concept, whether by research or by knowledge transfer through language planning, raises the issue of the concept's determination, and *ipso facto* delimitation from others which may be evoked, by spreading activation, on the basis of relationships of content or of form. The translation experiments reported in Chapter 3 showed quite clearly how the absence of definitions is conducive to the activation of wrong knowledge bases or to the abuse of world knowledge. With respect to the setting aside of glossary solutions, this is not just a question of a particularly difficult bunch of translators who would not accept equivalents proposed in their reference glossary. The point is that translators have a need to control, to balance off what is proposed in a dictionary against what is contained in the text being processed. But the importance of definitions does not begin and end with the user. As the miscellaneous section (3.3) of Chapter 3 shows, it also is of concern upstream, in the production of multilingual glossaries such as the Nigerian one that was reviewed. Clearly, the problems of coordination would not have arisen if there had been definitions.

The import of concept theory is evident in the conditions to be met by the definition type that is described as terminological, as opposed to lexicographical or encyclopaedic.[23] According to Sager (1990: 39) "a terminological definition provides a unique identification of a concept only with reference to the conceptual system of which it forms part and classifies the concept within that system". This view finds expression, for instance, in the frame-based definition structures that have been proposed in the literature (see McNaught 1988; Sager & L'Homme 1994; Eck & Meyer 1995; Strehlow 1997). The environment for developing and implementing these structures is typically computational (see Chapter 7.5). At any rate, whether or not a definition fits this description narrowly by virtue of relating a definiendum (concept to be defined) to a proximate superordinate, then stating the definiendum's restricting characteristics, the point is that concept theory provides, among others, a framework for determining what characteristics need to be verbalised. It would be recalled that the notions of essential and non-essential characteristics were made relative because what is trivial in one context may become important in another. There is therefore cause to speak of the modularity of definitions (that is, the verbalisation of characteristics from different standpoints), a construct that would coincide with the multidimensionality of concepts put forward by Bowker & Meyer (1993) to describe the various standpoints of classifying concepts in concept systems. These issues are revisited in the discussion on textual updates and shifting motivations in Chapter 8 (Section 8.8.1.3).

4.9.3 *Conception of domain*

By focusing on the characteristics of concepts and on the relationships between concepts, concept theory ultimately sensitises persons who develop terminology resources to the issue of domain relevance when they have to decide what to include or leave out. As was mentioned in Section 4.7, the epistemological commitment of terminology does not mean that, to be relatable, concepts have to be derived from the same point of the object spectrum. It rather means that there be a basis in the given knowledge structure to justify relations declared between concepts or groups of concepts, relations that are tacitly declared when concepts appear together in a resource. It certainly would be interesting to know the relationship into which the following terms in the glossary evaluated in Chapter 3 enter: *adjournment motion, aspirin, basic travelling allowance, tattoo, vegetative propagation,* and *zoom lens.* The latter terms are entered when terms like *recommit a bill, negative a motion,* etc. are not included. The coincidence

---

23. This triple distinction is credited to de Bessé. See Sager & Ndi-Kimbi (1995).

between the foregoing and the view expressed below by Arntz & Picht is particularly striking:

> It is not uncommon to find terminological collections that are simply inventories of terms that are presented alphabetically. Without a clear-cut methodology, it is impossible to determine whether all the concepts in a subject field have been recorded. Furthermore, terms from outside the subject field are frequently included. In choosing terms to be used in the collection, the authors depend on their own experience, which means they proceed for the most part on the basis of intuition [...]. Under these conditions, we cannot speak of terminology management per se (Arntz & Picht 1989:222; transl. from the German by Sue Ellen Wright).

The entering in the Nigerian glossary of the various senses of polysemous terms like *division*, *teller*, etc. (see Chapter 3.3.4) — including domain-irrelevant ones — is at once an indication of the problem of domain conception. While in certain contexts it may be difficult to implement all aspects of the onomasiological methodology associated with concept theory, this methodology nonetheless creates a decision-making framework for determining what is relevant and worth including in a terminology resource.

4.9.4 Knowledge transfer

For long, the pedagogical potentials of terminological activity remained barely exploited, no doubt because of the conception of terminology as a vocabulary list. Beaugrande (1994), whose comment on this view was cited earlier on, notes that a "terminology is an organisational and pedagogical tool for offering or acquiring competence and fluency in a (subject) field".

In the knowlege experiment reported in Chapter 3 (Section 3.2), the relative poverty of H. G.'s knowledge protocol stemmed from the fact that the constellation of terms in the reference glossary did not exhibit significant conceptual relations, as a result of which the experimental subject was unable to extract any significant chunk of knowledge.

In recent studies on knowledge transfer in the classroom, in speed-training for professional and non-professional purposes, etc., attention has been drawn to the important role of terminological methods (Humbley 1995; de Schaetzen 1993). Increasing use of these methods is a reflection of another application of concept theory. These methods are based on concept analyses and relations, and deviate from the propositional or discursive patterns of traditional instruction.

What is true of *terminology*, seen above as a method, is also true of *a terminology*, that is, a product. Thus a terminology may be regarded as a structured didactic material. Indeed, Eisele (1993: 74) has observed that the terminologist's method of explaining and ordering a field of knowledge confers on him/her the status of a producer of teaching materials. The premise is in part summed up by the idea that (German) *Bildung ist, wenn man weiß, wo's steht* which equates knowledge of a concept to knowledge of its place and links within a system. The picture is completed by definitions.

The next chapter provides a framework for examining those issues in the evaluation in Chapter 3 that relate to word combinations.

Chapter 5

Collocations and Communication

The study on translation reported in Chapter 3 revealed a number of problems some of which invite a consideration of the syntagmatic dimension of natural language (LGP or LSP). Experimental translators, it would be recalled, found the processing of word combinations particularly difficult. Whether in respect of the specialised "substantive motion for the adjournment of the House", "that the chairman do leave the chair" or the non-specialised "confine debate", the results were often the same: time-consuming error-laden decisions. Now, a recommendation (to improve the glossary) that merely urged the inclusion of word combinations would hardly be helpful because the glossary in many cases does include such combinations (there is "substantive motion"; there is also "adjournment of the House").

In discussing the environment of words, or the company words keep, this chapter seeks to provide a theoretical basis for understanding the problems of the translating subjects in Chapter 3. It is also the goal of the discussion to theoretically ground decisions that will have to be taken in respect of the terminology resource described in Chapter 8.

To begin with, let us consider accounts of the importance of word combinations for research on Language for General Purposes (LGP) and Language for Special Purposes (LSP) respectively.

5.1 LGP views on word combinations

The importance of word combinations in LGP discourse is examined below from two standpoints, namely, communication and knowledge.

5.1.1 *Communication perspective*

Kjellmer (1991) attempts to correlate patterns of speech with knowledge of what he refers to as *collocations*. As basis for the correlation, he cites research evidence comparing the speech output of moderately fluent *native speakers* of a language (group A) and moderately fluent *learners* of the same language (group B). The typical group A subject would normally make hesitation pauses between considerably long stretches of words, whereas the typical group B subject would pause after every two or three words. From these observations, Kjellmer makes the following inference, the interest of which explains the length of the quotation:

> It seems reasonable to believe that the difference between them in this regard can be ascribed largely to a difference in the automation of collocations. The native speaker has acquired an automatic command of substantial portions of speech and uses his pauses to plan one or more thought units ahead. In building his utterances he makes use of large prefabricated sections. The learner, on the other hand, having automated few collocations, continually has to create structures that he can only hope will be acceptable to native speakers; he, too, will of course have to plan his thought units, but we can assume that his pauses are to a great extent used for decision-making at this fairly trivial word-structure level. So even if he is not diffident, uncertain or hesitant he will inevitably be hampered in his progress, and his output will often seem contrived or downright unacceptable to native ears (Kjellmer 1991: 124).

Kjellmer expects an analogy in the written outputs of both groups, and pleads for a collocational strategy in the teaching and learning of vocabulary.

Hausmann (1979, 1989) discusses the environment of words, and the importance of this environment in text production. He also calls word combinations *collocations*. His context is the organisation of dictionary entries. Where the perspective taken in the dictionary is primarily one of comprehension, Hausmann argues that the independent element of the collocation, that is the base (he actually speaks of the entire collocation), ought to be entered under the collocate (the dependent element), otherwise the latter is not understood. As an example, the collocate 'confirmed' as an entry does not make much sense without a base such as 'bachelor'. On the other hand, in a dictionary entry on the German *Junggeselle* (bachelor), the qualifier *eingefleischter* (confirmed) contributes nothing to the understanding of this entry. That is to say, *Junggeselle* is not defined in relation to *eingefleischter*, whereas the latter requires the former if it is to suggest what is meant in English by *confirmed bachelor.*

In a production perspective, however, entering the collocate under the base is of great importance because the producer of discourse proceeds from the base to the collocate. In a sense, Hausmann's analysis is reminiscent of the theme-rheme distinction where the rheme corresponds to the collocate, and says something about the theme, correlate of the base. In what might be considered as levels in the incorporation of a base into norm-conforming propositions, collocate assignment would be an important first level of predication. This is perhaps why Hausmann affirms elsewhere (Hausmann 1994) that the learning of vocabulary for active purposes must go *pari passu* with the learning of collocates.

The foregoing accounts presumably put into perspective some of the issues that arose in the translation protocols in Chapter 3. Seen from the perspective taken by Kjellmer, the numerous hesitations (time) and errors (quality) associated with the processing of certain word combinations casts the experimental translators in the mould of learners of the Hausa language of legislative procedure, learners for whom "confine" and "proposes" were still to be automated in the context of "debate" and "amendment" respectively. In the Hausmann perspective, the translators would be akin to text producers whose reference dictionary had failed to list the collocates under their respective bases.

Let us now turn to the so-called knowledge perspective to collocations in LGP, a perspective which is not without importance to communication.

5.1.2 Knowledge perspective

There is a knowledge dimension to the environment of words which quite naturally affects communication. To the extent that it helps in sense disambiguation, the environment of words is relevant to communication in a very profound sense. Firth (1957) describes several "modes of meaning" of which "meaning by collocation" is a category. If this category is understood in terms of one collocational element helping to restrict the other element which, otherwise, is polysemous, then Firth's construct could very easily be one of the earliest insights into what is now an important field of research: lexical sense disambiguation. In the evaluation in Chapter 3, it was seen that, on occasion, the polysemous nature of certain items in the source-language term lists resulted in contextually non-relevant choices being made in the target-language. Again, using the previous examples, if "debate" and "amendment" had appeared by the words "confinement" and "proposal" in the glossary, these words may not have been understood as "seclusion" and "advice/counsel" respectively.

Let us now consider word combinations from the standpoint of research on Language for Special Purposes.

5.2 LSP views on collocations and other word combinations

The same two perspectives as in the previous section are examined.

5.2.1 Communication perspective

Picht (1987: 150) expressly prefers not to use the concept and term *collocation* in his analysis of the environment of terms in LSP. In (1987), but particularly elsewhere (1988, 1990a, 1990b, and with Arntz 1989), Picht stresses the importance of what he refers to as *LSP phrase* in the production of specialist texts. Indeed, it is largely to Picht that the terminology community owes the explicit theoretical formulation, in recent times, of the problem of terms and text production. Consider the following remarks:

> In text production, integrating terms into specialist texts, that is, choosing the correct verbs, prepositions, etc. presents considerable difficulties (Arntz & Picht 1989: 34; my translation from the German).

> In the course of correcting translation exercises of technical texts, I remarked time and time again that the LSP vocabulary had been correctly researched, but that it was when it came to incorporating the terms in stretches of target language that the problems started. In most cases the wrong verbal element was selected, and this led either to constructions that were comprehensible from the point of view of the subject field, but unusable, or else to distortions of meaning which invalidated the usefulness of the resultant translation (Picht 1990a: 49).

As to the attribution of the phenomenon observed, he notes as follows:

> This kind of error, as inquiries and error analyses have indicated, must be largely laid at the door of the special dictionaries; generally special dictionaries will prove helpful in the solving of terminological problems, but when it comes to incorporating the terms in the appropriate linguistic context, the dictionaries leave seekers in the lurch, or else mislead them by offering information that is too general and too vague (Picht 1990a: 49).

The foregoing could very well be a description of some of the data in the translation protocols, and of the relationship between these data and the glossary used by experimental subjects.

5.2.2 Knowledge perspective

As in LGP, the environment of subject field terms also has a knowledge dimension. Since what was said in Section 5.1.2 holds true for LSPs (see, for instance, Roberts 1993a, Meyer & Mackintosh 1994), I examine other aspects of this knowledge dimension. Meyer & Mackintosh find it expedient for their specific discussion to collapse *collocation* (*sensu* Benson *et al.* 1986; see Section 5.3) and *noun compound* into one construct which they label *phraseme*.

They admit that generally a compound designates a single concept while a collocation does not. From items in the word combination which constitutes a phraseme, several kinds of information may be gleaned. One type of information is useful for investigating links existing between the domain whose phrasemes are being studied and some other domain. Meyer & Mackintosh's data on optical storage technologies yields phrasemes such as: (1) *author a* CD-ROM, *subscribe to* CD-ROM, *publish on* CD-ROM; (2) *cut a* CD-ROM, *record a* CD-ROM, CD-ROM *juke-box*, CD-ROM *player*. The italicised items show this domain as having paper-based publishing (list 1) and audio-recording (list 2) as "ancestral domains".

It is also instructive to note that word solidarities are a component of Ahmad's research programme which uses "terminology dynamic" as a heuristic framework within which to observe the evolution of knowledge in a given field over a period of time, and as evidenced by terminological preferences in the works of scholars (Ahmad 1996).

These, then, are some of the factors that have driven theoretical explorations of word combinations. The next section examines some theories that have been proposed.

5.3 Theoretical accounts in perspective

A common concern among many of the authors reviewed is with the environment of words/terms. This common concern might suggest that the differences between the accounts are merely terminological (collocation, LSP phrase, co-occurrence). While Cowie (1981: 225), writing on the subject of collocations and idioms, is right in noting that the "lack of a standardized terminology continues to bedevil the work of lexicologists [...]", it might be added that the varied terminology should be suspected of designating different concepts. This could of course also be the case even when common terminology is used.

With reference to the terms and concepts used by the authors reviewed, and a few others, I propose to provide a restricted account of theories of word combination. The goal is to investigate differences in the theoretical underpinnings of the views held by authors cited, and to distil elements of a theoretical framework for the terminology project described in Chapter 8. The LGP side of the account will deliberately omit the rich documentation on what has been specifically labelled *phraseology*. The interested reader is referred to the "Europhras" conference proceedings, and to work by Burger, Fleischer, etc. in which issues like (non) substitutability and semantic componentiality are common. I concentrate, rather, on collocations (more as an end concept than as a process), cognisant nonetheless of the fact that, like phraseology, collocation can hardly be described as a homogenous construct, and that *phrase* appears even in collocational discourse.

5.3.1 *LGP theories of word combinations*

In the following sections, the theoretical underpinnings of the collocational frameworks of Kjellmer (1991) and Hausmann (1979, 1984, 1985) are investigated.

5.3.1.1 *Kjellmer and British contextualism*

Kjellmer uses *set expressions* and *collocations* as synonyms. Table 5.1 below is an interpretation of Kjellmer's typology of collocations. The broad conception of collocation revealed by the Table in turn makes it obvious what Kjellmer considers as the environment of words. Kjellmer argues that made-up constructions form a significant part of the mental lexicon of a competent speaker of a language. To demonstrate this point, Kjellmer submits a piece of ordinary expository prose to collocational mark-up, using, as basis, a corpus of collocations derived from the one-million word Brown corpus. Kjellmer defines collocations as "structured patterns which recur in identical form", and views recurrence as two times and above.

Not surprisingly, in the light of this definition and the above typology, word combinations in the prose passage are extensively marked-up. While acknowledging the limitations of formal analogy and semantic parallelism, Kjellmer uses these criteria to compare unmatched combinations in the text with attested combinations in the reference collocation corpus. The comparison allows for the conjecture that the passage contains even more collocations than the reference corpus makes evident. Establishing the significance of collocational phenomena in text allows Kjellmer to posit the existence of semi-automated routines in speaking and writing (see the quotation in Section 5.1.1).

Kjellmer's very broad view of collocations is also shared by such scholars as Sinclair (1966, 1991; with Renouf 1991), Cowie (1978), Mackin (1978), all working within a paradigm that is traditionally referred to as British contextualism (Hausmann 1985). Sinclair (1966: 411), acknowledging the influence of Halliday and others, notes that there "are virtually no impossible collocations, but some are much more likely than others". Halliday defines collocation as follows:

> Collocation is the syntagmatic association of lexical items, quantifiable textually, as the probability that there will occur, at n removes (a distance of n lexical items) from an item x, the items a, b, c… Any item thus enters into a range of collocation, the items with which it is collocated being ranged from more to less probable; […] (Halliday 1961: 276).

Table 5.1: *Interpretation of Kjellmer's collocational typology (elements predicted are in italics)*

Types of collocations	General/structural description	Cohesion level & predictability direction	Example
Fossilized phrases	Unassimilated loans typically, but not exclusively belong here. Variation rare, limited to inflection.	Very high cohesion a) right-left predictive b) right predictive c) left predictive	a) *nouveau riche* b) ball point *pen* c) *ad* infinitum
Semi-fossilized phrases	Idioms in the narrow sense of semantic non-compositionality belong here.	High cohesion a) right predictive b) left predictive	a) Achilles' *heel/tendon* b) *jump/grant/stand* bail
Variable phrases	a) Combination of two or more lexical words, including function words. Commonality accords them near lexemic status. b) Sequence of one lexical word and one or more function words	Low cohesion	a) *glass of* water b) a number *of*

Practical (lexicographical) interpretation of aspects of this broad way of looking at collocations, would be dictionaries by Cowie & Mackin (1975) and by Benson, Benson, Ilson (1986). A recent attempt at constructing a coherent theory of the contextualist view of collocation is Sinclair (1991).

Drawing on previous work, Sinclair posits two principles or models to account for the interpretation of meaning in discourse, or in the production of such discourse. The *open-choice principle* views discourse as a set of paradigms each of which offers a variety of options. Discourse being a stretch of slots, producing or comprehending it according to the open-choice principle means taking major decisions after each paradigmatic slot. The only restraint is grammaticalness, and there is a tacit assumption of the semantic independence of members of a paradigm. The other model, *the idiom principle*, has ontological and other premises. It is held that: (1) in the extralinguistic world there is to be observed certain *object* co-occurrences; (2) that scholarly fields or registers impose certain views on these ontological object co-occurrences; and (3) that humans have certain inclinations (e.g. towards economy). These are all believed to be reflected in language. These phenomena drastically cut down the number of slots that would otherwise have required major decision-making in order to be filled. The phenomena suggest that major decisions, which imply a switch to the open-choice model, would then be taken at critical junctures, such as change in line of thought.

Sinclair sees discourse as a combination of the open-choice principle and the idiom principle, the latter being the more natural and hence more frequently trodden path. Evidence for this assertion comes from observation. A comparison of senses attributed to words by introspection (as in an intuition-based dictionary) with senses of words as they naturally occur in discourse (as may be investigated through text corpora) clearly invalidates intuitive assumptions of sense frequencies, and even of our ability to identify senses. This evidence challenges the tacit assumptions of the open-choice model in at least two ways. It questions the semantic basis of the slot-by-slot decision routine of this model. Following from this, it refutes the suggestion that choices at each slot are fundamentally unwieldy. Semantic dependency is what the evidence points to, and this dependency leads to degrees of predictability. Stated syllogistically, the upshot of all of this is that: the idiom principle prevails in language; collocations illustrate the idiom principle; therefore, collocations prevail in language.

Another theoretical construct developed by Sinclair contrasts *downward collocation* with *upward collocation* — a distinction to which the concepts 'node' and 'collocate' are central. In a collocation (in any of the contextualist senses examined), the element being studied is the node and the element that occurs in the defined environment of this node is the collocate. But node and collocate change status depending on the analytical standpoint or point of departure. In a combination, x (e.g. good) + y (e.g. omen), where the analysis proceeds from x (known to be a very frequent word), x is the node, and y the collocate. Here one speaks of downward collocation. The less frequent y can also provide the analytical angle, in which case it becomes the node and x the collocate. Here one speaks of upward collocation. The perspective-dependent interpretation of node and collocate is strikingly reminiscent of Halliday's underlining of the fact that the theme of a clause, while realised position-initially in English clauses, is not defined in this manner. As a variety of points of departure are possible, a given clause can be severally structured so that the rheme of one clause becomes the theme of the other, and *vice versa* (Halliday 1994: 37–8). It would seem that Sinclair's perspective-dependent interpretation of node and collocate is necessary to support the concept of *collocational range*. By this is meant the degree to which components of a collocation combine, this degree being measured in statistical terms. Thus, 'omen' has a limited collocational range (good, bad) whereas the range of 'good' is in principle unlimited.

Now let me attempt to use Sinclair's theoretical formalisation to reinterpret

Kjellmer (reviewed earlier on), and to account for problems in the translation protocols (chapter 3). Cohesion (*sensu* strength of solidarity), which is an important feature of Kjellmer's typology as seen in Table 5.1, is a question of collocational range. With respect to the communication problems of my experimental translators, they were, as seen earlier, comparable to learners of Hausa on account of the technical subject matter. As a result, they did not possess the basis to operate within the idiom mode according to which "a language user has available to him or her a large number of semi-preconstructed phrases that constitute single choices, even though they might appear to be analysable into segments" (Sinclair 1991: 110). Recall the search for several components of the term "substantive motion for the adjournment of the House". Although not mentioned previously, in this same example 'House' was curiously looked up by the dTAP team after they had seen "adjournment of the House". To the extent, then, that it can explain "any occasion where one decision leads to more than one word in text", the idiom principle, Sinclair argues, is easily able to account for "idioms, proverbs, clichés, *technical terms*, phrasal verbs, and the like" (my italics). The iTAP subject's better bracketing of multi-word terms could be described in terms of his possessing the knowledge required to operate the idiom principle.

5.3.1.2 *The Hausmann perspective*

Specificity or non-triviality may be considered central to Hausmann's concept of collocation. Word combinations which satisfy this criterion, the only ones deserving of the label collocation, are fewer than the non-specific word combinations (Hausmann 1985: 118). Hausmann reviews a number of dictionaries of German that claim to be rich in collocations, and observes that many of them list trivial, that is non-specific, co-occurrences, in addition to clause-type metaphorical expressions. Thus, in the dictionary, *Stilduden*, the article *Kakao* (cocoa) has: (1) *Kakao bereiten* (prepare, that is, entire process, as opposed to, say, (2); (2) *Kakao kochen* (bring to/come to simmering or boiling point); (3) *Kakao trinken* (drink); and (4) ***Jemanden durch den Kakao ziehen*** (idiomatically: to pull somebody's leg).

Hausmann's association of collocation exclusively with the instantiation of a word in (a non-trivial environment of) discourse makes him assert that the *Stilduden*'s subtitle makes a spurious claim: *Die Verwendung der Wörter in Satz* (How words are used in sentences). A metaphorical construction in which a given word occurs in a changed or unidentifiable sense is no instance of the use of that word. One of the two tasks Hausmann sets for a theory of collocations is related to the foregoing, that is, distinguishing between specific word combinations (collocations) and non-specific or trivial combinations. The second task is clarifying the status of the combining elements. Each task is taken up in turn below.

For Hausmann, knowledge of collocations situates at the level of *langue*. But *langue* is understood, not as a system accessible to all (including grammar-confident non-native speakers), but as norm conventionalised by usage. Placing collocations at, as it were, a level intermediate between *langue* and *parole* allows for the exclusion of:

1. trivial co-occurrences like 'buy a book' which belong to the *langue* level;
2. co-occurrences deriving from individual creativity like 'colourless green ideas' belonging to the parole level.

Further restriction would come from two defining criteria, *viz.*

3. transparency/ease of comprehension (not coterminous with ease of prediction/production) which would exclude all compositionally opaque sequences; and
4. the structural frame of collocations postulated to be: substantive + adjective, substantive + verb, verb + substantive, verb + adverb, adjective + adverb, substantive + (preposition) + substantive.

The resulting field is so restricted that the criterion of specificity, when applied, generates more acceptable candidate collocations, that is, the norm-determined and limited word combination samples of a language.

To move on to Hausmann's second task for a theory of collocations: it is in the normal run of things for the processes of text composition/comprehension, and the sequence of these processes, not to vary. (Recall from Halliday that, in English at least, the clause as message requires the theme to be fronted.) This being the case, collocations (which are text microcosms) must be made up in a way that reflects these processes, and respects their sequence. As seen earlier, Hausmann labels the components of a collocation as (German) *Basis* (base) and *Kollokator* (collocate). The former would be the correlate of theme, while the latter would correlate with rheme. In any given word sequence the importance of components must be ranked, in order to determine and fix the base and its collocate. Formulated interrogatively, Hausmann's rule-of-thumb is: under which component is it indispensable, if this component is not to be misunderstood, that the entire collocation appear? This component would be the less important one, and, therefore, the collocate of the base. This test of course presupposes that the word combination first meet the collocational criteria posited.

Hausmann (1984) proposes criteria for identifying collocations, and for distinguishing them from other types of word combinations. Figure 5.1 presents Hausmann's typology of word combinations. I have adapted a few of Hausmann's original German examples.

Combinations of the type 'strongroom' and 'pull somebody's leg' which

```
                    Word combination
                   /              \
              fixed                not fixed
              /                       \
                                    types of relationships
  compounding                       /      |       \
  figurative expressions    counter-affinity  affinity    free
  ***strongroom***              |              /           |
  ***pull somebody's leg***  counter-creation  collocation  co-creation
                             ***watch your height***  ***confirmed bachelor***  ***buy a book***
```

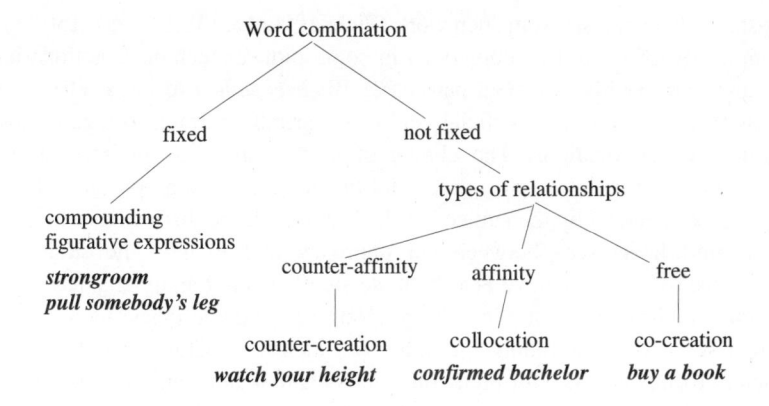

Figure 5.1: *English adaptation of Hausmann's (1984) typology of word combinations*

would be labelled compound and figurative expression respectively are by Hausmann treated as fixed word combinations, and excluded from any discussion of collocations. Combinations such as 'buy a book' with very few combinatorial constraints, and deriving from knowledge of the rules of a language are labelled free co-creations. A combination like 'confirmed bachelor' would be labelled a collocation because it is formed by unique semantic rules, and its components occur together more frequently than might otherwise have been expected. Combinations that present these features of 'confirmed bachelor' are seen as semi-processed combinations of a language, and are therefore not perceived as marked or striking. Combinations like 'handsome girl' or 'watch your height!' with scant regard for semantic rules governing what can be combined are called counter-creations. They are perceived as marked because of a statistically verifiable lack of affinity among their components.

The Hausmann account suggests how the glossary might have listed word combinations, assuming the parameters for distinguishing between, say, a compound (a multi-word term) and the collocate of this compound were straightforward or easily applicable. What is the base and what is the collocate (if one exists) in "substantive motion for the adjournment of the House"? See Section 5.4.2 for a discussion of the problem of identifying base and collocate.

Let us now turn to an account of LSP word combinations.

5.3.2 An LSP theory of word combinations

Picht's analysis of the environment of terms in LSP discourse takes research in LGP, particularly collocations, as its point of departure. In doing this Picht seeks to distance his analysis from such work (Picht 1990a: 35; Picht 1987: 150). Given examples of LSP word combinations in some pioneer technical dictionaries — examples akin to his own (German) *einen Wechsel ziehen* (draw a bill) — Picht claims that it would be superficial, and only partially correct, to regard these as instances of collocations. The choice of verbs cannot be entirely, if at all, explained by linguistic imperatives, to the total exclusion of the referential framework provided by the subject field. To maintain the distinction which Kjaer (considered later) sees between her approach and Picht's, the subject field framework referred to above is to be understood as the domain characteristics of concepts. Picht is interested in concept relational characteristics — in the newly posited sense of determining the value or valency structure of concepts. This structure forms the basis for predicting elements that can combine. The relational characteristics of the term "forge" should point to "iron", "copper" and *vice versa*. Picht writes:

> Since the concern of LSP phraseology is the combinatory properties of concepts, (their combinability or connectability), it is of prime importance to trace these characteristics which may be assumed either to promote or to hinder the possible combination of elements (Picht 1990a: 36).

He defines the LSP phrase as "the product of a syntactic linkage between at least two LSP elements in a proposition with an LSP content, whose inner coherence depends upon conceptual connectability" (Picht 1990a: 43). Only the form of, or configuration of elements in, the LSP phrase is determined by language. At a deeper level, the co-occurrence of elements of the phrase is said to stem from conceptual "combinability".

It seems safe to infer that there are two explanations of conceptual combinability in the LSP phrase. In the first, one element (the verb in Picht's research programme) undergoes transformation occasioned by a need for it to appear in the environment of another element, a noun-term. The transformation implies that, in this new context, the verb will be partly or totally emptied of its LGP semes, then acquire an LSP acceptation. This would be the case with *einen Wechsel ziehen* (draw a bill). In the second, both elements (verb concept and noun concept) have mutually attracting inherent characteristics. No transformation is called for. Both elements could be candidate terms in their own right. An example would be "forge copper".

Given the assumption in the second explanation, the likelihood is that even traditional dictionaries would record both, and the user could confidently use definitions or equivalents proposed. The communication problem, therefore, is associated with the first scenario in which assumptions of the *LGPness* of the verbal element may well be wrong. In Picht's view, then, the element constituting the environment of the LSP term is conceptually determined, and the problem of integrating the term in discourse derives from either of two factors: non-recognition of the terminological status of this environment, or of a (slight) modification of its LGP acceptation. The questions below, posed by Picht (1987), are intended to reflect these factors, in addition to being the basis for Picht's rejection of the collocational framework:

1. To what semantic influences/modifications are the linguistic elements which cluster around an LSP collocational nucleus, a term, subject?
2. Is it, in fact, reasonable to posit a semantic influence or modification at all?
3. Or are such elements clustered around the LSP collocational nucleus not in fact already independent LSP elements? (Picht 1987: 150).

Even though he himself does not use the collocational framework, he does admit that the findings of this framework could even turn out to be "more useful for the study of LSP phraseology than phraseological studies have proved to date".

5.4 Appraisal, and an eclectic framework for LSP

Kjellmer's maximalist theory and Hausmann's minimalist theory of collocations were apparently not formulated to deal specifically with LSP. This will be evident in some of the issues raised below. But as the references in this chapter to the translation experiments show, Kjellmer and Hausmann have relevance for LSP. On the other hand, Picht's LSP phrase construct, formulated exclusively with LSP in mind, will be shown to require extension. A case can therefore be made for a framework that selectively draws insights from these accounts, and combines these with other approaches to produce a more generally applicable account. I use parliamentary discourse as my LSP case study. In the discussion, [US] and [GB] refer respectively to American and British data sources.

5.4.1 *Variously conditioned term environments*

In the following word combinations, the italicised elements all predicate the non-italicised items, and are, therefore, environments of the latter.

a. *prorogue* Parliament [GB]
b. *engross* a bill [US]
c. *defeat* a bill [GB]
d. *kill* a bill [US]

e. i *select* an amendment [GB]
   ii *choose* an amendment* [?]
f. i *offer* an amendment [GB]
   ii *make* an amendment [GB]
   iii *propose* an amendment [GB]
   iv *introduce* an amendment [GB]

As environments, the italicised words do not all have the same conditioning. If Picht's account were likened to a frame approach to concept modelling — as Martin (1992) does in discussing a comparable construct — *prorogue* and *engross* in (a) and (b) would have object slots which only 'Parliament' and 'bill' respectively could fill. Similarly, if the frames for 'Parliament' and 'bill', particularly the latter, had enough slots, *prorogue* and *engross* respectively would show up as fillers. In other words, the relational characteristics of one concept predicts an association with another concept.

In (c) and (d) the collocates are clearly strange as they seem to have undergone transformation (loss of a class of objects that is typically animate) in order to fill the slots in the frames of their respective nodes. Thus, it might be said that the environments in examples (a–d) can be explained in terms of Picht's relational conceptual characteristics (of combinability or inclusion).

However, in the examples in (e), which remind of "confine debate" in the translation protocols, no semantic modification takes place, and it is only in a very loose sense that the italicised words in these examples can be explained by relational characteristics. Even with such elasticity, the concept combinability account does not explain why the environment is *select* and hardly ever *choose* in (d) or even *pick*. A plausible explanation, rooted in usage, may be found in Collins Cobuild's *English Usage* (1992: 130) which notes that "*Select* is more formal than *choose* or *pick*".

Kjaer (1990a) takes issue with Picht's theory and all others that seek to "predict or explain restrictions on combinability by means of semantic markers and distinguishers [...] unless the restrictions are due to lack of compatibility". In her study of word combinations in German legal language, Kjaer (1990a) finds that, with respect to the modification of actions or suits (German *Klage*), the form employed is *Klage ändern*, and it never is *Klage verändern*. On the basis of data such as these, Kjaer proposes a theory of context conditioning, and shows how word combinations, whose degree of invariability is not quite explicable from a linguistic standpoint, may be linked to circumstances in the non-linguistic world of the law: express prescription (the law states how a concept is to be invariably expressed if the concept is not to be voided); indirect prescription (a departure from established pattern might call for an interpretation by the court); convention (conformity to a pattern motivated by desire to maintain the linguistic integrity of the law, or not to be out of line); and expediency (patterns whose use is explained by the need for economy in expression). The first two factors would appear to be more centred on the law, while the other two are more user-centred. The degree of variability increases as one goes down the list of factors. Not surprisingly, therefore, these circumstances taper in terms of their explanatory adequacy, as Kjaer herself seems to admit.

Paradoxically, this admission is an important source of strength for the Kjaer model. One might, for instance, be inclined to view those word combinations that are accounted for by convention (a minimal context conditioning factor) as deriving merely and exclusively from knowledge of a language. Indeed, that might have been the interpretation for the variability of (synonymous) collocates in (f): "*offer, propose,* ... an amendment". In spite of this variability, it did not appear that any word from a pertinent entry in Roget's Thesaurus, for instance, could serve as collocate without eyebrows being raised. Consider: *give* an amendment*.

Martin (1992) proposes a model of restricted word groups according to which the collocates in example f would derive from knowledge of a language. Evidence for this claim are his references to Mel'cuk's lexical functions, arbitrariness, lexical non-computability. The items in example f would be labelled *lexeme-bound collocations*. These form a category in Martin's scheme, which also has a place for the Picht-type analysis as well as Kjaer's contextual conditioning. Of lexeme-bound combinations that may occur in an LSP, Martin notes that the "more they are expressible in terms of general lexical functions, the more their restriction is extraordinary [*i.e. unlike concept- and context-conditioned combinations?*], the more they are prototypical collocations" (Martin 1992: 162; italicised remark mine). Commenting on the salience of the three types of combinations, Martin notes that sublanguages (specialised languages) "will show, per excellence, *concept*-bound and *context*-bound 'collocations', without excluding the 'central' lexeme-bound ones" (p. 163). The challenge of course is with cases such as in example f where the distinction between lexeme-bound and context-conditioning (in its stronger version) is difficult to make. Therein lies the usefulness of Kjaer's weaker context conditioning factors.

To summarise, my data on legislative procedure support a collocational framework that acknowledges a variety of conditioning factors — even if the lines dividing these factors are at times difficult to draw. Because it does not rely exclusively on linguistic conditioning, such a framework would provide answers like the following to the first two questions posed by Picht (see Section 5.3):

1. There does not have to be any influences or modifications, but when there are, they will be due to the terminological concept and to the subject field context.
2. It is reasonable in the light of 1 above to posit modification or semantic influence, but ostensibly this thesis cannot always hold as there are other factors.

An answer to the third question is offered in Section 5.4.2. The results of Picht's own investigations of Spanish verbs (Picht 1987: 153) more or less support the answer in 1. Similar evidence is to be gleaned from Draskau (1986). The implications of all of these for communication is that problems do not always have to be explicable in non-linguistic terms.

5.4.2 Problems of term delimitation

It is commonly admitted in terminology that subjective judgement is not infrequently the basis for deciding what is to be considered a term (Roberts 1993a; Meyer/Mackintosh 1994). Commonly used rules-of-thumb (existence of definition, position in a concept system, statistics, etc.) in principle apply equally well to terms as to LSP phrases. In positing a collocational framework for LSP, or in distinguishing terms from other LSP word combinations, criteria established for categorisations in the Kjellmer and Hausmann typologies are not of much help (see Table 5.1 and Figure 5.1). The use of stress in English is, besides the native-ear-like requirement, not very reliable (see Weissenhofer 1995). With a few exceptions — e.g. where concept-bound combinations yield a series of concept types (see Martins 1992: 163; Meyer & Mackintosh 1994: 5) — it is also not very helpful probing the source of conditioning. For one thing, the tendency of some LSPs to avoid synonymy makes it difficult, except in very peculiar situations, to determine whether the conditioning is conceptual, contextual or linguistic.

The problem of term delimitation is vividly illustrated by what might be called *term expansion* or the phenomenon of expansion in LSP. Crystal (1985: 115) defines expansion as "a grammatical process in which new elements are added to a construction without its base structure being affected". This definition could be reformulated as follows from a terminological perspective in order to describe term expansion in LSPs: a process (variously conditioned) in which new elements are added to a given term without the concept underlying the original term becoming irretrievable. To comment on this definition: the concept underlying the original term, while remaining retrievable, is capable of losing its status as base with repeated expansion. Illustrative examples must be preceded by the admission that this way of looking at term expansion erroneously assumes that in successive additions to an initial concept — where the additions themselves are, or comprise, terminological concepts — the resulting surface construction must be transparent or motivated. This need not be the case. I take the following example of expansion from my British parliamentary data:

(1) bill
(2) bring in bill
(3) leave to bring in bill
(4a) grant leave to bring in bill
(4b) motion for leave to bring in bill
(5) move motion for leave to bring in bill

(1) is incontrovertibly a term. If "bring in" in (2) is considered a trivial co-occurrence of bill with 'introduce' as one of several synonyms, does this phrasal verb also have the same status in (3) and (4 a & b)? Is 'leave to bring in' in (3) a term, or should it be simultaneously considered an expansion of 'bring in' and a trivial co-occurrence of bill, or is the entire phrase in (3) rather considered a multi-word term? If 'bring in' in (2) and 'leave to bring in' in (3) were considered as trivial co-occurrences of bill: how would we deal with the prospect that (4b) would be listed as it is in an exercise in which it was attempted to exhaustively list terms designating procedural motions? Are the verbs 'grant' and 'move' in the verbal phrases in (4a) and (5) expansions of their respective conceptual kernels (however these are analysed), or are they integral parts of conceptual and terminological wholes? Just how many terms are there in this list?

In effect, there exist contexts in which models of base and collocate in some of the accounts reviewed earlier become simplistic, and hence of limited use. Besides conditioning, the second feature of a word combination framework that is adequate for my data must be its acknowledgement of, and search for pragmatic solutions to, the problem of term delimitation. One terminographical implication of this feature is that, in cases of uncertainty or other practical exigency, it provides a basis for tentatively entering a variety of combinations (potential terms) as collocates of a given kernel, the entry term. The condition, however, must be that, unlike the *Jemanden durch den Kakao ziehen* example (see Section 5.3.1.2), the resulting combinations (entry term plus collocates) be verifiable as expansions of the main entry term, not so much at a surface level as conceptually. An answer to Picht's third question (see Section 5.3.2), then, would be:

3. The elements clustering around the LSP collocational nucleus can also be independent LSP elements, that is, terms.

The collocation field of a term record therefore serves communication and the identification of related terms.

5.4.3 *Rethinking the trivialisation of grammatical collocations*

Within communication in LSP, the issue of grammatical collocations would on occasion assume greater importance than one may infer from Hausmann's LGP account, or from critical comments directed at collocational dictionaries such as Benson/Benson/Ilson (1986) and Cowie/Makin (1975) — both of which were produced within the contextualist framework. Consider the following test of prepositions (statements (a) and (b) are taken from my parliamentary data, (c) and (d) from Meyer & Mackintosh on optical storage technologies, (e) and (f) from Picht on finance).

a. The bill originated — the Senate [US] *Context: Legislative/Congress*
b. The bill originated — the House of Commons [GB] *Context: Legislative/ Parliament*
c. Publish — CD-ROM [both US and GB] *Context: Optical storage technology*
d. Master (data) — CD-ROM [both US and GB] *Context: Optical storage technology*
e. Draw a bill — somebody [both US and GB] *Context: Finance*
f. Einen Wechsel — jemanden ziehen [DE] *Kontext:Wirtschaftssprache*

In an informal test, respondents from Great Britain, Germany and USA (all connected to the University of Bielefeld) were asked to supply the missing prepositions in statements that applied to them (see country codes in brackets). English language respondents all attempted (a) and (b), but rarely (c–e). Responses to (a) and (b) revealed the prepositional versatility of the verb "originate", at least in general language. Answers offered included 'in', 'from' and 'with'. The preposition used frequently in the legislative context (in both legislatures) is 'in'. For (c), 'on' was expected (see Meyer & Mackintosh). One of two subjects who attempted (c) proposed 'as' (a smart solution), while the other gave 'on', but added a question mark and the comment "not good English". Of (d), where the answer expected was 'to' (Meyer & Mackintosh), this same subject wrote the comment: "not English at all". In (e) no answers were provided. The equivalent German sentence in (f) elicited a number of prepositions from German students of German language: 'gegen', 'für' and 'von'. The preposition expected was 'auf'.

Two simple points emerge from these results. First, the dynamic interface between LGP and LSP, if nothing else, makes it difficult to consider native-speaker competence as a clearly circumscribable construct. Second, context-conditioning (*sensu* Kjaer) is not restricted to lexical items, but can also involve prepositions. Now, while a good many examples of Kjellmer's word combinations would, from a number of native-speaker perspectives, be considered trivial, and indeed patronising if recorded in certain kinds of dictionaries, the theory underlying Kjellmer's work is, of the two other theories (Hausmann, Picht), about the only one that makes for the identification of the prepositional collocates in the above examples. Although the role of prepositions in specialist communication is recognised by Picht (see Section 5.2.1) they do not appear to be accounted for in his theory of conceptual combinability. The importance of prepositions suggests that a collocational framework adequate for LSP communication must not exclude *a priori* certain word classes.

Perhaps further investigation could reveal other issues, but the three points of appraisal in the foregoing paragraphs suffice to show why an LSP communication-focused account of word combinations, particularly collocates of terms or of other term collocates, requires flexibility in its theoretical commitments. Figure 5.2 presents my proposed typology of LSP word combinations. It might be noted that, in the diagram, collocates (i.e. environments) rather than collocations are spoken of. It is immaterial if these collocates are themselves terms. The requirement of flexibility is in part evident in what the three curved lines stand for. The two lines (labelled 3) converging at the box labelled 'multiword terms' suggest that the result of some collocates combining with certain terms/bases may not be distinguishable from multiword terms. A typical example would be a collocate that also had a subcategorising function of its base (bill–*public* bill– admissible public bill). The curved line (6) reflects the point made previously concerning the grey area between minimal context conditioning and language system/knowledge-determined combinability. These and other comments are made against corresponding numerical notations in the Diagram.

136 TERMINOLOGY AND LANGUAGE PLANNING

```
                    ┌─────────────────────┐
                    │ LSP word combinations│
                    └─────────────────────┘
                           /  |  \
                          /   |   \
                         /    │  (class)
                        /     |     \
                       /      |      \
                   (class) (class)  ┌──────────┐
                                    │collocates│
                                    └──────────┘
                                         │
                                      (class)
```

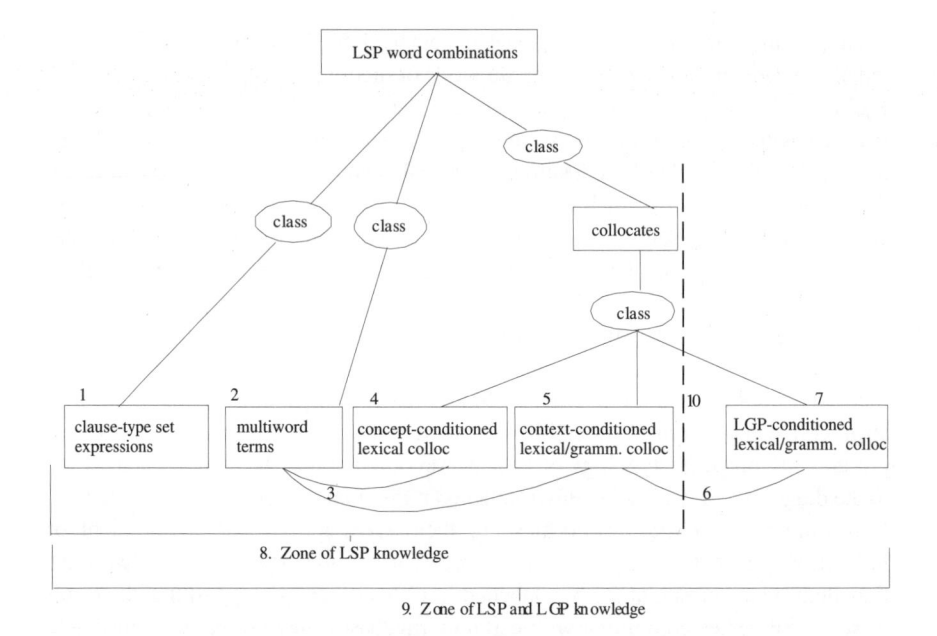

1	2	4	5	10	7
clause-type set expressions	multiword terms	concept-conditioned lexical colloc	context-conditioned lexical/gramm. colloc		LGP-conditioned lexical/gramm. colloc

8. Zone of LSP knowledge

9. Zone of LSP and LGP knowledge

Figure 5.2: *A typology of LSP word combinations, with special reference to legislative discourse*

1. The LSP correlate of LGP sayings and formulaic expressions. Examples: (a) [GB] a ceste bille avecque des amendemens les seigneurs sont assentus; (b) [GB] ceste bille est remise aux seigneurs avecque des raisons.
2. Concepts whose linguistic representation makes use of several words. Examples: (a) [US] joint resolution; discharge a committee; (b) [GB] motion to report progress and ask leave to sit again.
3. Curved lines suggest that it might be difficult to distinguish between 2 and the outcome of the collocational processes (lexeme-related) in 4 and 5.
4. Without prejudice to the relevance of other analyses, the collocate or term environment here can be analysed as being conceptually conditioned, in the sense of the definition of the collocate necessarily implying the base or vice versa. Examples: (a) [GB] prorogue Parliament; (b) [GB] move a motion.
5. Without prejudice to the relevance of other analyses, the collocate or term environment here can be viewed as displaying features (e.g. uniqueness, frequency) for which facts in the subject field hold *an* (not *the*) explanation. Examples: (a) "originate *in*" as in: [GB] "the bill originated in the House of Commons"; (b) [US] adjourn to a day certain.
6. Curved line suggests that some collocates that are analysed as minimally conditioned by context could very well be the outcome of knowing a given language. Examples: (a) confine debate (see translation protocol in Chapter 3); limit debate (restrict debate might have been as equally valid); (b) [GB] propose an amendment.
7. Collocates or parts thereof that derive from a communication need whose solution relies more on linguistic knowledge than anything else. Examples: See 6.

8. Describes 1–5 as word combination types that are of interest to the linguistic subject with a good command of the given language in which unfamiliar specialised knowledge is expressed.
9. Describes 1–7 as word combination types of interest to a subject who is diffident in both the specialised subject matter and in the LGP.
10. Separates the extent of interest of the linguistic subject described in 8 from that mentioned in 9.

5.5 Sources of collocates

Having now established the importance of collocates for a variety of communication and knowledge goals, and placed them within a working theory of LSP word combinations, the question may be posed as to how these collocates can be obtained. A variant of this discussion is to be found in Chapter 7 on terminology, text and technology.

5.5.1 Introspection and reference

Using the term *phraseology* under which she subsumes collocations, Roberts (1993: 6) writes that, as sources of phraseological information, lexicographers use "other dictionaries, their own linguistic competence, and occurrences encountered in the course of reading and listening". In an LSP, the use of introspection as a means of eliciting collocates almost certainly suggests that subject experts are the authors, not just collaborators, of the terminographical resource

5.5.2 Concept modelling and systematic elicitation

Traditionally, terminologists routinely rely on human experts in a given field for terminographical data. But experience has shown that these experts require a lot of guidance to generate the data desired. This is true of terms, but perhaps even more so of collocational data. The concept of lexical functions is one of several novelties in evidence in dictionaries elaborated by Igor Mel'cuk and associates (Mel'cuk *et al.* 1992). A lexical function is a semantic abstraction. Mel'cuk calls a "key word" (French: *mot clé*) or "argument" (*argument*) a lexeme or phrase to which is (are) assigned, in a given language, (a) certain value(s) on the basis of function. The descriptive formula is as follows:

$$f(X) = Y$$

where f is the lexical function, X its argument, and Y the value of the lexical function f pertinent to this argument. By value is meant the totality of expressions (institutionalised in a language) that convey a given sense or syntactic role (expressed by *f*) in the environment of *X*. Fifty-three simple (and standard) lexical functions are identified. *Ver* (expected/appropriate form), *Magn* (great, etc.), *Sing* (a quantity of), *Culm* (the summit, peak), *Anti* (opposite) are some examples. Complex lexical functions are obtained by combining two simple functions, e.g. *AntiVer* (contrary of expected/appropriate form). These LFs (some of which actually yield derived forms as opposed to collocates) may not entirely be satisfactory for LSPs. But to the extent that they can be made suitable for a particular LSP, or to the extent that they can in part apply to a given LSP, LFs can guide the introspective identification of collocates by subject specialists assisting a terminologist. The important point to note is that it is only the subject specialist that can use these LFs to generate 'unmarked' collocates, except the totality of generable and admissible collocates is linguistically motivated, as opposed to being conceptually or contextually conditioned. For the term 'amendment' [US], a specialist informant would probably indicate a number of collocates using the corresponding LFs. Examples:

1. *Ver* (amendment) = germane, relevant, admissible
2. *AntiVer* (amendment) = non-germane, hostile, inadmissible

The next chapter examines issues of knowledge representation in terminology.

CHAPTER 6

Terminography and Knowledge Representation

Some of the problems observed in the knowledge and translation experiments reported in Chapter 3 can be discussed in terms of knowledge representation challenges. In the knowledge protocol, N. S.'s handling of "reject a bill" and "defeat a bill" typifies an apparent challenge of representing synonymy in a terminology resource. In their translation, the dTAP team treated as free variants the two Hausa equivalents for "adjournment" as a component of two different concepts, *viz.* "adjournment of the House" and "adjournment of debate". This point exemplifies the challenge of reflecting a field's knowledge structure, or the place of concepts in a given knowledge space. H. G.'s relatively poor knowledge protocol, compared with that of N. S., illustrates on a higher level the same issue of knowledge structure, in this case, contents of the knowledge space revolving around "bill", and of spaces around other nuclei but into which "bill" enters.

Different dimensions of these representation challenges are captured by the following dichotomies: (1) representation of language-based relations (full synonymy, orthographic variants, etc.) *versus* representation of concept-based relations (hierarchical, associative); and (2) micro-structuring of knowledge (at the level of information categories in an entry) *versus* macro-structuring of knowledge (at levels higher than what is captured in a single entry).

This chapter explores comparable challenges of representation elsewhere, and examines how solutions found in such areas recommend themselves to terminography, the multi-stage activity that culminates in a structured collection of concepts and terms of a specialised field. The task in this chapter amounts to finding out how insights provided by concept theory can be translated into strategies that ensure that terminology resources have enhanced knowledge-mediating potentials.

6.1 Notional representation in lexicography

In the introduction to his dictionary, *Der Deutsche Wortschatz nach Sachgruppen* which was first published in 1933,[1] Dornseiff gives a detailed account, dating from Greek antiquity, of lexicographical collections that do not structure their material alphabetically. The organising principle is expressed by one or the other of the following terms: ideas, internal logic, concepts, themes, contexts, etc.

6.1.1 *Motivations and theoretical premises of non-alphabetical representation*

In articles and/or introductions to lexicographical works they have authored, Roget, Wartburg, Dornseiff and Baldinger justify their preference for non-alphabetical ordering. Four major points may be distilled.

The first may be labelled *precision and stylistic aptness in communication*. This very practical objective indeed underlies Roget's eponymous thesaurus. *Roget's Thesaurus of English Words and Phrases*[2] offers the user words and phrases "arranged, not in alphabetical order as they are in a Dictionary, but according to the *ideas* which they express" (p. xxi). This structure enables the user to "readily select, out of the ample collection spread out before his eyes [...] those expressions which are best suited to his purpose, and which might not have occurred to him without such assistance" (*ibid.*). As Dornseiff who also makes the same point in his *Deutsche Wortschatz nach Sachgruppen* notes, only an onomasiological or conceptual structure enables a user to find answers to questions such as: How would a school pupil express this idea? How would adults put it, etc.? (p. 55). The alphabet is clearly a hindrance in the attainment of these objectives.

The second motivation may be labelled *pedagogical* and refers to arguments why the lexicographical work ought to be valued of and by itself, and not simply as an ancillary to communication. Dornseiff views his work in the context of the following opinion expressed by Hermann Paul:

> Given that a dictionary ought to be a work of intrinsic value, not a mere reference tool resorted to during reading, any departure from happenstance alphabetical ordering that can bring about real context-based classifications must be viewed as an effort worthy of commendation (Paul, quoted by Dornseiff 1970: 29; my translation from the German)

---

1. All references here are to the 1970 edition.

2. The first edition of the Thesaurus appeared in 1852. Except otherwise stated, all references in this work are to the 1982 edition prepared by Susan M. Lloyd.

Baldinger (1956: 380f) argues that any 'scientific' dictionary that seeks to instruct must be conceptually structured. His premise, (German) *Erkenntnis bedeutet Erkennen von Zusammenhängen*, treats knowledge as being all about knowing how things are interrelated. Compare the formulation of this premise to the one by Eisele (see Section 4.9.4). Roget similarly speaks of "the sphere of mental vision" being greatly expanded as a consequence of reviewing words of analogous signification, presenting an idea from diverse standpoints (p. xxiii).

The third point has to do with *research applications*. As a consequence of developments in field theory in linguistics in the early decades of the 20th century, the structure of the vocabulary increasingly came to be seen not just as a reflection of the world picture of a language community, but also (often through the latter) as a more effective strategy for studying meaning change. Writing in 1939, Wartburg (1939 [1972: 10]) deplored the fact that lexicographical practice of the time hardly reflected the ideas of structure and system. Commenting on what was required of a *scientific descriptive dictionary* (by which he, like Baldinger, seems to mean a dictionary for diachronic and synchronic linguistic research), Wartburg notes as follows:

> A scientific descriptive dictionary must abandon the meaningless and unscientific principle of alphabetical order. It will never be possible to understand the true nature of the vocabulary *qua* manifestation of the world-picture current in the community at a particular period, or to discern the general pattern of its internal economy, until alphabetical order is replaced by a system dictated by the state of the language itself at a given moment in time. Alphabetical order is obviously indispensable for purposes of reference, but as a principle of classification its place is in the index (Wartburg 1969: 174; see also Wartburg 1972: 10).[3]

The fourth point relates to the search for a *universal framework of knowledge*; stated differently, a universally applicable framework for the classification of (pre-scientific) knowledge. Rather than contradict the third point which emphasises peculiar world visions, this fourth point may be seen as extending it. Synchronic and diachronic concerns remain, but there is no restriction of application to a particular language and community. This clearly explains the pains which Hallig & Wartburg take in their joint work, *Begriffssystem als Grundlage für die Lexikographie* (1952), to distinguish between words (meanings) and concepts (see Section 4.4). At the end of their introduction to this work, Hallig and Wartburg write thus:

---

3. It may however be noted that even within this particular preoccupation alphabetical order is of more use than is admitted here. See Baldinger (1956: 383ff).

We hope that the concept system presented here provides lexicography with a scheme for representing vocabulary as a structured whole, irrespective of the language, dialect or the epoch to which this vocabulary belongs (p. xxii; my translation from the German).

Roget also hoped that his thesaurus would contribute to the search for a universal scheme for classifying knowledge. He sets his thesaurus against the background of earlier unsuccessful attempts at creating a universal or philosophical language. He thus identifies with concerns of seventeenth-century philosophers like Descartes, Leibniz, George Dalgarno, John Wilkins, etc.[4] These four points call to memory the following knowledge tasks associated with terminology in the contexts of translating, standardisation, teaching and research:

1. consulting a subject specialist in respect of the correct term to be used for one in a series of closely related, and difficult to distinguish, concepts; (recall the problem of distinguishing between closely related or synonymous terms in the translation and knowledge experiments in Chapter 3);
2. the use of terminological methods in speed-training, or the reference to concept schemes to verify concept/term equivalence interlingually;
3. the use of concept schemes to identify lacunae in the conceptual and terminological systems of two languages or schools of thought *vis-à-vis* a given subject field;
4. proceeding from the last point, the use of concept schemes to harmonise the concept systems of a subject area internationally.

With goals akin to terminology's, conceptual lexicography in principle should be of great interest here. Let us examine the structure of one of these conceptually organised lexicographical resources.

6.1.2   *A plan of classification: Roget's Thesaurus*

Roget establishes six primary classes, each of which subdivides into a number of sections (see Figure 6.1).

These classes, like the categories established by Hallig-Wartburg and others, have been criticised as *a priori* and difficult to justify (Lyons 1977: 300). The logic claimed in the thesaurus is most apparent at deeper levels of classification. This is seen better in the tabular synopsis of categories than in the text. See Figure 6.2 below.

---

4. See Robins (1969).

Class	Section	Heads	Class	Section	Heads
1 Abstract relations	1 Existence	1–8	5 Volition: the exercise of the will	1 volition in general	95–616
	2 Relation	9–25		2 Prospective volition	617–616
	3 Quantity	26–59	*Division one:*	3 Voluntary action	676–699
	4 Order	60–84	*Individual volition*	4 Antagonism	700–724
	5 Number	85–107		5 Results of action	725–732
	6 Time	108–142			
	7 Change	143–155	*Division two:*	1 General social volition	733–755
	8 Causation	156–182		2 Special social volition	756–763
				3 Conditional social volition	764–770
				4 Possessive relations	771–816
2 Space	1 Space in general	183–194			
	2 Dimensions	195–242	6 Emotion, religion and morality	1 General	817–823
	3 Form	243–264		2 Personal emotion	824–879
	4 Motion	265–318		3 Interpersonal emotion	880–912
				4 Morality	913–964
3 Matter	1 Matter in general	319–323		5 Religion	965–990
	2 Inorganic matter	324–357			
	3 Organic matter	358–446			
4 Intellect: the exercise of the mind	1 General	447–452			
Division one:	2 Precursory conditions and operations	453–465			
Formation of ideas	3 Materials for reasoning	466–474			
	4 Reasoning processes	475–479			
	5 Results of reasoning	480–504			
	6 Extension of thought	505–511			
	7 Creative thought	512–513			
Division two:	1 Nature of ideas communicated	514–521			
Communication of ideas	2 Modes of communication	522–546			
	3 Means of communicating ideas	547–594			

Figure 6.1: *Roget's Plan of classification*

Class one

Abstract:	1 Existence	2 Nonexistence
Concrete:	3 Substantiality	4 Insubstantiality
Formal (internal/external):	5 Intrinsicality	6 Extrinsicality
Modal (absolute/relative):	7 State	8 Circumstance

Figure 6.2: *Extract from Roget's tabular synopsis of categories*

As can be seen from Figure 6.2, the 'heads' in a section are presented in contrasting pairs. The two-column layout of the original thesaurus precisely served to visually indicate these relationships.[5] This relation between heads may be described as horizontal. A look at the italicised facets shows that horizontal pairs follow one another according to some (non-orthographic) logic. In the texts of revised editions, each head is followed by its negative, where there is one. It is under these heads that English words and phrases were placed by Roget. Entries under each head are further grouped according to their grammatical classes (nouns, adjectives, etc).

Let us examine another kind of thesaurus for further strategies of knowledge representation.

6.2 Non-alphabetical representation in document classification

The field of Information Science or Documentation has developed idea- or theme-centred structuring devices. Classification schemes that divide up areas of knowledge iteratively, such as the Universal Decimal Classification System (UDC) or systems for specific applications, are used by document managers, who would normally implement them to those levels of depth at which specific cataloguing and retrieval needs are deemed to be best served. While establishing

---

5. In his introduction, Roget writes: "For the purpose of exhibiting with greater distinctiveness the relations between words expressing opposite and correlative ideas, I have, whenever the subject admitted, placed them in two parallel columns in the same page, so that each group of expressions may be readily contrasted with those which occupy the adjacent column, and constitute their antithesis" (p. xxix). This layout is (regrettably) changed in revised editions because the "philosophical interest in classification and analysis of words and their relationships, which had played an important part in Roget's conception of his book [...] was now thought to be of negligible interest to most modern readers, who looked on the work as a purely practical aid in communication" (Llyod 1982: xii; on the edition of the thesaurus prepared by her).

relationships between small areas of knowledge or subject headings, these hierarchical schemes may not reach deep enough to the level of individual concepts or terms (Sager 1990: 37).

6.2.1 *Motivation for information retrieval thesauri*

Incidentally the classic versions of these document ordering devices presented problems for classification researchers. For instance, Foskett (1973: 107) observes that a common criticism of classification schemes is that "their linear structure cannot reflect the polyhierarchical relationships which occur between concepts; only one hierarchy can be displayed at the same time".

A solution that has since established itself is the information retrieval thesaurus, which is believed to have been first conceptualised and so called in 1957, possibly with inspiration drawn from Roget's eponymous work (see Gilchrist 1971: 4f). Aitchison & Gilchrist (1972: 26) note that an information retrieval thesaurus is characterised by "its ability to show structural relationships between terms, including hierarchical and non-hierarchical as well as equivalence and associative relationships". From their specification of these relationship classes, the following type-token equations can be established: *equivalence* (corresponds to true synonyms, quasi-synonyms); *hierarchical* (corresponds to generic, polyhierarchy); *non-hierarchical* (corresponds to part/whole, thing/process, thing/application, process/thing, etc.).

Much of the foregoing is strikingly reminiscent of Chapter 4 of this work on concept theory, and shows that classification science is indeed one of the ancestral domains of terminology. The concern with polyhierarchical relationships is what Bowker & Meyer (1993) have popularised within the terminology community under the label of 'multidimensionality'. The knowledge implications of the foregoing are obvious, and call for a close examination of the structure of information retrieval thesauri. It should not matter much that thesauri share with traditional classification schemes the shortcoming of not operating with individual concepts or terms.[6]

6.2.2 *Structure of information retrieval thesauri*

Earlier thesauri, according to Aitchison & Gilchrist (1972: 26, 50), were alphabe-

---

6. Some disagreement may exist on this point. Suggesting that some of the criticisms levelled against the UDC were unfounded, Foskett (1973: 125) notes: "It is also important to remember that thesauri often contain very specific terms which one would not expect to find in a classification scheme".

tically arranged, and made use of cross-references to indicate relationships between descriptors (recommended index/search terms). It was subsequently realised that classification could be used to give "an overall view of (a) subject field and to facilitate the display of hierarchies and other relationships" (Aitchison & Gilchrist 1972: 26). Although in several thesauri there is at least an alphabetical display and a hierarchical display, the latter could be alphabetically structured, and must not therefore be confused with a systematic display, or with thesauri that seek to give an overall view of a field.

6.2.2.1 *Structure of a non-classified thesaurus*
The thesaurus, *A Women's Thesaurus* (1987), has six displays (alphabetical, rotated, hierarchical, subject group, use/do not use, delimiters) which are all alphabetised. Now, in spite of what might be suggested by some display names (e.g. hierarchical), this thesaurus does not seek to reflect a general structure of knowledge about women. By the admission of the editor, the thesaurus "is not itself a classification system, nor is it intended to replace existing classification and cataloguing systems" (p. xiii). To use one of the dichotomies suggested at the beginning of this chapter, it must be at a micro level that this thesaurus captures 'document-concept' relations. The differences which this thesaurus makes between its alphabetical and hierarchical displays may be illustrated by reference to Figure 6.3 and 6.4. It bears repeating that features associated with each display reflect no more than conventions adopted by the thesaurus.

The alphabetical display is by design made to contain the most information for each term: SN (scope note) — often a clarification of acceptation; SG (subject group) — the (sub)field to which the entry term (in bold) belongs; BT (broader term) — a theme under which the entry term is subsumed; NT (narrower term) — a theme that is subsumed in the main entry term; RT (related term) — a theme related to the main entry term in a manner that differs from the (presumably) hierarchical nature of BT and NT. The hierarchical display has a much trimmer record. The entry term is in bold. A theme that is superordinate to the entry term is indicated by a colon, and successively higher levels are indicated by double, triple, ... n colons. A theme that is subordinate to the entry term is indicated by a period, and should there be successive levels of subordination (not the case in Figure 6.4), this would be indicated by a succession of periods.

While the alphabetical display contains maximum information for each main entry term, it limits superordinate and subordinate cross-references (BT and NT) only to one level, that is, the main entry term has no 'grandparents' nor 'grandchildren'. The hierarchical display is not given any such restriction. The fact of this display not having an information category like SN must be seen in terms of

pay equity

    SN *Basing compensation on education, skills, effort, training, and responsibility rather than nonrelevant classifications of sex, age, racial or ethnic background, or other discriminatory classifications.*

    SG Economics and Employment, Law, Government, and Public Policy
    BT equity
    NT comparable worth
         equal pay for equal work
    RT back pay
         careers
         economic equality
         equal pay
         Federal Equitable Pay Practices Act of 1987
         labor legislation
         low pay
         occupational sex discrimination
         sexual division of labor
         wage discrimination
         wage gap
         wages

Figure 6.3: *Extract from alphabetical display to* A Women's Thesaurus

         :electronic media
           television
           . cable television
           . commercial television
           . educational television
           . public television

Figure 6.4: *Extract from hierarchical display to* A Women's Thesaurus

displays complementing one another.

    The foregoing shows how a thesaurus is able to reflect concept relationships at a micro level even though it does not proceed from a general classification of knowledge in its field. It is not obvious in the extracts presented above, but this thesaurus also fully reflects the other dichotomy proposed, that is, (the representation of) concept-based relations *versus* language-based relations. As in other thesauri, *A Women's Thesaurus* also has information categories labelled USE and UF (use for) that often express synonymy of various kinds. USE is the reciprocal of UF. A USE indication suggests that the concept designated by the main entry term is more properly referred to by the term after the USE indication. Thus, "heroic women USE **heroes**" and "heroes UF heroic women, heroines". Besides correcting biases, synonymy-based cross-references may concern abbreviations, acronyms, orthographic variants, the need to standardise indexing terms, etc. It is not too difficult to see how problems in the translation and knowledge protocols might have been avoided by a representation akin to this format. Let us now examine a thesaurus that proceeds from a general structuring of its subject area.

6.2.2.2 *Structure of a classified thesaurus*

The *Thesaurus of Sociological Research Terminology* (Merwe 1974) is described as "a structured and classified vocabulary of terms grouped according to subject headings" (p. 7). It is noted further that even though "an alphabetical list of terms has been added as an extra aid, the thesaurus in a more narrow sense consists of terms that have been arranged in a logical order by subject rather than in an alphabetical order" (*ibid.*).

The domain covered is split into twelve main categories, whose order of presentation more or less mirrors the stages in social research. Thus, the category on *types of research* precedes the one on *selection of research units*, which in turn precedes the category on *data collection*. After this comes the category on *measurement and scale analysis*, etc. A complementary principle, 'junction classification principle', is employed for topics relevant to all, as opposed to, one phase of research. Each of the twelve categories is divided into subcategories some of which have branches. These subdivisions are often arranged in decreasing order of generality. Figure 6.5 below shows how the category on *types of research* is organised.

Each term record consists of a descriptor, unauthorised terms and related terms, as seen in Figure 6.6 below.

The descriptor is the preferred index term. The unauthorised terms were candidate descriptors that fell short of the criteria for the selection of descriptors. Therefore they are "often synonyms or near synonyms of the descriptors" (p. 11). They have other functions not relevant to the current discussion. Related terms show relationships between descriptors belonging to different categories. The thesaurus' justification for related terms is based on the need to address the issue of polyhierarchy raised earlier by Foskett. The thesaurus notes that while classified indexes bring together logically related themes in order to show relationships among various subjects, it "is impossible [...] to group in the same category all the descriptors related in some way" (Merwe 1974: 11). Hence the need for a listing of related terms.

To conclude, the *Thesaurus of Sociological Research Terminology* mediates a structure of its subject matter at macro and micro levels. If the latter level is perceived as doing so less effectively, it would no doubt be as a result of the

C.	Types of research		
C. 0	Types of research	C. 222	Action research
		C. 223	Community self-survey
C. 1	*Types of research (design)*		
C. 11	Descriptive research		
C. 111	Public opinion poll	C. 3	*Types of research (focus)*
C. 112	Marketing research	C. 31	Case study
C. 12	Exploratory research	C. 311	Gestalt research
C. 121	Pilot study	C. 32	Comparative research
C. 122	Survey of literature	C. 321	Cross-section survey
C. 13	Hypothesis testing research	C. 322	Dynamic research
C.131	Explanatory research	C. 323	Cross-national research
C. 132	Experimental research		
C. 132.1	Types of experiments		
C. 132.2	Experimental design	C. 4	*Types of research (units)*
C. 132.21	Control group designs	C. 41	Behavioral research
C. 132.22	Comparative designs	C. 42	Small group research
C.132.23	Representative design	C. 43	Organizational research
		C. 44	Mass communication research
C. 2	*Types of research (objectives)*	C. 45	Community study
C. 21	Basic research	C.46	Aggregative research
C. 211	Methodological research		
C. 22	Applied research		
C. 221	Policy research		
C. 221.1	Evaluation research		
C. 221.2	Prediction research		
C. 221.3	Operations research		

Figure 6.5: *Organisation of a category in the* Thesaurus of Sociological Research Terminology

Category	Descriptors	Unauthorized terms	Related terms
C. 121	*Pilot study*	Test-tube survey	Testing of instruments (C.211)
Pilot study		Trial survey	Unstructured observation (E.15)
		Scouting phase	Pretest of questionnaire (E.234)
		Preliminary investigation	
		Pretest	
		(use *pilot study* if a preliminary investigation is meant; otherwise use *pretest of questionnaire*)	

Figure 6.6: *A descriptor record from category C of* Thesaurus of Sociological Research Terminology

principle of complementary functions. It is also obvious that both concept- and language-based relations are captured. In Section 6.1.1 the motivations for notional representation in lexicography were shown to have parallels in terminology and in its applications. These motivations are strikingly similar to the claims made in the *Thesaurus of Sociological Research Terminology*, for which reason the views of its author are quoted below *in extenso*:

> Because the user's attention is drawn to related subjects which are possibly also of interest, he may discover relationships that he himself had not thought of in the first instance (Merwe 1974: 12).

> It may help the individual researcher with tracing approaches and techniques pertinent to the research he is engaged in. If one is studying specific themes in the field, one may use parts of the thesaurus as a guide for preliminary orientation. Furthermore, as a frame of reference the classification scheme may reveal existing gaps in the craft of research, and stimulate methodological thinking and research on specific topics (Merwe 1974: 14).

6.3 A (systematic) thesaurus model for terminography

General language thesauri *à la* Roget are distinguishable from information retrieval thesauri in a number of respects including data dealt with (words versus documents). But in terms of some of their broad objectives, they overlap with each other, and also with those objectives that are normally assigned to a terminological resource. Seen in the light of these goals, many of the difficulties encountered by experimental subjects in Chapter 3 suggest that a thesaurus-like format recommends itself to terminography. In recommending systematic ordering of specialised dictionaries, Picht & Draskau (1985: 132) could very well have been referring to the problems of the experimental subjects in Chapter 3. Picht & Draskau write that such dictionaries facilitate the selection of appropriate terms during translation because they enable the user to "understand conceptual coherence". In other words, a translator is less likely to "lose his bearings in the immediate conceptual environment of the concept to be translated". When the difficulty of the experimental subjects with "adjournment" terms is recalled, the significance of the latter view is better appreciated. Sager (1990: 203) indeed notes that "the most appropriate form of classifying and presenting terms is via a format which owes much to the principles of thesaurus construction".

In terminological resources elaborated by such pioneers as Schlomann, Wüster, or produced under the auspices of standards bodies like the DIN, certain features associated with thesaural formats are in evidence. Specially developed classifications, the UDC classification, or a combination of both serve as ordering device in these resources. Figures 6.7 and 6.8 are sample term records from sources cited in Felber (1984).

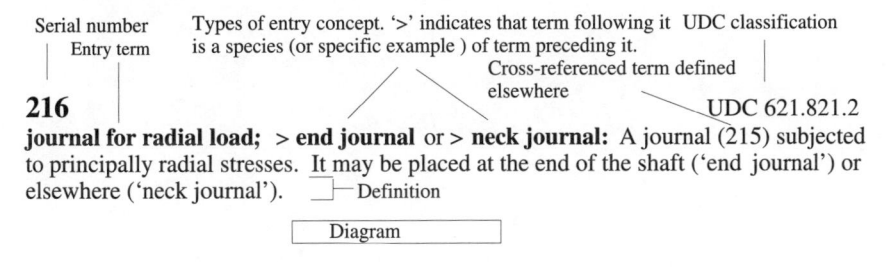

Serial number — Types of entry concept. '>' indicates that term following it is a species (or specific example) of term preceding it. — UDC classification
Entry term
Cross-referenced term defined elsewhere

216   UDC 621.821.2
journal for radial load; > end journal or > **neck journal:** A journal (215) subjected to principally radial stresses. It may be placed at the end of the shaft ('end journal') or elsewhere ('neck journal').   ⟵ Definition

Diagram

Figure 6.7: *A commented term record from Wüster's* The Machine Tool

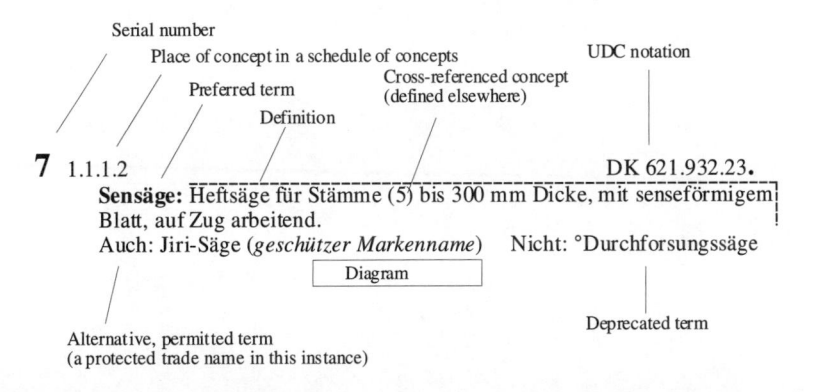

Serial number
Place of concept in a schedule of concepts   UDC notation
Preferred term   Cross-referenced concept (defined elsewhere)
Definition

7   1.1.1.2   DK 621.932.23.
Sensäge: Heftsäge für Stämme (5) bis 300 mm Dicke, mit senseförmigem Blatt, auf Zug arbeitend.
Auch: Jiri-Säge (*geschützer Markenname*)   Nicht: °Durchforsungssäge

Diagram

Deprecated term
Alternative, permitted term
(a protected trade name in this instance)

Figure 6.8: *A commented term record from a 1964 DIN standard on handsaws for wood*

Whichever classification is adopted, and however (other) thesaural features are specifically interpreted, the net result is the mediation of knowledge on concept- and language-based relations among terms at both macro and micro levels. At the latter level, Wüster indeed uses an elaborate symbolic notation system for expressing language- and concept-based relations: synonym/quasi-synonym [;], bad term [°], parts of a term that may be optionally omitted [( )], species-genus relationship (<), genus-species relationship (>), etc.

CHAPTER 7

Terminology, Text and Technology

The discourse on, and practice of, terminology is presently in a phase of rapid evolution. With the experiments reported earlier in retrospect, and the terminology resource described in Chapter 8 in prospect, this chapter will report on aspects of this evolution.

The last three chapters sought to provide a framework for understanding the issues raised in the translation and knowledge experiments. The chapters also made it possible to infer how terminology practice might deal with these issues. For instance, it would have been inferred that solution pathways to problems raised in the translation experiments lie in: (1) subject delimitation (i.e. defining the scope of resources, etc.), and (2) in involving subject experts (to obtain terms, collocations, etc.). Besides also sharing in the issue of subject delimitation, the knowledge experiment raised the question of representation, for which formats in thematic lexicography and document classification systems recommended themselves.

Useful as these solution pathways may be in and of themselves, recent advances suggest that many of these paths would have to go through other frameworks for enhanced results of terminology management.

7.1 Complementary frameworks

Let us examine the bases for broader frameworks. With respect to the acquisition of concepts and terms, concept relations, collocations, insights were offered in Chapters 4, 5 and 6 that help the terminologist to better manage the introspection or intuition of resource persons, that is, subject specialists. But it still is the case that the terminologist, being often an outsider to the field, remains dependent all through on the resource person or specialist in whose field a resource is being produced. Most terminologists with some experience of involvement in language planning (specifically, large scale creation of terms) have a tale or two to tell on their ordeal in getting the cooperation of subject specialists. Now, while not contesting expert collaboration, the sense of a report on a cost-benefit evaluation of several terminology management scenarios is actually that a less subject specialist-centred approach is more economical (time, cost). Qualitatively, the result of this strategy is not seen as inferior to that obtained in a more specialist-focused setting (Nykänen 1993).[1] Given the optimism expressed in Nykänen's study, and the case thus made for a more terminologist-centred approach, the following question then arises: how can the terminologist take on more of the expert's responsibilities and less of the expert's time?

With respect to the representation of concepts and terms, insights from classification systems as well as from language and documentation thesauri were offered that provide an alternative to alphabetisation, thereby improving the claims of any 'systematically' ordered terminology to being a knowledge resource. Ahmad & Rogers (1993) are right in noting that, traditionally, when terminologists speak of systematic or conceptual ordering they have generally meant ordering according to classification systems, etc. Now, leaving aside the subjectivity (see Sager 1990; Merwe 1974) that are inherent in them, these schemes offer a largely fixed or static model of, and access to, knowledge; they do not easily allow for the representation of multidimensional concept relations (several valid relations or categorisations of a given concept); they also do not easily permit the representation of non-hierarchical concept relations. The question that arises, then, is: how can the representation of terminology better reflect a theory of concept relations as well as allow for a more efficient management of, and means of reasoning over, terminological concepts?

Answering the questions posed in the preceding two paragraphs takes us into some of the more recent areas of research and development in terminology. Frameworks examined below include text linguistics, *Fachsprache* (study of special languages), corpus linguistics, information technology, language engineering and artificial intelligence.

7.2 Knowledge in text: Inferences from text linguistics

It has been observed that, often, when people come into contact with text, "the knowledge which they acquire is [...] highly structured, consisting of complex

---

[1]. It is of course assumed that the terminologist (who is not a subject specialist) is sufficiently grounded in the theory and practice of terminology to be able to easily unlock the ontology of knowledge in the specialised domain in question.

networks of concepts and semantic relations that connect concepts into highly propositional structures" (Frederiksen 1977: 57). Consistent with this observation is the thinking that a text's structure may reflect the structure of the knowledge in the producer of the text.

Now, agreeing with the above views does not have to lead to a naive claim that knowledge in a scientific text, for instance, is in all particulars isomorphous with the corresponding extra-lingual/textual reality. Budin (1993) sees any such assumption as a fiction. In the sociology of knowledge where there has been some concern with textual analysis, the evidence which Budin finds points consistently to one fact: contexts have an impact on the shape of written knowledge. There is of course also the issue of textualisation and its knowledge transforming effects.

Nonetheless, support for Frederiksen's view of texts as knowledge sources can be found in several sources. Hoffmann (1991: 160), although clearly aware of the impact of communication context on LSP text production, makes the point that "most scientific subjects can only be treated according to their inherent logic, so that part of the communicational framework is neutralized". The latter qualification would seem quite important, as is easily confirmed by readers familiar with the distinction which Greg Myers makes between the *narrative of nature* and the *narrative of science* (Myers 1990).

Similarly supportive of Frederiksen's views would be the correlation of (some) standards of textuality with discourse production models. Seven standards of textuality are postulated in Beaugrande & Dressler (1981 [1994]), Beaugrande (1980), etc. They are:

1. *cohesion*, which measures the degree to which grammatical dependencies or connectivities activated by a surface text conform to the preferential connectivities that constitute the syntactic norms of a language;
2. *coherence*, which describes the particular knowledge configuration (concepts and their connectivity) to which the surface text gives expression, and is assessed by reference to preferential conceptual configurations in the worlds of general and specialised knowledge;
3. *intentionality*, which examines the *raison d'être* of the text, that is, the existence of a goal (entertainment, edification, instruction, etc.) in the pursuit or realisation of which the text is expected to contribute;
4. *acceptability*, which describes the text receiver's determination of the usefulness and relevance of the text for the purpose of attaining a given goal;
5. *informativity*, which seeks to determine how the knowledge choices made in the creation of a text translate into the recipient's perception of text-conveyed knowledge (as known *versus* unknown, given *versus* new), and what

the implications of these choices are in the processing resources expended on the text, *ipso facto*, on the level of reader-interest the text is able to sustain;
6. *situationality*, which describes the context from which the text derives its relevance, and that helps to resolve surface text ambiguities;
7. *intertextuality*, which investigates what pre(textual)knowledge might be required if the processing of a current text is to be facilitated.[2]

In discourse production models, a text is normally seen as the outcome of a series of communicative decisions made by a speaker or a writer. In Frederiksen's model, the decisions involve:
1. selection of a *message domain* from the wide array of domains comprised in the speaker or writer's store of facts about the world;
2. formation of a *message base* by retrieving (from the message domain) information units intended for verbalisation in text;
3. formation of a *text base* through the structuring of information units from the message base;
4. text generation through production in writing or speech according to grammatical rules.

In a correlation of the textuality standards with these four stages, there might be some discussion as to what standard belongs (exclusively or not) to what stage. The standard of coherence would be a strong candidate for the text base stage. This is evident when one thinks of constructs like frames, schemas, plans and scripts which are knowledge formatting patterns, and, in a sense, illustrations of text base processes. Studies of textual coherence are investigations of the concepts and the concept relations instantiated in these knowledge formats as captured in text. From a writer's perspective, the selection of 'bill' as a *message base* from the *message domain* of legislative concepts could raise *text base* questions relating to whether one wishes to essentially discuss types of bills (frame), the standard processing of a bill (schema), or railroading the passage of a bill that is controversial (plan). To each format, particularly the first two, there would correspond a more or less unique set of concept relations (partitive, sequential, etc.) which would be retrieved by an analysis of textual coherence.

Flowing from the foregoing is the plausible thesis that a substantial part of

---

2. Now, it is a moot point what stretch of language is text or not text, and how usable these criteria are in a variety of research preoccupations with the text (see the criticism in Sager 1994: 89f). There is however no disputing the point that the formulation of these largely interdependent standards of textuality advances our understanding of the text.

the knowledge possessed by an expert and needed by a terminologist can in fact be obtained in the relevant text produced by the expert.

7.3 Objectifying knowledge in text: Insights from corpus linguistics

Establishing that an expert-authored text is source of (structured) knowledge evidence is not to vouch for the quality of this evidence — its reach, representativeness or skewness, epistemological validity, etc. Indeed, the setback suffered in the 1960s and 1970s by corpus linguistics — a methodology for studying language on the basis of a statistical analysis of empirical data — was occasioned by Chomsky's deprecation of performance data along similar lines: non-representativeness, biased, incorrect, unfaithful reflection of competence, etc. (McEnery & Wilson 1996: 8ff).

The rebirth of corpus linguistics in the 1980s, and its growing popularity is not just a reflection of the widespread availability of computers, with the entailed possibilities of faster processing of data that are larger than could have been imagined in the 1960s.[3] The growth of corpus linguistics is also the outcome of considerable thought having been given to data collection procedures that address some of Chomsky's criticisms. Perhaps most importantly, it reflects acceptance of a certain conception of the nature of the object (i.e. language) being investigated. For instance, Halliday's probabilistic approach to grammatical description provides a theoretical status for corpus frequencies in some kinds of language investigation (see Halliday 1992).

To connect the above two points: sampling and representativeness are crucial in the building of a corpus from which it is intended to infer tendencies and the proportions of these tendencies in a language (McEnery & Wilson 1996). A thoughtful diversification of text sources ensures that source-specific idiosyncrasies are statistically insignificant, and therefore obscured (see Sinclair 1991: 17). But these activities do not by themselves wholly establish that the results obtained can be generalised. It is a theory of the nature of the object under investigation — in the construction of which these activities and results no doubt contribute — that really says, when taken together with these results, just how much of a reliable *explicandum* of language the corpus really is.

The implications of the foregoing for knowledge in specialised language or

---

3. Indeed the term 'corpus' is increasingly less frequently encountered in an acceptation other than machine-readable.

texts are obvious. Given the theory of lexical closure of LSPs — discussed in Section 7.4.1 below — a corpus of specialised texts can lay claims to objective evidence, perhaps to a degree that cannot be claimed by an LGP corpus. A further basis for this suggestion, and for why size of the specialised corpus may not be too crucial, stems from another feature of LSPs. While the production of LSP texts, like those of an LGP, is governed by various communicative circumstances (intentions, receiver, situation, etc.), Hoffmann, as was seen in the previous section, makes the point that the inherent logic of scientific subjects is only partly affected by the communicational framework. To the extent that this is correct, the advantage of building very large specialised corpora in well defined areas may lie more in the identification of synonymous designations and in explicating (assisting inferencing) rather than in the generation of new and substantive knowledge; that is, knowledge not found in a smaller but carefully sampled corpus. For the building of specialised corpora for terminology, Ahmad (1993: 61) has suggested three text genres worth considering: instructional (textbooks, technical manuals, encyclopaedic texts), informative (learned papers, advanced treatises, etc.), imaginative (public information materials, 'made-simple' texts, etc.).

7.4 Specialised text and Artificial Intelligence: Heuristics and tools for terminological knowledge acquisition

However peculiar it might be, the language of the specialised text remains an integral part of general language. The specialised text is therefore an admixture of domain-specific language and knowledge, and general language and knowledge. Given this reality, then, identifying means of objectifying specialised knowledge is not coterminous with actually identifying this knowledge. This is true for man, but even more so for a machine which is to simulate the human expert. Indeed without some heuristics, or rules-of-thumb, and appropriate tools, the putative gains in economy of a textual or 'less specialist-centred approach' to terminology management can hardly be realised.

A convenient starting point is to recall the kinds of specialised knowledge required by the terminologist. First, the terminologist is interested in the concepts and terms of a domain, and these have to be filtered out from non-domain items. Terms could be single-unit or multi-unit. Secondly, the terminologist is interested in acquiring the relations obtaining between extracted concepts or terms. Thirdly, the terminologist would require some descriptive or definitional data on the concepts extracted. Fourthly, for purposes of facilitating the use of terms in discourse, the terminologist requires information on the environment (collocates, presence or absence of determiners, etc). What heuristics and tools could be of help here?

7.4.1 *Statistics, LSP texts and term extraction*

In descriptions of languages for special purposes (LSPs), statistical analyses of word classes are common. Hoffmann (1985: 136ff), for instance, provides the following descriptions held to be generally valid for several West European languages and Russian: nouns constitute up to 40% of LSPs while accounting for 28% in LGP; adjectives account for over 16% of LSP texts compared to 10% in LGP; adverbs in LSP come to about 4% compared to 8% in LGP; verbs are anywhere between a half and a third less frequent in LSP compared to LGP; there are no significant differences between LGP and LSP as far as determiners, prepositions and conjunctions are concerned. For more language-specific descriptions, see Fluck (1991) for German; Kocourek (1982 [1991]) for French; and Sager, Dungworth & McDonald (1980) for English.

On the face of it, nothing in these figures indicates the proportion of LSP or domain-specific concepts actually comprised in each of these classes. However, with respect to nouns at least, theoretical evidence — reification in subject fields (Hoffmann 1985) of certain text types — and empirical data (Ahmad/Davies/Rogers 1993: 29) confirm that domain-specific concepts are the items mostly comprised in this class.

It has been hypothesised by Ahmad that, in English, closed class words (determiners, pronouns, prepositions, modals, conjunctions) are statistically not very significant as forms taken on by, or entering into the formation of, terms. But in any statistical enumeration of words in a text (LGP or LSP) these closed class words would have the highest frequency ratings. This is confirmed by Tables 7.1a and 7.1b taken from Ahmad, Davies & Rogers (1993).

How the foregoing yields a rule-of-thumb for identifying terms should be obvious momentarily.

LSPs, in contrast to general language, are characterised by lexical closure. Because, comparatively speaking, LSP vocabularies allow for less linguistic creativity, they tend to be more finite than those of LGP. McEnery & Wilson (1996: 147ff) test this lexical closure hypothesis in three corpora (one suspected specialised and two suspected general). The type/token ratios for the general language corpora were 1:53.14 and 1:17.18 respectively (i.e., each word in the first corpus is repeated 53 times, and 17 times in the second). On the other hand, the type/token ratio of the specialised text was 1:139.69. This means that each

Table 7.1a: *Frequency ratings of closed class words in general language corpus*

General language corpora

COBUILD Birmingham 17,900,000 words			Brown University 1,013,644 words			Lancaster-Oslo/Bergen 1,013,737 words		
Word	Abs. freq	Rel. freq (%)	Word	Abs. freq	Rel. freq (%)	Word	Abs. freq	Rel. freq (%)
the	1,023,506	5.72	the	69,971	6.90	the	68,351	6.74
of	503,284	2.81	of	36,411	3.59	of	35,745	3.53
and	475,869	2.66	and	28,852	2.85	and	27,873	2.75
to	448,378	2.50	to	26,149	2.58	to	26,781	2.64
a	388,354	2.17	a	23,237	2.29	a	22,647	2.23
in	311,996	1.74	in	21,341	2.11	in	21,248	2,1

Table 7.1b: *Frequency ratings of closed class words in special language corpus*

Special language corpora (Surrey collections)

Mammography corpus 24,458 words			Automotive engineering corpus: 372 274 words			Hydrology corpus 34,698 words		
Word	Abs. freq	Rel. freq (%)	Word	Abs. freq	Rel. freq	Word	Abs. freq	Rel. freq (%)
the	1,683	5.91	the	26,634	7.15	the	2,255	6.50
of	1,074	3.77	of	12,434	3.34	to	1,334	3.84
a	789	2.77	and	8,792	2.36	of	1,226	3.53
in	710	2.49	to	8,319	2.23	and	912	2.63
and	710	2.49	in	7,823	2.10	a	886	2.55
is	654	2.30	a	7,157	1.92	that	750	2,16

Abs. freq = absolute frequency; Rel. freq = relative frequency

word is repeated 139 times. The specialised text was found to reach lexical closure, or to enumerate itself, within the first 110,00 words counted; that is, after this threshold no new words occurred. On the other hand, the general language corpora continues to grow with no indications of reaching lexical closure. The foregoing is evidence of the relatively limited lexical resources used in LSP.

To tie these findings into the word class analysis: the high incidence of repetition of LSP-specific tokens (which to a large extent are open class words) means that in a statistical count of undifferentiated tokens in an LSP corpus, the domain-specific tokens would have enhanced prospects of showing up within the high frequency bracket which is otherwise occupied exclusively by closed class words. One heuristic for terms in specialised texts may therefore be formulated thus: in a frequency count, an open class word token occurring in the environment of (that is, competing for ranks with) closed class words is a candidate term. Referring back to Tables 7.1a and 7.1b, the tokens 'breast' and 'cancer' (certified as terms) rank 11th and 21st respectively in the mammography corpus, but place 5000th and 8000th respectively in the (general language) Lancaster/Oslo-Bergen corpus (Ahmad/Davies/Rogers 1993: 20).

System Quirk, the kit developed by Khurshid Ahmad's Artificial Intelligence (AI) Research Group at Surrey, has a function in its text analysis tool that operates on the foregoing premises. The 'weirdness' command assumes that open class words in LSP texts have a uniqueness in their frequency that is not encountered in LGP texts, and it exploits this difference to output candidate terms. A relative frequency is computed for each word form in the LSP text that is read into the system. For each word in the system's reference LGP corpus there is also a stored relative frequency value. Where a word form in the LSP corpus also exists in the selected LGP corpus, its relative frequency is divided by the stored relative frequency of the same word form in the LGP corpus. The further away a word form is from unity (zero) the higher is its coefficient of weirdness. This in turn suggests that the word's claims to terminological status are stronger. Words not found in the LGP corpus are labelled 'infinity' and have the strongest claims, while closed class words would have a value close to zero because of their stable frequency in both kinds of texts. Figure 7.1 is a sample coefficient of weirdness result generated by System Quirk.

The foregoing describes the procedure for extracting single-word terms. For multi-word terms, System Quirk has a function, 'ferret', which runs on the premise that the positioning in text of open class words relative to closed class words and punctuation marks is a heuristic. It is held that terms in specialised texts tend to be particularly sandwiched between closed class words, or punctuation, or a combination of both (Fulford 1992). As it runs, ferret attempts to match words and punctuation in text on the basis of a specified lexicon of selected closed class words, any LGP words that may be predetermined to be non-term elements, and punctuation. A hit that is not followed by another hit signals a candidate term whose length (but for a default maximum of 5 words) is only determined by another lexicon hit in the string. An illustration: if the word 'important' had been previously determined as a non-term element, and included in a lexicon along with punctuation marks and closed class words, then the three terms (in bold) would be output by a ferret run over the following text sample:

Lead and **tetramethyl lead** are important **fuel additives**.
(Source: Fulford 1992).

7.4.2   Statistics, LSP texts and concept relations

Besides terms, there are other kinds of terminologically-relevant knowledge embedded in text. Concern with the linguistic manifestations of conceptual

=== /a/anorien/vol/mcs/ai/corpus/Lex_Res/analyses/bassey/American/billaw.txt ===

Abs.freq	Rel.freq	
7	inf	adjourns
1	inf	allot
1	inf	amendable
1	inf	amendatory
3	inf	apportionment
1	inf	authorizes
1	inf	bicameralism
2	inf	buzzers
34	inf	cloture
46	inf	conferees
3	inf	engrossment
1	inf	excerpted
1	inf	expeditiously
1	inf	expires
3	inf	filibustered
2	inf	filibustering
12	inf	filibusters
1	inf	foment
5	inf	germaneness
14	inf	gopher
77	4346.904785	quorum
26	2935.572021	appropriations
132	1862.959229	senators
442	1217.188477	senate
245	1063.927734	amendments
114	0.985857	their
16	0.984472	together
1058	0.828595	and

Comments
- Notice the low coefficient of the last three items (closed class/invariable words).
- The various tokens of certain types (amend..., filibuster..., etc) show that our corpus was not lemmatised.
- Besides the last three items, there are some false candidates (e.g. gopher).

Figure 7.1: *Coefficient of weirdness result generated by System Quirk, with comments*

relations leads Ahmad & Fulford (1992) to posit knowledge probes as heuristics. Knowledge probes are akin to diagnostic frames (Cruse 1986: 13f) and formulae (Lyons 1981) — both being labels for linguistic signals of semantic relations: X is a type of Y, X is made from Y, X is part of Y, etc. Ahmad & Fulford build an archive of these knowledge probes, and investigate their efficiency in the automatic acquisition of relations holding between concepts or terms of a specialist corpus. Some results of their test of the efficiency of these probes are presented in Table 7.3 taken from Ahmad & Fulford (1992). I reflect only results that show an efficiency of 60% and above.

Table 7.3: *Efficiency of select knowledge probes*

	Number of experimental probes	Probes above 60% efficiency	Hits	Frequency of probe in corpus	Efficiency (%)
Causal relations	23	affect*	3	3	100.00
		cause*	12	12	100.00
		causing	2	2	100.00
		change%	4	4	100.00
		lead* to	4	4	100.00
		let	1	1	100.00
		effect*	11	13	84.62
		influenc*	3	5	60.00
		produce%	6	10	60.00
Material relations	9	composed of	2	3	66.67
		material	2	3	66.67
Partitive relations	17	consist*	5	5	100.00
		constituent%	1	1	100.00
		factor%	1	1	100.00
		zone%	1	1	100.00
		contain*	70	72	97.22
		component%	11	12	91.67
		compris*	8	9	88.89
		incorporat*	4	6	66.67
		includ*	9	14	64.29

'*' is a wildcard denoting any number of characters while '%' denotes any single character

Based on the hits from the more efficient probes, the terminologist is able to declare valid relationships between the concepts in the working specialised corpus with minimal help from a domain expert.

Given that definitions typically declare relationships between domain concepts, it is easy to understand Ahmad & Fulford's optimism that knowledge probes could be further refined to assist in the assembling of definitions — perhaps in a way that is more efficient than the running of large span concordances.

7.4.3 *LSP texts and extraction of term collocates*

The importance of collocates was stressed in Chapter 5. Collocates being words that occur in some proximity to a term (single or multiword), they are spotted by methods which identify the textual neighbourhood of terms. Figure 7.2 is a sample System Quirk concordance result (text span definition of five words right and left of node).

```
==Command::concordance Date::Tuesday, 13 August 1996 CPU used:: 0:2:2
==Vocabulary: 161
==Total words: 45242
==File:1/vol/mcs/ai/corpus/Lex_Res/analyses/bassey/American:billaw.txt
===============================================================
              = = = = = bill 582 = =
1_1037             bill originating in senate xvii .
1_3518     bill originating in senate the preceding
1_60   when a bill reaches a committee it is
1_203  the whole cannot pass a bill ; instead it reports the
1_351  a president vetoes a bill by refusing to sign it
1_401  he or she may write a bill in such a way that
1_403  any different places where a bill may die .
1_423         allow a markup of a bill that does not command enough
1_524  the floor to discharge a bill from the committee of jurisdiction
```

Figure 7.2: *Extract of a concordance output from System Quirk*

It might be pointed out that besides the largely statistics-based heuristics and tools discussed so far, other term extraction strategies have been reported. Two of such strategies may be designated 'linguistic' and 'conceptual' respectively. The linguistic approach described by Heid *et al.* (1996) assumes that, when applied to a corpus, operations such as morphosyntactic analysis, part-of-speech (POS) tagging, lemmatisation, etc. prepare the corpus for complex querying; they in fact yield information which, when combined with some other knowledge, provide a heuristic for performing searches to obtain candidate terms. Single terms are automatically extracted by searching the lemmatised text, taking into account affixes resulting from morphosyntactic analyses, and/or by using a set of independently obtained domain-specific roots. For Heid's test-language (German) and -field (automobile engineering), some of these recurrent roots are *fahr*, *trieb*, *motor*, *brems*, etc. For multiword terms the tool generates the POS shapes formulated in the query via searching the POS-tagged text. The absence of a phrase-level parser in German (Heid 1996: 142, 147) — the reason for the POS search — yields significant noise betraying false bracketing.

The conceptual approach reported by Nkwenti-Azeh (1994) applies only to the automatic extraction of multiword terms. The strategy derives from an in-depth study of the positional and combinatorial properties of terms in a specific field as evidenced by a representative corpus of either texts or lists of multiword terms. An important assumption of this strategy is that there is a high incidence of reuse of lexical items in multiword terms, at least in the field of satellite communications which is used as case study. Elements of multiword terms are found to occur in several unique (initial, medial and final) as well as multiple positions. Through a study of these distribution patterns, it is held that inferences can be drawn on crucial positions revealing conceptual or domain imposed constraints. In the satellite communications data, two key positions identified are P1–2 (i.e. lexical items occurring as the first element of two-element compounds) and P1–3 (lexical items occurring in the final position of two-, three- or n-element compounds). Two kinds of combinatorial constraints — grammatical and conceptual — determine what sequence of positionally tagged lexical items is a candidate term. Some sample conceptual constraints are expressed by the following rules:

> Rule: Any sequence of lexical item 1 + lexical item 2 is a candidate term if lexical item 1 has a positional value P1–2 and lexical item 2 has a positional value P3–3. From a positionally tagged corpus this rule would generate (a) and (b) as acceptable candidate terms but not (c):
> a. spectral[P1–2] components[P3–3]
> b. baseband[P1–2] channels[P3–3]
> c. standard[P2–3, P3–3] stations[P3–3]
>
> Rule: Any sequence of lexical item 1 + lexical item 2, ..., + lexical item n is a candidate term if: the positional values for lexical item1 include P1–2, the positional values of the last item P3–3; and the positional value for the intervening items include P2–3. This rule would generate (d) and (e) as acceptable, but not (f):
> d. first[P1–1] [P1–2]
>   commercial[P1–2] [P2–3]
>   geostationary[P-1] [P1–2] [P2–3]
>   communication [P1–2] [P2–3] [P3–3]
>   satellite[P1–1] [P1–2] [P2–3] [P3–3]
> e. first[P1–1] [P1–2]
>   commercial[P1–2] [P2–3]
>   direct[P1–2] [P2–3]
>   broadcasting[P1–2] [P1–2] [P2–3] [P3–3]

f. first[P1–1] [P1–2]
    operational[P1–2]
    broadcasting[P1–2] [P1–2] [P2–3] [P3–3]
    satellite[P1–1] [P1–2] [P2–3] [P3–3]
    system [P1–2] [P2–3] [P3–3]

The tools and procedures discussed (statistical, linguistic and conceptual) are all based on heuristics, which means their success rates cannot be unqualified. To quote Pearl (1985: 73), "it is often said that heuristic methods are unpredictable; they work wonders *most* of the time, but may fail miserably some of the time". To limit the discussion to term extraction: the heuristics upon which a tool functions must be such that the error margin in results generated is small enough to limit the terminologist's reliance upon a domain expert, at least initially. Indeed from the practising terminologist's standpoint, the amount of domain knowledge required by each tool might be considered a crucial criterion. In determining the statistical threshold for frequency queries or in striving for optimal ferret runs, the user of Ahmad's tool would be helped by some knowledge of terms in a domain (e.g. degree of LGP-LSP lexical interface). The user of Heid's tool would need to know domain-recurrent radicals. Nkwenti-Azeh's tool requires a study of combination patterns of terms. Some degree of computational support can be relied upon to meet these preliminary requirements.

7.5 Knowledge structure-simulated representation of terminology

In his *Dream Machine*, Ted Nelson who coined the term 'hypertext' writes that "[i]ntertwingularity is not generally acknowledged — people keep pretending they can make things hierarchical, categorizable and sequential when they can't. Everything is deeply intertwingled" (quoted by McKnight *et al.* 1991).

In Section 7.1 it was claimed that representation formats in traditional thematic lexicography and documentation systems had shortcomings as attempts at modelling knowledge. The question was posed as to how the representation of terminology could better reflect the multidimensionality of concepts, the diversity of relations into which concepts enter (and not just relations that are hierarchical), the non-static nature of knowledge, etc.

In computer environments, the question of knowledge representation has arisen in such specific contexts as on-line software documentation, development of expert systems, computer-assisted learning, Internet search engines, etc. Representation formalisms adopted in most cases reflect certain hypotheses concerning the very nature of human knowledge, how it is created, retained or stored in the memory, accessed, manipulated, applied, etc. Now, if some of the knowledge hypotheses underlying the representation formalism in one or the other application are relevant to terminological conceptions of knowledge, then the relevant formalism(s) would quite naturally be worth considering in terminology.

Associativity, non-linearity, (re)generation may be taken as key words that express some hypotheses about knowledge. Associativity will be used here to refer to the nature of stored knowledge (particularly in long term or conceptual memory); non-linearity to how knowledge is accessed; and (re)generation to how new knowledge is created and applied. Associativity, under which might be subsumed constructs like interconnectedness, network, web, etc., describes knowledge elements as existing, not as discrete entities, but in chunks, such that the activation of one element in the chunk is capable of activating others. Of the many reasons why these chunks or subspaces may be difficult to define, there is the fact that the motivation for chunked elements can be conceptual/semantic (e.g. types of a concept) or formal (homonyms referring to different concepts), or combinations of both. Non-linearity holds that because of the non-static interconnectedness of knowledge — an attribute which allows for different valid knowledge configurations — access to knowledge must permit some randomness. The apt metaphor employed by Dede (1988) to describe an aspect of this randomness is that of "the first needle found in the haystack acting as a magnet which then collects the remaining needles". Because non-linearity also involves movement in different directions, including returning to paths already traversed, the magnet-needle(s) will have to be directionally versatile. (Re)generation posits creativity as an attribute of knowledge. Inferencing is a process by which new knowledge is created by deductively reasoning over a given store of knowledge. A representation formalism that seeks to approximate the creative attribute of knowledge must, therefore, allow for inferencing.

When the experiments described in Chapter 3 are recalled, the relevance of these knowledge hypotheses becomes evident. For instance, if 'bill', the first needle found in the Nigerian glossary haystack, had been able to act as magnet, picking up related concepts located elsewhere, then the knowledge protocol of the Nigerian subject might have been much richer.

One or the other of the hypotheses described above underpins such computational knowledge representations as semantic networks, frames, hypertext, conceptual graphs, production rules (if/then) etc., the actual choice depending on the goals of the computational application. For instance, the 'slot' and 'filler' structure of frames would be ideal in an application that sought to represent conceptual characteristics in a way as to make possible the automatic generation of detailed definitions, or the determination of concept equivalents, etc. Two representations are used in connection with the terminology resource developed in this work (see Chapter 8). They are conceptual graphs and hypertext. Below they are briefly described from the standpoint of the knowledge hypotheses they represent.

7.5.1 *Conceptual graphs*

The conceptual graph formalism is used in modelling data for the terminology resource described in Chapter 8. Although the modelling medium is paper, those attributes that make the graph a flexible representation formalism intended for computation are not completely eroded by the shortcomings of the paper medium. This formalism was developed by Sowa (1984), and first applied to terminology by Ahmad and his colleagues (Hook & Ahmad 1992; Ahmad 1994, etc.). The formalism allows for the representation of the interconnected structure of knowledge, and it does so in a flexible way that makes possible different configurations of, and access points to, the same knowledge data ('associativity'/'non-linearity'); by virtue of the foregoing, it supports inferencing ('(re)generation').

In their display form, conceptual graphs are expressed as boxes representing concept-types (substitutable by individuals) and circles representing concept relations, both of which are connected by directed arcs. The circles may be seen as representing the so-called 'typed' links. Figures 7.3a and 7.3b are sample graphs.

Meaningful, true graphs are called canonical graphs. From a starting set of such graphs, other graphs (more complex, for instance) can be obtained through the application of some of the so-called formation rules, in a manner that is partly reminiscent of transformational generative grammar. The join formation rule merges canonical graphs that share a concept node at the point of this common node. By this rule, all the relations which the given concept has with other concepts are displayed, thus revealing links and concept configurations that may not have been evident at the time the simple canonical graphs were entered. The graphs in Figure 7.3a and b are the building blocks for Figure 7.4 below which would be generated by the join rule.

Figure 7.4 shows some of the relationships into which the concept 'joint resolution' enters.

On the interpretation of the graphs, two conventions obtain. In reading in the direction of the arrows, the convention is: "the *relation* (in circle) of *concept$_1$* [box from which arrow originates] is *concept$_2$* [box to which arrow is pointing]". As indicated, Figure 7.3a reads: "type of resolution is joint resolution", while 7.3b reads: "analogy of joint resolution is bill". When reading in the opposite direction of the arrows, the convention requires that the arrow pointing away from the circle be read as "*is (a)* (+ name of relation in circle)", and the one

```
resolution ──▶ (type) ──▶ joint resolution
```

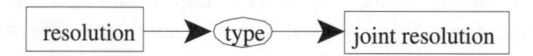

Figure 7.3a: *A canonical graph: 'a type of resolution is joint resolution'*

```
bill ◀── (anal) ◀── joint resolution
```

Figure 7.3b: *A canonical graph: 'an analogy of joint resolution is bill'*

```
           joint resolution
           ▲            ▲
       (anal)        (type)
         │              │
         ▼              │
        bill         resolution
```

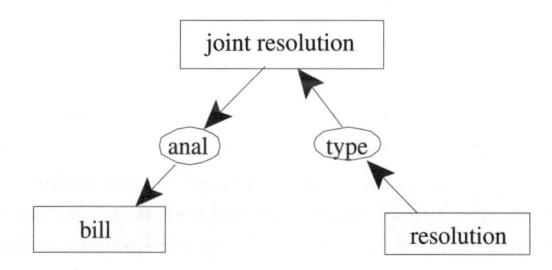

Figure 7.4: *A complex graph*

pointing towards it as "*of*". Thus, Figure 7.3a reads as "joint resolution is type of resolution", and 7.3b as "bill is analogy/analogous to joint resolution". The language of the readings does not have to be impeccable. It is worth stressing that the direction of the arrows, not the positioning of the boxes, is what is important.

The extreme flexibility of the formalism and its suitability for representing terminology stems in part from the fact that it allows for a reinterpretation of concept characteristics as relation nodes. A prototype of the formalism intended as a graphical complement to a textually represented terminology in a management system has been implemented at Ahmad's Artificial Intelligence Research Group in Surrey. In that application, the knowledge in a terminology database (as expressed in simple graphs) can be searched and browsed. The functions of two important commands in this prototype application are described thus:

> The *build* function is designed to take a concept name as input and then search the knowledge base for any relationships that include that concept, outputting a graph for that concept to the user. Using the formation rules, the build function will then create a graph including all of the relations it has found. The *extend* function is designed to take an existing graph, and, given a concept node, to again search the knowledge base for more relationships that include the concept, outputting these as an extension to the graph (Hook & Ahmad 1992: 15).

Because it is arguably more expressive than traditional (tree) formats, the conceptual graph formalism is used for a second-tier data modelling in the resource developed in this work (see Section 8.6). The formalism also makes it possible for the different activities of modelling and representation to be served by the same artefact. In part at least, the limitations of traditional modelling formats presumably explain the observation by Sager (1990: 160) that, although "the terminologist builds a model of the structure of a subset of the subject field", this structure "is not normally presented nor preserved in the dictionary or terminology bank".

7.5.2   Hypertext

In its database environment, the terminology resource developed in this work is presented as a hypertext document *via* the technology in the application with which the resource is managed. As a knowledge representation, hypertext uses the same basic architecture of nodes and links seen in conceptual graphs, the difference being that in the case described here the implementation is in textual environment, as opposed to a graphical one. From a terminology standpoint, a hypertext system frees concepts (the building blocks of propositionally expressed knowledge) from the so-called constraints of sequential access and perusal that are imposed by sentences, paragraphs, pages, sections, different texts, among other boundaries in surface textual world. The shortcomings of linear text need not be exaggerated. Object-oriented documenting, a feature of hypertext, involves the use of such document elements as sentences, paragraphs, etc. and, in the current case, words as "keys and references to other parts of a document or other documents entirely" (McGrew & McDaniel 1989: 89).

Using these keys or nodes, as well as links which serve as pointers, hypertext systems simultaneously create parallel configurations to, and an alternative perusal of, text-conveyed knowledge. This other configuration is based on the principle of modularity of information, according to which "the same node of information can be referenced from multiple locations" (Dede 1988: 97). This is in consonance with the earlier observation that knowledge elements are not static in their interconnectedness. A given concept can occur in a number of different configurations, just like related/relatable concepts may be spatially scattered in text. A linear mode of perusal is clearly a disadvantage here.

7.6   Terminology management systems

Terminology software have high visibility in the range of products originating from the so-called language industries. A 1994 survey identified about eighty of such software (see *TermNet News* 43 & 44). A number of these programs are described in some detail in the proceedings of the 3rd TermNet Symposium on Terminology in Advanced Microcomputer Applications,[4] among other TermNet symposia on the subject. The development of these tools is an acknowledgement of the increasingly widespread access to information technology in the workplace. This obviously suggests that terminology resources are not just being created on, and with substantial assistance from, the computer, but that they are also increasingly being maintained and consulted 'on-line'. There is of course also the influence of the machine (assisted) translation sub-industry.

7.6.1 An overview

A terminology management system (TMS) could support any or a combination of the following stages or substages of work on terminology: (1) acquisition/ extraction of terminological data from text corpora; (2) storage of such data in a manner that facilitates consultation, modification, etc.; (3) construction of concept systems or graphic representation of the relations obtaining among terms in the term base; (4) publishing. Given the importance of all of these (sub)stages to the overall process, it certainly is a strange quirk to exclusively refer, as is commonly the case, to tools associated with (2) and (4) as TMSs. Perhaps this is the case because these tools are the most frequently encountered. In this skewed acceptation, a TMS could allow for all or a combination of the following: user-defined entry structure (that is, fields in a given term/concept record), a variety of query modes (fully specified or fuzzy searches, all or only some fields of the record, language combinations), printing of the stored data (according to a default format or user-specification), modification of data, import and export of data, etc.

A change in the perception of what constitutes a TMS has been underway for a while now. Some years ago, the Artificial Intelligence Laboratory at the University of Ottawa developed a knowledge management system, CODE (conceptually-oriented description environment), which was integrated into a terminology environment, COGNITERM. COGNITERM is a hybrid term bank and knowledge base. The aim is to have the construction of definitions an integral part of a TMS. System Quirk, the software package developed in Khurshid Ahmad's AI group at the University of Surrey, is conceived as an integral workbench. This suite of subprograms supports all of the aforementioned

---

4. Published in 1995 by TermNet (Vienna, Austria).

stages of the terminology management cycle, and related activities like text management. There is reason to expect many more integrated systems modelled after, or combining features of, these pioneering examples. Integration also appears headed in the direction of language processing workbenches in which TMSs and translation systems share a common platform. For now, let us examine MultiTerm®, a tool that addresses concerns (2) and (4) above. This is the tool used in managing the resource described in Chapter 8. MultiTerm® is a product of the language engineering firm, TRADOS.[5]

7.6.2 *MultiTerm: A Case Description of a TMS*

The version of the product used is MultiTerm '95 Plus (professional edition). The description below is a selective and brief presentation that is done with a view to facilitating the account of my actual interaction with the system as reported in Chapter 8.

7.6.2.1 *Database definition*

Effective management of terminology in a TMS environment depends on the definition of the database structure. MultiTerm's flexibility allows for a user-driven definition of the database structure. Three fields are available to the user for this purpose, a fourth being generated automatically by the system.[6] The *index fields* would typically list the languages to be managed by the system. In an entry, a given language's term or synonymous terms for a concept are entered in the corresponding language index field. As the index field is the only sortable field,[7] it can also be used to store other kinds of information (e.g. aspects of bibliographic data) for which rapid access will be required. This is the practice, for instance, in the terminology course run by Schmitz at Cologne's University of Applied Sciences.[8] As not all languages are adequately catered for by the rather restricted 255 characters associated with fonts used in Windows® environments, MultiTerm allows for user-installed fonts. The user is able to specify what index fields (among other kinds of fields) are to be used with what fonts. Twenty

---

5. Coordinates: (Surface-mail in Germany) Hackländerstraße 17, 70184 Stuttgart, Germany; (URL) http://www.trados.com

6. The system (generated) fields reflect administrative information categories like entry number, creation date, creator of the entry, date on which entry was changed, etc.

7. Sorting may be performed according to a default sequence or according to a user-specified order.

8. Professor Dr. Klaus-Dirk Schmitz is thanked for making his course materials available.

index fields are permissible.

Text fields allow for information in free-format text, and such information could apply to an entire entry (*global text field*) or to a specific term (*term-level text field*). Definitions, examples of usage, notes are typical instances of such text fields. Bibliographical information categories (e.g. title of work, etc.) might also be entered here. Up to 62 text fields are permissible. *Attribute fields* allow for further information specification, typically but not exclusively in non free-format text. Information managed as an attribute would usually be of a recurring kind. It could relate to questions of reliability, geographical provenance, etc., and apply to the entire term record (*global attribute*), an individual term in the record (*term attribute*), or to a text field (*field attribute*). A number of values can be specified for each attribute field (e.g. *geographical provenance*: Great Britain, USA, India, Australia, New Zealand; *subject*: political science, zoology, educational administration, veterinary pathology, human medicine, environmental engineering, physical oceanography, language planning).

The user determines, to a large extent, what information is managed in what field. It is on the basis of the defined database structure that users are able to manage (enter, search, etc.) their terminology. Data may be entered into a MultiTerm database in a variety of ways: by directly keying in entries into the defined fields of the database, by importation following a specified routine, or by using the cut & paste strategy to insert data from a word processor document.

7.6.2.2 *Searching*

MultiTerm provides for a variety of search options. *Browsing* is a search strategy that enables the user to view all entries in the selected database one after the other, the sequence being determined by the sort order specified during the database structure definition. The only other constraint to this non-directed search is the language direction (that is, what language has been set as source language, target language). Buttons allow the user to browse forward and backward.

Simple search in non-filter mode allows the user to look up a term in the entire database. Here the user keys a term into the search field, and the term is displayed if it exists. Keying in a truncated form is often enough for the intended search term to be recognised by MultiTerm. The user may also use concept numbers automatically generated by the system for search purposes.

Wildcard search or *global search* enables the user to call up from the entire database all entries that match the criterion entered into the search field. The search parameter would normally be a combination of a limited string of characters and asterisk(s), serving as place holder for other characters. Entries in the database that match the search parameter all appear at once as a list of terms, the so-called Hit list, from where the user can proceed to examine the full records associated with each hit on the list. A typical situation where one would perform a global search would be the following. I have opened a database on sports, and wish to see all concepts in the database that have 'ball' in their designation. This may well be the starting point for my ultimate goal which is to identify all ball games. By typing *ball* in MultiTerm's search field, the hypothetical database returns the following in a Hit list: *base ball, football, basketball, hand ball, volley ball*, but also the obviously non-relevant *ball boy*, etc.

Another search strategy, *fuzzy search*, allows for a margin of tolerable error in the spelling and structure of the term to be searched. As a user I may be aware that I do not know the spelling of an intended search term because it is somewhat difficult, or because I have come across the term only aurally; I may simply be suspicious of the way I write the search term, because I regularly use the phonology of my own language to reinterpret the phonology of the language of the search term (a fact which occasionally affects my spelling); I may also be merely gambling, calquing the search term on the syntax of my own language; it could also be that the orthography of the language of the search term is not yet stable. However my uncertainty is explained, by typing (into the search field) a pound sign (#) before, say, *week-end, week end, weakend, veekend*, or *end of week*, MultiTerm will find the intended **weekend**, if it exists in the database.

MultiTerm has a filter function, a functionality that allows the user to impose constraints on what is searched, displayed, printed, exported, etc. As a result, the searches described above can be customised, that is, limited to a subset of the database, as opposed to the database in its entirety. This can be particularly useful when a database contains homonyms having, say, different subject attributes. To avoid having to examine each homonym, a user familiar with the database structure definition can filter on 'subject', with the result that the only searchable entries in the entire database will be those that match the selected subject attribution.

Searching of a different kind is represented by hyperlinks or cross references. An entailed term, that is, a term with its own entry record, that appears in a text field like definition, etc. is a good candidate for cross reference. Multi-Term allows for the creation of a hyperlink from the entailed term in text field to the point where this term is an index field.

7.6.2.3 *Printing*
Although a TMS presupposes an on-line environment for creating, but also for consulting, a database, this does not foreclose the option of deriving hardcopies — for which there will always be a need. MultiTerm's flexibility indeed makes

for the generation of hardcopies in a variety of pre-specified and user-defined formats through a variety of procedures. To print, but also for such other purposes as rapid lookup during writing, or term insertion during translating, MultiTerm has to be able to communicate with other Windows applications (e.g. word processor). Its integration of the Dynamic Data Exchange facility, the data exchange standard for Windows applications, makes this communication possible. From a standard Windows word processor the user is able to select any of four printing options.

7.7 Language engineering applications: Implications for Africa

Paradoxically, the point that terminology planning in less widely used languages stands to benefit from language engineering applications is perhaps not the most important implication of this chapter. Neither am I that concerned about the dearth of information technology infrastructure. What is perhaps most crucial in this context is the question of corpus evidence, the very basis for much of the language engineering technologies described in this chapter.

A language with little or no record of functionality in a domain in which it is sought to create a terminology resource simply has no textual corpora to support the semi-automatic extraction of terms, collocates, concept and term relations, definitions, contextual examples, etc. At the launching of the Pan-African Centre for Terminology in Addis Ababa in 1986, the need to provide definitions in terminology resources was pointed out. Given that in certain domains the working languages of the producers of such resources had no textual corpus evidence, the following question posed by a delegate was only quite natural: *Where do we obtain the definitions?* It might also have been asked: *Where do we obtain the contextual examples? Without intensive expert involvement or without being experts ourselves, how do we identify concept relations?*

There are obviously many domains in which corpus evidence exists, mainly, but by no means exclusively, in oral form. In such domains, corpus tools and the work methods they imply are directly applicable, and lead to quality resources. To take an example from LGP: the African Languages Lexicon Project (ALLEX) has recently concluded work on a Shona language dictionary, produced on the basis of transcribed oral corpora and some written corpus (Ridings 1996).

It is to address non-conforming scenarios that a proposal is made here for 'greater initial source-language corpus focus' ('initial source-language focus,' or other permutations for short). Two justifications are provided — for 'initial source-language focus' and 'greater' respectively.

'Initial source-language' because it would appear to be an indispensable preparatory stage in those contexts where terminology planning is motivated by concerns of knowledge transfer. There would typically exist an abundance and a variety of textual evidence in the languages of the transfer source. In the African context, this would be English, French, Portuguese, Spanish and Arabic, languages with which the continent has come in contact as a result of an admixture of commerce, politics and culture. Besides being a source of terms and concept or term relations, the evidence in the languages of the transfer source also does the following:

1. reveals the company terms keep, information which could be useful in deciding what shape a target language (TL) term that is about to be created must have (see 8.8.1.1 and 8.8.2.2);
2. provides a basis on which to focus attention on the company which TL equivalents have to keep if they are to be used in discourse;
3. yields material for the crafting of definitions and contextual examples.

All of these data are vital in a terminology resource. The richness of the source language (SL) is crucial because a corpus, as *explicandum* of the various facets of terminological knowledge, makes sense if it is diversified. Here is an illustration of this point. It was difficult to find text sources for the terminology resource described in Chapter 8. Although Hansard and Standing Orders were easily accessible in one or the other Nigerian language, these texts could not by themselves (particularly Hansard) significantly support the kind of terminology resource envisaged, that is, on forms of substantive and procedural action. It was a delight to have confirmed the observation that, as text type, Hansard does not qualify as specialised (McEnery & Wilson 1996: 155ff). Although lexical closure, the basis of the conclusion reached by these authors does not tell the whole story, physical examination of Hansard of several national legislatures supports the spirit of the conclusion. The case for an initial source-language focus is therefore not invalidated by attestation of some textual evidence in the TL. There is more on texts in Chapter 8.

My proposal adds 'greater' to 'initial source-language focus' because in the knowledge transfer settings described above, terminology planners typically refer to English, French, etc., in other words, to the intuition of experts trained in, or dictionaries/texts written in, these languages. Indeed a good many terminology resources are bilingual, with the language of the transfer source being the SL. The proposal therefore calls for an exploitation of evidence sources (documentary in particular) that goes beyond terms to encompass other facets of terminological knowledge.

Evidently, then, the integration of language engineering technology into terminology planning in corpus-poor languages, so as to obtain the benefits of efficient and quality work, will often be possible only in an indirect manner, through a corpus-rich language of reference. An implication of the proposal is that the terminology planner would often be producing a SL resource in addition to the TL one.

The next chapter illustrates the foregoing. It describes the making of a model terminology resource that draws on theoretical insights, procedures and tools contained in Chapters 4, 5, 6 and 7.

CHAPTER 8

Applications
The Making of a Legislative Terminology Resource

This chapter has two objectives. First, to report on how the theory and technology described in preceding chapters were applied to the creation of a terminology resource. Second, to report on other matters arising from the process of creating the resource, particularly those matters that have implications for further theorisation and practice. The resource, a bilingual (English — Efik) terminology on forms of legislative action and their processing, must not be confused with the one evaluated in Chapter 3. In the two-volume dissertation on which this book is based, a print-out of the resource provided much of the material for the second volume.

8.1 Set of justifications

Some major decisions taken in respect of the resource call for explanation. Below, comments are made on decisions relating to the choice of domain, target language and sources of data. Having based the appraisal in Chapter 3 on the quadrilingual glossary of legislative terms, it is only proper that data from this same domain serve as basis for developing a model resource in order to test the alternative framework proposed. It is hoped that the exemplary value of the resource would stimulate comparable efforts aimed at bringing about implementation of the policy and constitutional provisions discussed in Chapter 2.

Besides being one in my repertoire of Nigerian languages, Efik was chosen as target language for the following reason: the assumption that terminology can play an important role in language revival. In the last two decades in particular, Efik has witnessed a downturn in its fortunes. Usage spheres of the language as well as competence levels are declining. Some factors for this decline include geo-political restructuring (creation of new states, i.e. new centres of political power, linguistic influence, etc.) and widespread access to an educational system in which English is perceived as offering prospects of upward mobility, to which mobility Efik is seen as a hindrance (Connell 1991).

Efik is classified as belonging to the Benue-Congo branch of the Niger-Congo language family. Within Benue-Congo, it belongs to the Lower Cross group of languages. It is spoken in the South-eastern part of Nigeria. In the 1996 (13th edition) of *Ethnologue*, Efik is said to have 2.3 million speakers, who apparently use it as mother, other or further tongue. Total number of mother tongue speakers is put at 360,000. Interestingly, Efik is one of 169 'critical' languages around the world which the U.S. government identified in 1985. By 'critical' is meant that knowledge of these languages "would promote important scientific research or security interests of a national or economic kind" (*Language and Technology* published in 1996 by the European Commission).

A combination of factors put Efik for some time in the league of what Connell (1991) describes as "Africa's most studied languages". Efik was the first Nigerian language into which the Judeo-Christian scriptures were translated — between 1862 and 1868. There was published in the 1880s a monthly newspaper in the language called 'Uñwana' (the light), and others followed in the 1930s and 1940s (Aye 1989). This latter period also saw the emergence of prolific and published writers like E. N. Amaku and E. E. Ñkaña. It is to this generation of writers that Efik continues to owe its very rich corpora of written ethnocentric literature.[1] For several decades until the 1980s, Efik was one of four Nigerian languages exclusively examined in tests conducted by the sub-regional African body responsible for secondary school certificate examinations (i.e. the West African Examinations Council).[2] Given the prestige which Efik has had historically, it is understandable why the downturn in the fortunes of the language should be of concern to many in the Efik community.

Be that as it may, a renaissance appears to be taking place, given a number of policy successes recorded by the Association for the Promotion of Efik Language, Literature and Culture (APELLAC). As a taught subject, Efik has been reinstated in the entire pre-university educational spectrum. Approval already exists for the tertiary level, but there is as yet no full degree course. The renaissance however runs the risk of being set back by the dearth of collaborators on the

---

1. Fifty-eight titles appear on a list of Amaku's works, and, although they reflect a range of concerns, there is a dominant preoccupation with the Efik view of the world. This is reflected in titles under many of the bibliography's subsections (school readers, mass education, general reading, poetry, drama, general information, etc.). I am grateful to Mrs. A. E. Asuquo (*née* Amaku) for this list.

2. The other languages were the major languages: Hausa, Igbo and Yoruba. See Brann (1990: 17 n. 6).

implementation side of things. Obviously, unless policy successes are followed by corpus planning activities and an attitudinal change, the whole enterprise of language promotion becomes imperilled. This terminology resource is a contribution towards the support of promotion efforts.

In a presentation to the APELLAC (Antia, 1997a), the point was made that the institution of new written and specialised discourses in Efik, to complement the existing ethnocentric literary corpora, was crucial to the success of the association's efforts. It was noted that there was a dearth of fresh material in Efik to cater to the varied tastes of otherwise willing readers. A plea was made for the modification of the school syllabus and the structure of tests in order to achieve a balance between traditional themes (cooking, processing garri — a Cassava based staple) and such themes as principles of radio broadcasting, flying an aircraft, etc. because the latter themes hold out prospects for keeping pupils interested in the language, besides also helping them in their other school tasks. Obviously, the institution of these new kinds of LSP calls for attention to terminological matters.

The final justification has to do with data sources. Obtaining (Nigerian) texts upon which to base term extraction and term elaboration was quite difficult. The reference here is to English texts (recall Section 7.7 on corpus requirements associated with language engineering technologies). Besides inaccessibility of texts presumed to exist, the difficulty may also have been explained by a real dearth of appropriate texts on Nigerian legislative practices. The brevity of each of the country's three post-independence national legislatures may not have particularly favoured the production of works akin to those by Erskine May (British Parliament), Beauchesne (Canadian House of Commons), etc. Texts that could be found were sociological analyses of legislatures rather than descriptions of procedures. Hansard, it would be recalled from Chapter 7, is not exactly a specialised text. The set of Hansard found in a private library (C. M. B. Brann's) in Maiduguri/Nigeria only confirmed this view. Standing Orders, while being a good source for pertinent concepts, generally lack definitions.

Against this background, I decided to use more readily accessible and terminological-knowledge rich texts of American and British origins, giving up as a result the goal of producing a uniquely Nigerian resource. But this hybrid resource is not without practical utility in Nigeria. Pre- and post-independence experiences of a parliamentary-cabinet system coupled with the embrace, beginning in the late 1970s, of American presidentialism suggest the following: in addition to whatever uniquely Nigerian legislative practices there might exist, the country has also been exposed to British and American influences. So, the resource is potentially a source of readily usable concepts in Nigeria. Besides this, the resource also serves the useful function of drawing attention to (subtle) differences between American and British procedural devices (see Antia, in prep.).

8.2 Delimitation of domain

The spectrum of what may be considered 'legislative concepts' is wide. In delimiting this field, the domain tree or map provided by Parc (1992) proved quite useful. A modified version of that tree is reproduced below as Figure 8.1 from Antia (1996b).

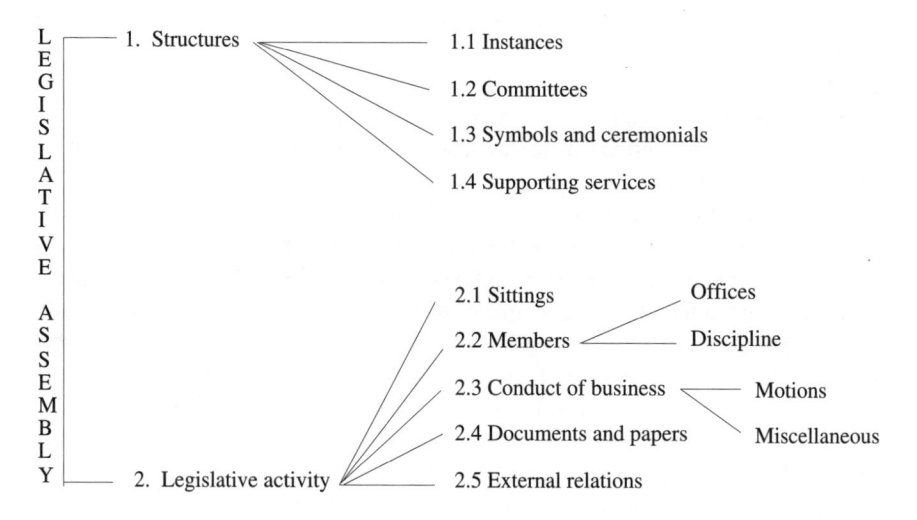

```
LEGISLATIVE      1. Structures ──────── 1.1 Instances
                                        1.2 Committees
                                        1.3 Symbols and ceremonials
                                        1.4 Supporting services

ASSEMBLY                                2.1 Sittings          Offices
                                        2.2 Members          Discipline
                                        2.3 Conduct of business  ── Motions
                                        2.4 Documents and papers   Miscellaneous
                 2. Legislative activity  2.5 External relations
```

Figure 8.1 *Tree structure of legislative domain*

The focus is on node 2.3, within which a specific area of interest is identified, namely, 'forms of substantive legislative action and procedural devices'. This area is further divided into a number of sections. In Antia (1996b) where the earliest draft of the resource was described, nine subsections were identified. In the version of the resource upon which this discussion is based, six sections are identified, namely, *legislative business and its management*; *substantive non-legislative business*; *modification to measure*; *management of time and debate*; *periods, breaks and discontinuation*; *deciding and voting*. Like other aspects reported in Antia (1996b) but which have now been overtaken, this disparity in subsections will be explained in the next section. Section 8.6 describes the modelling of terminological data in each of the six divisions.

8.3 From initiation corpus to definitive corpus

Text acquisition for terminological exploitation turned out to be a process rather than a once-and-for-all action. In general, while collaboration with a domain-expert facilitates text identification and acquisition, the terminologist's perception may change continuously as to text variables such as the suitability of information, format of presentation, language, etc. In effect, while there may be practical reasons for defining a corpus *ab initio*, other practical exigencies may later compel reference to evidence sources not comprised in the initial corpus. If the terminology resource is in computer environment, the review of texts is obviously an easy task. The implications of such textual updates is discussed under Section 8.8.1.3.

Besides some of the titles listed in Table 8.1 below, the corpus of texts that served as initiation to legislative procedure and practice also included the following American texts: *Demeter's Manual of Parliamentary Law and Procedure* and an on-line/Internet tutorial based on *Robert's Rule of Order* (under the auspices of the National Council of Black Engineers and Scientists). While these texts gave invaluable introduction and insight into practice and procedure in deliberative fora or assemblies, they do not describe the practices of any specific legislature. They ought to have remained as initiation corpora and should neither have influenced data modelling nor have been used to extract terms, definitions, etc. as they were in the draft reported in Antia (1996b).

In preparing the version of the resource described here, other texts in the initial corpus, together with texts recommended or discovered subsequently, served as basis for data extraction. It is possible to classify the final corpora according to several criteria:

a. *source*: [a1] American or [a2] British;
b. *level of technicality/presumed readership*: [b1] specialised (text) book/document and reader or [b2] public information material/general reader;
c. *usage goal*: [c1] term extraction or [c2] term elaboration or [c3] extraction and elaboration;
d. *format in which obtained*: [d1] electronic or [d2] paper

In Table 8.1 below, the texts are identified by sources/authors/titles (depending on brevity or availability of information) and criterial codes.

In some cases, text processing (for terms and elaboration data) was based on full texts, and in others on sections of texts. In some instances, processing was manually done while in others it was done with the help of computer software. The corpus size was over a million words.

Table 8.1: *Text corpora*

a1	a2
How our laws are made: b2, c1, d1	May: b1, c3, d2
Rules of the House of Reps.: b1, c1, d1	Griffith/Ryle: b1, c3, d2
Goehlert/Martin: b1, c1, d2	Silk: b1, c2, d2
Oleszek: b1, c3, d2	Heater: b2, c2, d2
Oleszek/Davidson: b1, c2, d2	Factsheet: b2, c3, d1
How Congress Works: b2, c3, d2	Hawtrey/Abraham: b1 & b2, c2, d2
CQ Washington Alert: b2, c2, d1	Taylor: b1, c2, d2
Senate: b2, c3, d1	
CRS Report for Congress: b2, c3, d2	
Legi.Slate: b2, c2, d1	

8.4 Manual processing

An initial manual extraction of terms was rendered necessary by two factors, namely: (1) the fact that it was inconceivable to create records for all the terms extracted in the over one million word corpus in any affordable time span (whether or not one was assisted by machine); (2) the fact that the resource had been divided into sections to which terms had to be assigned, a task that cannot be easily done automatically. Leaving out many of the candidate terms from texts in the initiation corpus texts, seventy-nine terms were extracted.[3] In some cases, elaboration data (like collocation, definition, contextual example, etc.) were also extracted.

8.5 Semi-automatic processing

Here, I describe the tests run on System Quirk (SQ), the text and terminology management tool described in Chapter 7. That chapter also had some sample results.

The thrust of the first set of analyses done was 'elaborational': co-occurrents of those terms elicited in the manual stage of my work were sought from the evidence sources read into SQ. I also sought to obtain text fragments that could serve as definitions and contextual examples for these terms. Both kinds of information were required to supplement or substitute data obtained manually. For co-occurrents, a concordance with a text width of five was performed. For

---

3. Many of the discarded terms (e.g. incidental main motion, restoratory motion) can be found in appendix one to Antia (1996b).

definition and usage data, a concordance with a text width of thirteen was performed. A constraint was imposed on both concordances by the use of a lexicon containing terms that had been extracted in the manual stage.

A second set of analyses had as object the extraction of term candidates, both single- and multi-word. The idea was to create a pool of term candidates for the following purposes: (1) to obtain statistical evidence for the terminological status of the items extracted manually; (2) to add terms which may have been missed out in the manual stage but which belong to the concept field previously defined, that is, forms of substantive parliamentary action and procedural devices; (3) to have preliminary working data in the event of the framework or scope having to be enlarged. For these extraction operations three complementary analyses were done:

1. wordlist, to obtain raw statistical information (frequency of occurrence) of words in the corpus. A constraint was imposed on this analysis: Surrey's lexicon of closed class words for SQ was used;
2. weirdness, to obtain processed statistical information;
3. ferret, to generate multiterm candidates.

The working of these extraction tools was described in Chapter 7.

8.6 Knowledge modelling

As texts from which terms were to be (semi-)automatically extracted could not be expected to contain only those concepts that fell within the purview of legislative areas of interest, it was apparent that in-depth knowledge modelling (that is, more detailed than the *a priori* identification of six sections (see Section 8.2)) could only come after the terms had been extracted. Indeed, the implication of automatic term extraction from text corpora is that an initially semasiological approach is adopted, after which a conceptual structure is built, that is, on the basis of extracted terms (Pozzi 1996: 77). As the following diagrams show, concepts and terms obtained by procedures described above are modelled in the conceptual graph format described in Chapter 7 (Section 7.5). With the exception of section I (*Legislative Business and Management*) which has two diagrams, the other five sections have a diagram each. To deal with one shortcoming of a paper implementation of the graphs, concept nodes are in a few instances repeated within and across sectional graphs. For example, in order to establish a relationship such as the impact of time management devices on the offering of amendments, diagram IV includes several 'amendment' terms, whose principal context is diagram III (*Modification to measure*).

The reading convention for the graphs was described in Chapter 7 (Section 5). The following are some sample readings. From Diagram I, part two: *bill [GB] has as (stage) readings [GB], committee [GB], recommit [GB],* etc. Conversely, *readings [GB], committee [GB], recommit [GB]* etc. *are (stage) of bill [GB]*. From Diagram IV: *debate [US] has as (limitatx) one-hour rule [US], open rule [US], special rule [US],* etc. Conversely, *one-hour rule [US], open rule [US], special rule [US], etc. (limit) debate [US]*. From Diagram V: *a session [GB] and a session [GB] have (between) them recess [session] [GB]; a session [GB] has as (terminatx) prorogation [GB]*.

There are nineteen relations in the catalogue of conceptual relations used. They are: anal (analogy/analogous); assoc. (associated with/association); between; break; class; death; extension; limitatx (limitation); locatx (location); means; part; prohibitx (prohibition); rslt (result); source; stage; syn (synonym); terminatx (termination); type; quasyn (quasi-synonym). As mentioned earlier, the language of the readings does not have to be impeccable. An initial set of conceptual relation primitives had to be extended in order to achieve greater differentiation. Although (terminatx), (death), and possibly (break) could have been subsumed under an abstraction or a primitive like *end*, such a decision would have concealed the fact that: (1) British 'adjournment of the House' and 'adjournment of debate' have different 'ending effects' on business (one supersedes and the other merely postpones); (2) US 'adjournment' has different ending effects on 'debate' and on 'legislative day' in the House of Representatives and in the Senate respectively.[4]

As for the knowledge modelling proper, besides showing concept relations, it yields information characteristic of exercises aimed at specifying or unlocking the ontology of domains. To the extent that the data is a reliable indicator, the following points are suggested by the modelling: (1) there are concepts/terms that are clearly instances of non-articulated superordinates (see the dummy concepts

---

4. The following is a definition of 'adjournment [US]' in the resource. Much of the text is taken from Legi.Slate. Cross references are indicated by italics: "The termination of a meeting, with a set date and time of the next meeting. [...]. In the Senate, adjournment creates a new *legislative day [US]*; so the Senate normally recesses, rather than adjourns, at the end of a day". [See *recess [US]*. The 'observation' on the entry, 'legislative day [US]', equally taken from Legi.Slate, reads: "The House usually adjourns at the end of each day's proceedings, and its legislative day therefore coincides with the calendar day. The Senate usually recesses instead of adjourns at the end of a day's proceedings, and its legislative day often extends over more than one calendar day".

APPLICATIONS 187

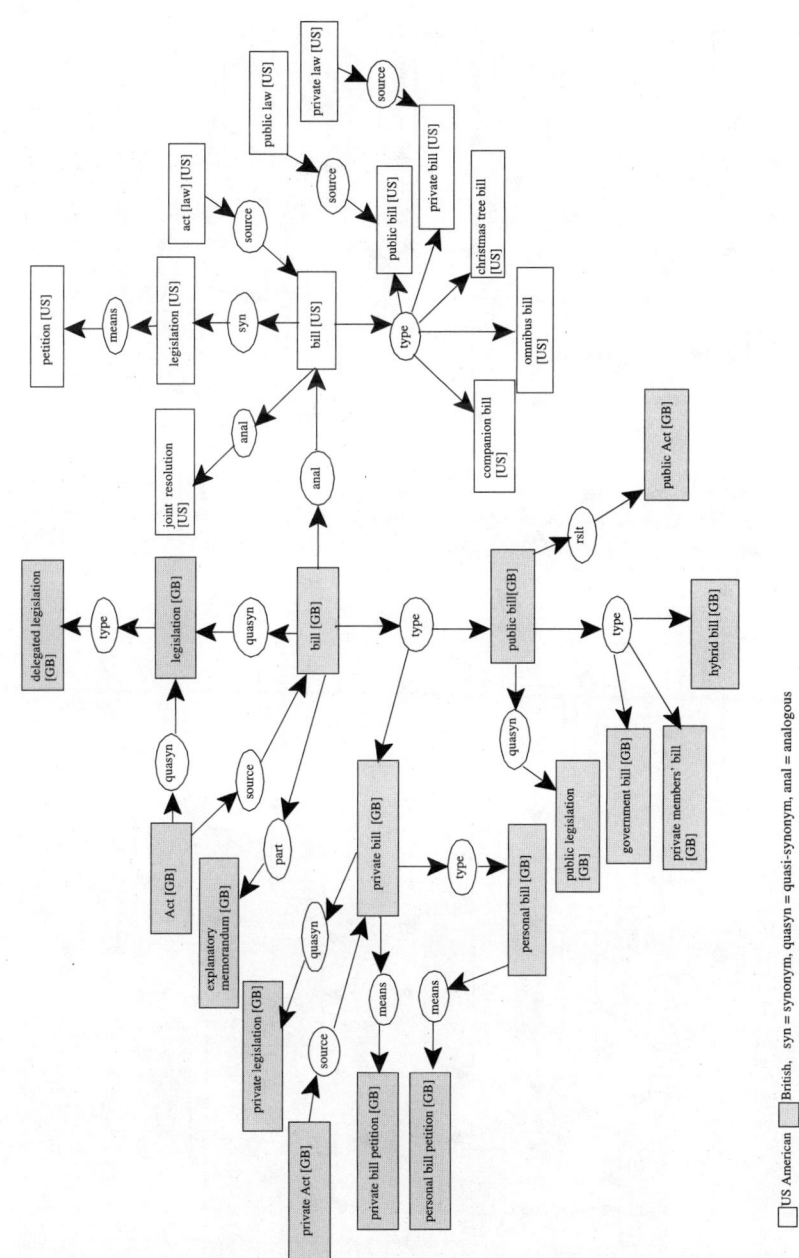

Diagram I. *Legislative business and management - Part one (business)*

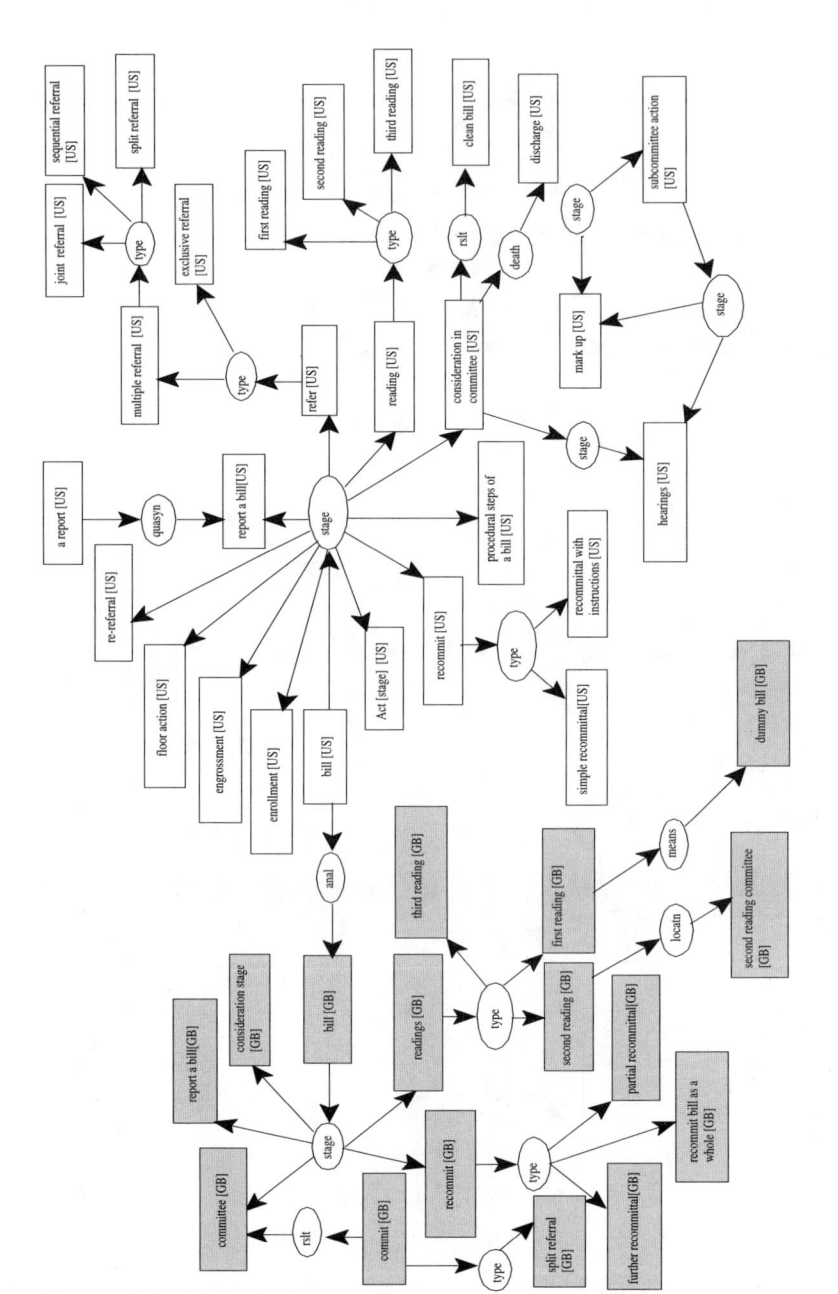

Diagram I. *Legislative business and management - Part two (stages)*

APPLICATIONS

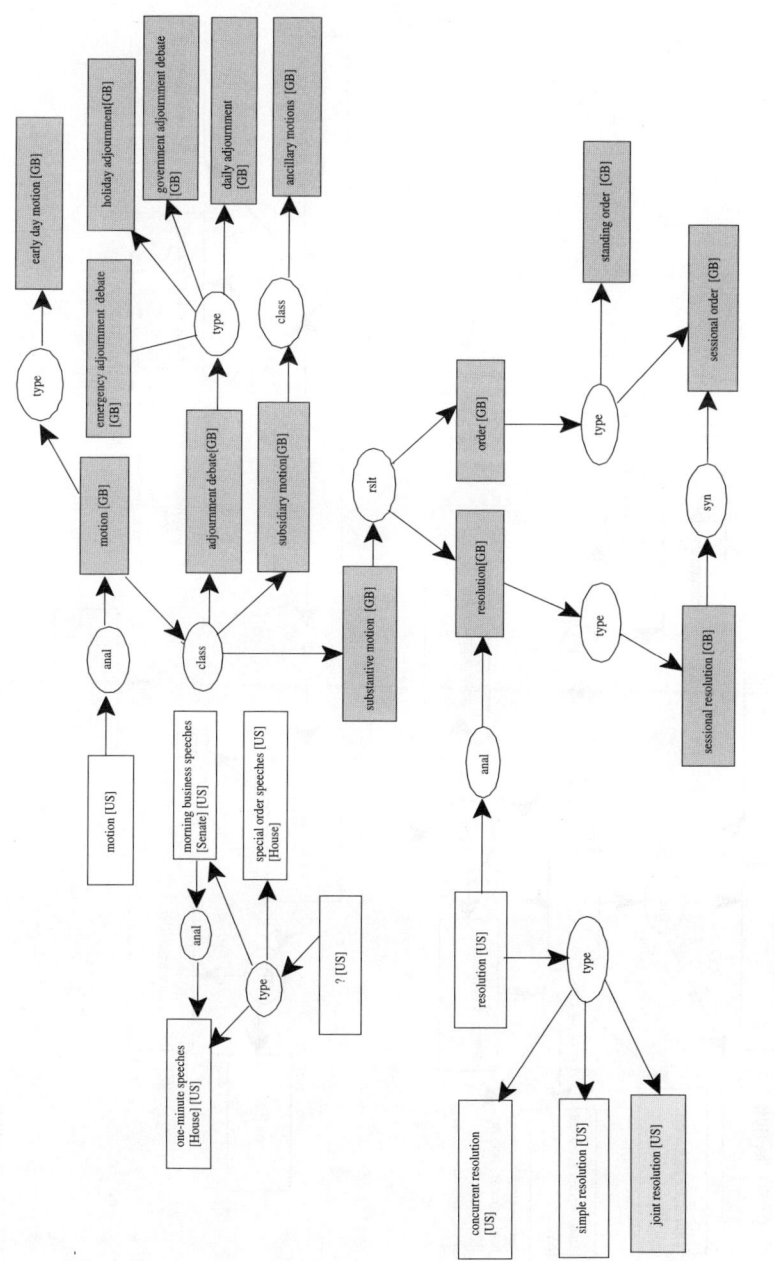

Diagram II. *Substantive non-legislative business*

190 TERMINOLOGY AND LANGUAGE PLANNING

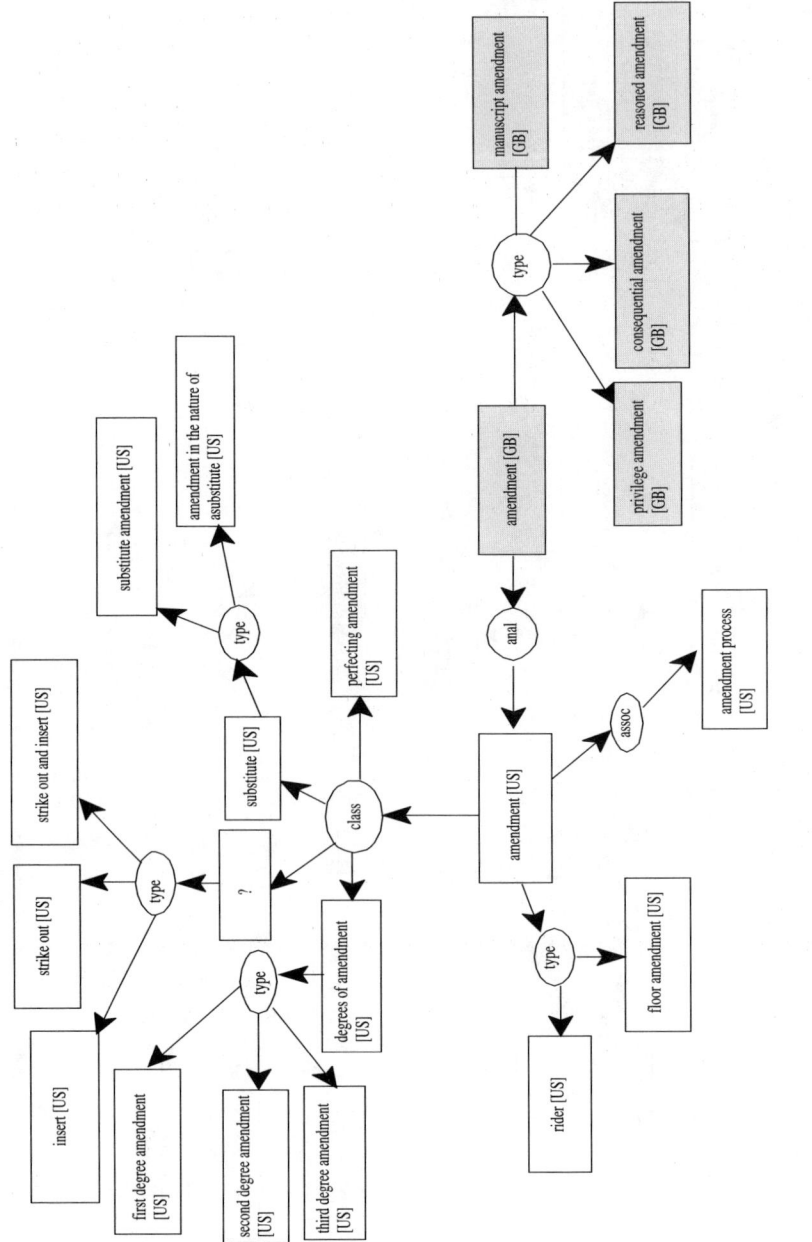

Diagram III. *Modification to measure*

APPLICATIONS 191

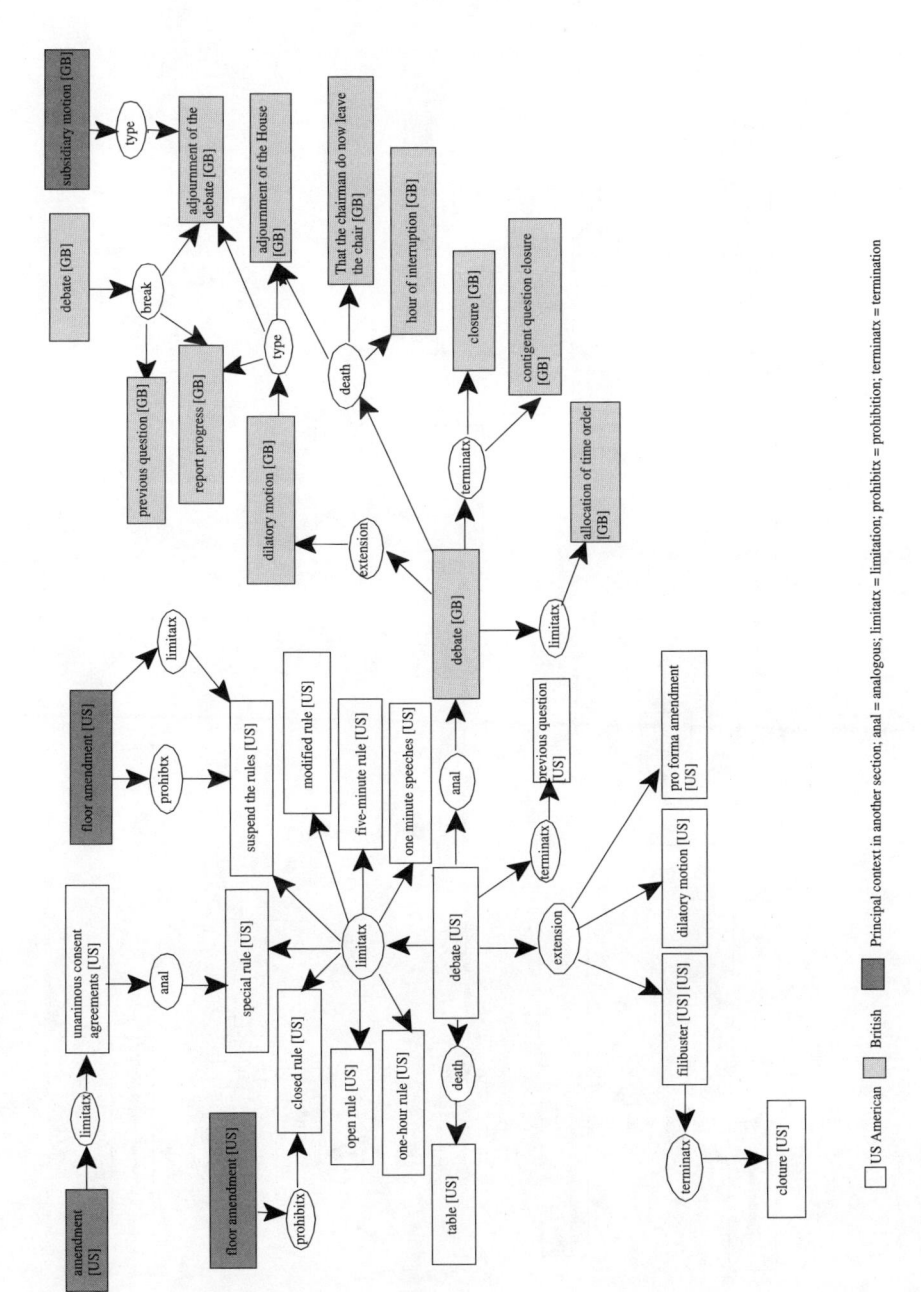

Diagram IV. *Management of time and debate*

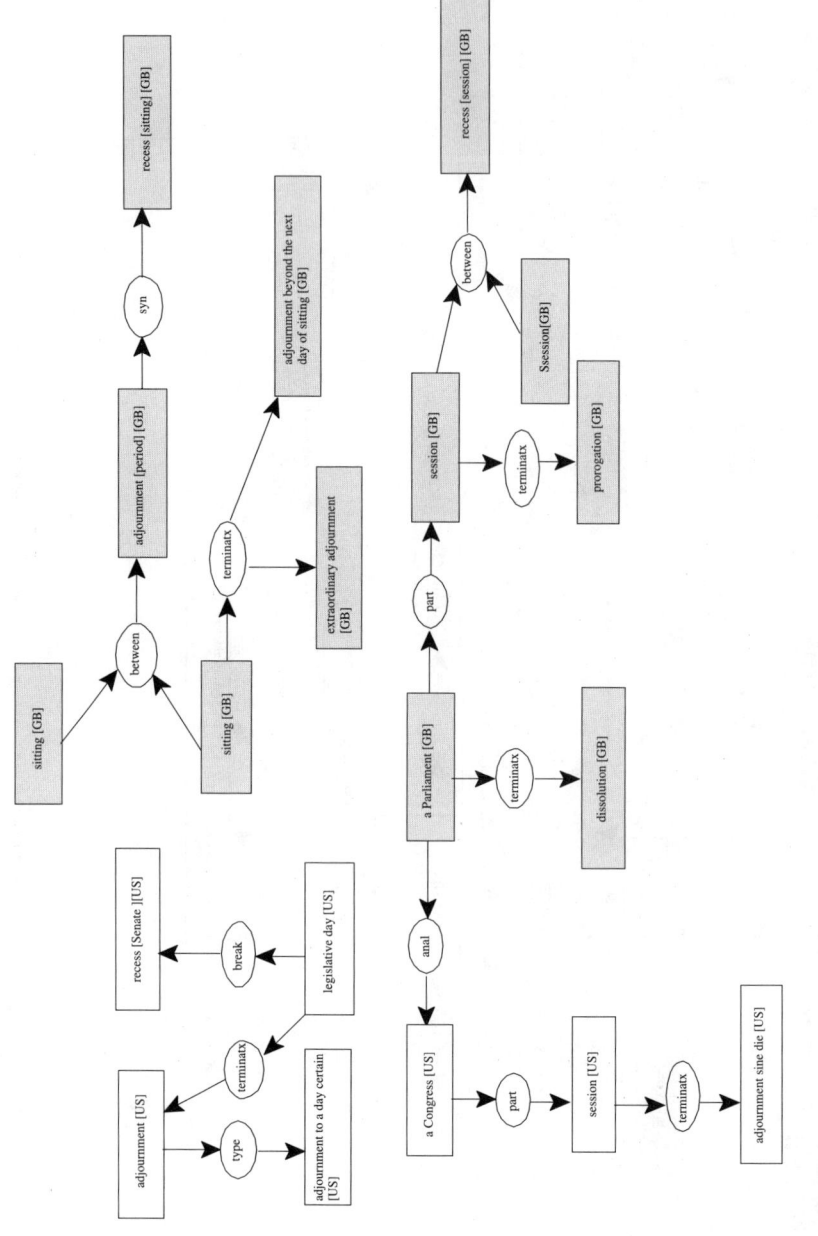

Diagram V. *Periods, breaks and discontinuation*

APPLICATIONS 193

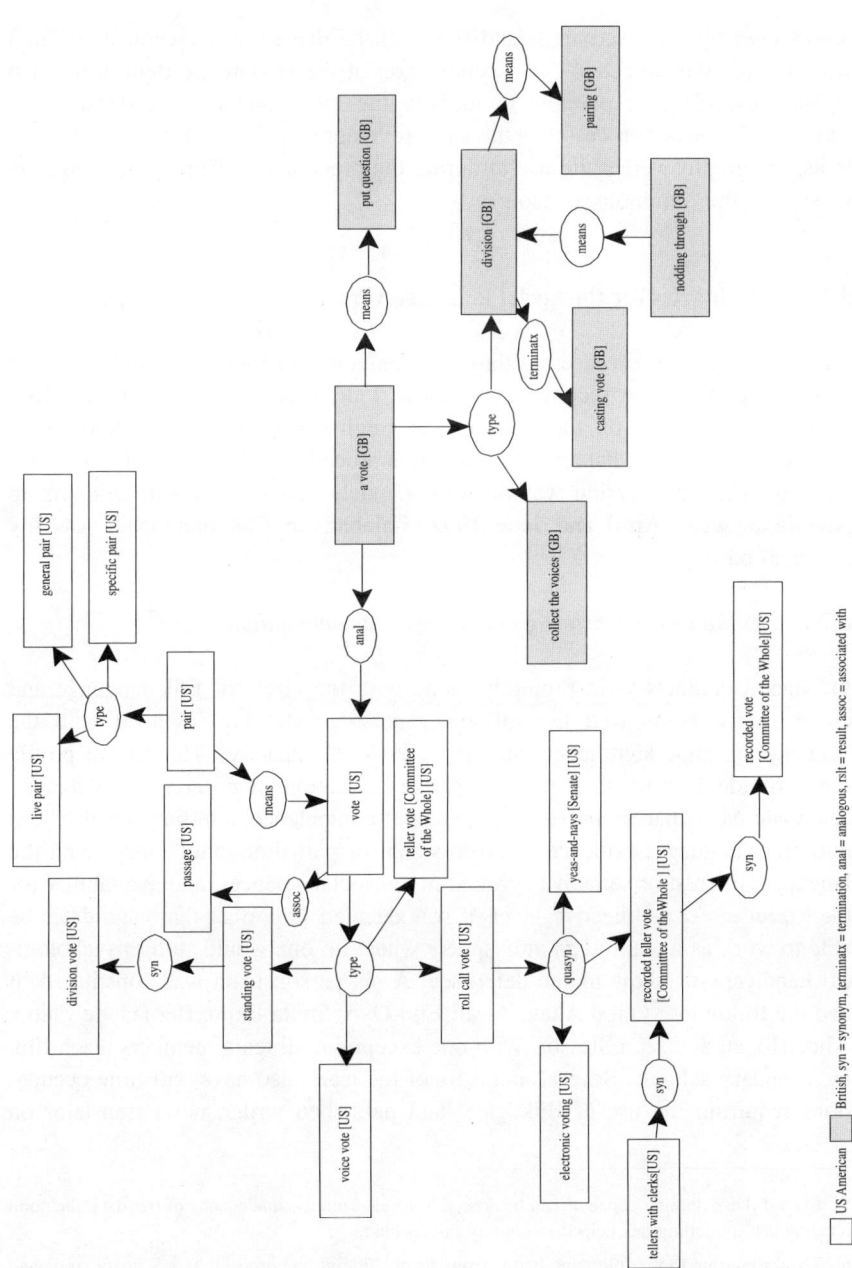

Diagram VI. *Deciding and voting*

represented by ? in sections II and III);[5] (2) the density of concepts associated with a particular procedure, or a subdivision of the resource, differs in the two legislatures; (3) it is possible to identify the kinds and relative densities of actions, relations or processes in the legislative domain. As knowledge-mediating tools, the graphs were quite useful during the preparation of the target language version of the terminology resource.

8.7 Preliminaries for the target language version

The account of the resource has thus far been concerned with the English source language part. In the sections that follow, I describe the making of the Efik target language part on the basis of the English. The context of knowledge transfer (as noted in Chapter 7.7) makes this procedure exceptional. The groundwork for the Efik version was done over much of a three-month field trip to Nigeria between April and June 1997. Calabar, an Efik homeland, was my principal base.

8.7.1 *Collaborators, briefing and process documentation*

In Nigeria contacts were promptly made with the circle of Efik language and culture activists as well as with other persons who are involved with the language in some significant way or professional capacity.[6] The mental profile I had of ideal co-workers required the specification of criteria to be met by candidate participants: native-speaker (-like) competence, a tertiary level tuition in/on the language, evidence of professional or part-time involvement with the language, interest or some background in the social sciences, and availability for the exercise. At a collective level, it was deemed important that candidates be able to work as a team in an atmosphere where no one would suffer psychological handicaps or show undue deference. A six-person team was constituted. It had the following: Ofiọñ Akak, Awaii Efio-Ọyọ, Stella Ekpo, Bernadette Etetta, Alice Hogan and Jean Slessor. With one exception, all team members teach Efik in secondary schools. Several members of the team also have part-time occupations requiring the use of Efik: poet and published writer, news translator on

---

5. Even if these dummy concepts can be argued to result from the inadequacy of our data, the point remains that modelling has helped to identify the problem.

6. Thanks are due to the following two persons for facilitating the process: Mrs. Christy Antia and Chief Dr. B. E. Bassey.

television, membership of Efik Bible translation review committee, etc.

A number of preliminary matters were settled at the inaugural session. A general overview of the resource was given (motivations, production of the source language version, expectations for a target language version, time frame). Agreement was reached on remuneration. The resource was split up into three parts, and the six participants formed three groups. Two plenary sessions per week were agreed upon. At each such plenary, reports from two groups were to be received and discussed. These preliminaries over, the final of inaugural sessions was devoted to technical briefings. Legislative procedure was described, mainly with the aid of conceptual graphs. A talk on term disputes and on resolving them, based on Gilreath (1995), served to give participants a working theory of terminology. This was followed by an outline of translation concepts hinged on the interpretative theory of translation (as articulated by Seleskovitch, Lederer and others at the E.S.I.T in Paris), and on Nida's dynamic equivalence. The one emphasises the knowledge processing side of translation, while the other stresses the sociological side. I was at once chair and participant at the plenaries.

Given that in a number of cases planners are normally not terminology theorists and vice versa, work on the resource was considered a very unique opportunity. In Chapter 2 (Section 2.5), one of the examples cited showed how vital it is for evaluation of terms to take into account some of the considerations underlying the creation of terms. Now, taking advantage of the favorable juncture of circumstances provided by the exercise meant developing procedures for documenting the planning process. Plenary sessions were audio-recorded. Collaborators were instructed to preserve all drafts originating from individual or team work sessions, as well as back and forth (editorial) comments. I took notes to supplement the above procedures.

8.7.2   Efik: Orthography and writing challenges

Efik has a history of writing dating back to about 1850 when the first orthography was devised by missionaries of the United Presbyterian Church of Scotland (Essien 1982). This orthography, commonly called Goldie's orthography, was used until 1929. A revised Goldie orthography then came into effect, and was used until the current one which is the outcome of a 1973 initiative of the Committee of Vice-Chancellors of Nigerian Universities. It is this latter orthography that is employed in the legislative terminology resource described in this chapter.

Efik has thirteen consonant and seven vowel phonemes. The orthography, however, has nine vowels, fifteen single consonant symbols, five consonant diagraphs and five loan sounds. In some respects the disparity between the phoneme inventory and the number of graphic symbols is hardly motivated, given that variations are very systematic and predictable (Essien 1982). In other respects, the disparity is well founded. For instance, the number of allophones of the phoneme /k/ is such that correct pronunciation would have been ill-served if this phoneme were represented by a single graphic symbol. Syllable-initially, /k/ is realised as a velar stop [k], and represented orthographically as k (e.g. eka [è-kà] 'mother'); ambisyllabically[7] after vowels other than the phoneme /i/, it is realised as a velar fricative [x], and represented orthographically as h (e.g. fehe [fèxé] 'run'); ambisyllabically after the high front vowel /i/ in closed syllable (orthographic i̩), it is realised as the velar fricative [ɣ], and represented orthographically in two free variants gh and g (e.g. ti̩gha [ti̩ɣá] 'kick').

Occasionally, the transition from spoken to written Efik is not a simple routine. Phonological processes in the language generate more than one acceptable (spoken) variant of a particular feature. Now, there are more or less formal guidelines concerning which specific variants are to be written. However, because of a dominant oral use of Efik, guidelines have, in the written practice of many, not entirely translated into intuition or become completely routine. The consequence is that differences of spelling, albeit minor, are quite common. To illustrate the foregoing, the phonological process of consonant weakening is discussed.

Consonant weakening would be said to obtain, for instance, when a plosive became non-released in certain environments. In Efik this is not a trivial matter. In several non-initial word positions, the Efik phoneme /d/ is weakened to a variety of forms: (a) an unreleased stop [t˺] syllable-finally in unconnected speech; (b) an apico-velar tap [r] ambisyllabically after vowels other than /i/; and (c) a syllabic trilled [r̩] ambisyllabically after /i/ (Cook 1969). The challenge for writing in Efik does not stem from the diversity of allophones, but from the observation that weakening in specific environments is idiolectal and linked to whether or not a syllable juncture is evident, a phenomenon which may not even be systematic in a given speaker. Under such circumstances attempting to draw isoglosses may not be worthwhile.

Now, the situation in (b) above (that is, a sequence of other-than /i/ vowels + /d/) is quite intractable. A [d] is realised where a speaker makes room for a syllable boundary. When no boundary is evident, an [r] is realised. Thus, the word meaning 'sheep' may be pronounced as [e-dɔ̀ŋ] with syllable juncture, or as [erɔ̀ŋ] without juncture. In terms of spelling, the dictionary by Adams *et al.* enters it as "erọñ", while Aye's dictionary enters it 'preferentially' as "edọñ"

---

7. A sound is said to be ambisyllabic if it is perceived as belonging equally to two syllables.

under which the concept is described. Because this word has two other homonyms, it is not quite clear whether just one or all of the homonyms are referred to in the following entry in Aye's dictionary: "eroñ, n. See Edọñ ". This entry has no tone marking, no definition, just the cross reference information. At any rate, according to Akpanyuñ (1978: 14f), in writing, d is to be preferred to r.

This variation is minimal, but can perhaps be deplored as one might in certain computational processing contexts deplore the variant spellings of, say, 'data bank' (solid, hyphenated, separate), or the fact of there being strong and weak forms of certain past participles ('spelled', 'spelt'). In the terminology developed in this work, spelling problems do not affect the (electronic) searching of terms because the management software used (MultiTerm) allows for fuzzy searches as seen in Chapter 7.6.

8.8 Process analysis of the target language version

As noted in Section 8.7.1, much of the process of creating the TL version of the resource was documented. Below, manually and electronically recorded protocols as well as drafts of the resource are analysed from a number of standpoints. For readers who may not be familiar with legislative concepts, brief descriptions are given of concepts cited, particularly when a given context appears to require substantial background information. Only the first mention of a concept is accompanied by a description. Concepts from British data sources are identified as [GB], while those from US American sources are identified as [US].

8.8.1 *Term motivation*

Previous work (e.g. Antia 1995b) did suggest that one difficult task in LP-oriented terminology management is that of identifying what features of a concept x are to be used in creating a term for this concept. The task is difficult because the SL and TL would often have very uneven knowledge structures. Let us assume that in language $L1$ a new concept y is easily given a term by referring to a related and named concept x. In another language $L2$, finding a term for concept y may be quite difficult where concept x is unknown. Nonetheless, previous discussions also pointed out the potential usefulness of term motivation profiles in several languages. The foregoing issues of motivation are illustrated below under three headings.

8.8.1.1 *Comparative term motivation models and decision-making*

In Antia (1995b), I discussed the potential usefulness, in a term creation exercise, of term motivation models in languages other than the reference or source language. While the procedure was not consistently applied here, for reasons having to do with the question of concept equivalence validation, its usefulness was borne out whenever confidence levels were high enough for attention to be drawn to it.

The team of terminology planners was particularly relieved when I communicated to them the solution reached by a non-member for the term 'bill'. A bill is a proposal for a law. In the course of discussing parts of my project with Chief E. U. Aye (current President of APELLAC and retired university teacher of History) and Chief B. E. Bassey (APELLAC member and a retired university teacher of Physics), I mentioned the term 'bill', and Chief Aye reached out for one of three types of Efik dictionaries he had just completed. As Efik equivalent for the legislative acceptation of 'bill' he had proposed *mbet emi mibopke owo kaña* (literally, a law that is yet to bind anyone). While this was a perfectly acceptable paraphrase solution, the chief saw the point I had been making about the implication for usability of term length. Term length was defined, not in an abstract and unabashed way *à la* Tauli (1968), but in the specific sense of frequently occurring concepts that have subtypes or manifest surface expansion. For example: *bill → public bill → public bill petition → public bill petition office*, etc. (see 8.8.2.2). It was the introduction of the comparative perspective an hour or so later that brought about the solution everyone was quite satisfied with. I gave Chief Aye glosses in English of the French and German equivalents of 'bill': *projet de loi* (proposal for law) and *Gesetzentwurf* (draft of law). Almost spontaneously, the Chief, working from the German, came up with *nsek mbet* (*nsek*: unformed, unripe, etc.;[8] *mbet*: law). At the plenary session, team members were able to test the suitability of this solution by applying concepts presented at the technical briefings: collocability, precedence, etc.

The comparative procedure need not always bring about as dramatic a solution as the preceding example. At other times, the procedure only helped to clear doubts or even justify a decision that seemed almost inevitable. Take the

---

8. *Nsek* could be described as an abstraction or a primitive whose specific sense is determined by the given context in which it occurs. In collocation with *eyen* (child), it has the sense 'baby'; in collocation with maize or other plants, it produces the sense 'tender', 'not ready for harvest', etc.

example of the term, 'reasoned amendment [GB]'.[9] While the motivation for this term could be inferred from the definition, there was concern in the team as to what the implications of an Efik calque would be on how other kinds of amendment might be perceived. All reservations petered out when it was realised that in Canadian French the same concept is referred to as *amendement motivé* in the Canadian Parliament.

Be that as it may, and as argued in Antia (1995b), term models cannot be indiscriminately adopted, no matter how widespread they have become. The term, 'previous question [US]', identifies a concept that has an exact equivalent in the English used in the Canadian Parliament.[10] In the French used in this Parliament, it is termed *question préalable*. But the fact of this motivation being attested elsewhere did not produce consensus in the team as to the acceptability of one participant's calque: *udañ mbume* (literally, stale, old question). Unlike the 'reasoned amendment' example, this proposal could not by any stretch of the imagination be justified on the basis of knowledge available to the team. We settled for *ebeñe owuri biop* (motion for ultimate halting).

8.8.1.2 *The place of metaphor*

In a sense, the level of challenge involved in creating a TL term for a SL concept is related to the existence in the TL (and/or proximity to the term creator's cognitive deck) of labels for (salient) characteristics of the SL concept. Indeed, for some concepts, as many as three hours spread over several plenaries went into the search for TL motivations that would be economical and more or less conceptually adequate. Such situations saw the team chair pose questions that led in many instances to the adoption of metaphorical solutions. A few of these metaphors were agriculture-based. The term, 'dummy bill [GB]', is designated *emine nsek mbet*, where *emine* is the Efik word for a plant 'bud/ shoot'. The dummy bill was viewed as standing in a relationship of 'forerunner and place holder' to the bill.

---

9. A definition of "reasoned amendment" in the resource (as obtained from Hawtrey/Barclay) reads: "This form of amendment seeks, by substituting other words for those of the question 'That the bill be now read a second (third) time', either to give reasons why the House declines to give a second or third reading to the bill, or to express an opinion with regard to its subject matter or to the policy the bill is intended to fulfil".

10. A definition in the resource, as obtained from CQ Washington Alert, reads: "A motion for the previous question, when carried, has the effect of cutting off all debate, preventing the offering of further amendments and forcing a vote on the pending matter".

British 'ancillary motions' are a class of 'subsidiary motions'.[11] The term 'motion' having been already called *ebeñe* (request, prayer), the qualifiers 'subsidiary' and 'ancillary' were labelled *ndisa* and *mbomi* respectively. In the local agricultural practice, the tendrils of climbing plants are often supported in their vertical growth by ropes tied around upright poles or long sticks stuck into the ground. The ropes are called *mbomi* and the solid upright support is termed *ndisa*. Generally, like motions described as subsidiary and ancillary, *mbomi* and *ndisa* are seen as facilitators, providing different degrees or types of support.

The term, 'consequential amendment [GB]', refers to an amendment that is made to, say, a clause of a bill by virtue of a previous amendment to some other clause. Although the TL proposal for this term, *unyik uneñede* (literally, forced straightening), occurred to the chair during editing, the team had considered many 'semantico-metaphorical' fields. In some cases no metaphors were found, in others metaphors found were adjudged inadequate. Some of the fields examined included:

1. inevitability, indispensability: nothing could be found other than the lengthy non-metaphorical phrase *ñkpo emi owo mikemeke ndinyaña* (something that one cannot help);
2. automation (i.e. automatic occurrence): nothing found;
3. predictability, co-occurrence: the metaphor *ekpat ubok* (hand bag — usually lady's) produced no consensus. In Efik, a child tied to its mother's apron strings can be said to be its mother's hand bag, to be seen wherever the mother is;
4. gradual expansion or spread, as of wax, oil, etc.: the leaf called *ntan* which has a dispersed or distributed itching effect when it touches the human skin did not produce any consensus; neither did *ntatara*, the reduplicated adjective expressing the property of spreading (as of oil).

8.8.1.3 *Textual updates and shifting motivations*

The motivation for terms was based on the descriptive text data available to us. The drawback of textual descriptions, as opposed to a listing or enumeration of a concept's properties, is that they tend to represent one of several possible views of the given concept. Rogers has made the point that in textual progression different dimensions or views of a concept may be focused on (Rogers 1998).

---

11. Subsidiary motions refer to the totality of actions taken in order for the House to appropriately dispose of a substantive business. Whereas some subsidiary motions do not have to be pre-planned, ancillary motions are tied to the advertised agenda of business for a particular day.

McNaught (1988) calls for concept descriptive data to be represented in machine environments in a form that can be manipulated, selected and combined to yield different views. Both of these views make it clear why it may sometimes be observed that two textual definitions of the same concept could have very little in common, even though they are offered within the same speciality. One implication of, or opportunity associated with, corpus-based extraction of terminology-related data and of managing such data electronically is that initial definitions, for instance, can be replaced when others that are deemed to be more apposite (simpler, clearer, etc.) are found. But terms cannot afford to be reviewed with each such textual update. The 'atom' after all has been maintained as the designation for a concept that is now known to be the exact opposite of what the etymology of this term suggests. Just like the motivation of 'atom' may cease to be obvious to future generations of science students with no knowledge of Greek, so might the motivation of terms in the resource be lost with textual updates. In the resource, the term proposed for the British, not the American, 'previous question' is *ebeñe mkpahaukot* (literally, motion that immobilises the feet; idiomatically, a restraining motion). This motivation is based on the italicised parts of Passage A.

Passage A.
A method occasionally employed *in order to withhold from the decision of the House a motion that has been proposed from the Chair* is to move the previous question. The form in which the previous question is put to the House is 'That the question be not now put'. The House is thus compelled to decide in the first instance whether the original motion shall or shall not be submitted to the House. If the previous question is agreed to, *the Speaker is prevented from putting the original question, as the House has refused to allow it to be put*. If the previous question is negatived, the original question on which it was moved must be put forthwith.

Passage B.
A procedure akin to that of a dilatory motion but which is now rarely used, is the 'previous question'. This is moved in the form. 'That the question be not now put' and if agreed to has the effect of aborting the debate on the original question (though it could be moved again on another day).

If the description in Passage A were replaced by the one in B (which applies to the same concept in the same legislature), the motivation for *ebeñe mkpahaukot* (as equivalent for British 'previous question') would become less apparent.

8.8.2 *Constraints on term decision*

Before they were adopted, term suggestions were subjected to all or a selection of the following tests (depending on pertinence and availability of data): derivability, collocability and series uniformity. Some illustrations.

8.8.2.1 *Derivability*

For British and American 'report a bill', the following suggestions were considered: **sian** *baña nsek mbet*; **bu̱k** *baña nsek mbet*; **ti̱ñ** *baña nsek mbet*; **to̱t** *baña nsek mbet* — all of which are capable of expressing the concept. The challenge, obviously, was one of agreeing on one verb. The team settled for the verb, *sian*, having eliminated the others because of concerns expressed over (possible) inappropriate connotation (*bu̱k*), overgenerality (*ti̱ñ*), strong contextual association/overspecification (*to̱t*). But when it was not apparent how, if at all, a noun could be derived from this verb, this option was dropped. In its place the more productive *to̱t* was adopted from which the noun *nto̱t* is derivable.

8.8.2.2 *Collocability*

By providing co(n)texts of various kinds, collocations were not only checks on usability of the main entry terms, that is their compatibility with regularly occurring terms or other LGP elements. They also served to illustrate modifications which the main entry term would have to undergo in specific contexts. Here are some examples. In Section 8.8.1, Chief Aye's initial proposal for 'bill' was mentioned. Now, building on that initial proposal, the term for British 'public bill petition' would have had to be rendered by a form glossed as *plea for a law that is yet to bind anyone that is for the entire community*. It would have had to be this long as well. Using that initial proposal to translate into Efik a sentence such as the following would have produced a nightmare: 'Constituents who wish to have the House consider a matter of interest may draft and sign a public bill petition, then submit it to the public bills office'. An alternative solution to the Chief's initial proposal was clearly inevitable.

A second example illustrates a related function of collocation or co(n)text. In the extract below, the team is considering whether the Efik equivalent they had just proposed for 'discharge [US]' (synonyms: 'discharge petition', 'discharge motion') can be sustained in the light of what would have to be Efik equivalents for collocates of the English 'discharge' terms. These collocates include: file, sign, offer, agree to, vote, etc. In the extract, English translations (italicised) follow the Efik utterances. Efik terms in the English lines are underlined.

Extract on collocates of 'discharge [US]'.

[1]BA: So in the light of edisio ubọk mfep inọde for discharge, ikpidọhọ didie to file a discharge petition? [...]
BA:.So in the light of <u>edisio ubọk mfep</u> the term for discharge, how would we say to file a discharge petition?

[2]AEO: Ndisịn ebeñe naña. BA: Ndisịn, ndisịn... Chrous: iñ SE: Ndisịn or ndinịm? [...] BE: Eñ, ndisịn
AEO: <u>Ndisịn ebeñe</u>, I'd say. BA: <u>Ndisịn</u> ... Chorus: yes SE: <u>Ndisịn</u> (to put) or <u>ndinịm</u> (to place)? BE:Yes, <u>ndisịn</u>

[3]ñwed ebeñe. AEO: Ndisịn ebeñe. BA: Ok, ok, yeah ok SE: Ẹsisisịn ebeñe mme ẹsininịm? AEO: Ẹsisịn.
petition application. AEO: Ndisịn petition. BA: Ok, ok, yeah ok SE:Do you <u>sin</u>(put) or <u>nịm</u>(place) petition? AEO:You sịn

[4]BA/AH: Ẹsisịn. BA: Ẹsisịn ebeñe, ẹsisịn ñwed AEO: Ndisịñ ebeñe ndisio OA: Ẹnyuñ ẹkeme ndinịm
BA/AH:You can <u>sịn</u> BA: One can <u>sịn</u> a petition or application. AEO:To <u>sịn</u> a petition to discharge OA:One can also nịm

[5]ebeñe ke iso... SE: Ndinịm ebeñe edi enyefe? Enye etịñdetịñ? JS: That is orally...Chorus: Orally...
an application before... SE: When does one <u>nịm</u> a petition? When presented orally? JS:That is orally... Chorus:Orally

[6]AEO: Ete ñkoyom ndinịm ebeñe emi ke iso mbufo. Edi emi ewetdewet akade file esịn ebeñe...
AEO: (As e.g.) Sirs, I wanted to <u>nịm</u> this petition before this body. But the one you write which is filed is <u>sịn</u>...

[7]BA: Ok. So, sịn ... AEO: Ndisịn ebeñe ndisio ubọk ... JS/AEO: ... mfep [...] AEO: Ndien sign a discharge petition.
BA: Ok. So, <u>sịn</u> (put) ... AEO:To <u>sịn</u> petition to hands .... JS/AEO:.. off [...] AEO: Next, sign a discharge petition.

[8]Ndisịn ubọk... BA: ... ke ebeñe... JS/AEO: ... ke ebeñe edisio ubọk mfep BA: Then ... well, to offer a discharge
To put hand... BA: ... in petition...JS/AEO: ... in petition to take hands off BA: Then ... well, to offer a discharge

[9]motion edi ukem ñkpọ nte ndifile a discharge petition. So there is no problem. Ndiadopt a discharge motion.
motion is the same thing as to file a discharge petition. So there is no problem.

The protocol shows that the Efik proposal for 'discharge' does not pose problems with respect to expected collocates. In other words, the collocates confirm that the Efik equivalent proposed for 'discharge' can indeed be used along with probable co-text segments. Interestingly, the uncertainty and debate over certain collocates simply reinforced the initial decision to give end-users of the terminology resource collocational information.

The third example of the function of collocates is related to the term, 'enrollment [US]'. The Efik equivalent proposed is the noun phrase *oyoho ndutim*. Now, in the verbal collocational environment, 'enroll a bill', *oyoho ndutim* exhibits two modifications (non-contiguity and reduplication). It becomes *tim **nsek mbet** oyoho oyoho*. The function of the collocate here is to show the modification which the main entry term would have to undergo in a certain environment. There was some debate as to whether this modification would have been obvious to the end-user, even if s/he readily perceived the problem. Let us now turn to a 'constraint' of a completely different kind.

8.8.2.3 *Series uniformity*

Gilreath (1995: 41) defines a uniform term series as a "group of related terms having common term elements". These related terms ought to be understood as related concepts. Decisions taken during the plenaries or editing were guided by three uniformity patterns. The most common pattern implied adherence to sets of SL term patterns. This was particularly evident in types of given concepts. Take the example of amendment in Table 8.2 below.

Table 8.2: *Uniformity through adherence to SL pattern*

consequential amendment [GB]	unyik uneñede [GB]
manuscript amendment [GB]	mbabuat uneñede [GB]
substitute [US]	ada itie uneñede [US]

The TL designation for 'amendment' (*uneñede*) is consistently used in all SL compounds where 'amendment' occurs. 'Substitute' is a generic name for two kinds of substitute amendments.

The second pattern involved the creation in the TL of a pattern that does not exist in the SL. The sectional organisation of the resource was particularly helpful in the establishment of this pattern. Consider the pattern in Table 8.3 below.

The Efik *ini ukama utom* literally means 'period of holding work', idiomatically 'tenure'. The modifiers *akwa*, *ekpri*, and *utit* mean respectively 'big' 'small' and 'end'.

Table 8.3: *Enhancing uniformity by creating in TL a pattern absent in SL*

[GB]	[US]	Efik
a Parliament session	a Congress session	akwa *ini ukama utom*
		ekpri *ini ukama utom*
prorogation	adjournment sine die	utịt ekpri *ini ukama utom*
dissolution		utịt akwa *ini ukama utom*

The third pattern is a hybrid of the foregoing two patterns. In the resource there are ten British concepts and two American concepts with designations in which 'adjourn/adjournment' appears.[12] However, these terms do not all belong together conceptually. Incidentally, two of the four conceptual systems to which these terms can be assigned also accommodate committee-related concepts which do not, however, have 'adjourn/adjournment' as part of their designation. Two such committee linked concepts are: (a) 'that the chairman do now leave the chair' and (b) 'motion that the chairman do report progress and ask leave to sit again'. Let us identify as follows the various concept systems to which the 'adjourn/adjournment' terms can be assigned:

1. substantive non-legislative matters;
2. conclusion of sitting and, simultaneously, final disposition of business at hand;
3. deferment of sitting/business; and
4. a period/duration.

In proposing Efik equivalents, we have sought to provide a more conceptually based uniform term series. System 1 and 2 terms share a common Efik word (*usuana*=closure); system 3 terms commonly use an existing Efik phrase for deferment (as of a court case or of a meeting), that is, the serial verb construction *sio nịm* (literally, *remove [and] place/keep*). With reference to the SL paradigm, system 4 has only one concept. Table 8.4 below presents the SL and TL series.

8.8.3 *The old and the new: Conflict and accommodation*

The knowledge transfer context of our project is perhaps one of the few admissible instances where work on terminology in one language can afford to be based on the conceptual system associated with another language. However, even where terminology planning is motivated by large scale knowledge transfer there still

---

12. As there are synonyms the actual number of 'adjournment' terms exceeds the number of concepts.

Table 8.4: *Enhancing uniformity through adhering to, and modifying, SL patterns*

System 1	adjournment debate [GB]	ebeñe nneme *usuana*
	daily adjournment debate [GB]	nneme *usuana* ke usen ke usen
	government adjournment debate [GB]	nneme *usuana* ukara
	holiday adjournment [GB]	nneme *usuana* ini nduk odudu
	emergency adjournment debate [GB]	mbabuat nneme *usuana*
System 2	adjournment of the House [GB]	*usuana* ufọk
	that the chairman do now leave the chair [GB]	*usuana* kọmiti
	adjournment [US]	*usuana* ufọk
System 3	adjournment of the debate [GB]	*usio* nneme *nnịm*
	motion that the chairman do report progress and ask leave to sit again [GB]	ntọt ye *usio* mbono kọmiti *nnịm*
	adjournment beyond the next day of sitting [GB]	*usio* usen mbono *nnịm*
	extraordinary adjournment [GB]	ọkpọ ọkpọ *usio* usen *nnịm*
	adjourn to a day certain [US]	*usio* usen mbono *nnịm*
System 4	adjournment [period] [GB]	ini idem owo

is the possibility that the TL conceptual universe is not a *tabula rasa* or clean slate. This suggests the possibility of a conflict between the source and target conceptual universes. Whether this conflict is resolved by substituting one conceptual universe for the other, or by accommodation, would depend on the specific circumstances. The protocol extract below shows one such conflict with the question of voting. The extract is a continuation of the previous one on the collocates of 'discharge'. The collocate being discussed is 'vote', which also happens to be an entailed term in the resource.

Extract on 'vote' as collocate of 'discharge' and as entailed term.

[1]BA: Mhi... To vote AEO: Ndi...ndiwụt ubọk mme ndimenede ubọk OA: Ndivote... ndimek BA: Ndi ..eñ ?
BA: Alright ... To vote AEO: To ...show hands or to raise hands OA: To vote ... to mek (choose) BA: To..what?

[2]AO: Because at the end of it BA: Em .. JS: Ndimek ... SE: Ndimek idụkke idi naña BA: No, ẹmek owo ...
AO: Because at the end of it BA:Em... JS: To mek .... SE:To mek (choose) is hardly relevant here BA: No, you mek people ..

[3]OA: at the end of the vote ... BA: Edi nsehe nte ẹkeme ndi... ndiọñoke o ... , ẹkeme ndimek ñkpọ?
OA: at the end of the vote ... BA:I am not quite sure that you could... well, I don't know... can you mek a thing?

[4]AO: Ẹmemek [...] AH: Owo imekke ñkpọ o. JS: Ẹmemek ñkpọ. Edieke ẹnọde fi options ediwak afo ẹmek emi
AEO: You can [...] ***AH****: You cannot* mek *a thing* ***JS****: You can. If given several options you choose the one*

[5]oyomde BA: E..eñ e..eñ AEO: Ẹmemek owo ẹmemek ñkpọ ... efen afiak edi ndi... voting?
you like ***BA****: Well,...* ***AEO****: You can* mek *a person or a thing ... another alternative is...talking about voting right?*

[6]BA: Eñ AEO: ... Ndimenede OA/AEO: ... ndimenede ubọk BA: Em ... mbon ẹnamde ñkpọ ẹbaña voting ẹyekụt
BA*: Right* ***AEO****: To raise...* ***OA/AEO****: raise hands* ***BA****: Em ... the group in charge of voting will see that*

[7]ete voting ẹdu ke utọ ke utọ. Enyene ubak voting ẹmenede ubọk, enyene ubak voting ẹdadeda ...
there are several types of voting. There is a type involving show of hands, involving standing ...

[8]Chorus: ẹmiñde ubọk ... OA: Edi enyemi nyiñ idiọñọde edi ndimenede ubọk. Ndimenede ubọk, ndimenede
Chorus*: thumb printing ...* ***OA****: But the one we know is raising hands. To raise hands, to raise*

[9]ubọk nnọ eyop. Ndimenede ubọk nnọ ekikọ. That was the language ke ini eset BE: But in this context mme
hands to the palm. To raise hands to the cock.That was the language in times past ***BE****:But in this context perhaps*

[10]ekpe ẹuse nte ndisọñọ because... JS: I think so **BA**: Yeah, just general vote koro edieke ẹsede, edieke ẹsede
to soñọ *(ratify) should be used because ...* ***JS****:I think so BA: Yeah, just general vote because if we look at, look at*

[11]that graph, under voting, voting ẹdu ke utọ ke utọ. And edieke itọñọde ndidọhọ nte vote idahaemi edi
that graph, under voting, voting comes in several forms. And if we now begin to say that vote

[12]ndimenede ubọk iyinyene mfana [...]. Edieke isede ñkañ America oro iminyene standing vote, voice vote, [...]
is raising hands we will run into problems [...]. If we look at the US side (of graph) we find standing vote, voice vote,[...]

[13]roll call vote ... BE: Yak ida ndisọñọ naña Chorus: Ndisọñọ [...] BA: Then well ebiet odụk, odụk there is no
roll call vote ... ***BE****:Let's use to* soñọ *(ratify) then* ***Chorus****: To* soñọ *[...]* ***BA****:*

> Then well, it appears to fit, it fits there is no
> [14]problem.
> problem.

Here, as in the previous protocol extract on other collocates of 'discharge', there is again uncertainty. This time, it relates to the kind of object (± animate) which a particular verb can take (lines 2–5). This uncertainty simply revalidates the initial decision to include collocates of terms in the resource, a decision which was itself the outcome of the translation experiments reported in Chapter 3. After attention is drawn in lines 6–7 to the fact that there are many types of voting, the discussion extends beyond a spontaneous problem of a collocate for the term 'discharge motion', etc. and reaches into the conceptual system represented by voting types. In lines 8–10, it is inferred that traditional forms of indicating preference at elections or at meetings are by thumb-printing and by a show of hands (presumably as well as a voice voting procedure but for which no term is known to exist). The reference in line 9 to palm (tree) and cock stems from the fact that in the 1960s the two dominant political parties in the Efik area used these items as their respective symbols.[13] ('Graph' refers to the conceptual graphs which gave an overview of concepts in different sections of the resource).

Now, the American and British conceptual universes collectively distinguish between four voting procedures at least. This contact with a more differentiated SL system meant that Efik had to adjust. As the motivation for the traditional Efik voting terms was quite transparent, we ruled out the possibility of according one of these terms generic status, then adding to it qualifiers to correspond to the SL specialisations or types. In Efik, the word, *soño* commonly means 'ratify', 'concur with' (as in *soño akam emi*: agree to, say Amen to, this prayer). As seen in Table 8.5 below, this word is severally qualified to produce equivalents for types of voting.

An affirmative vote would be *soño ke iñ* (vote with yes), while the obverse would be *soño ke iñiñ*. The reduplicated form means 'no'.

8.8.4 More terms than bargained for

It is no doubt a reflection of the 'intertwingularity' of knowledge that one has to be concerned with terms other than those one had planned for. Definitions and contextual examples of terms often make use of many other terms. Guidelines for selecting contextual examples to elaborate terms perhaps have greater

---

13. Ọfiọñ Akak is thanked for this information.

Table 8.5: *Vote types*

collect the voices [GB]	sọñọ ke uyo (*vote with voice*)
voice vote [US]	sọñọ ke uyo (*vote with voice*)
roll call vote [US]	sọñọ ke enyiñ (*vote by name*)
teller vote [US]	nsaña mbe edisọñọ (*passing-by voting*)
division [GB]	nsaña mbe edisọñọ (*passing-by voting*)
standing vote [GB]	edisọñọ ke ndidada (*voting by standing*)

significance in the context of LP-oriented terminology management. In Fulford & Rogers (1990), as discussed by Ahmad & Fulford (1991), it is recommended that one should avoid "examples which contain more than two other technical terms (i.e. other terms which may need to be clarified by the reader before the contextual example can be fully understood)". While the concern of these authors is with the information processing load of the user of a resource, in the LP context the processing load is also at the producer's end. The problem of course is that at times the terminologist can do very little about what illustrative texts are used. In the language planning context, this means that the planner would routinely have to create more terms than had been envisaged, or prepared for.

With the exception of 'second reading committee [GB]', it was not intended to reflect names or types of committees in the resource. But we had to deal with 'select committee [GB]', 'standing committee [GB]' etc. occurring in definitions, contextual examples, etc. The time taken out to research these unplanned terms was in some cases well worth it. Without this research, 'standing committee', for instance, would most certainly have been rendered in a way to suggest it was a long-lasting committee. In the British Parliament, standing committee is quite the opposite (Antia, in prep.). While an initial outline of the above discussion (i.e. Antia, in prep.), drawn up in the course of work on the resource, sensitised me to such mine fields, the inability to research every such term (no thanks to time constraints) and/or give collaborators insights on each case necessarily implies the following:

1. in the TL only the main entry terms (including entailed terms) have term status;
2. TL equivalents proposed for other SL terms occurring in free text fields must be flagged as translation labels which would have to await systematic research to acquire term status;
3. certain collocate slots in the TL have been left blank;
4. free text fields (definitions, contextual examples, observations) produced by collaborators required utmost editorial attention, as collaborators could not be expected to identify such mines.

The next section is devoted to the team's work on free text fields.

8.8.5 *Knowledge of language, subject-matter and of translating*

What is suggested by some of the errors identified in Chapter 3 is that terminology planning, like translating or other instances of language-mediation, calls for much more than language competence. Obviously, knowledge of the subject matter is vital. Inadequate subject knowledge becomes particularly evident when a terminology resource has definitions that have to be translated or adapted from a SL. Bell (1991: 37) rightly specifies the translator's competence as requiring the integration of "linguistic knowledge of [...] two languages with specific and general knowledge of the domain and of the world via comparative and contrastive linguistic knowledge".

The earliest experience of conflict arising from the unevenness of these kinds of knowledge was at the plenary where a decision was to be taken on Efik equivalents for names of term fields. Here we were not yet dealing with knowledge of legislative business, but with the metalanguage of terminology. The field on 'observations' generated some debate. Pleas that what was intended were 'tips', 'remarks' or 'comments' on the main entry term were only reluctantly heeded after members had to be reminded of the authorship of the SL version! The designation, *ndausụñ* (guide), was eventually adopted. Previously as project chair I had given in on some less controversial points.

Let us now turn to knowledge of the domain of legislation and to translational skills. It might be recalled that the technical briefing given to collaborators comprised discussions on the interpretative theory of translating and on Nida's dynamic equivalence. In a restricted sense, the former addresses questions of subject knowledge while the latter relates to translation-procedural knowledge. Consider the challenge posed by the processing of the definition in the entry below.

> *Source text*
> Main entry term: contingent question closure [GB]
> Definition: [Commons] Without some further provision, the House might, even with the help of the closure, be unable to complete the matter then immediately in hand. [...].[A]fter a closure motion has been moved and acted upon, any Member may claim that such further questions be put forthwith as are requisite to bring to a decision the question already proposed from the Chair, no second closure being necessary. Source: May 406; 407
>
> *Back translation into English of collaborator's initial draft of the definition*
> With closure the House cannot end the business which members are considering at the given time: after the moving of a closure motion, any member may

request that questions be posed so that they serve as conclusion to the questions that existed. There is no need for second closure.

Post edited version (back translation into English)
The House voting affirmatively for a closure motion [**closure motion [GB]**]) does not mean that the House can conclude the main business being considered. It is possible that conclusion is first required on smaller items attached to the main business. Rather than waste time on moving closure motions on each of these smaller items, it is possible to use a contingent question closure to stop them, so a decision can be taken on the main business.

The language and style of the collaborator's initial draft was hardly impeachable. Yet, the text (particularly the second half) hardly communicated. What emerges here is that the knowledge base and text analysis skills required for an interpreting-oriented translation were lacking. The editorial process involved in improving these TL draft texts varied. Depending on the specific circumstances, editing called for: 'enabling' or retouching the English text field in order to facilitate translation into Efik; rewriting the entire Efik text; and making minor modifications.

8.9 Linguistic analysis of target language terms

One dimension of language planning has to do with intervening in the form or structure of language. It is therefore in order to document how we intervened in the structure of Efik in the course of creating the legislative resource. First, an overview. Table 8.6 is a summary of the resource's 187 TL terms as distributed over two sets of criteria: status and source.

The Table shows: (1) that 82% of the 187 terms had to be created; (2) that 70% of the new TL terms are based on endogenous resources; and (3) that 87% of these endogenously based terms are multi-unit terms, that is, they consist of more than one word. This latter finding can be further specified. The more detailed breakdown from which the above summary was abstracted shows that the 23 one-unit terms belong to the category of pre-existing terms. This, in effect, means that none of

Table 8.6: *Distribution of terms according to status and source*

Status of term		Source of term		
Neologism	Pre-existing	Endogenous		Exogenous
		multi- unit	one- unit	
154	33	160	23	4

the newly created endogenous terms was a one-unit term.

Consistent with these figures, much of the analysis that ensues focuses on the multi-unit endogenous terms. However, a comment on the exogenous as well as the one-unit terms should be in order here. The forms borrowed, that is, the exogenous terms, are: 'order', 'committee' (which occurs twice) and 'guillotine'. These forms are borrowed respectively as *ọda, kọmiti* and *kiotịn*. In the latter example, the phoneme /g/ is substituted for /k/ because this obtains in the speech of monolingual speakers of Efik. Because we have borrowed from the correct French pronunciation (as opposed to some English adulteration), the glide represented orthographically by 'uillo' is interpreted in Efik as the diphthong /io/.

Of the 23 endogenous one-unit terms which were said to be comprised in the pre-existing set, only one, *mbet*, had a domain-specific acceptation. It is the TL equivalent of 'act'/'law'. Very many others like *ediomi* and *iwụk* (synonyms for 'resolution'), *ntọt* ('report'), *nneme* ('debate') have had to be semantically extended, or terminologised, terminologisation being the process whereby an existing LGP word is used to designate a concept in a given LSP field (Picht & Draskau 1985; Arntz & Picht 1989: 120). In the following paragraphs, the multi-unit endogenous terms are analysed from the standpoint of form and function.

But for two verbal phrases,[14] all the other instances of multi-unit terms can, broadly speaking, be assigned to the class of nominals (derived or non-derived). The diversity of processes and categories involved in creating terms is highlighted better by an analysis of the modifiers, rather than the heads, of these multi-unit nominals. Table 8.7 is a categorial distribution of modifiers in the 160 multi-unit terms found in the resource.

It is interesting to note that much of the load of modifying the head nouns is borne by nominals, with adjectives accounting for only 27%.

The two categories 'adjective' and 'nominals' are quite broad, and may be discussed in terms of types. In examples cited, the heads of the constructions are in brackets. Let us begin with the category on adjectives.

Table 8.7: *Categorial distribution of modifiers*

Adjectives	Nominals	Prepositional phrases	Adverbs
44	109	8	1

---

14. That is, *nọ esọk* [GB] and *nọ esọk* [US], literally 'send to', for the term, 'commit'. To commit a bill is to send it to a committee.

8.9.1 *Simple adjectives*

These are single words, and may be derived as in 1 below or non-derived as in 2:

(1) ntaha [uneñede]
    worthless straightening
    'Pro forma amendment'[15]

(2) akamba [ọda]
    big order
    'Standing order'[16]

8.9.2 *Partially and totally reduplicated adjectives*

Reduplication is associated with (many) Efik adverbs. These adverbs are formed by doubling a noun or an adjective, as Essien notes in respect of a closely related language (Essien 1990: 23). Be that as it may, there are in Efik: (a) attributive adjectives that are inherently reduplicated; (b) adjectives that are reduplicated to emphasise a given quality, or reduplicated forms that can in abstraction be assigned to the category of adjectives or adverbs; and (c) adverbs used as attributive adjectives.[17] Building on one or the other precedent, we have put in the resource reduplicated forms that function as adjectives, some presumably for the first time. Some examples:

(3) ibio ibio [edifiak nnọ esọk]
    short short (or) brief brief to again send to
    'Simple recommittal'[18]

---

15. A definition in the resource, taken from Legi.Slate, reads: "Pro forma amendments are 'nonsense' amendments in the House which may be offered only during the amendment process in the Committee of the Whole to obtain five additional minutes of debate time".

16. Unlike sessional orders which have to be renewed on the first day of a new parliamentary session, standing orders remain in force until vacated by the House.

17. Example for (a): *obubụt* 'black' as in *obubụt owo* 'black person'. But the predicative variant of this adjective *bre* is not reduplicated (*enye ebre* = 'he is dark complexioned'), except when serving to emphasise this quality. Example for (b): *ñkịm ñkịm* 'dark' as in *ñkịm ñkịm itie* 'a dark place', or as in *itie oro etie ñkịm ñkịm* 'that place is dark'. Example for (c): *ikpọñ ikpọñ eyen* 'an only child'.

18. Unlike the motion, 'recommit with instructions [US]', through which a bill is sent to a committee for it to carry out specific tasks within a given time frame, a 'simple recommital [US]' gives no such tasks and is, in principle, a summary verdict on (or adverse disposal of) the bill. The motion, in other words, kills the bill.

(4)   ọkpọ ọkpọ   [usio   mbono nnịm]
      single single (or) unique unique postponement of   meeting
      'extraordinary adjournment'[19]

(5)   ket ket   [nsek   mbet]
      IDEOPHONE   orderly bill
      'clean bill'[20]

8.9.3 Adjectival phrases

An example of one such phrase qualifying the head noun is:

(6)   [ikot]   ọyọhọ   ikata
      reading   number (or ordinal adjective formant) three
      'third reading'

Let us turn now to subdivisions in the category of nominal qualifiers.

8.9.4 Simple nouns

Following a pattern attested in the language, nouns intended to function as modifiers have been juxtaposed to heads. Some of these modifier single nouns are derived (as in 7), while others are not (as in 8).

(7)   [ñwed]   uñwana
      book (or) document.for light
      'explanatory memorandum'[21]

Uñwana derives from the verb *ñwaña* (enlighten, illuminate).

---

19. In the British Parliament, an adjournment occasioned by say, the death of a Member, of some important personality, or due to a royal ceremony.

20. In the terminology resource, part of the entry on 'clean bill [US]', taken from CQ Washington Alert, reads: "Frequently after a committee has finished a major revision of a bill, one of the committee members, usually the chairman, will assemble the changes and what is left of the original bill into a new measure and introduce it as a 'clean bill'".

21. Part of the relevant entry in the resource gives the following definition, taken from Hawtrey/Barclay: "The member introducing a bill may have printed with it, at the beginning, a memorandum explaining its purposes, or its financial proposals. This is known as an explanatory memorandum".

(8) [nsek mbet] isụñutom
     bill.of   messenger/emissary
     'delegated legislation' (synonym: secondary legislation).[22]

8.9.5 Complex noun phrases

These can also serve as modifiers, as in example 9:

(9) [ikọ]   minịk kiet
     talk.of minute one
     'one minute speech'

8.9.6 Agentive prefix

Efik is able to nominalise verb phrases in such a way as to make the resulting construction have the sense of '*doer of* the verb complement'. Thus, *aka isañ*: 'goer on a journey (traveller)'. Besides expressing the agent, the vowel prefix can also specify a state or function of the noun to which it is juxtaposed. Some examples:

(10) anana   ebuana   [uneñede]
     lacker.of relation straightening
     'rider' (synonym: 'non-germane amendment')

(11) ebeiso   [nsek mbet]
     goer.in.front bill
     (one of the TL synonyms proposed for 'dummy bill')

Although *ebeiso* in 11 is written as one word, it actually consists of two, namely, *be* (the verb for 'pass'), and *iso* (front). The particular nominalising vowel prefix is determined by vowel harmony. Thus, in (10) the vowel prefix is *a* because the disyllabic verb root to which it is attached (*nana*) has this same vowel on both syllables. In (11), the monosyllabic verb root *be* has the vowel *e*, hence the vowel prefix is *e*. There are rules governing less straightforward cases.

---

22. In the British Parliament, this is law made by persons or authorities under powers accorded by an Act of Parliament. Delegated legislation is therefore law that is not directly made by Parliament.

8.10 Creation of a MultiTerm database

To create a MultiTerm database with the data obtained by procedures described earlier in this chapter, the structure of the database had to be first defined. Three MultiTerm index fields were defined — for English, Efik and Source ID. The Source ID index field, inspired by Schmitz's model at Cologne's University of Applied Sciences, contains full bibliographical information on sources of data for the terminology resource. As I had to represent Efik with a special font but wished to use the system's default font for English, these language index fields were assigned different fonts. Figure 8.2 presents the structure of the legislative database (called 'legis'). The foregrounded box titled 'Database definition' shows that the language highlighted (Efik) has AfroRoman® as default font. Text fields were then defined for available data, and in a few cases (e.g. Formulaic expressions, pronunciation, Comment) for anticipated data.

The font considerations in respect of the index fields equally apply to text fields. Separate text fields, which would otherwise have been unnecessary, had to be defined for text information attached to both languages. English text fields have an initial upper case, while the Efik fields have an initial lower case.[23]

Currently, the English and Efik index fields do not have an identical list of text fields. For example, all bibliographical text fields are attached to the English index field (see discussion in Chapter 7.7 on implications of language engineering applications). The list of text fields, inspired in part by Schmitz's Cologne model, is as follows: *Definition, Source, Contextual example, Collocations, Observation, Formulaic expressio(n), definition, contextual example, collocations, observation, pronunciation, source, Title, Place of publicatio(n), Publisher, Responsibility, Source author/URL, Year, Edition, Pages, In:journal, In:issue+ pages, In:editor, Rank/affiliation, Date of info, Comment.* See Figure 8.2. A few less obvious text fields invite brief comments. *Rank/affiliation* applies to the author of a source consulted. *Date of Info* applies to the date information was obtained at a given Uniform Resource Locator (URL) or Internet location.

Four attribute fields are currently defined as Figure 8.2 also shows. They are: *Subject, Term Category, Usage Label* and *Chamber*. It would be recalled from the system presentation in Chapter 7 that attribute fields allow for the specification of values. These values form a picklist. The picklist displayed in

---

23. Technical considerations led to the abandonment of the Efik field names for English ones. In the definition of a database structure in MultiTerm there is a limit to the number of characters (including spaces) which a field name may have. A few English field names are truncated (e.g. Place of **publicatio**).

APPLICATIONS 217

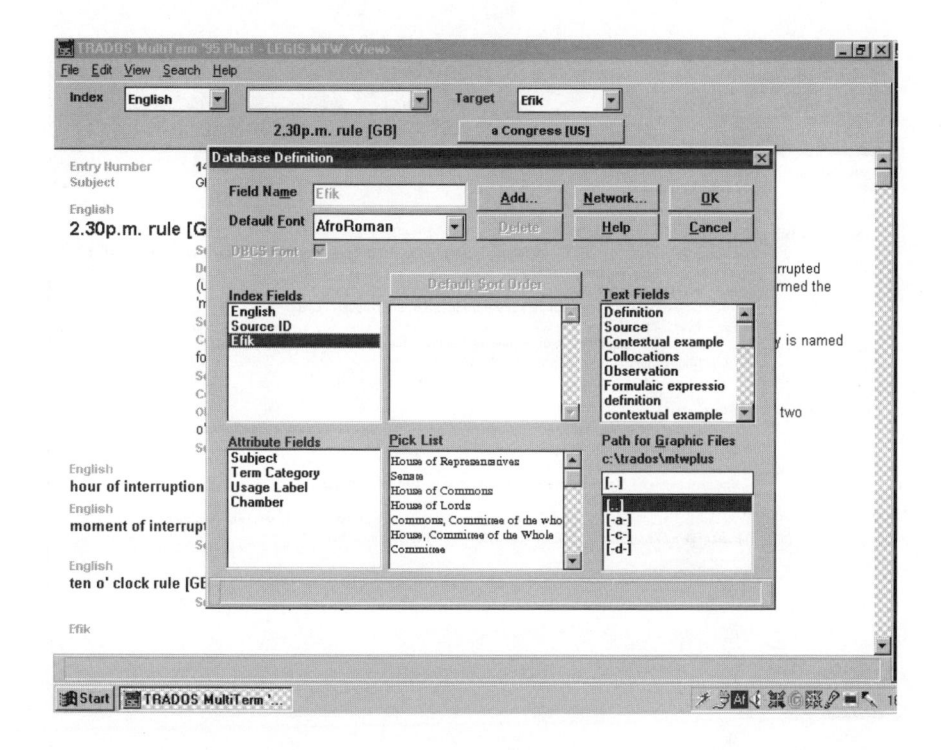

Figure 8.2: *Definition of the database structure for 'legis'*

Figure 8.2 is in respect of *Chamber*, by which I mean the deliberation forum (in the two legislatures treated) with which a particular concept is associated. The picklist values for this attribute are: House of Representatives; Senate; House of Commons; House of Lords; Commons, Committee of the whole; House, Committee of the Whole; Committee. The other attributes also have their picklist values, the names of which have (occasionally) been shortened for technical reasons. Thus, *Subject* has: GB legbiz & mgt, US legbiz & mgt, GB subst non-legbiz, US subst non-legbiz, GB modification, US modification, GB time & debate mgt, US time & debate mgt, GB periods & breaks, US periods & breaks, GB deciding & voting, US deciding & voting. (See Section 8.2 for the full names). As values, *Term Category* has: long form, short form, abbreviation, quasi-synonym, legal terminology, proposed. *Usage Label* has: official, informal, obsolete, standardised, preferable, recommended, acceptable. Many of these values currently represent anticipated needs. Since the version of MultiTerm used supports the

218   TERMINOLOGY AND LANGUAGE PLANNING

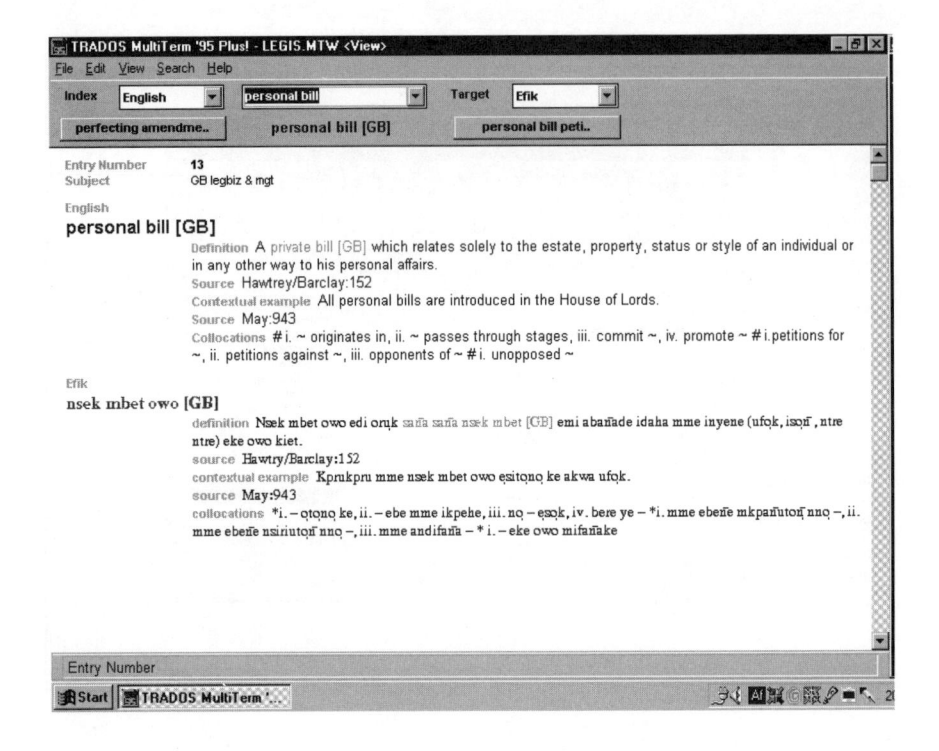

![Screenshot of TRADOS MultiTerm '95 Plus! showing a sample entry]

TRADOS MultiTerm '95 Plus! - LEGIS.MTW <View>
File Edit View Search Help

Index: **English**   personal bill   Target: **Efik**

perfecting amendme..   personal bill [GB]   personal bill peti..

Entry Number   13
Subject   GB legbiz & mgt

English
personal bill [GB]
Definition A private bill [GB] which relates solely to the estate, property, status or style of an individual or in any other way to his personal affairs.
Source Hawtrey/Barclay:152
Contextual example All personal bills are introduced in the House of Lords.
Source May:943
Collocations # i. ~ originates in, ii. ~ passes through stages, iii. commit ~, iv. promote ~ # i.petitions for ~, ii. petitions against ~, iii. opponents of ~ # i. unopposed ~

Efik
nsek mbet owo [GB]
definition Nsek mbet owo edi oruk saña saña nsek mbet [GB] emi abañade idaha mme inyene (ufok, isoñ, ntre ntre) eke owo kiet.
source Hawtry/Barclay:152
contextual example Kprukpru mme nsek mbet owo esitono ke akwa ufok.
source May:943
collocations *i. – otono ke, ii. – ebe mme ikpehe, iii. no – esok, iv. bere ye – *i. mme ebeñe mkpañutoñ nno –, ii. mme ebeñe nsiriutoñ nno –, iii. mme andifaña – * i. – eke owo mifañake

Entry Number

Start   TRADOS MultiTerm '...

Figure 8.3: *Sample MultiTerm entry (personal bill)*

display of graphics, a path (the default) for graphic files was specified.

Having thus defined the database, the terminology resource (which existed previously in word processor files) was customised to the database definition, then imported into MultiTerm. The English part of the resource posed no problems. For reasons having to do presumably with improvisation during the creation of the Efik resource, the imported Efik data revealed significant integrity loss. This compelled the adoption of a complementary data transfer strategy, one that would allow for the easy identification and correction of problems. Editing was done in the AfroRoman font environment (which was not the environment in which the resource was created initially). Cut and paste (from a word processor file into a selected MultiTerm record field) was employed, followed by post-editing. Figure 8.3 above is a display of an entry (personal bill). The number of data fields an entry has depends on what information was available.

Geographical provenance, as might be recalled, is typically managed as an

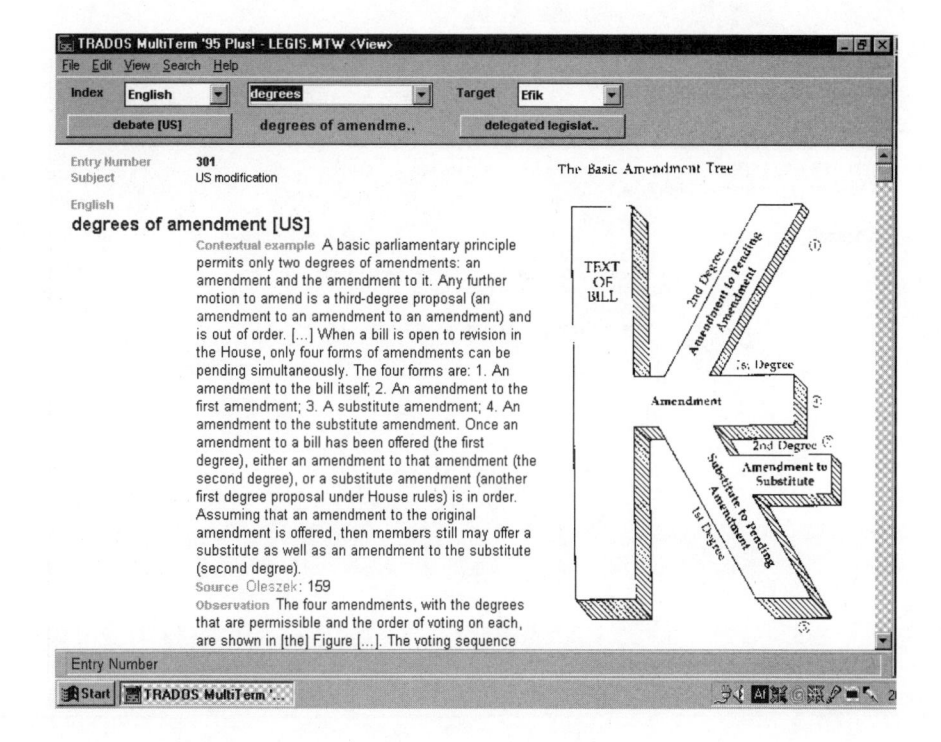

Figure 8.4: *Sample entry with graphic illustration*

attribute in MultiTerm. The unconventional representation of this information in a way that makes it part of terms is explained by several factors, none the least of which is the need to create correct hyperlinks. Because of several facts — (1) MultiTerm (95' Plus, professional edition) uses index fields as basis for cross references; (2) data for the terminology is taken from American and British legislatures; (3) the data shows (a) instances of identical concepts having identical labels and (b) different concepts having identical labels — it became compelling to integrate some discrimination-enhancing marker into the terms in order for hyperlinks to be properly understood by the system.

Let us examine other aspects of the database. Figure 8.4 above is an entry that has graphic illustration. As mentioned in the discussion on database definition, the 'legis' database also has bibliographical data which can be searched as one would look up terms. A mouse click on Oleszek (the name written against the *source* field) in Figure 8.4 takes the user to the bibliographical entry in Figure 8.5.

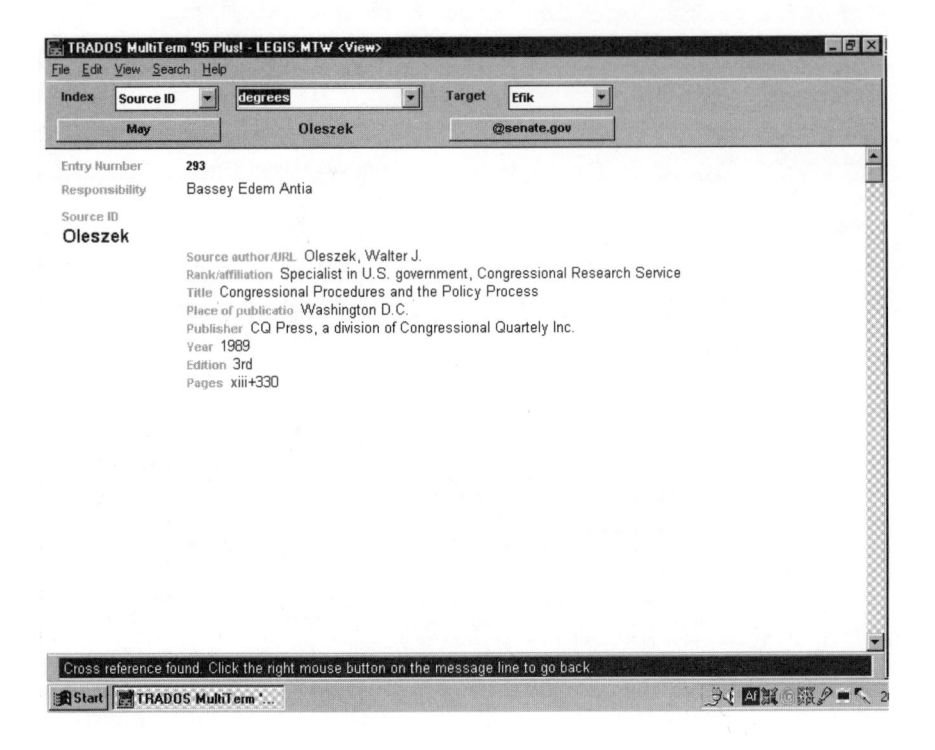

Figure 8.5: *Sample bibliographical entry*

8.11 The terminology resource, MultiTerm and the experiments

In the translation and knowledge experiments reported in Chapter 3, a number of issues were raised from the standpoint of the reference resources. It may be worthwhile speculating on whether these or other issues would arise in a hypothetical re-creation of the experimental settings in which the changed variables would be: (1) the fact that the resource consulted is the one developed in this work; (2) that it is managed in a MultiTerm environment; and (3) that it is consulted on-line. What weights should attach to these variables can be determined by the reader. In the discussion below, MultiTerm, the software (note uppercases in spelling), must not be confused with word combinations variously referred to as multi-unit term, multiterm or multi-word term.

Identifying and parsing of multi-unit terms was a problem common to the two translation protocols. It would be recalled from the dTAP that, in formulating or verbalising searches, experimental subjects occasionally gave the impression (that is, before the glossary was actually consulted) that they would be quite happy if they found only part of a multi-unit term (recall 'adjournment of the house'). This assumption was of course quite exaggerated, and in the specific instance cited here, the glossary helped to avoid a probable error by entering the form 'adjournment of the house'. But as noted earlier, the error evident in the translation of 'substantive motion for the adjournment of the house' (where 'for' is rendered as a causal conjunction rather than as a genetive preposition) is the result of the glossary not entering this form, thus not helping the subjects to identify it as a single multi-unit term.

Interestingly, using the software, MultiTerm, to manage the legislative resource described in this chapter makes it possible to address two matters arising from the translation experiments, namely: (1) the minimal or truncated-word search instincts of the translators; and (2) the challenge of correct recognition of multi-unit terms. As the foregrounded box in Figure 8.6a (on page 222) shows, by typing *substanti* into the search field a Hit List is displayed. This list contains two matching items: (1) the text segment that had not been reckoned with, that is, had not been the focus of the search ('substantive motion for the adjournment of the house'), and (2) the term the user actually searched ('substantive motion'), which, on inspection, turns out to be a different concept from the one s/he in fact had in mind.

A mouse click on any of the two matches leads to the corresponding entry record in which the target language equivalents are to be found. The problem of interpreting the acceptation of *for* (causal conjunction or genetive preposition) does not therefore arise.

Similarly a global search performed on 'amendment' or a truncation thereof would have prevented the iTAP subject from erroneously conflating two amendment types ('leave out words' and 'insert words') into their conjunctive cognate ('leave out and to insert words') which the subject had seen earlier (see §3 & §4 of translation text). The use, not of a conjunction that translates as 'and', but of a phrase that translates as 'in order to', makes this conflation matter. Figure 8.6b (on page 223) is a Hit List on *amend* matches. To reduce the sense of information overload, a filter on subject might have been defined that would have excluded amendment terms of a particular legislature.

Another issue in the translation protocols was the question of search misses, that is, of terms in the source language text that could not be found in the reference glossary. It bears repeating that what matters is not so much how exhaustive a resource actually is, but the potential for exhaustiveness of the methodologies underlying the resource. It is in the nature of hardcopy and

222   TERMINOLOGY AND LANGUAGE PLANNING

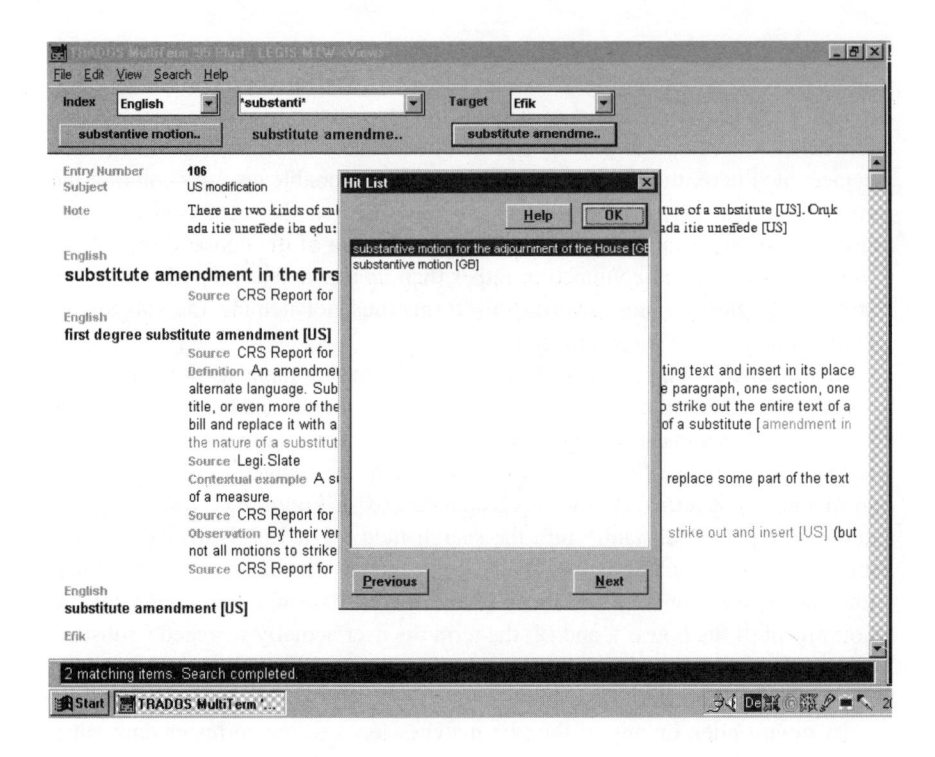

Figure 8.6a: *Wildcard search in support of minimal search instinct and correct term identification*

privately-owned resources that user interactions with them provide at best haphazard and limited data on what improvements need to be made. A MultiTerm database, particularly in network environment, stresses the process and co-operative nature of terminology resources, and allows for a systematic harnessing of otherwise difficult-to-track data from user interaction with a given terminology. The important information resource represented by terms not found in the glossary in the experiments is completely lost to the producers of the glossary. In MultiTerm such misses can be logged and used as basis for adding new entries. If one searched the 'legis' database for 'appropriation bill', one would not find it. If one logged this term, on the prompting of MultiTerm, one could retrieve it (along with other logged terms) from a word processor. The information retrieved would look like this:

    appropriation bill ⟨English⟩ super

APPLICATIONS 223

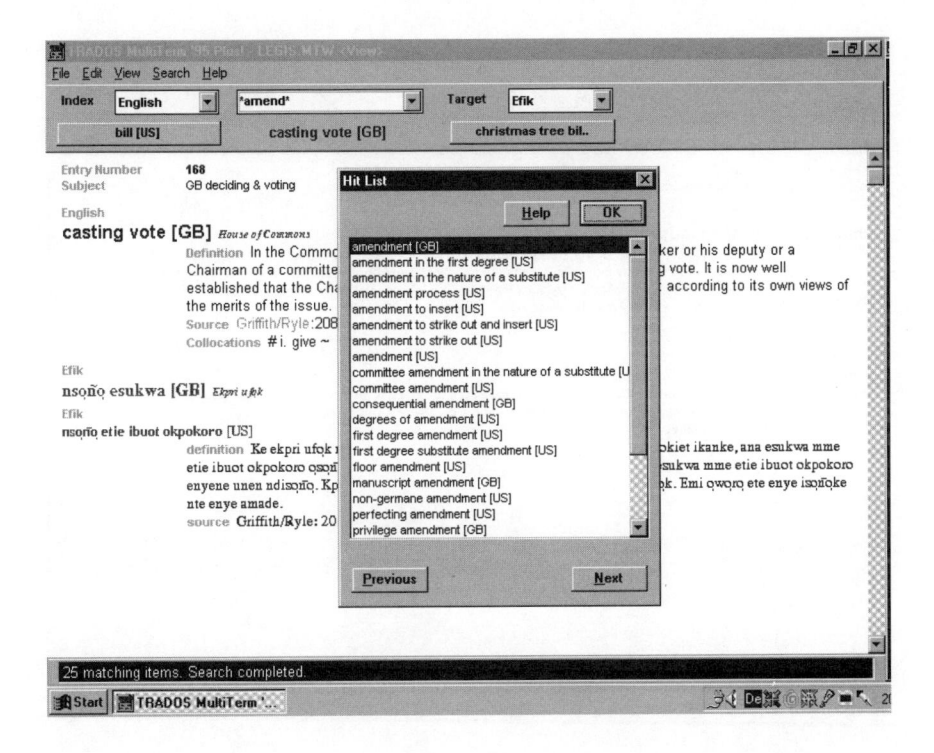

Figure 8.6b: *Wildcard search in support of minimal search instinct and correct term identification*

The first item refers to the search term, the second to the index at the time of search (the English index field in this case), and the third item refers to the identification of the user who performed the unsuccessful search.

A further issue raised by the translation protocols was that of the self-commendation of solutions proposed by the glossary. Arising from this were a number of issues like the creation or modification of knowledge models in the heads of experimental subjects, processing time, and wrong decision-making. The dTAP and iTAP teams, respectively, were seen to have problems with the glossary solutions for 'adjournment of the House' and 'adjournment of debate'. It would be recalled that the processing done by the dTAP subjects led to the erroneous belief that the Hausa proposals in each case were free variants, a belief which in turn led to a wrong decision. While the solution proposed by the iTAP subject could not exactly be faulted, the logic underlying this solution (and for that reason, the rejection of the glossary entry) was wrong. The knowledge

TERMINOLOGY AND LANGUAGE PLANNING

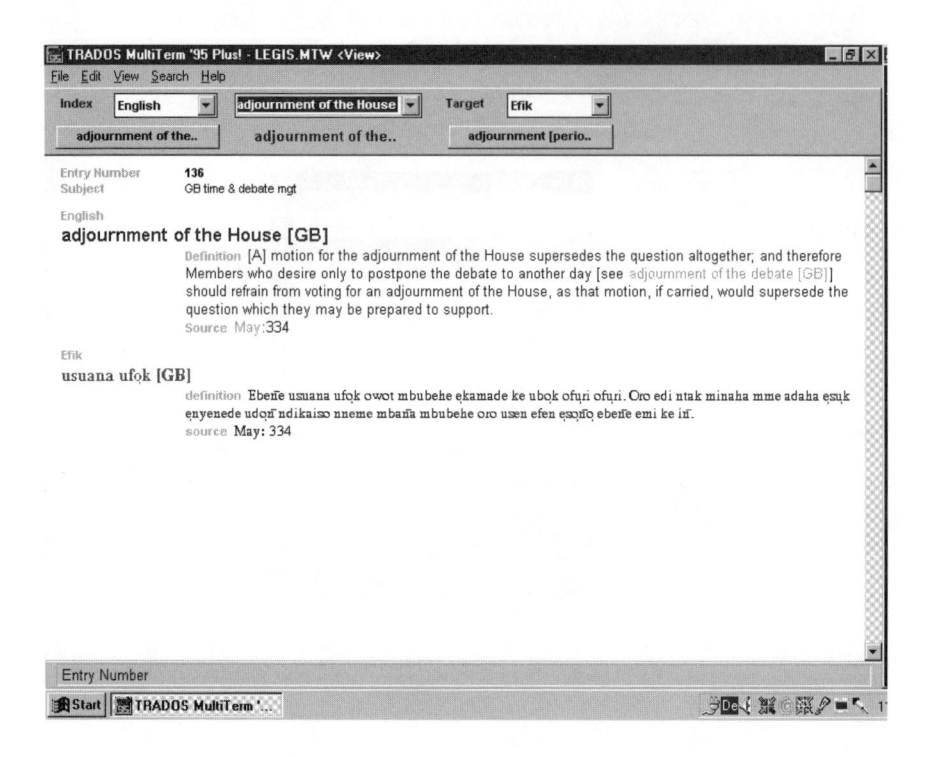

[Screenshot of TRADOS MultiTerm '95 Plus! - LEGIS.MTW window]

```
Index: English    adjournment of the House    Target: Efik
       adjournment of the..    adjournment of the..    adjournment [perio..

Entry Number    136
Subject         GB time & debate mgt

English
adjournment of the House [GB]
        Definition [A] motion for the adjournment of the House supersedes the question altogether; and therefore
        Members who desire only to postpone the debate to another day [see adjournment of the debate [GB]]
        should refrain from voting for an adjournment of the House, as that motion, if carried, would supersede the
        question which they may be prepared to support.
        Source May:334

Efik
usuana ufọk [GB]
        definition Ebeñe usuana ufọk owot mbubehe ekamade ke ubọk ofụri ofụri. Oro edi ntak minaha mme adaha esụk
        enyenede udọñ ndikaiso nneme mbañā mbubehe oro usen efen esọñọ eberie emi ke iñ.
        source May: 334
```

Figure 8.7: *Entry on 'adjournment of the House [GB]' with hyperlink to partial cognate*

system set up by the subject, and within which he evaluated glossary finds, saw an invalid distinction being made between a more substantial kind of termination and a less substantial one (e.g. intra-*diurnal* or daily termination).

The foregoing problem was said to lie fundamentally in the fact that the glossary provided no descriptive data for its entries. The resource developed here provides for various categories of concept/term descriptive data as seen in the database structure definition. The facility for creating hyperlinks in MultiTerm makes it possible for a certain configuration of knowledge to be imparted to users. Figure 8.7 above is the British entry on 'adjournment of the House'. By clicking on the node represented by 'adjournment of the debate [GB]' the user is able to inspect this concept, and compare it to the former.

Turning to the knowledge experiments, the absence of descriptive data in respect of entries was also a problem. This was particularly evident in the German subject's richer protocol. A number of the subject's inferences were seen

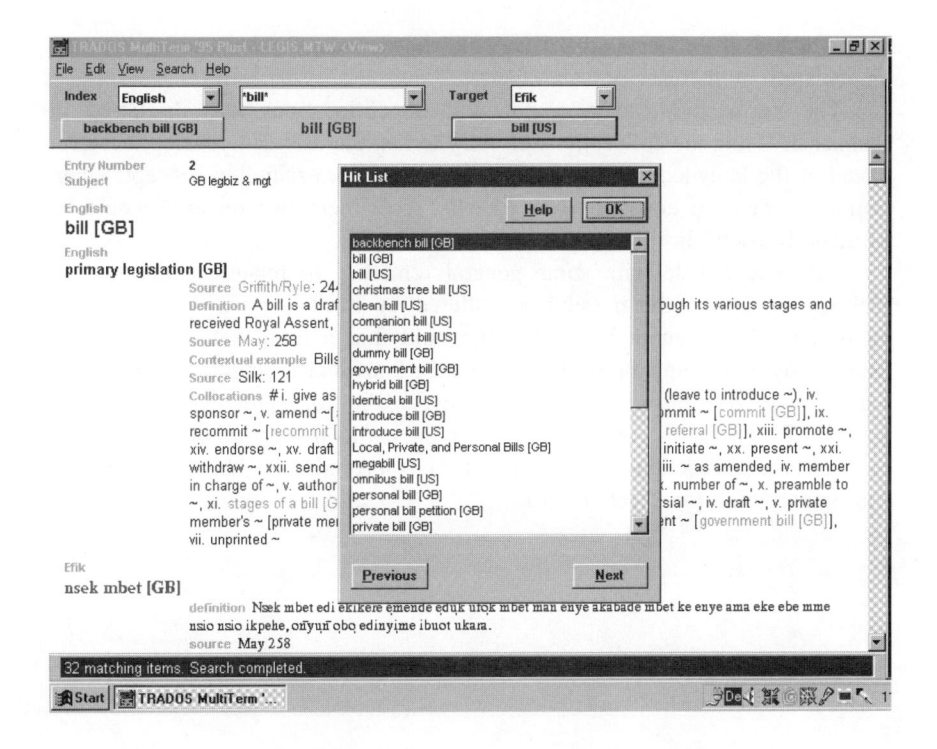

Figure 8.8: *Wildcard search for 'bill'*

to be inaccurate, a situation that might have been averted if two types of descriptive information had been available: clues on relationships between synonymous terms, and descriptions of the (specialised) acceptation of terms. For the Nigerian subject, a significant problem was that of access to the relevant information available in the glossary, a problem which was explained by the alphabetical representation strategy adopted in the glossary. A relationship was also established between tautology in this subject's protocol and the dearth of data.

From preceding sections it may already be obvious how the resource developed in this work and managed as a MultiTerm database addresses the problems in the knowledge protocols. The concept orientation of the resource means that all terms that are synonymous are contained in the same entry. Textual description means that user-inferred and error-prone senses (based generally on knowledge of the LGP) are excluded. Hyperlinks ensure guided access around the resource. A wildcard search such as Figure 8.8 (on page 225) means that all the concepts that have 'bill' in their designation can be accessed immediately by the user.

The knowledge-mediating potential of collocations was discussed in Chapter 5. Using the collocations of entry terms, the user can develop a correct model of the knowledge subspace into which the corresponding concepts enter. Collocates that are entailed terms (that is, have their own records) would be particularly useful in this respect.

Let us conclude with some general remarks. To relate the question of spelling in Efik to the possibilities offered by MultiTerm: a user who was mindful of the potential for variation would find a term that existed in the database by first typing a pound sign, then the known or preferred spelling of the search term. As for the relationship between the conceptual graphs and the resource, it is perhaps worth noting that in the hardcopy version of the resource, each of the six sections (see Section 8.2) is preceded by the corresponding conceptual graph (see Section 8.6).

Conclusion

This book sought to establish the bases for alternative needs analysis, work methodologies as well as modes of theorisation in the area of general and African *language planning* (LP), specifically planning in respect of terminology. A review of discourse and product samples connected with this activity revealed that: (1) there often is a gap between the stated goals of terminology planning and the actual products; (2) an inadequate theoretical framework is employed in conceptualising the goals and challenges of terminology planning as well as in evaluating the products of this planning; (3) there is insufficient understanding of (i) the nature of specialised language (in particular from science theory perspectives, discourse/syntagmatic dimensions, etc.), (ii) of the mission of specialist language and (iii) of the place of terminology in this agenda.

To obtain a framework for understanding these observations as well as for addressing the issues they raise, the book drew from a variety of theoretical sources: translation process analysis; (LSP) text linguistics; aspects of knowledge theory; theory of word combinations; thematic lexicography; documentation science; corpus linguistics; knowledge representation; and natural language processing technology. But in all of these, the ultimate goal has been practical, informed as it is by a need to deregulate access to specialised knowledge, and therefore to enhance popular participation in society in its local, national, regional or global dimensions.

Besides opening up the academic communities of LP and terminology to each other (through an exploration of their respective concerns), the book makes specific contributions to these two fields and to a number of other areas. This is evident in the following: application of translation process analysis studies to terminology evaluation; exploration of the textual status of terminologies; examination of the dichotomy 'general language' and 'specialised language' from the standpoint of corresponding sign models or model constellations (particularly the ontical and epistemic bases of these models); provision of process data on terminology creation — much sought after in the scientific communities of terminology management and language planning; development of a flexible model of word combinations for technical legislative discourse; modelling of knowledge on legislative practice; and proposal of a methodology for terminology planning in languages with limited written specialised corpora.

The shift implied in the book, from the realm of virtual models (of specialised communication, knowledge) to real, empirical representations, is an expression of the need for increased social relevance of LP-oriented terminology scholarship and practice. In the several ways the book has linked terminology to knowledge, its sustained thrust has been that LP-oriented terminology management is the basis for the creation, transfer and communication of specialised knowledge.

The point can be made, as have indeed Fishman (1974) and Budin (1990), that national macro-planning would do well to notice the system linkages which language and terminology planning and policy maintain with educational planning and policy, cultural planning and policy, agricultural planning and policy, science and technology planning and policy, etc. In an age where rapid access to specialised information and knowledge is crucial, knowledge and discourse-inflected terminologies in indigenous languages are a key to the intellectual, economic and political empowerment of marginalised populations all over the world.

Some of the foregoing propositions are illustrated in the book by the specialised discourse and knowledge connected with legislative practice. The terminology resource developed in the course of research on this book (and described in Chapter 8) provides knowledge and discourse 'infrastructures', not just for the conduct of aspects of technical legislative business in the Efik language, but also for authoring or translating texts in the language. On the basis of this terminology, a text such as the following, presumably without precedent, can be authored in Efik. The text is preceded by a poem, a literary form most cherished by the Efiks and useful for generating interest in a variety of discourses.

Source language
Ukara ekọñ, ukara ikañ
Enyene ikañ otop, afo ọbọ ukara
ọbọde ukara, anam se amade
Ke mbono, kpukpru owo ẹnyek ye ndịk
Oyomde ẹwụk ñkpọ, onyụñ obụp mme ẹwụk
Mbon utom fo ẹda ikwo ẹbọrọ ẹwụk
Mme unyụñ umaha ẹwụk, obụp mme ẹfre
Mmọ ẹnyụñ ẹbọrọ ẹfre
Edi ukara mbon obio itiehe ntem o!

Ke America ye ke Britain, usụñ nte ẹsidade ẹnam mbet ayak mbon obio me mme adaha emi mmọ ẹkẹmekde ẹnọ ekikere mmọ. Ke

Translation into English
Military rule, rule of the gun
Have one to shoot, and take over power
In power, you do as you please
At meetings, your colleagues quake with fear
To have a policy enacted, you ask: approved?
In unison your colleagues chorus: approved!
To kill an initiative you ask: disapproved?
Again in unison they chorus: disapproved!
Legislative democracy is not like this.

In America as in Britain, the law-making process allows for input from citizens and from their elected representatives. In both of

CONCLUSION

idụt mbiba emi, ufọk mbet esinyene mbak iba - ekpri ufọk ye akwa ufọk. Nsek mbet emi etịmde odụk ufọk enyene ndibọ se ẹdiọñọde nte akpa edikot. Ke ekpri ufọk ke America, ẹma ẹkụre ye ikpehe emi ana ẹnọ nsek mbet oro aka kọmiti, ndien kọmiti onyụñ ekeme ndinọ nsek mbet aka ñkọk esie kiet. Ke kọmiti me ke ñkọk kọmiti, mme adaha ẹyẹneme nsek mbet oro, ẹnyụñ ẹdụk mbono ẹdiọñọde nte mkpañutọñ. Mbono emi ọnọ mbon obio ifet nditịñ se mmọ ẹkerede ẹbaña nsek mbet anade kọmiti ke iso. Kọmiti me ñkọk kọmiti amakụre ndụñọde, nneme ye uneñede esie, ana enye ọtọt ubiere esie kabaña nsek mbet oro ọnọ ofụri ufọk. Do ndien ke ẹdinọ nsek mbet oro udiana edikot. Ke akwa ufọk ke America, udiana edikot esida itie ke ini ẹnọde nsek mbet ẹsọk kọmiti.

Ke ufọk mbet mbiba ke Britain, udiana edikot esinyụñ ada itie mbemiso ẹnọ nsek mbet ẹsọk kọmiti. Ke Britain udiana edikot edi ata akpa nneme ẹnyenede ẹbaña nsek mbet. Ikpehe emi edi ufañ ndineme ntak ẹdade nsek mbet edi ufọk. Ke mfaña odude, ẹsisọñọ ke nneme ama okụre. Edieke mmọ emi ẹsọñọde ke iñiñ ẹwakde ẹkan, nsek mbet oro idikaha aba iso. Edieke ẹbierede ndika iso ye nsek mbet oro, ẹyẹnọ enye ẹsọk kọmiti. Do ke ẹditịm ineme enye ke ikpehe ke ikpehe. Kọmiti ọnode ntọt, ana ufọk ọtọñọ ntak eneme abaña nsek mbek oro.

Ke mbak mbiba ẹdude ke ufọk mbet eke idụt iba emi, akpatre ikpehe emi nsek mbet enyenede ndibe edi se ẹdiọñọde nte ikot ọyọhọ ikata. Ikpehe emi edi akpatre ini ẹdisọñọde nsek mbet nte ẹma ẹkẹneñede enye enịm. Nsek mbet ebede kpukpru mme ikpehe emi ke ufọk emi enye ọkọtọñọde, enye enyene nditọñọ ntak mbe mme ukem ikpehe emi ke ufok enyeken. Ke akpatre, ufọk mbiba ẹyẹnọ nsek mbet oro ẹsọk edidem (ke Britain) mme ibuot ukara (ke America). Nsek mbet oro edikabare ata mbet ke ini edidem ọnọde edidiọñ esie (ke Britain) mme ke ini ibuot ukara esịnde ubọk (ke America).

these countries the national legislature has two chambers. A bill that is properly brought into the legislature receives what is known as first reading. In the U.S. House of Representatives, the first reading stage is followed by referral to committee, and the committee may in turn refer the bill to one of its subcommittees. In committee or subcommittee, members discuss the bill, and summon sessions known as hearings. These meetings afford citizens the opportunity to give their opinion on the bill that is pending in the committee. After its investigations, debates and amendments, the committee reports its decisions on the bill to the entire House. The bill then receives its second reading. In the U.S. Senate, second reading takes place when the bill is referred to a committee.

In both Houses of the British Parliament, second reading also takes place prior to committal of the bill. In this Parliament second reading is the very first debate over a bill. This stage is an opportunity to discuss the justification for the bill. Where there is controversy, a vote is taken after the debate. If opponents of the bill outnumber those in favour, the bill is dropped. If it is decided that the bill should go ahead, the bill is committed. In committee, the bill is discussed thoroughly, clause by clause. On receiving the committee's report, the House again considers the bill.

In the two Chambers of both national legislatures, the last stage a bill has to go through is known as third reading. This is the stage at which the bill as amended is voted on for the last time. A bill that has gone through all of the above stages in the Chamber in which it originated has to go through these same stages in the other Chamber. At the end, both Chambers send the bill to the Crown or to the President. The bill becomes law after it has received royal assent or has been signed by the president.

In a report on a conference (Antia 1996c), it was noted that the contemporary history of terminology as a practice and as a discipline was one of two-directional interface in which terminology at once drew from, and served a variety of, disciplines. This paradoxical relationship is evident in some of the following concluding propositions.

In serving the educational or instructional enterprise as in the above text, terminology also depends on educational structures for its psychological anchor within a language community. Evaluations of new terms phrased in questions such as *What do you think this term means?* or *What is the English equivalent of this term?* proceed from a widespread fallacy that is actually quite consistent with *austere* appreciation or knowledge of the nature of LSPs, and of their relationship to LGP. It is typically assumed by critics that terms must have a primary motivation, or be instantly self-explanatory, without which they are to be rejected. In doing so, such critics forget the role of education in the associations which they themselves make between specialised concepts and the Western languages in which they, the critics, were educated. It is also conveniently forgotten that there are millions of terms in English, French, German, etc. that are unknown by native speakers of these languages who are not initiated into the specialities to which concepts identified by these terms belong. The point is that, although LSP is based on LGP, it is unique in its use of LGP resources, with the implication that LGP-based assessments of how LSPs fulfil their mission of communicating specialist knowledge will be routinely error-laden (see Sections 1.2.2 and 2.5).

So, whether it is construed in classroom or in less formal terms, or seen from the standpoint of written texts or structured TV/radio broadcasts, the educational enterprise is what creates the opportunity for concept–term associations to be made. It is this enterprise that provides a more objective framework for critiquing concept–term assignment. A terminology planning effort that is concurrent with, or otherwise linked to, text production is to be commended.

While serving to develop written texts, terminology itself regularly requires written textual corpora. Chapter 7 described terminology extraction as being increasingly based on written corpora. Chapter 8 referred to the problem of obtaining texts on Nigerian legislative practice that were rich in 'terminological knowledge'. While this difficulty was explained in terms of an actual dearth, given the iterative character of military presence in Nigerian politics, the abuse of available textual evidence is, scientifically speaking, felonious. One day, over the period of time I was hunting for texts in Nigeria, my niece walked in with an item bought from a small retail outlet. The sheet in which the item had been wrapped turned out to be part of the Standing Orders of the defunct state legislature. Equally felonious is the fact that several electronic media establishments keep no records (taped or written) of translations of English news bulletins into Nigerian languages. Such translations, particularly those concerning reports on legislatures when they were still operational, would have been of particular interest to this work. Media translators spoken to in different parts of Nigeria said they customarily left the studios with their hand-written scripts after casting the news. It follows from the fact of terminology being corpus-dependent that these text management practices need to be checked.

But text management for terminology planning calls for much more than preservation. There are two urgent conversion tasks. The first involves reducing to writing, and in machine-readable form, the indigenous language corpora generated orally in such specialised domains as phamarcognosy, brewing, textile production, etc. The second involves capturing in machine-readable form the vast corpora of indigenous (and foreign) language texts that were produced using offset lithography or other technologies that limit the manipulation and reuse of textual resources. Such conversion activities hold out prospects for natural language processing that is related to terminology as well as to other pure or applied activities (e.g. corpus annotation). Conversion allows for the reuse of textual resources. As an instance of resource reuse — one that is applied to terminology — it should be possible to reconfigure (along lines of subject domain) the data in the Nigerian glossary that was evaluated. Two frameworks for such reuse could be proposed: *optimisation* and *re-engineering*. Optimisation refers to enhancing a given resource for it to better serve the functions motivating its creation. Re-engineering is concerned with 'retooling' a resource so as to make it serve a new or extended function — at any rate, a function not envisaged at the time the resource was created. Optimisation presupposes a 'situated' needs analysis (such as the experiments described in Chapter 3), while re-engineering calls for strategies that are able to support functional shifts, that is a change in the function of terminology resources. In this respect, the usage situations described by Kühn (see Chapter 3) are of interest.

For reasons of cost, the foregoing proposal clearly implies that the environment in which terminology planning is conducted would have to be substantially computerised. Such computerisation would not be limited to terminology extraction, but would include other aspects of terminology management. Language engineering technologies such as described in Chapters 7 and 8 must be seen as indispensable components of terminology work environments because of the economies (in time, manpower, effort, money, etc.) they bring to the task. Network utilisation of terminologies, either in the environment of a terminology management system exclusively, or in conjunction with the Internet, is a promising method of, say, rationalising term creation and use. Previous work (Antia 1992, 1995a, 1996a) has shown that the use of uniform terminology is a serious concern in African languages that are spoken across national boundaries as much as it is a problem within national frontiers, and even within the same establishment (e.g. the mass media). Comparable problems have been reported in respect of Spanish.

As a practice and as a discipline, terminology has legitimate claims to an independent place in the research programme and teaching curriculum of African tertiary education. Indeed, the putative benefits of terminology planning would be a perpetual mirage without investment in systematic and sustainable programmes of manpower development. In pure research, the paradigm represented by terminology could be further articulated from African perspectives. In applied research, concerns might relate to the re-engineering of existing terminological and lexicographical works; to terminology as a factor of productivity and quality in such areas of industry as spare parts administration, product localisation, translation, etc.; to terminological methods and how they could reverse falling levels of attainment in schools, and high drop-out rates; to issues of sensitivity and specificity of the terminology employed by health planners, health workers and mothers or other caretakers in their bid to give or receive specialised knowledge — indispensable for checking the high levels of child morbidity and mortality caused by acute respiratory infections, diarrhoea, among other child-killer diseases. In teaching, an important pay-off would be terminology projects carried out by students for their bachelors' and masters' degrees, for instance. Given the steady flow of students, such projects would be a most important source of new terminologies, or for the terminological documentation of traditional conceptual universes. Such theoretically sound projects would relieve language planning agencies — active, moribund or otherwise inert — of an important technical task, and contribute rapidly to the development of indigenous languages concerned.

But such projects must be undertaken within frameworks that are much broader than merely fulfilling conditions for earning one's degree. The demands of producing a terminology on the one hand, and, on the other, the need to avoid repeating work on domains already covered (when there are millions of others in need of attention) require that coordinating mechanisms be put in place. In a country like Nigeria with thirty-odd universities, each of which has a national, as opposed to a local, student population base, an important challenge would be how to ensure that an Efik-speaking student studying in Maiduguri (where Kanuri is natively spoken) does not repeat, unknowingly, work done by another Efik student registered at the university in Calabar, Calabar being an Efik homeland. Whatever measures are considered (a centralised deposit programme for project proposals, etc.), the structures that grow from them must not be bureaucratic. As it gains ground in African centres of scholarship, the Internet should become a coordinating structure *per excellence*. A sense of needs, domains covered, etc. can be obtained from an Internet discussion forum or a website patronised by interested parties.

Measures such as outlined above should increase the pace at which indigenous languages adapt to the rapidly changing social circumstances with which their speakers are confronted. Without such rapid adaptation, there is little hope that speakers of such languages can move away from their peripheral position in the political, economic and social realities of their immediate environments, and of the world at large.

Bibliography

ACCT. 1989. *Coopération linguistique: actes de la conférence internationale* [Abidjan, 22–26 February 1988]. Paris: ACCT/Université Nationale de Côte d'Ivoire.

Adams, R. F. G., Akaduh, E. and Abia-Bassey, O. 1981. *English–Efik Dictionary*. Oron: Manson.

Afolayan, A. 1976. "The Six-Year Primary Project in Nigeria". In *Mother Tongue in Education: The West African Experience*, A. Bambose (ed.), 113–134. London: Hodder & Stoughton; Paris: UNESCO.

Ahmad, K. and Davies, A. 1992. Knowledge processing 2: Terminology Management: A Corpus-Based Approach to Eliciting and Elaborating Specialist Terms. Computing Sciences Report, No CS-92–05, University of Surrey.

Ahmad, K., Davies, A., Fulford H. and Rogers, M. 1992. Knowledge Processing 3: Introduction to (Semi-) Automatic Terminology Acquisition and Elaboration. Computing Sciences Report, No CS-92–06, University of Surrey.

Ahmad, K. and Fulford, H. 1992. Knowledge Processing 4: Semantic Relations and Their Use in Elaborating Terminology. Computing Sciences Report, No CS-92–07, University of Surrey.

Ahmad, K. and Fulford, H. 1993. "Terminology of Interdisciplinary Fields: A New Perspective". In *Terminology Work in Subject Fields* [Proceedings of the Third Infoterm Symposium, 12–14 Nov. 1991], M. Krommer-Benz and & A. Manu (eds), 568–587. Vienna: TermNet.

Ahmad, K. 1993. "Terminology and Knowledge Acquisition: A Text Based Approach". In *TKE '93: Terminology & Knowledge Engineering*, K-D. Schmitz (ed.), 56–70. Frankfurt/M: Indeks.

Ahmad, K. and Rogers, M. 1993. "Terminology and Knowledge Processing". In *Translation and Knowledge* [SSOTT IV], Y. Gambier and J. Tommola (eds), 167–181. Turku: University of Turku Centre for Translation and Interpreting.

Ahmad, K. 1994. "Terminology Workbenches and the Engineering of Special Languages". In *TAMA '94: Proceedings of the Third TermNet Symposium on*

Terminology in Advanced Microcomputer Applications, TermNet (ed.), 5–52. Vienna: TermNet.

Ahmad, K., Holmes-Higgin, P., Abidi, S. R., Rogers, M. and Griffin, S. M. 1995. Terminology Management: The Extraction, Representation and Retrieval of Specialist Terms. Computing Sciences Report, No CS-95-08, University of Surrey.

Ahmad, K. 1996. "A terminology Dynamic and the Growth of knowledge: A Case Study in Nuclear Physics and in the Philosophy of Science". In: *TKE '96: Terminology and Knowledge Engineering*, C. Galinski and K-D. Schmitz (eds), 1–11. Frankfurt/M: Indeks.

Aijmer, K. and Altenberg, B. (eds). 1991. *English Corpus Linguistics*. London & New York: Longman.

Aitchison, J. and Gilchrist, A. 1972. *Thesaurus Construction: A Practical Manual*. London: Aslib.

Akpanyuñ, O. A. 1978. *An Efik Language Handbook for Teachers*. Lagos: Macmillan.

Akpanyuñ, O. A. 1979. *A Study of Efik for Schools and Colleges*. Lagos: Thomas Nelson.

Alisjahbana, S. T. 1971. "Some Planning Processes in the Development of the Indonesian-Malay Language". In *Can Language be Planned?*, J. Rubin and B. H. Jernudd (eds), 179–187. Hawaii: East-West Center/The University Press.

Alisjahbana, S. T. 1974. "Language Policy, Language Engineering and Literacy in Indonesia and Malaysia". In *Advances in Language Planning*, J. A. Fishman (ed.), 391–416. The Hague: Mouton.

Alloni-Fainberg, Y. 1974. "Official Hebrew Terms for Parts of the Car: A Study of Knowledge, Usage and Attitudes". In *Advances in Language Planning*, J. A. Fishman (ed.), 493–517. The Hague: Mouton.

Andrzejewski, B. W. 1983/84. "Language Reform in Somalia and the Modernization of the Somali Vocabulary". In *Language Reform* [vol.1], I. Fodor and C. Hagège (eds), 60–84. Hamburg: Helmut Buske.

Antia, B. E. 1991. "An Areal Approach to Terminological Neologisms in Nigerian Languages". *Neoterm* 13 (16): 145–152.

Antia, B. E. 1992. "Translating in the Electronic Media in Borno State". *Translatio: FIT Newsletter* xi (3): 256–279.

Antia, B. E. 1993. "Temps, aspect, mode: La problématique des catégories grammaticales en classe de traduction". *Le Linguiste* 2: 1–7.

Antia, B. E. 1995a. "A Survey of Institutional Terminology Work in Nigeria". *TermNet News* 49: 1–7.

Antia, B. E. 1995b. "Comparative term records: Implications for decision-making in secondary term formation". In *Multilingualism in Specialist Communication* [vol. 2], G. Budin (ed.), 933–963. Vienna: TermNet.

Antia, B. E. 1996a. "Situation audiovisuelle dans un pays multilingue: Le Nigéria". In *Les transferts linguistiques dans les médias audiovisuels*, Y. Gambier (ed.), 61–72. Villeneuve d'Ascq (Nord): Presses universitaires du Septentrion.

Antia, B. E. 1996b. "Towards a Terminological Resource on the Language of Parliamentary Proceedings". In *TKE '96: Terminology and Knowledge Engineering*, C. Galinski and K-D. Schmitz (eds), 381–390. Frankfurt/M: Indeks.

Antia, B. E. 1996c. "TKE '96 as seen by Bassey Antia". *TermNet News* 54–55: 40.

Antia, B. E. and Haruna, A. 1997. "Language in Ethnicity in Nigeria". In *New Strategies for Curbing Ethnic & Religious Conflicts in Nigeria*, F. U. Okafor (ed.), 136–151. Enugu: Fourth Dimension.

Antia, B. E. 1997a. Outline of Some Strategies for Promoting Efik: a discussion paper presented to the Association for the Promotion of Efik Language, Literature and Culture (APELLAC). Calabar, 29th April, 1997.

Antia, B. E. 1997b. "A Review of Peter Weissenhofer's Conceptology in Terminology Theory, Semantics and Word-formation. A morpho-conceptually based approach to classification as exemplified by the English baseball terminology". *Babel* 43(4): 375–379.

Antia, B. E. 1998. "A Text Linguistics Analysis of Terminology-mediated Knowledge Transfer". *Terminology Science & Research* 9(1): 5–17.

Antia, B. E. *Forthcoming*. "Terminology and the Social Dimensions of Language: The Brann Impact". In *Festschrift for Professor C. M. B. Brann*, S. Ajulo (ed.). Lagos: University Press. Also in: *TermNet News*, 58–61 (1998), 3–11.

Antia, B. E. 1999. "Terminology under the Magnifying Glass". *Translatio: FIT Newsletter* xviii(4): 463–473.

Antia, B. E. *In prep*. Westminster in Washington and Elsewhere.

Arntz, R. and Picht, H. 1989. *Einführung in die Terminologiearbeit*. Hildesheim, Zürich, New York: Georg Olms.

Askira, M. G. 1994. A Linguistic Analysis of the Translation of English into Kanuri and Hausa by the Borno State Electronic Media. Unpub. M.A. Dissertation, University of Maiduguri.

Auroux, S. 1995. "The Semasiological Sources of Semantics". In *Historical Roots of Linguistic Theories* [Studies in the History of Language Sciences, 74], L. Formigari and D. Gambarara (eds), 221–232. Amsterdam/Philadelphia: John Benjamins.

Awobuluyi, O. 1989. "The Development of Standard Yoruba". In *Language Reform* [vol.4], I. Fodor and C. Hagège (eds), 25–42. Hamburg: Helmut Buske.
Aye, E. U. 1989. A Brief History of the Efik Language. Manuscript.
Aye, E. U. 1991. *A Learner's Dictionary of the Efịk Language* [vol. 1]. Ibadan: Evans.
Baldinger, K. 1956. "Grundsätzliches zur Gestaltung des wissenschaftlichen Wörterbuchs". In *Deutsche Akademie der Wissenschaften zu Berlin 1946–1956*, 379–388.
Baldinger, K. 1957. "Die Semasiologie. Versuch eines Überblicks". *Deutsche Akademie der Wissenschaften zu Berlin* [Vorträge und Schriften: Heft 61].
Baldinger, K. 1960. "Alphabetisches oder begrifflich gegliedertes Wörterbuch"? *Zeitschrift für Romanische Philologie* 76: 521–536.
Baldinger, K. 1980. *Semantic Theory: Towards a Modern Semantics* [Transl. W. C. Brown; ed. R. Wright]. Oxford: Basil Blackwell.
Bambgose, A. (ed.) 1976. *Mother Tongue in Education: The West African Experience*. London: Hodder & Stoughton; Paris: UNESCO.
Bambgose, A. 1976. "Introduction: The Changing Role of the Mother Tongue in Education". In *Mother Tongue in Education: The West African Experience*, A. Bamgbose (ed.), 9–26. London: Hodder & Stoughton; Paris: UNESCO.
Bambgose, A. (ed.) 1984 [1992]. *Yoruba Metalanguage: A Glossary of English-Yoruba Technical Terms in Language, Literature, and Methodology* [2nd edition]. Ibadan: University Press.
Bamgbose, A. 1984 [1992]. "Introduction". In *Yoruba Metalanguage: A Glossary of English-Yoruba Technical Terms in Language, Literature, and Methodology* [2nd edition], A. Bamgbose (ed.), viii-xiv. Ibadan: University Press.
Bamgbose, A. 1987. "When is Language Planning not Planning?" *Journal of West African Languages* XVII (1): 6–14.
Bamgbose, A. 1989. "Issues for a Model of Language Planning". *Language Problems and Language Planning* 13 (1): 24–34.
Bamgbose, A. 1991. *Language and the Nation: The Language Question in Sub-Saharan Africa*. Edinburgh: Edinburgh University Press for International African Institute.
Barnes, J. 1982. *Aristotle*. Oxford: Oxford University Press.
Bauer, L. 1983. *English Word-formation*. Cambridge: University Press.
Beaugrande, R. 1984. *Text Production. Toward a Science of Composition* [vol. XI of Advances in Discourse Processes]. Norwood: Ablex.
Beaugrande, R. 1988. "Special Purpose Language as a Complex System: The Case of Linguistics". In *Special Language: From Humans Thinking to*

Thinking Machines, C. Laurén and M. Nordman (eds), 3–29. Clevedon & Philadelphia: Multilingual Matters.

Beaugrande, R. 1994. "International Terminology: Prospects for a New Agenda". In *Terminology Science & Terminology Planning/Theoretical Issues of Terminology Science* [IITF Series 4], J. K. Draskau and H. Picht (eds), 6–23. Vienna: TermNet.

Beaugrande, R. and Dressler, W. 1994. *An Introduction to Text Linguistics*. London & New York: Longman.

Beaugrande, R. 1997. *New Foundations for a Science of Text and Discourse: Cognition, Communication, and the Freedom of Access to Knowledge and Society* [vol. LXI of Advances in Discourse Processes]. Norwood: Ablex.

Bell, R. T. 1991. *Translation and Translating. Theory and Practice*. London & New York: Longman.

Benson, M., Benson, E. and Ilson, R. 1986. *Lexicographic Description of English*. Amsterdam/Philadelphia: John Benjamins.

Benson, M., Benson, E. and Ilson, R. 1986. *The BBI Combinatory Dictionary of English: A Guide to Word Combinations*. Amsterdam/Philadelphia: John Benjamins.

Bolton, N. 1977. *Concept Formation*. Oxford: Pergamon.

Bowker, L. and Meyer, I. 1993. "Beyond Textbook Concept Systems: Handling Multidimensionality in a New Generation of Term Banks". In *TKE '93: Terminology & Knowledge Engineering,* K-D. Schmitz (ed.),123–137. Frankfurt/M: Indeks

Brann, C. M. B. 1983. *Language Policy, Planning and Management in Africa: A Select Bibliography*. Québec: CIRB [Publication H-2].

Brann, C. M. B. 1989. "Lingua Minor, Franca and Nationalis". In *Status and Function of Language Varieties*, U. Ammon (ed.), 372–385. Berlin: Walter de Gruyter.

Brann, C. M. B. 1990. "The Role and Function of Languages in Government: Language Policy Issues in Nigeria". *Sociolinguistics* 9: 1–19.

Brann, C. M. B. 1991. "National Language Policy and Planning: France 1789, Nigeria 1989". In *History of European Ideas* [special issue on Rise and Development of National European Languages, C. M. B. Brann, ed.], 13 (1/2): 97–120.

Brann, C. M. B. 1995. Language Choice in the Nigerian State Houses of Assembly. Manuscript.

Budin, G. 1990. *The Role of Terminology Planning in International Science & Technology Planning Policies*. Infoterm paper no. 18–90en.

Budin, G. 1993. "Wissenschaftstheoretische Aspekte der Erforschung von Wissenschaftssprachen". In *Fachtextpragmatik*, H. Schröder (ed.), 19–30. Tübingen: Gunter Narr (FFF vol. 19).

Budin, G. 1994. "Do We Need An Object Theory?" In *Terminology Science & Terminology Planning/Theoretical Issues of Terminology Science* [IITF Series 4], J. K. Draskau and H. Picht (eds), 203–208. Vienna: TermNet.

Budin, G. (ed.) 1995. *Multilingualism in Specialist Communication* [2 vols] Vienna: TermNet.

Budin, G. 1996. *Wissensorganisation und Terminologie. Die Komplexität und Dynamik wissenschaftlicher Informations- und Kommunikationsprozesse.* Tübingen: Gunter Narr (FFF, vol. 31).

Budin, G., Galinski, C., Nedobity, W. and Thaller, R. 1988. "Terminology and Knowledge Data Processing". In *Proceedings, International Congress on Terminology and Knowledge Engineering* [29 Sept. — 1 Oct. 1987], H. Czap & C. Galinski (eds), 50–60. Frankfurt/M: Indeks.

Cabré, T. M. 1996. "Terminology Today". In *Terminology, LSP and Translation. Studies in Language Engineering in honour of Juan C. Sager*, H. Somers (ed.), 15–33. Amsterdam/Philadelphia: John Benjamins.

Caney, J. 1984. *The Modernisation of Somali Vocabulary, with Particular Reference to the Period from 1972 to the Present* Hamburg: Helmut Buske.

Capek, M. E. S. (ed.) 1987. *A Women's Thesaurus*. New York: Harper & Row.

Chumbow, B. S. 1987. "Towards a Language Planning Model for Africa". *Journal of West African Languages* XVII (1): 15–22.

Clas, A. (ed.) 1985. *Guide de recherche en lexicographie et terminologie*. Paris: ACCT.

Cobarrubias, J. and Fishman, J. A. (eds). 1983. *Progress in Language Planning*. Berlin: Mouton.

Connell, B. A. 1991. Phonetic Aspects of the Lower Cross Languages and Their Implications for Sound Change. Ph.D Dissertation, University of Edinburgh.

Cook, T. L. 1969. *The Pronunciation of Efik for Speakers of English*. Indiana University: African Studies Programme and Intensive Language Training Centre.

Cook, T. L. 1994. Grote Structuurcursus Efik. Course stencils. University of Leiden.

Corbeil, J.-C. 1980. *L'aménagement linguistique du Québec*. Montreal: Guérin.

Coserieu, E and Geckeler, H. 1981. *Trends in Structural Linguistics*. Tübingen: Gunter Narr.

Coulmas, F. 1988. "What is a National Language Good for"? In: *With Forked Tongues: What are National Languages Good for?* F. Coulmas (ed.), 1–23. Singapore: Karoma.

Cowie, A. P. and Mackin, R. 1975. *Oxford Dictionary of Current Idiomatic English* [vol.1: Verbs with Prepositions and Particles]. Berlin: Cornelson & Oxford University Press.

Cowie, A. P. 1978. "The Place of Illustrative Material and Collocations in the Design of a Learner's Dictionary". In *In Honour of A. S. Hornby*, P. Strevens (ed.), 127–139. Oxford: Oxford University Press.

Cowie, A. P. 1981. "The Treatment of Collocations and Idioms in Learners' Dictionaries". *Applied Linguistics* II (3): 223–235.

Cruse, D. 1986. *Lexical Semantics*. Cambridge: Cambridge University Press.

Crystal, D. 1985. *A Dictionary of Linguistics & Phonetics*. Oxford: Blackwell.

Cyffer, N., Schubert, K., Weier, H-I. and Wolff, E. (eds). 1991. *Language Standardization in Africa*. Hamburg: Helmut Buske.

Czap, H. & Galinski, C. (eds). 1987. *Proceedings, International Congress on Terminology and Knowledge Engineering* [29 Sept.-1Oct. 1987; main volume + supplement]. Frankfurt/M: Indeks.

Czap, H. & Nedobity, W. (eds). 1990. *TKE '90: Terminology and Knowledge Engineering* [vol. 2]. Frankfurt/M: Indeks.

Dahlberg, I. 1976. "Über Gegenstände, Begriffe, Definitionen und Benennungen. Zur möglichen Neufassung von DIN 2330". *Muttersprache* 86: 81–116.

Dahlberg, I. 1978a. *Ontical Structures & Universal Classification*. Bangalore: Sarada Ranganathan Endowment for Library Science.

Dahlberg, I. 1978b. "A Referent-Oriented, Analytical Concept theory for INTERCONCEPT". *International Classification* 5 (3): 142–151.

Dahlberg, I. 1981. "Conceptual Definitions for Interconcept". *International Classification* 8 (1): 16–22.

Dahlberg, I. 1985a. "Begriffs- und Definitionstheorie in Ihrem Zusammenhang". In *Studien zur Klassifikation, Systematik und Terminologie*, K. D. Dutz (ed.), 93–110. Munster: Institut für Allgemeine Sprachwissenschaft of the Westfällischen Wilhelms University & MAKS Publications.

Dahlberg, I. 1985b. "Begriffsbeziehungen und Definitionstheorie". In *Terminologie und benachbarte Gebiete 1965–1985*, Infoterm (ed.), 137–148. Vienna, Cologne, Graz: Böhlau.

Dahlberg, I. 1995. "Conceptual Structures & Systematicization". *International Forum on Information & Documentation* 20 (3): 9–24.

Dahlberg, W. (ed.) 1978. *Kooperation in der Klassifikation I*: Frankfurt: Ges. für Klassifikation.

Dede, C. 1988. "The Role of Hypertext in transforming Information into Knowledge". In *Proceedings NECC '88* [Dallas, Texas, June 15–17, 1988], W.C. Ryan (ed.), 95–102. Eugene: International Council on Computers for Education/Univ. of Oregon for Nat. Educ. Computing Conf.

Diki-Kidiri, M. and Don, D. 1989. *Dimo-Lexis. Outils logiciels pour le linguiste*. Paris: CNRS-LACITO/ACCT.

Diop, C.A. 1975. "Comment enraciner la science en Afrique: exemples walafs (Sénégal)". *Bulletin de l'I. F.A.N* [B series], 37(1): 154–233.

Diop, C.A. 1979. *Nations nègres et culture II* [3rd edition]. Paris: Présence africaine.

Dornseiff, F. 1970. *Der Deutsche Wortschatz nach Sachgruppen* [7th edition]. Berlin: Walter de Gruyter & Co.

Draskau, J.K. 1986. "A Valency-Type Analysis of Four Monolexical Verbs and two Polylexical Verbs in English LSP texts from two Subject Fields, Marine Engineering and Veterinary Science". *ALSED-LSP Newsletter*, 9(2–23): 25–42.

Draskau, J.K. & Picht, H. (eds). 1994. *Terminology Science & Terminology Planning/Theoretical Issues of Terminology Science* [IITF Series 4]. Vienna: TermNet.

Dubow, F. 1976. "Language, Law and Change: Problems in the Development of a National Legal system in Tanzania". In *Language and Politics*, W.M. O'Barr and J.F. O'Barr (eds), 85–99. The Hague/Paris: Mouton.

Ducháček, O. 1960. *Le champ conceptuel de la beauté en français moderne*. Prague: Státné Pedagogické Nakladatelství.

Durham, W.H. 1991. *Coevolution: Genes, Culture and Human Diversity*. Stanford: Stanford University Press.

Eade, J. 1997. *Living the Global City. Globalization is a Local Process*. London: & New York: Routledge.

Eck, K.E. and Meyer, I. 1994."Bringing Aristotle into the 20th century — Computer-Assisted Definition Construction in a Terminological Knowledge Base". In *Standardizing and Harmonizing Terminology: Theory and Practice*, S.E. Wright & R.A. Strehlow (eds), 83–101. Philadelphia: American Society for Testing and Materials.

Edmonds, I.G. 1975. *Ethiopia: Land of the Conquering Land of Judah*. New York: Holt, Rinehart & Winston.

Eisele, H. 1993. "Speed Training via Terminology". In *TKE '93: Terminology & Knowledge Engineering*, K-D. Schmitz (ed.), 71–77. Frankfurt/M: Indeks.

Ekefre, N.U. 1986. *Efik Language Course for G.C.E. O'Level*. Ibadan: Evans.

Emenanjo, E. N. 1991. "Language Modernization from the Grass-roots: The Nigerian Experience". In *Language Standardization in Africa*, N. Cyffer, K. Schubert, H-I. Weier, and E. Wolff (eds), 157–164. Hamburg: Helmut Buske.

Essien, O. E. 1982. "Efik Orthography". In *Orthographies of Nigerian Languages* [manual 1], A. Bamgbose (ed.), 4–30. Lagos: National Language Centre (Fed. Ministry of Education).

Essien, O. E. 1992 *A Grammar of the Ibibio Language* Ibadan: University Press.

Federal Government of Nigeria 1979. *Constitution of the Federal Republic of Nigeria*. Lagos.

Federal Government of Nigeria 1981. *National Policy on Education* [revised]. Lagos.

Felber, H. 1984. *Terminology Manual*. Paris: UNESCO/Infoterm.

Felber, H. and Budin, G. 1989. *Terminologie in Theorie und in Praxis*. Tübingen: Günter Narr.

Felber, H. 1994. "The Correspondence of Object, Concept & Symbol". In *Terminology Science & Terminology Planning/Theoretical Issues of Terminology Science* [IITF Series 4], J. K. Draskau and H. Picht (eds), 209–216. Vienna: TermNet.

Felber, H. 1995. *Allgemeine Terminologielehre und Wissenstechnik: theoretische Grundlagen* [2nd edition, IITF Series 1]. Vienna: TermNet.

Ferguson, C. A. 1968. "Language Development". In *Language Problems of Developing Nations*, J. A. Fishman, C. A. Ferguson and J. Das Gupta (eds), 27–36. New York: John Wiley & Sons.

Firth, J. R. 1957. *Papers in Linguistics 1934–1951*. London: Oxford University Press.

Fishman, J. A., Ferguson, C. A. and Das Gupta, J. (eds). 1968. *Language Problems of Developing Nations*. New York: John Wiley & Sons.

Fishman, J. A., Das Gupta, J., Jernudd, B. H. and Rubin, J. 1971. "Research Outline for Comparative Studies of Language Planning". In *Can Language be Planned?*, J. Rubin and B. H. Jernudd (eds), 293–305. Hawaii: East-West Center/The University Press.

Fishman, J. A. (ed.) 1974. *Advances in Language Planning*. The Hague: Mouton.

Fishman, J. A. 1974. "Language Planning and Language Planning Research". In *Advances in Language Planning*, J. A. Fishman (ed.), 15–33. The Hague: Mouton.

Fishman, J. A. 1974. "Language Modernization and Planning in Comparison with other types of National Modernization and Planning". In *Advances in Language Planning*, J. A. Fishman (ed.), 78–102. The Hague: Mouton.

Fishman, J. A. 1983. "Modeling rationales in corpus planning: Modernity and Tradition in Images of the Good Corpus". In *Progress in Language Planning*, J. Cobarrubias and J. A. Fishman (eds), 107–118. Berlin: Mouton.

Fishman, J. A. 1987. "Conference Comments: Reflections on the Current State of Language Planning". In *Proceedings of the International Colloquium on Language Planning*, L. Laforge (presentation), 405–428. Quebec: University of Laval Press.

Fishman, J. A. (ed.) 1993. *The Earliest Stage of Language Planning: The 'First Congress' Phenomenon*. Berlin: Mouton de Gruyter.

Fluck, H-R. 1991. *Fachsprache*. Tübingen: Francke.

Foskett, A. C. 1973. *The Universal Decimal Classification*. London: Clive Bingley.

Frederiksen, C. H. 1977. "Semantic Processing Units in Understanding Text". In *Discourse Production and Comprehension* [vol. 1, Discourse Processes], R. O. Freedle (ed.), 57–87. Norwood: Ablex.

Fulford, H. 1992. Knowledge Processing 6: Collocation Patterns and Term Discovery.' Computing Sciences Report, No. CS-92-09, University of Surrey.

Galinski, C. and Schmitz, K-D. (eds). 1996. *TKE '96: Terminology and Knowledge Engineering*, Frankfurt/M: Indeks.

Gambier, Y. and Tommola, J. (eds). 1993. *Translation and Knowledge* [SSOTTIV]. Turku: University of Turku Centre for Translation and Interpreting.

Gambier, Y. 1993. "Présupposés de la terminologie: vers une remise en cause". *TextConText* 8 (3/4): 155–176.

Gambier, Y. 1994. "Vers une histoire sociale de la terminologie". In *Translation Studies. An Interdiscipline*, M. Snell-Hornby, M, F. Pöchhacker and K. Kaindl (eds), 255–266. Amsterdam/Philadelphia: John Benjamins.

Garvin, P. L. 1973. "Some Comments on Language Planning". In *Language Planning: Current Issues and Research*, J. Rubin and R. Shuy (eds), 24–33. Washington D. C.: Georgetown University Press.

Gaudin, F. 1990. "Socioterminology and Expert Discourses". In *TKE '90: Terminology and Knowledge Engineering* [vol. 2], H. Czap and W. Nedobity (eds), 631–641. Frankfurt/M: Indeks.

German Bundestag 1997. *Rules of Procedure of the German Bundestag* [published and translated respectively by the Administration and the Language Service of the German Bundestag].

German Bundestag 1984. *Parlamentarische Terminologie (Deutsch — Englisch/ Französisch)*.

Geeraerts, D. 1985. "Les données stéréotypiques, prototypiques et encyclopédiques dans le dictionnaire". *Cahiers de lexicologie et de lexicographie* 46 (7): 27- 43.

Gbery, E. A. 1993. "Terminologie de la pêche lagunaire en pays Adioukrou et Ébrié". *Terminologies nouvelles* 9: 66–70.

Gerzymisch-Arbogast, H. 1994. "Identifying term variants in context: the SYSTEXT approach". In *Translation Studies. An Interdiscipline*, M. Snell-Hornby, M, F. Pöchhacker and K. Kaindl (eds), 279–290. Amsterdam/Philadelphia: John Benjamins.

Gerzymisch-Arbogast, H. 1996. *Termini im Kontext. Verfahren zur Erschließung und Übersetzung der textspezifischen Bedeutung von fachlichen Ausdrücken*. Tübingen: Gunter Narr (FFF, vol 31).

Gilchrist, A. 1971. *The Thesaurus in Retrieval*. London: Aslib.

Gillam, L. & Ahmad, K. 1996. "Knowledge-Engineered Terminology (Data) Bases". In *TKE '96: Terminology and Knowledge Engineering*, C. Galinski and K-D. Schmitz (eds), 205–214. Frankfurt/M: Indeks.

Gilreath, C. T. 1994. "Resolving Term Disputes with Weighted Onometrics". In *Standardizing and Harmonizing Terminology: Theory and Practice*, S. E. Wright and R. A. Strehlow (eds), 25–52. Philadelphia: American Society for Testing and Materials.

Gorman, T. P. 1973. "Language Allocation and Language Planning in a Developing Country". In *Can Language be Planned?*, J. Rubin and R. Shuy (eds), 72–82. Hawaii: East-West Center/The University Press.

Grossmann, R. 1992. *The Existence of the World. An Introduction to Ontology*. London & New York: Routledge.

Guespin, L. 1990. "Socioterminology facing Problems in Standardization". In *TKE '90: Terminology and Knowledge Engineering* [vol. 2], H. Czap and W. Nedobity (eds), 642–647. Frankfurt/M: Indeks.

Halaoui, N. 1989. *Questions de méthode en terminologie des langues africaines*. Paris: ACCT.

Halaoui, N. 1990. "La terminologie des langues africaines aujourd'hui". *Terminologies nouvelles* 4: 12–24.

Halliday, M. A. K. 1961. "Categories of the Theory of Grammar". *Word* 17: 241–292.

Halliday, M. A. K. 1966. "'Lexis as a linguistic level". In *In Memory of J. R. Firth*, Bazell, Catford, Halliday and Robins (eds), 148–162. London: Longman.

Halliday, M. A. K. 1992. "Corpus studies and probalistic grammar". In *English Corpus Linguistics*, K. Aijmer and B. Altenberg (eds), 30–43. London & New York: Longman.

Halliday, M. A. K. 1994. *An Introduction to Functional Grammar.* London: Arnold.
Hallig, R. & Wartburg, W. von 1952. *Begriffssystem als Grundlage für die Lexikographie* [Abhandlungen der deutschen Akademie der Wissenschaften zu Berlin]. Berlin: Akademie.
Hartmann, R. R. K. 1989. "Sociology of the Dictionary User. Hypotheses and Empirical Studies". In *Wörterbücher: Ein internationales Handbuch zur Lexikographie* [vol.1], F. J. Hausmann, O. Reichmann, H. E. Wiegand & L. Zgusta (eds), 102–111.Berlin & New York: Walter de Gruyter.
Haugen, E. 1966a. *Language Conflict and Language Planning: The Case of Modern Norwegian.* Cambridge, Massachusetts: Harvard University Press.
Haugen, E. 1966b. "Linguistics and Language Planning". In *Sociolinguistics. Proceedings of UCLA Sociolinguistics Conference, 1964*, W. Bright (ed.), 50–71. The Hague: Mouton & Co.
Haugen, E. 1969. "Review of V. Tauli (1968)". *Language: Journal of the Linguistic Society of America* 45: 939–949.
Haugen, E. 1971. "Instrumentalism in Language Planning". In *Can Language be Planned?*, J. Rubin and B. H. Jernudd (eds), 281–289. Hawaii: East-West Center/The University Press.
Haugen, E. 1983. "The Implementation of Corpus Planning: Theory and Practice". In *Progress in Language Planning*, J. Cobarrubias and J. A. Fishman (eds), 269 -289. Berlin: Mouton.
Haugen, E. 1987. "Language Planning". In *Sociolinguistics* [vol.1], H. Ammon, N. Dittmar and J. Mattheier (eds), 626–637. Berlin: Walter de Gruyter.
Hausmann, F. J. 1979. "Un dictionnaire des collocations est-il possible?" *Travaux de linguistique et de littérature* xvii (1): 187–195.
Hausmann, F. J. 1984. "Wortschatzlernen ist Kollokationslernen". *Praxis des neusprachlichen Unterrichts* 1.84 (January-March): 395–406.
Hausmann, F. J. 1985. "Kollokationen im deutschen Wörterbuch. Ein Beitrag zur Theorie des lexikographischen Beispiels". In *Lexikographie und Grammatik*, H. Bergenholtz and J. Mugdan (eds), 118–129. Tübingen: Max Niemeyer.
Hausmann, F. J., Reichmann, O., Wiegand, H. E. and Zgusta, L. (eds). 1989. *Wörterbücher: Ein internationales Handbuch zur Lexikographie* [3 vols]. Berlin & New York: Walter de Gruyter.
Hausmann, F. J. 1989. "Le dictionnaire de collocations". In *Wörterbücher: Ein internationales Handbuch zur Lexikographie* [vol. 1], F. J. Hausmann, O. Reichmann, H. E. Wiegand and L. Zgusta (eds), 1010–1019. Berlin & New York: Walter de Gruyter.
Heid, U., Jauss, S. and Hohmann, A. 1996. "Term Extraction with Standard Tools for Corpus Exploration — Experience from German". In *TKE '96:*

Terminology and Knowledge Engineering, C. Galinski and K-D. Schmitz (eds), 139–150. Frankfurt/M: Indeks.

Heger, K. 1965. "Les bases méthodologiques de l'onomasiologie et du classement par concepts". *Travaux de linguistique et de littératures romanes* III(1): 7–32.

Heger, K. 1969. "La sémantique et la dichotomie de langue et parole. Nouvelles contributions à la discussion sur les bases théoriques de la sémasiologie et de l'onomasiologie". *Travaux de linguistique et de littératures romanes* VII(1): 47–111.

Heger, K. 1976. *Monem, Wort, Satz und Text*. Tübingen: Max Niemeyer.

Hessen, J. 1947. *Lehrbuch der Philosophie* [vol.1]. Munich: Reinhardt.

Hoffmann, L. 1985. *Kommunikationsmittel Fachsprache*. Tübingen: Gunter Narr.

Hoffmann, L. 1991. "Text and Text Types in LSP". In *Subject-oriented Texts: Languages for Special Purposes and Text Theory*, H. Schröder (ed.), 158–166. Berlin: Walter de Gruyter.

Hohnhold, I. 1982. "Grundbegriffe im Bereich und im Umfeld übersetzungsorientierter Terminologiearbeit". *Lebende Sprachen* 27 (1): 1–5.

Hook, S. and Ahmad, K. 1992. Knowledge Processing 10: Conceptual Graphs and Term Elaboration: Explicating (Terminological) Knowledge". Computing Sciences Report, No. CS-92-13, University of Surrey.

House, J. 1988. "Talking to Oneself or Thinking with Others? On Using Different Thinking Aloud Methods in Translation". *Fremdsprachen lehren und lernen* 17: 84–98.

Humbley, J. 1995. "Terminological methods as an aid to learning a new subject in a multilingual setting: Examples in the field of insurance". In *Multilingualism in Specialist Communication* [vol. 2], G. Budin (ed.), 1011–1020. Vienna: TermNet.

International Standards Organization ISO/CD 1087-1. 1995. *Terminology Work-Vocabulary: Part 1: Theory & Application* [partial revision of ISO 1087: 1990].

International Standards Organization ISO/CD 704.2. 1995. *Terminology Work-Principles & Methods*.

Issoufi, A.O. 1993. "Terminologie grammaticale en Zarma". *Terminologies nouvelles* 9: 71–79.

Jernudd, B.H. and Das Gupta, J. 1971. "Towards a Theory of Language Planning". In *Can Language be Planned?*, J. Rubin and B.H. Jernudd (eds), 195–215. Hawaii: East-West Center/The University Press.

Jernudd, B.H. 1973. "Language Planning as a type of Language Treatment". In *Language Planning: Current Issues and Research*, J. Rubin and R. Shuy (eds), 11–24. Washington D.C.: Georgetown University Press.

Jernudd, B. H. 1977. "Agency Man". In *Language Planning processes*, J. Rubin, B. H. Jernudd, J. Das Gupta, J. A. Fishman, C. A. Ferguson (eds), 131–139. The Hague: Mouton.

Jernudd, B. H. 1983. "Evaluation of Language Planning — What Has the Last Decade Accomplished?" In *Progress in Language Planning*, J. Cobarrubias and J. A. Fishman (eds), 345–378. Berlin: Mouton.

Jernudd, B. H. and Neustupný, J. V. 1987. "Language Planning: For Whom?" In *Proceedings of the International Colloquium on Language Planning*, L. Laforge (presentation), 69–84. Quebec: University of Laval Press.

Jernudd, B. H. 1993. "Language Planning from a Management Perspective: An Interpretation of Findings". In *Language Conflict and Language Planning*, E. H. Jahr (ed.), 133–142. Berlin: Mouton de Gruyter.

Jernudd, B. H. and J. V. Neustupný 1991. "Multi-Disciplined Language Planning". In *Language Planning* [Focusschrift in honor of Joshua A. Fishman], D. F. Marshall (ed.), 29–36. Amsterdam/Philadelphia: John Benjamins.

Jernudd, B. H. 1997. "New Agencies in Language Planning". *TermNet News* 56/57: 14–17.

Ka, O. 1993. "Senegalese languages in education: The First Congress of Wolof". In *The Earliest Stage of Language Planning: The 'First Congress' Phenomenon*, J. A. Fishman (ed.), 305–320. Berlin: Mouton de Gruyter.

Karam, F. X. 1974. "Toward a Definition of Language Planning". In *Advances in Language Planning*, J. A. Fishman (ed.), 103–124. The Hague: Mouton.

Kennedy, C. ed. 1983. *Language Planning and Language Education*. London: George Allen & Unwin.

Khamisi, A. M. 1986. "Language Planning Processes in Tanzania". In *Language Planning: Proceedings of an Institute*, Annamalai, Jernudd, and Rubin (eds), 259–278. Mysore/Honolulu: Central Institute of Indian Languages/East-West Centre.

Khamisi, A. M. 1991. "Language Promotion Activities in Tanzania" In *Language Standardization in Africa*, N. Cyffer, K. Schubert, H-I. Weier and E. Wolff (eds), 215–220. Hamburg: Helmut Buske.

Khubchandani, L. M. 1983. "Language Planning Processes for Pluralistic Societies". In *Language Planning and Language Education*, C. Kennedy (ed.), 93–110. London: George Allen & Unwin.

Kjaer, A. L. 1990a. "Context-conditioned Word Combinations in Legal Language". *Terminology Science & Research* 1(1–2): 21 -32.

Kjaer, A. L. 1990b. "Phraseology Research — State-of-the-Art". *Terminology Science & Research* 1(1–2): 3–20.

Kjellmer, G. 1991. "A mint of phrases". In *English Corpus Linguistics*, K. Ajimer and B. Altenberg (eds), 111–127. London & New York: Longman.
Kleiber, G. 1990. *La sémantique du prototype*. Paris: Presses universitaires de France.
Kloss, H. 1969. *Research Possibilities on Group Bilingualism: A Report*. Québec: International Centre for Research on Bilingualism.
Kocourek, R. 1982[1991]. *La langue française de la technique et de la science*. Wiesbaden: Oscar Brandstetter.
Königs, F. G. 1988. "Auf der Suche nach dem richtigen Wort. Analysen zum lexikalischen Suchverhalten beim Schreiben in der Fremdsprache und beim Hinübersetzen". *Fremdsprachen lehren und lernen* 17: 99–117.
Krings, H. P. 1986. *Was in den Köpfen von Übersetzern vorgeht*. Tübingen: Gunter Narr.
Kühn, P. 1989. "Typologie der Wörterbücher nach Benutzungsmöglichkeiten". In *Wörterbücher: Ein internationales Handbuch zur Lexikographie* [vol. 1], F. J. Hausmann, O. Reichmann, H. E. Wiegand and L. Zgusta (eds), 111–127. Berlin & New York: Walter de Gruyter.
Kuhn, T. 1996. *The Structure of Scientific Revolutions* [3rd edition]. Chicago & London: The University of Chicago Press.
Kummer, W. 1983. "Probleme des Sprachausbaus in Entwicklungsländern. Terminologieprägung im Swahili". In *Sprache im politischen Kontext (Ergebnisse aus Bielefelder Forschungsprojekten zur Anwendung linguistischer Theorien)*, P. Finke (ed.), 77–118. Tübingen: Max Niemeyer.
Kussmaul, P. 1995. *Training the Translator*. Amsterdam/Philadelphia: John Benjamins.
Kozelka, P. R. 1985. *Community-Based Language Planning: A Movement Needed and Starting in West Africa*. Laval: University Press (CIRB).
Laforge, L. (presentation). 1987. *Proceedings of the International Colloquium on Language Planning*. Quebec: University of Laval Press.
Lauren, C., Myking, J. and Picht, H. 1998. *Terminologie unter der Lupe* [with additional contributions by Anita Nuopponen & Nina Pilke]. TermNet: Vienna.
Leech, G. 1991. "The state of the art in corpus linguistics". In *English Corpus Linguistics*, K. Ajimer and B. Altenberg (eds), 8–29. London & New York: Longman.
Lloyd, S. M. (ed.) 1982. *Roget's Thesaurus of English Words and Phrases*. Essex: Longman.
Lörscher, W. 1988. "Modelle des Übersetzungsprozesses: Anspruch und Wirklichkeit". *Fremdsprachen lehren und lernen* 18: 62–83.

Lörscher, W. 1991. *Translation Performance, Translation Process and Translation Strategies: A Psycholinguistic Investigation*. Tübingen: Gunter Narr.

Lörscher, W. 1993 "Translation Process Analysis". In *Translation and Knowledge* [SSOTTIV], Y. Gambier and J. Tommola (eds), 195–212. Turku: University of Turku Centre for Translation and Interpreting.

Lyons, J. 1977. *Semantics* [vol.1]. Cambridge: Cambridge University Press.

Mackey, W. F. 1994. "La politique linguistique dans l'évolution d'un État-Nation". In *Langues et Sociétés en Contact. Mélanges offerts à Jean-Claude Corbeil*, P. Martel and J. Maurais (eds), 61–70. Tübingen: Max Niemeyer [Canadiana Romanica 8].

Mackin, R. 1978. "On Collocations: 'words shall be known by the company they keep'". In *In Honour of A. S. Hornby*, P. Strevens (ed.), 149–165. Oxford: Oxford University Press.

MacWilliam, A. 1985. "Some thoughts on Translation of Scientific Terminology in Kiswahili". *Kiswahili* 52(1 & 2): 114–128.

Martin, W. 1992. "Remarks on Collocations in Sublanguages". *Terminologie et Traduction* 2/3: 157–164.

Maiga, A. 1991. "La place de la terminologie dans l'alphabétisation fonctionelle". *Terminologies nouvelles* 9: 32–36.

Mbodj, C. 1994. "L'activité terminologique au Sénégal". *Terminologies nouvelles* 11: 154–233.

McEnery, T. & Wilson, A. 1996. *Corpus Linguistics*. Edinburgh: Edinburgh University Press.

McGrew, P. C. & McDaniel, W. D. 1989. *On-line Text Management. Hypertext and other Techniques* [J. Ranade IBM Series]. New York: Intertext Publications/McGraw Hill.

McKnight, C., Dillon, A. and Richardson, J. 1991. *Hypertext in Context*. Cambrige: Cambridge University Press.

McLuhan, E. and Zingrone, F. (eds). 1997. *Essential McLuhan*. London: Routledge.

McNaught, J. 1988. "Computers and Terminology". In *Parallèles* [special issue; B. de Bessé & J. C. Sager, eds.]10: 37–49.

Mdee, J. S. 1983. "The Policy of Adapting Loan Words in Kiswahili as conceived by BAKITA: A Critique". *Multilingua* 2-2: 109–112.

Mel'cuk, I., Arbatchewsky-Jumanie, N., Iordanskaja, L, Mantha, S. 1992. *Dictionnaire explicatif et combinatoire du français contemporain. Recherches lexico-sémantiques III*. Montreal: Presses de l'Université de Montréal.

Merwe, C. van de 1974. *Thesaurus of Sociological Research Terminology*. Rotterdam: Rotterdam University Press.

Meyer, I. and MacKintosh, K. 1994 "Phraseme Analysis and Concept Analysis: Exploring a Symbiotic Relationship in the Specialized Lexicon". On the Internet at http://www.csi.uottawa.ca/~ingrid/cogniterm.html.

Meyer, P. G. 1997. "Hedging Strategies in Written Academic Discourse: Strengthening the Argument by Weakening the Claim". In *Hedging and Discourse: Approaches to the Analysis of a Pragmatic Phenomenon in Academic Texts*, R. Markkanen and H. Schröder (eds), 21- 41. Berlin: Walter de Gruyter.

Minako, O'. 1996. *The Coming Industry of Teletranslation*. Clevedon/Philadelphia/Adelaide: Multilingual Matters.

Mönke, H. 1978. "Definitionstypen und Definitionsmatrix". *Nachrichten für Dokumentation* 29 (2): 51–50.

Mtintsilana, P. N. and Morris, R. 1988. "Terminography in African languages in South Africa". *South African Journal of African Languages* 8(4): 109–113.

Myers, G. 1990. *Writing Biology. Texts in the Social Construction of Scientific Knowledge*. Winsconsin: The University of Winsconsin Press.

Myking, J. 1997. "The Sign Models of Terminology — Recent Developments and Current Issues". *Terminology Science & Research* 8 (1/2): 51- 62.

Ndukwe, P. 1982. "Standardizing Nigerian Languages". *Journal of the Linguistic Association of Nigeria (JOLAN)* 1: 141–146.

Neustupný, J. V. 1974. "Basic Types of Treatment of Language Problems". In *Advances in Language Planning*, J. A. Fishman (ed.), 37–48. The Hague: Mouton.

Nida, E. A. 1964. *Toward a Science of Translating*. Leiden: E. J. Brill.

Nida, E. A. and Taber, C. R. 1969. *The Theory and Practice of Translation*. Leiden: E. J. Brill.

Nigerian Educational Research Development Council 1991. *Quadrilingual Glossary of Legislative Terms* [English, Hausa, Igbo & Yoruba]. Ibadan: Spectrum Books for NERDC.

Nkwenti-Azeh, B. 1994. "Positional and combinational characteristics of terms: Consequences for corpus-based terminography". *Terminology* 1(1): 61–95.

Nkwenti-Azeh, B. 1995. "The Treatment of Synonymy and Cross-references in Special-language Dictionaries (SLDs)". *Terminology* 2(2): 325–350.

Nuopponen, A. 1992. "On Causality and Concept Relationships". In *Terminology Science & Terminology Planning/Theoretical Issues of Terminology Science* [IITF Series 4], J. K. Draskau and H. Picht (eds), 217–230. Vienna: TermNet.

Nuopponen, A. 1994. *Begreppssystem för Terminologisk Analys* [Acta Wasaensia, no. 38]. Vaasa: University of Vasa.

Nykänen, O. 1993. "Cost Analysis of Terminology Projects". *TermNet News* 42/43: 20–23.

O'Barr, W. M. & O'Barr, J. F. (eds). 1976. *Language and Politics*. The Hague/ Paris: Mouton.

O'Barr, J. F. 1976. "Language and Politics in Tanzanian Governmental Institutions". In *Language and Politics*, W. M. O'Barr and J. F. O'Barr (eds), 69– 84. The Hague/Paris: Mouton.

O'Barr, W. M. 1976. "Language Use and Language Policy in Tanzania: An Overview". In *Language and Politics*, W. M. O'Barr and J. F. O'Barr (eds), 33–48. The Hague/Paris: Mouton.

Oeser, E. 1978. "Die Dynamik wissenschaftlicher Begriffsformen". In *Kooperation in der Klassifikation I*, Dahlberg, W. (ed.), 34–45. Frankfurt: Ges. für Klassifikation.

Oeser, E. 1992. "Terminology & Philosophy of Science". In *Terminology Science & Terminology Planning/Theoretical Issues of Terminology Science* [IITF Series 4], J. K. Draskau and H. Picht (eds), 24–34. Vienna: TermNet.

Öhman, S. (1953). "Theories of the Linguistic Field". *Word* 9: 123–134.

Ogden, C. K. and Richards, I. A. 1969. *The Meaning of Meaning*. London: Routledge & Kegan Paul.

Ojerinde, A. 1978. The Use of a Mother Tongue, Yoruba, as a Medium of Instruction in Nigerian Schools. Unpub. Ph.D thesis, Cornell University.

Okonkwo, E. C. J. 1977. Towards an Integrated Theory of Language Planning (With Special Emphasis on Africa). Unpub. Ph.D thesis, S. U. N. Y. Buffalo.

Oredugba, F. C. 1977. Mathematics and Science Terminologies: Publishing in Nigerian Languages. Paper presented at Language Symposium, Kaduna.

Oyelaran, O. O. n.d. "Yoruba". In A Glossary of Technical Terminology for Primary Schools in Nigeria [Pre-publication version of *Primary Science and Mathematics Vocabulary*]. Lagos: Federal Ministry of Education.

Palmer, F. R. 1995. *Mood and Modality*. Cambridge: University Press.

Paepcke, F. 1985. "Pour une communicativité transnationale". *Neoterm* 2/3, 3/4: 7–11.

Parc, F. 1992. "Phraséologie terminologique dans les textes législatifs et réglementaires". *Terminology & Traduction* 2/3: 219–236.

Paulston, C. B. 1983. "Language Planning". In *Language Planning and Language Education*, C. Kennedy (ed.), 55–65. London: George Allen & Unwin.

Pearl, J. 1985. *Heuristics: Intelligent Search Strategies for Computer Problem Solving*. Reading, Massachussets: Addison-Wesley.

Picht, H. and Draskau, J. K. 1985. *Terminology: An Introduction*. Surrey: University of Surrey.

Picht, H. 1987. "Terms and their LSP environment — LSP Phraseology". *Meta* xxxii (2): 149–155.

Picht, H. 1988. "Fachsprachliche Phraseologie — Die terminologische Funktion von Verben". In *Proceedings, International Congress on Terminology and Knowledge Engineering* [29 Sept.-1Oct. 1987], H. Czap and C. Galinski (eds), 21–34. Frankfurt/M: Indeks.

Picht, H. 1990a. "A Study of LSP Phraseological Elements in Spanish Technical Texts". *Terminology Science & Research* 1 (1–2): 49–58.

Picht, H. 1990b. "LSP Phraseology from the Terminological Point of View". *Terminology Science & Research* 1 (1–2): 33–48.

Picht, H. 1997. "Zur Theorie des Gegenstandes und des Begriffs in der Terminologielehre". *Terminology Science & Research* 8 (1/2): 159–177.

Polomé, E. C. 1983/4. "Standardization of Swahili and the Modernization of the Swahili Vocabulary". In *Language Reform* [vol.3], I. Fodor and C. Hagège (eds), 53–77. Hamburg: Helmut Buske.

Pozzi, M. 1996 "Quality assurance of terminology available on the international computer networks". In *Terminology, LSP and Translation. Studies in Language Engineering in honour of Juan C. Sager*, H. Somers (ed.), 67–82. Amsterdam/Philadelphia: John Benjamins.

Putnam, H. 1975. "The Meaning of 'Meaning'". In *Language, Mind, & Knowledge* [vol. 7, Minnesota Studies in the Philosophy of Science], K. Gunderson (ed.), 131–193. Minneapolis: Univ. of Minnesota Press.

Ray, P. S. 1963. *Language Standardization: Studies in Prescriptive Linguistics*. The Hague: Mouton.

Renouf, A. and Sinclair, J. McH. 1991. "Collocational Frameworks in English". In *English Corpus Linguistics*, K. Ajimer and B. Altenberg (eds), 128–143. London & New York: Longman.

Rey, A. 1996. "Beyond Terminology". In *Terminology, LSP and Translation. Studies in Language Engineering in honour of Juan C. Sager*, H. Somers (ed.), 99–106. Amsterdam/Philadelphia: John Benjamins.

Ridings, D. 1996. Interim report on the Standard Shona Corpus. On the Internet at: http: //svenska.gu. se/"ridings.

Riggs, W. F. 1991. "Nomenclators: A new Kind of Service". *International Classification* 18(2): 110–121.

Ringland, G. A. and Duce, D. A. 1988. *Approaches to Knowledge Representation: An Introduction*. Hertfordshire: Research Studies Press/New York: John Wiley & Sons.

Ritzel/Bücker 1995. *Handbuch für die Parlamentarische Praxis mit Kommentar zur Geschäftsordnung des Deutschen Bundestages*. Neuwid, Kriftel, Berlin: Luchterhand.

Roberts, R. P. 1993a. "Identifying the Phraseology of Languages for Special Purposes". In *Proceedings of the XVth International Congress of Linguists* [Quebec, University of Laval], A. Crochetiere-Andre, *et al.* (eds), 197–200. Sainte-Foy: University of Laval Press.

Roberts, R. P. 1993b. "Phraseology: The State of the Art". *Terminology Update* 26 (2): 4–8.

Roberts, R. P. 1993c. "Phraséologie: état des connaissances". *Terminologies nouvelles* 10: 36–42.

Robertson, R. (ed.) 1992. *Globalization: Social Theory and Global Culture.* London: Sage.

Robertson, R. 1994. "Globalisation or glocalisation?" *The Journal of International Communication* 1(1): 33–52

Robins, R. H. 1969. *A Short History of Linguistics.* London: Longmans, Green & Co.

Rogers, M. 1997. "Review of H. Gerzymisch-Arbogast (1996)". *Lexicology* 2: 319–329.

Rogers, M. 1998. Establishing Concept Systems: films, photographs and diagrams (a view from bilingual text analysis). Talk given at the Conference on Professional Communication & Knowledge Transfer. Vienna, August 1998.

Rubin, J. and Jernudd, B. H. (eds). 1971. *Can Language be Planned?* Hawaii: East-West Center/The University Press.

Rubin, J. and Shuy, R. (eds). 1973. *Language Planning: Current Issues and Research.* Washington D. C.: Georgetown University Press.

Rubin, J. 1973. "Language Planning: Discussion of some current issues". In *Language Planning: Current Issues and Research,* J. Rubin and R. Shuy (eds), 1–10. Washington D. C.: Georgetown University Press.

Rubin, J., Jernudd, B. H., Das Gupta, J., Fishman, J. A. and Ferguson, C. A. (eds). 1977. *Language Planning Processes.* The Hague: Mouton.

Rubin, J. 1977. "Textbook Writers and Language Planning". In *Language Planning processes,* J. Rubin, B. H. Jernudd, J. Das Gupta, J. A. Fishman and C. A. Ferguson (eds), 237–253. The Hague: Mouton.

Rubin, J. 1983. "Evaluation Status Planning: What has the Past Decade Accomplished?" In *Progress in Language Planning,* J. Cobarrubias and J. A. Fishman (eds), 329–343. Berlin: Mouton.

Sager, J. C., Dungworth, D. and McDonald, P. F. 1980. *English Special Languages.* Wiesbaden: Oscar Brandstetter.

Sager, J. C. and Nkwenti-Azeh, B. 1989. *Terminological Problems Involved in the Process of Exchange of New Technology between Developing & Developed Countries.* Reports & Papers in the Social Sciences, no. 59. UNESCO: Paris.

Sager, J.C. 1990. *A Practical Course in Terminology Processing*. Amsterdam/ Philadelphia: John Benjamin.

Sager, J.C. and L'Homme, M.C. 1994. "A Model for the Definition of Concepts". *Terminology* 1(2): 351–373.

Sager, J.C. 1994. *Language Engineering and Translation. Consequences of Automation*. Amsterdam/Philadelphia: John Benjamins.

Sager, J.C. and Ndi-kimbi 1995. "The Conceptual Structure of Terminological Definitions and their Linguistic Realizations". *Terminology* 2(1): 61–81.

Samsom, R. 1991. "The Dynamics of Car Engineering in Swahili". In *Language Standardization in Africa*, N. Cyffer, K. Schubert, H-I. Weier and E. Wolff (eds), 235–244. Hamburg: Helmut Buske.

Saussure, F. 1973. *Cours de Linguistique générale*. Paris: Payot.

Schaetzen, C. 1993. "The Use of Terminology to Prevent Failure in Science & Medical Courses". In *TKE '93: Terminology & Knowledge Engineering*, K-D. Schmitz (ed.), 92–104. Frankfurt/M: Indeks.

Schmitt, P.A. 1986. "Die Eindeutigkeit von Fachtexten. Bemerkungen zu einer Fiktion". In *Übersetzungswissenschaft — eine Neuorientierung*, M. Snell-Hornby (ed.), 252–282. Tübingen: Francke.

Schmitt, P.A. 1999. "Kultur in der Terminologiearbeit? Zum Konflikt zwischen Begriffsorientiertheit und Kulturgeprägtheit". In F. Meyer and U. Reisen (eds), *Deutsche Terminologie im internationalen Wettbewerb*, 81–104. Bolzano/Köln: Deutscher-Terminologie Tag, e.V.

Schifko, P. 1975. *Bedeutungstheorie. Einführung in die linguistische Semantik*. Stuttgart-Bad Cannstatt: Frommann-Holzboog.

Schmitz, K-D. (ed.) 1993. *TKE '93: Terminology & Knowledge Engineering*. Frankfurt/M: Indeks.

Seleskovitch, D. 1976. "Interpretation: A Psychological Approach to Translating". In *Translations: Applications & Research*, R. Brislin (ed.), 92–116. New York: Gardner Press.

Seyoum, M. 1985. The Development of the National Language in Ethiopia: A Study of Language Use and Policy. Vols 1 & 2. Unpub. Ph.D Dissertation, Georgetown University.

Seyoum, M. 1988. "The Emergence of the National Language in Ethiopia: An Historical Perspective". In *With Forked Tongues: What are National Languages Good For?*, F. Coulmas (ed.), 101–145. Singapore: Karoma.

Sinclair, J. McH. 1966. "Beginning the Study of Lexis". In *In Memory of J.R. Firth*, C.E. Bazell, J.C. Catford, M.A.K. Halliday, R.H. Robins (eds), 410–430. London: Longman.

Sinclair, J. McH. 1987 "Collocation: A Progress Report". In *Language Topics. Essays in honour of Michael Halliday*, R. Steele and T. Threadgold (eds), 319–331. Amsterdam/Philadelphia: John Benjamins.

Sinclair, J. McH. 1991. *Corpus, Concordance, Collocation*. Oxford: University Press.

Snell-Hornby, M, Pöchhacker, F. and Kaindl, K. (eds) 1994. *Translation Studies. An Interdiscipline*. Amsterdam/Philadelphia: John Benjamins.

Somers, H. (ed.) 1996. *Terminology, LSP and Translation. Studies in Language Engineering in honour of Juan C. Sager*. Amsterdam/Philadelphia: John Benjamins.

Sonaiya, R. 1991. "Vocabulary Acquisition as Process of Continuous Lexical Disambiguation". *International Review of Applied Linguistics in Language Teaching*, xxix(4): 273–284.

Sowa, J. 1984. *Conceptual Structures*. Reading: Addison-Wesley.

Stefanink, B. 1995a. "L'ethnotraductologie au service d'un enseignement de la traduction centré sur l'apprenant". *Le Langage et l'Homme* XXX (4): 265–293.

Stefanink, B. 1995b. "Review of Lörscher (1991)". *Fremdsprachen Lehren und Lernen* 24: 271–277.

Stoberski, Z. 1987. "International Seminar on Terminology and Pan African Centre for Terminology". *Neoterm* 5/6: 3–10.

Strehlow, R. A. 1997. "Frames and the Display of Definitions". In *Handbook of Terminology Management* [vol.1], S.E. Wright and G. Budin (compilers), 75–79. Amsterdam/Philadelphia: John Benjamins.

Tauli, Valter 1968. *Introduction to a Theory of Language Planning*. [Acta Universitatis Upsaliensis, Studia Philologiae Scandinavicae Upsaliensia, 6.] Uppsala: University of Uppsala.

TermNet News 46/47. 1994 & *TermNet News* 48. 1995.

Thagard, P. 1992. *Conceptual Revolutions*. Princeton, New Jersey: Princeton University Press.

Tirkkonen-Condit, S. (ed.) 1991. *Empirical Research in Translation and Intercultural Studies*. Tübingen: Gunter Narr (LIP series 5).

Toury, G. 1991. "Experimentation in Translation Studies: Achievements, Prospects and Some Pitfalls". In *Empirical Research in Translation and Intercultural Studies*, S. Tirkkonen-Condit (ed.), 45–66. Tübingen: Gunter Narr (LIP series 5).

Tubiana, J. 1983/84. "Aperçus sur l'enrichissement du vocabulaire amharique". In *Language Reform* [vol.3], I. Fodor and C. Hagège (eds), 331–365. Hamburg: Helmut Buske.

Tumbo, Z. 1982. "Towards a Systematic Terminology Development in Kiswahili". *Kiswahili* 49(1): 87–98.
Ullmann, S. 1956. "The Concept of Meaning in Linguistics". *Archivum Linguisticum* 8: 12–20.
Ullmann, S. 1957. *The Principles of Semantics*. Oxford/Glasgow: Basil Blackwell/Jackson, Son & Co.
Ullmann, S. 1970. *Semantics: An Introduction to the Science of Meaning*. Oxford: Basil Blackwell.
Van Laer, H. P. 1963. *Philosophy of Science* [Part 1: Science in General. An introduction to some general aspects of science]. Pittsburg: Duquesne Univ. Press.
Vollmer, G. 1978. "Erkenntnistheorie und Wissensordnung". In *Kooperation in der Klassifikation I*, Dahlberg, W. (ed.), 12–32. Frankfurt: Ges. für Klassifikation.
Vygotsky, L. S. 1971. *Thought and Language* [edited & transl. by E. Hanfmann and G. Vakar]. Cambridge, Massachussets: M. I. T. Press.
Wartburg, W. 1939 [1972]. "Betrachtungen über das Verhältnis von historischer und deskriptiver Sprachwissenschaft". In *Mélanges de linguistique offerts à Charles Bally* [Sous les auspices de la Faculté des lettres de l'université de Genève par des collègues, des confrères, des disciples reconnaissants], 2–18. Geneva: Slatkine Reprints.
Wartburg, W. 1969. *Problems and Methods in Linguistics* [transl. by J. Reid]. Oxford: Basil Blackwell.
Weissenhofer, P. 1995. *Conceptology in Terminology Theory, Semantics & Word-Formation* [IITF 6] Vienna: TermNet.
Wierzbicka, A. 1996. *Semantics, Primes and Universals*. Oxford: Oxford University Press.
Wilss, W. 1993. "Projekt übersetzungsdidaktische Grundlagenforschung". *Lebende Sprachen* XXXVIII (2): 53–54.
Wright, S. E. and Strehlow, R. A. (eds). 1994. *Standardizing and Harmonizing Terminology: Theory and Practice*. Philadelphia: American Society for Testing and Materials.
Wright, S. E. and Budin, G. (compilers). 1997. *Handbook of Terminology Management* [vol. 1]. Amsterdam/Philadelphia: John Benjamins.
Wüster, E. 1959/60. "Das Worten der Welt. Schaubildisch und terminologisch dargestellt". *Sprachforum* 3: 183–204.
Wüster, E. 1968. *The Machine Tool — An Interlingual Dictionary of Basic Concepts*. London: Technical Press.

Wüster, E. 1971. "Begriffs- und Themaklassifikationen". *Nachrichten für Dokumentation* 22(3): 98–104, & (4): 143–150.

Wüster, E. 1974a. "Die allgemeine Terminologielehre — ein Grenzgebiet zwischen Sprachwissenschaft, Logik, Ontologie, Informatik und den Sachwissenschaften". *Linguistics: An International Review* 119: 61–106.

Wüster, E. 1974b. "Die Umkehrung einer Begriffsbeziehung und ihre Kennzeichnung in Wörterbüchern". *Nachrichten für Dokumentation* 25(6): 256–263.

Wüster, E. 1991. *Einführung in die Allgemeine Terminologielehre und terminologische Lexikographie* [3rd edition]. Bonn: Romanistischer Verlag.

Zawada, B. & Swanepoel, P. 1994. "On the Empirical Adequacy of Terminological Concept Theories: The Case for Prototype Theory". *Terminology* 1(2), 253–275.

Subject Index

A
ACCT (Agence de Coopération Culturelle et Technique) 27, 28

B
British contextualism 122

C
cognitive categorisation
  prototype 108, 110
  stereotype 108
collocation 122
  base 126
  co(n)text 202
  collocate 126
  collocational range 124
  downward collocation 124
  trivial combinations 125
  upward collocation 124
concept 81, 82
  challenge of description 81, 82
  characteristics 96, 98, 99
  controlled indeterminacy 85, 106
  negotiated 82, 84, 85, 96
  transaction 84
  valency structure 128
concept creation
  models 93-95
concept relations
  logical 101
  ontological 101
  pragmatic 102
corpus linguistics 157
corpus, corpora 157-160, 164, 165, 171, 175, 176
initiation 183
Critical Realism 89, 110

D
discourse processing
  idiom principle 123
  open-choice principle 123
discourse production
  model 156

E
Efik 179-181, 195, 211-213, 215
  consonant weakening 196
  newspaper 180
  vowel harmony 215
Efik term creation
  Agentive prefix 215
  Comparative term motivation models 198
  Complex noun phrases 215
  metaphor 199
  reduplication/reduplicated forms 204, 213
  Series uniformity 204

SUBJECT INDEX

F
font 216, 218

G
globalisation xvi, xvii, xviii, xx
  localisation xx
  glocalisation xx

H
Hypothetical Realism 89

K
knowledge
  (re)generation 167, 168
  Associativity 167
  non-linearity 167, 168
knowledge modelling 185, 186
  catalogue of conceptual relations 186
knowledge protocols 66
  Epistemic modality 70
  factual correctness 68
  inferences 70, 71
  problem of cognitive activity 68
knowledge representation
  conceptual graph 168, 170
  frame 130, 167
  hypertext 170
  thesaurus 140, 144-148

L
language planning
  alternative model 2
  evaluation 10, 11, 13, 15, 43, 46, 47
  language management 3, 8, 10
  rational model 2
  sociology, see also 2.4.3 & 2.5 12, 15
language policy
  Ethiopia 25
  ethno-linguistic self-assertion xxi
  Europe xxi
  Nigeria xxii, 22
  Post-Revolutionary France xx
  Somalia 17
  South Africa xxii
  Tanzania 19, 20
  Zimbabwe xxii
legislatures, procedures & languages
  Hausa 23
  Swahili 20
  British 186, 209
  Hausa 24
  Igbo 24
  Nigeria xxii, 181
  South Africa xxii
  US 186
  Yoruba 24
  Zimbabwe xxii
  Bundestag 70
lexical functions 137
LSP phrase 128
  concept combinability 130
  context conditioning 130
  lexeme-bound 131

M
MultiTerm 172
  Database definition 172, 216
  fuzzy search 174
  knowledge experiments 225
  translation experiments 221
  Wildcard search 173

N
naive realism 86, 88, 105, 109, 110
Neo-Positivism 88

O
object 90
  formal 90
  material 90
objectivist epistemology 109
Onomasiology 84
ontology 84, 88, 97, 103, 186

SUBJECT INDEX

R
Radical Constructivism 88

S
semiotic models
  dyadic model 85
  Schifko's sign model 92
  triadic model 86
specialised knowledge
  access xviii, xxi, 227, 228
  communication 228
  democratisation xxi
  empowerment xxi, 228

T
term xv, 96, 132
  delimitation 132
  term disputes (see also 8.8.3 & 8.8.5) 195
  usability 44, 198, 202
term expansion 132
term extraction
  coefficient of weirdness 161
  concordance 164, 184
  knowledge probes 162
  multi-word terms 161
  relative frequency 161
single-word terms 161
System Quirk 161, 184
terminography 139
terminological knowledge 158
terminology management 171
  scenarios 154
  systems 171
  MultiTerm 172
terminology resource
  optimisation 231
  re-engineering 231
tertiary education 232
texts (specialised)
  lexical closure 159
  reification 159
  textuality 155
think-aloud protocols
  term parsing 56
translation success 51
translation think-aloud protocols
  adoption of glossary solutions 59
  dTAP 50, 53
  iTAP 50, 53
  non-adoption of glossary solutions 64
  term identification 54

Name Index

A
Abbé Grégoire xx, xxi
Ahmad 158, 161, 168, 169
Ahmad & Fulford 162
Ahmad & Rogers 154
Ahmad, Davies & Rogers 159
Aitchison & Gilchrist 145
Akpanyuñ 197
Alloni-Fainberg 14
Andrzejewski 17, 18, 39
Antia 181, 198, 199, 230
Antia & Haruna 22
Aristotle 110
Arntz & Picht 90, 103, 115
Askira 42, 46, 47
Aye 180, 196, 198

B
Baldinger 88, 113, 141
Bamgbose 2, 24
Beaugrande 68, 98, 100, 155
Beaugrande & Dressler 65, 155
Brann xxi
Budin 88, 89, 110, 155, 228

C
Cabré 49, 107
Caney 17, 35, 39
Connell 180
Cook 196
Corbeil 3
Cruse 162

D
Dahlberg 94, 98
Dede 167, 170
Diop 29, 30

E
Essien 195, 213

F
Felber 90, 92
Felber & Budin 90
Fishman xxi, 11, 12, 228
Frederiksen 155

G
Gerzymisch-Arbogast 51, 85, 93, 107
Gilreath 195, 204

H
Halaoui 27, 34, 37
Halliday 64, 122, 124, 157
Hallig & Wartburg 93, 105, 141
Haugen 1, 9
Hausmann 118, 125-127
Hoffmann 155, 159

I
Issoufi 34, 35

NAME INDEX

J
Jernudd 3, 8, 10, 15
Jernudd & Das Gupta 3, 10
Jernudd & Neustupný 9, 10, 79
Jernudd and Neustupný 3

K
Khamisi 21, 34
Khubchandani 3, 9
Kjaer 130, 131
Kjellmer 117, 118, 122
Kleiber 88, 110
Krings 51
Kuhn xvi, 49
Kummer 14, 33, 40, 41, 43, 47

L
Laurén, Myking & Picht 83
Leibniz xx, 142
Lörscher 51
Lyons 104, 162

M
Mackey 3
Martin 130, 131
Mazrui 20
McEnery & Wilson 157, 159
McNaught 201
Mel'cuk 137
Merwe 148, 150
Meyer & Mackintosh 112, 120, 121, 132, 134
Mill 111

N
Nuopponen 101

O
O'Barr 19, 21

O'Hagan xviii
Oeser 100
Ogunseitan xviii

P
Picht 82, 83, 90, 93, 99, 107, 120, 128, 129, 131, 134
Picht & Draskau 81, 103, 150
Polomé 20

R
Rey 106, 107
Robertson xx
Rogers 200
Rubin 2, 14

S
Sager 99, 105, 150
Samson 47
Schifko 86, 89, 92
Schmitt 108
Schmitz 172, 216
Seyoum 12, 25
Sinclair 123, 124
Sowa 110, 168
Stoberski 26, 33, 37

T
Thagard 99, 107

W
Weissenhofer 111
Wittgenstein 110
Wüster 81, 84, 88, 98, 101

Z
Zawada & Swanepoel 108, 110

In the series TERMINOLOGY AND LEXICOGRAPHY RESEARCH AND PRACTICE (TLRP) the following titles have been published thus far or are scheduled for publication:

1. CABRÉ, M. Teresa: *Terminology*. Theory, methods and applications. 1999.
2. ANTIA, Bassey Edem: *Terminology and Language Planning. An alternative framework of practice and discourse.* 2000.
3. TEMMERMAN, Rita: *Towards New Ways of Terminology Description. The socio-cognitive approach.* 2000.
4. SAGER, Juan C.: *Essays on Definition.* n.y.p.